D0025521

Manual de gramática

Grammar Reference
for Students of Spanish

Eleanor Dozier
Zulma Iguina

Cornell University

 Heinle & Heinle Publishers, Inc.
Boston, Massachusettes 02116 U.S.A.

I T P ® An International Thomson Publishing Company

New York • London • Bonn • Boston • Detroit • Madrid • Melbourne • Mexico City • Paris
Singapore • Tokyo • Toronto • Washington • Albany NY • Belmont CA • Cincinnati OH

The publication of *Manual de gramática* was directed by the members of the Heinle & Heinle College Spanish and Italian Team:

Vincent R. Di Blasi, Team Leader, Vice President of Sales & Marketing
Carlos Davis, Editorial Director
Patrice Titterington, Production Services Coordinator
Marisa Garman, Marketing Development Director

Also participating in the publication of this program were:

Publisher: Stanley J. Galek
Director of Production: Elizabeth Holthaus
Manufacturing Coordinator: Barbara Stephan
Project Manager/Compositor: Christine E. Wilson, IBC
Interior and Cover Designer: Barbara Goodchild

Dozier, Eleanor.
    Manual de gramática: Grammar Reference for Students of Spanish
Spanish students / Eleanor Dozier, Zulma Iguina
        p.   cm.
    Cover title: Manual de gramática = Grammar manual.
    Includes index.
    ISBN 0-8384-5888-2
    1. Spanish language—Grammar.   2. Spanish language—Textbooks for
foreign speakers—English.   I. Iguina, Zulma.   II. Title.
III. Title: Grammar manual
PC4112.D690   1994
468.2'421—dc20   94-26367
                                                        CIP

Copyright © 1995 by Heinle & Heinle Publishers
All rights reserved. No part of this publication may be reproduced or transmitted in any form or by any means, electronic or mechanical, including photocopy, recording, or any information storage and retrieval system, without permission in writing from the publisher.

Heinle & Heinle Publishers / A Division of International Thomson Publishing, Inc.

Manufactured in the United States of America
ISBN 0-8384-5888-2

10 9 8 7 6 5 4 3

CONTENTS

CHAPTER 4. Prepositions and Conjunctions

CHAPTER 5. Verbs I

CHAPTER 6. Verbs II

CHAPTER 7. *Ser, Estar, Haber, Hacer,* and *Tener*

PREFACE

Over the past decade, it has become increasingly out of style to include grammar as part of the curriculum of a language program. Textbooks are being marketed with less and less information on grammatical points, placing the focus of practice of the language on its use within situations, in context, broken down into notions or tasks. This is indeed a healthy turn of events for those who had not already been pressing the practice of the language within contexts closer to reality. Unfortunately, these new textbooks resemble more an instructor's set of class preparation notes than practical instruments of study for the student.

Accordingly, we have constructed what we consider to be a useful study tool for the intermediate level student who needs to review, or in many cases, relearn, specific areas of grammar. Over the past ten years, this Manual has seen more than a dozen versions, with changes based on students' comments, instructors' suggestions, and any evidence of need for improvement which arose. Despite the unavoidable conceptual difficulties contained in the grammar points covered in this Manual, and the expected fear or repulsion of students to approach them, we have found that, after the initial shock of opening the pages, our students respond well to the lessons therein, and even comment on the relative clarity of explanations, the quality of the examples, and the ease of use of the Manual as a whole.

Our goal has been to provide our intermediate level students with a means to understand very difficult conceptual distinctions between English and Spanish, and, when there is no graspable concept involved, to learn particular differences between the two. Our choice of points to cover has been made for us by the variety of students which has made its way to our classes, from such diverse backgrounds as our own second or third semester courses, high school, other universities and colleges, or a bilingual upbringing.

It should be understood that this Grammar Manual is not our only text for the courses we teach. We provide our students with a large amount of reading material, writing exercises, as well as listening and oral practice. Grammar is perceived within our curriculum as a tool, the nuts and bolts which will aid in holding the edifice together, or keep the student's expression of the language as understandable to the native speaker as possible.

We have decided to include some elements in this Manual which, although unrelated to grammar, do fit within our contrastive conceptual approach. These elements are lexical in nature, but we have observed them to be so useful to our intermediate level students that we chose to include them in an appendix.

This first publication would be incomplete without the recognition of the many friends and colleagues whose invaluable suggestions have made this Manual as useful as it has proven to be year after year in our intermediate courses. Our gratitude goes first to Margarita Suñer for the inspiration of her crystal-clear lectures on grammar, for her contagious fascination with the mysteries of language, for her guidance and friendly support throughout this decade. Our gratitude toward David Cruz de Jesús is unmeasurable, for continuously keeping us alert to inadequacies in the text, always basing his observations on his students' needs. Other generous contributors over the years, without whose help this project would have been impossible, have been Susana Sainz, Amalía Tió, Jeannine Routier, Judith Némethy, Ingrid Goobar, Anabel Echávarri-Dailey, Jorge Hernández, Cecelia Burke-Taylor, Luis Morató, Regina Roebuck, Rahul Maitra,

Reyna Proman, Karen Galinsky, Carmen Lizardi, and all of those who have taught or taken Spanish 200, 203, 213 and 204 over the past decade at Cornell University.

This text would still be unpublished were it not for Carlos Davis, of Heinle & Heinle: he has impressed us with his exceptional efficiency and unerring diplomacy and has encouraged and supported all of our efforts. We are also grateful to Patrice Titterington of Heinle & Heinle for assigning this project to Christine E. Wilson of IBC. In her role as project manager and compositor/typesetter she proved to be as precise as any author could hope for in her critiques of this work.

Subdivisions of *Manual de gramática*

Grammar: Chapters 1–7
Each segment of a Chapter has exercises for practice, indicated with the following graphic reminder:

Appendix 1: Lexical Variations
These are some of the most frequently encountered lexical difficulties for English speakers. These too have exercises for practice in *Appendix II.*

Appendices 2 & 3: Exercises and Answer Key
These are practice exercises for the grammar and lexical portions of the *Manual,* all self-correcting with an answer key following the exercises.

Appendix 4: Tables of Verb Conjugations
We placed these tables at the end of the text for easy reference by students who want to double-check their verb conjugations easily.

Eleanor Dozier
Zulma Iguina
Department of Modern Languages
   & Linguistics
Cornell University

Chapter 1

Overview

A. SENTENCE COMPONENTS

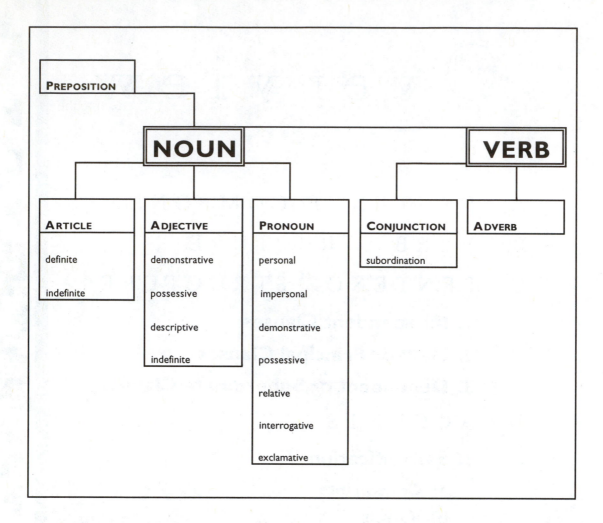

A sentence is a self-contained unit of communication that may be formed with combinations of the following eight types of words: nouns, verbs, prepositions, articles, adjectives, pronouns, conjunctions, and adverbs. Each of these types of words has its own particular function to perform in a sentence.

NOUN: may serve as the subject of a verb, its direct or indirect object, or the object of a preposition. In Spanish, equivalents of nouns (i.e., words or groupings of words that may have the same grammatical functions as a noun) are pronouns, infinitives, and nominalized words or groups of words.

VERB: the grammatical core of a sentence; expresses an action or state; its form changes in agreement with subject, tense, mood, aspect, and voice.

ARTICLE: accompanies and modifies as to specificity a noun or its equivalent.

ADJECTIVE: accompanies and modifies a noun or its equivalent.

ADVERB: modifies a verb, an adjective, another adverb, or a sentence.

PRONOUN: is used to avoid repeating a noun whose reference is clear.

PREPOSITION: relates a noun or its equivalent to another noun, to the verb, or to the rest of the sentence.

CONJUNCTION: joins two parts of a sentence. Conjunctions of subordination introduce subordinate clauses.

The following table enlarges on what we've just covered and gives the Spanish terms.

WORD TYPE	TIPO DE PALABRA	SUBCATEGORÍAS Y EJEMPLOS	GRAMMATICAL FUNCTION	FUNCIÓN GRAMATICAL
Noun	Nombre o sustantivo	Propio *(España...)*	Subject; direct/indirect object; prepositional object	Sujeto; objeto directo/indirecto; objeto de preposición
		Común *(libro...)*		
Pronoun	Pronombre	Personal *(yo, me, mí...)*	Same as the noun	Igual que el nombre
		Impersonal *(se, uno...)*		
		Demostrativo *(éste, esto...)*		
		Posesivo *(el mío, el tuyo...)*		
		Interrogativo *(¿qué?, ¿quién?...)*		
		Exclamativo *(¡qué!, ¡quién!...)*		
		Indefinido *(alguien, algo...)*		
		Relativo *(que, el que, cuyo...)*	Replaces the noun and introduces a relative clause. Subject or object of verb in the subordinate clause, or prepositional object	Reemplaza el nombre e introduce una cláusula relativa. Sujeto u objeto del verbo de la cláusula subordinada, u objeto de preposición
Article	Artículo	Definido *(el, la; los, las)*	Accompanies and modifies the noun or its equivalent	Acompaña y modifica el nombre o su equivalente
		Indefinido *(un, una; unos, unas)*		
Adjective	Adjetivo	Calificativo *(verde, grande...)*	Accompanies and modifies the noun or its equivalent	Acompaña y modifica el nombre o su equivalente
		Demostrativo *(ese, esta...)*		
		Posesivo *(mi, tu, su...)*		
		Indefinido *(algún, ningún...)*		

WORD TYPE	TIPO DE PALABRA	SUBCATEGORÍAS Y EJEMPLOS	GRAMMATICAL FUNCTION	FUNCIÓN GRAMATICAL
Preposition	Preposición	*(a, de, en, por, para, con, desde...)*	Introduces the noun or its equivalent	Introduce el nombre o su equivalente
Verb	Verbo	Transitivo/ Intransitivo	Provides action or description; is the core of the sentence	Proporciona acción o descripción; es el núcleo de la frase
		1ª, 2ª, 3ª conjugación		
Adverb	Adverbio	*(rápidamente, bien, mal, muy...)*	Modifies a verb, an adjective, another adverb, or a sentence	Modifica un verbo, un adjetivo, otro adverbio o una frase
Conjunction	Conjunción	De coordinación *(y, o, pero, sino...)*	Links two parts of speech or clauses	Une dos palabras o grupos de palabras
		De subordinación *(que, aunque...)*	Introduces a subordinate clause	Introduce una cláusula subordinada

(See Appendix II for exercises.)

B. VERB STRUCTURE

MODO	MOOD	TIEMPO Y ASPECTO	EJEMPLO	EXAMPLE
Infinitivo	*Infinitive*	Presente	**estudiar**	*to study*
		Perfecto	**haber estudiado**	*to have studied*
Participio	*Participle*	Presente	**estudiando**	*studying*
		Pasado	**estudiado**	*studied*
Indicativo	*Indicative*	Presente	**estudio**[1]	*I study*
		Presente perfecto	**he estudiado**	*I have studied*
		Futuro	**estudiaré**	*I will study*
		Futuro perfecto	**habré estudiado**	*I will have studied*
		Pretérito	**estudié**	*I studied*
		Imperfecto	**estudiaba**	*I studied, would study, was studying*
		Pluscuamperfecto	**había estudiado**	*I had studied*
Condicional[2]	*Conditional*	Presente	**estudiaría**	*I would study*
		Perfecto	**habría estudiado**	*I would have studied*
Subjuntivo	*Subjunctive*	Presente	**estudie**	
		Presente perfecto	**haya estudiado**	
		Imperfecto	**estudiara**	
		Pluscuamperfecto	**hubiera estudiado**	
Imperativo	*Imperative*	(sólo una forma)	**¡Estudien!**	*Study!*

APPENDIX II
Práctica

---

1. The examples for the indicative, conditional, and subjunctive are given in the first-person singular *(yo)*. The example for the imperative is given in the *ustedes* form.
2. Some grammarians consider the conditional to be a tense of the indicative mood, not a mood in itself. Because it is used for contexts that are modally different from those in which other moods are used, and because it has two tenses itself, we have chosen to consider it a mood. The only situation where it could be considered a tense of the indicative is when it is used as a future of the past.

C.   SENTENCE STRUCTURE

A sentence may be composed of one or many clauses. These clauses can be identified by the fact that they have a verb that is conjugated (not in the infinitive or participle form).

I. Independent Clauses

Independent clauses are not dependent upon another, nor do they have other clauses depending upon them. They may be found alone . . .

> **Conocimos a Juan en la fiesta.**
>
> *We met John at the party.*

or they may be attached to one another by means of conjunctions of coordination.

> **Conocimos a Juan en la fiesta y hablamos con él sobre la universidad.**
>
> *We met John at the party and spoke with him about the university.*

2. Main or Principal Clauses

A main clause is a clause that could be independent by its meaning, but that has one or more clauses that are its dependents.

> <u>**Vamos a quedarnos en un hotel**</u> **para que nuestros amigos no se incomoden.**
>
> *We are going to stay in a hotel so that our friends are not inconvenienced.*

3. Dependent or Subordinate Clauses

In Spanish, a subordinate or dependent clause is introduced by a subordinating conjunction or adverbial phrase *(que, porque, cuando, tan pronto como…)* or by a relative pronoun *(que, el que, lo que, cuyo…)*. Dependent clauses "depend" on a main clause. The relationship of the dependent clause to the main clause varies according to the type of dependent clause: nominal, adverbial, or adjectival.

A **nominal** clause is one that behaves like a noun and can serve the function of subject, direct or indirect object to the verb of the main clause, or object of a preposition.

> **Quiero <u>pan</u>.**   *I want bread.*
>
> **Quiero <u>que me ayudes</u>.**   *I want you to help me.*

Both *pan* and *que me ayudes* function in these sentences as the direct object of the main verb *Quiero*.

An **adverbial** clause is one that behaves like an adverb and modifies the verb of the main clause by indicating manner (how?), purpose (what for?), reason (why?), time (when?), condition (under what condition?), etc.

> **Salió <u>rápidamente</u>.**   *She left quickly.*
>
> **Salió <u>tan pronto como pudo</u>.**   *She left as soon as she could.*

Both *rápidamente* and *tan pronto como pudo* modify the main verb *Salió* by indicating how the action took place.

An **adjectival** clause behaves like an adjective and modifies a noun. Adjective clauses are also called relative clauses because they always begin with a relative pronoun, which replaces a noun in the main clause (its antecedent) and introduces the subordinate clause that modifies the antecedent.

> **Quiero leer una novela <u>divertida</u>.**
>
> *I want to read a fun novel.*
>
> **Quiero leer una novela <u>que me haga reír</u>.**
>
> *I want to read a novel that will make me laugh.*

Both *divertida* and *que me haga reír* modify the noun *novela*.

English/Spanish Terminology

ENGLISH	SPANISH
sentence	*frase, oración*
phrase	*expresión*
clause	*cláusula*
main clause	*cláusula principal*
subordinate or dependent clause	*cláusula subordinada*
independent clause	*cláusula independiente*
relative clause	*cláusula relativa*

TYPE OF CLAUSE	SUBCATEGORY	INTRODUCED BY	FUNCTION
Independent		(Nothing)	(Exists on its own)
Main clause		(Nothing)	(Could exist on its own)
Subordinate	Nominal	Conjunction of subordination	Subject or direct object of verb of main clause
	Adverbial	Conjunction of subordination or adverbial phrase	Modifies the verb of the main clause, by describing manner, purpose, reason, time, condition, etc...
	Adjectival	Relative pronoun	Modifies the antecedent of the relative pronoun

The following chart gives examples of main and dependent or subordinate clauses.

MAIN CLAUSE	SUBORDINATE CLAUSE
	Introduced by
	CONJUNCTION [NOMINAL CLAUSE]
Le dije a Elsa *I told Elsa*	**que me gustaba la universidad.** *(that)[3] I liked the university.*
	CONJUNCTION [ADVERBIAL CLAUSE]
Nos fuimos *We left*	**porque hacía mucho frío.** *because it was very cold.*
	RELATIVE PRONOUN [ADJECTIVAL or RELATIVE CLAUSE]
Fuimos a una fiesta *We went to a party*	**que dieron nuestros amigos.** *(that)[4] our friends gave.*

In some complex sentences one clause may be broken into two parts with another subordinate inserted in between.

> **El libro que leí ayer fue muy interesante.**
>
> *The book I read yesterday was very interesting.*

Main clause: **El libro (…) fue muy interesante.**

Subordinate clause: **que leí ayer** [relative clause]

In some complex sentences, a subordinate clause may serve as a main clause to yet another subordinate (sub-subordinate) clause.

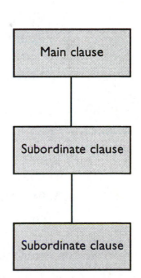

> **La clase de español que recomendaste que tomara me ha interesado mucho.**
>
> *The Spanish class (that) you recommended (that) I take has interested me a lot.*

Main clause: **La clase de español (…) me ha interesado mucho.**

Subordinate clause #1: **que recomendaste** [relative or adjectival clause]

Subordinate clause #2 (subordinate clause #1 serves as its main clause): **que tomara** [nominal clause]

---

3. In English, the conjunction may be omitted. This is impossible in Spanish, where all conjunctions must be stated.
4. In English, the relative pronoun may be omitted within certain contexts. In Spanish, the relative pronoun is always stated.

One main clause may have two subordinates of equal value connected with a conjunction of coordination *(y, o, pero, sino)*.

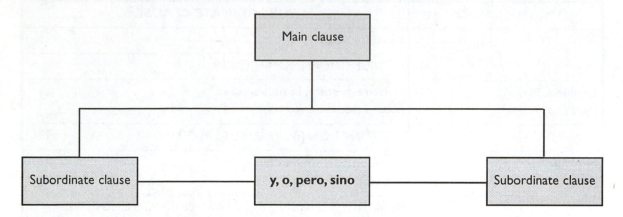

Me dijo que lo haría y que[5] me lo daría.

She told me (that) she would make it and (that she would) give it to me.

Main clause: **Me dijo**

Subordinate clause #1: **que lo haría** [nominal]

Subordinate clause #2: **que me lo daría** [nominal]

Conjunction of coordination: **y**

Yo sabía que Juan lo había hecho o que había ayudado a sus amigos a hacerlo.

I knew that Juan had done it, or that he had helped his friends do it.

Main clause: **Yo sabía**

Subordinate clause #1: **que Juan lo había hecho** [nominal]

Subordinate clause #2: **que había ayudado a sus amigos a hacerlo** [nominal]

Conjunction of coordination: **o**

Me dijo que vendría, pero que llegaría tarde.

He told me that he would come, but that he would arrive late.

Main clause: **Me dijo**

Subordinate clause #1: **que vendría** [nominal]

Subordinate clause #2: **que llegaría tarde** [nominal]

Conjunction of coordination: **pero**

No le dije que viniera, sino que me llamara.

I did not tell her to come, but rather to call me.

Main clause: **No le dije**

Subordinate clause #1: **que viniera** [nominal]

Subordinate clause #2: **que me llamara** [nominal]

Conjunction of coordination: **sino**

---

5. This conjunction may be omitted because it is a repetition of the previous one: *Me dijo que lo haría y me lo daría.*

One sentence may have two main clauses connected with conjunctions of coordination, each main clause having its subordinate clause(s).

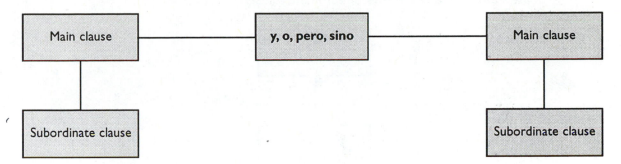

Lamento que no puedas venir, pero estoy contento que tus amigos te hayan invitado a cenar.

I am sorry you cannot come, but I am glad (that) your friends invited you to dinner.

Main clause #1: **Lamento**

Subordinate clause #1: **que no puedas venir** [nominal]

Main clause #2: **estoy contento**

Subordinate clause #2: **que tus amigos te hayan invitado a cenar** [nominal]

Conjunction of coordination: **pero**

Me dijo que necesitábamos boletos y luego llamó para que nos reservaran dos.

She told me that we needed tickets, and then she called so that they would reserve two for us.

Main clause #1: **Me dijo**

Subordinate clause #1: **que necesitábamos boletos** [nominal]

Main clause #2: **luego llamó**

Subordinate clause #2: **para que nos reservaran dos** [adverbial]

Conjunction of coordination: **y**

The complexity of a sentence is practically limitless. The following diagram is an example of a sentence with one main clause and four subordinates, three of which are subordinated to the first subordinate clause.

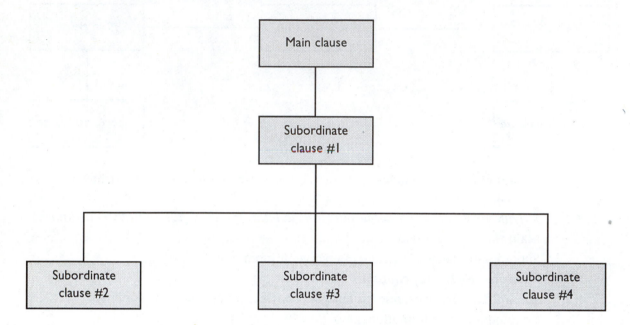

Mis amigos me habían dicho que cuando regresaran para las vacaciones me llamarían para que pudiéramos salir juntos a pesar de que tuviéramos poco tiempo.

My friends had told me that when they returned for vacation they would call me so that we could go out together, in spite of the fact that we might have little time.

Main clause: **Mis amigos me habían dicho**

Subordinate Clause #1: **que me llamarían** [nominal]

Subordinate Clause #2: **cuando regresaran para las vacaciones** [adverbial]

Subordinate Clause #3: **para que pudiéramos salir juntos** [adverbial]

Subordinate Clause #4: **a pesar de que tuviéramos poco tiempo** [adverbial]

APPENDIX II

Práctica

D. ACCENTS

1. Syllabification

The division of a word into syllables aids in the application of rules on accents.

a) Consonants (*Consonantes*)

Single intervocalic consonants: one consonant between two vowels joins the following vowel to form a syllable. (Remember that in Spanish *ch*, *ll*, and *rr* represent one consonant.)

ta/za	me/sa	mi/sa	ma/ce/ta	ca/la/ba/za
ta/lla	me/cha	ba/rro	fe/rro/ca/rri/le/ro	

Two intervocalic consonants: these are separated (except *ch*, *ll*, and *rr*).

lám/pa/ra	pan/ta/lla	an/gus/tia	com/pu/ta/do/ra
per/so/na	en/ca/rar	dic/cio/na/rio	

Do not separate the consonants *b, c, f, g,* and *p,* followed by *l* or *r,* or the combinations *dr* and *tr.*

ta/**bla**	fe/**bre**/ro	te/**cla**	re/**cre**/o	a/**flo**/jar
a/**fren**/ta	re/**gla**	a/**grio**	re/**ple**/to	de/**pri**/mir
po/**dri**/do	re/**tra**/to			

Three or more intervocalic consonants: with three or more consonants between vowels, only the last consonant joins the next vowel (unless it is *l* or *r*):

cons/ta	ins/pi/ra	ins/tan/te	in/**glés**	com/**prar**

b) Vowels (*Vocales*)

STRONG VOWELS	WEAK VOWELS	VOWEL COMBINATIONS
a	i	**Hiato:** two vowels forming two syllables
e	u	**Diptongo:** two vowels forming one syllable
o		**Triptongo:** three vowels forming one syllable

Hiatus (*Hiato*): two vowels of equal strength represent two syllables. Each strong vowel represents one syllable; when combined with another strong vowel, they are separated.

ca/e/mos	le/en	em/ple/o	em/ple/a/do

If a weak vowel before or after a strong vowel is stressed, there is a separation; a stressed weak vowel in combination with a strong vowel will always have an accent mark.

ca/í/da	re/í/mos	ma/ú/lla	gra/dú/en	tí/os
sa/lí/an	rí/en	grú/a	re/ú/no	

Diphthong *(Diptongo)*: a combination into one syllable of two weak vowels or one strong and one weak represents a diphthong and is not separated.

I/ta/lia	bai/le	vie/nen	rei/no	re/me/dio
vio/lín	cuan/do	au/la	rue/da	deu/da
rui/do	ciu/dad	cuo/ta	es/ta/dou/ni/den/se	

Stressed strong vowel: if the strong vowel in a diphthong is stressed, there is no separation.

diá/fa/no	tam/bién	na/ció	guár/da/lo	fué/ra/mos
quó/rum[6]	bai/láis	die/ci/séis	ói/ga/me	cáu/sa/me
Éu/fra/tes				

Triphthong *(Triptongo)*: a triphthong is one syllable formed by three vowels.

a/ve/ri/guáis   lim/piéis

More than one syllable occurs if there is more than one strong vowel or a stressed weak vowel in the combination.

se/áis   ca/í/an   re/í/a/mos

The *h* in Spanish is not pronounced; if it is enclosed between two vowels, these two vowels will interact as if they were next to each other.

No accent:	a/ho/rrar	re/ha/cer	re/ho/gar
	ahi/ja/do	rehi/lar	rehun/dir
With accent:	pro/hí/bo	bú/ho	

2. Stress

Every word with more than one syllable in Spanish has one syllable with more stress than the rest. Depending on the type of word it is, or where the stress falls, the word may or may not require a written accent.

---

6. Words imported from other languages follow the same accentuation rules as other Spanish words.

a) Categorization of Words by Stress

In Spanish, words with more than one syllable are categorized as follows.

TYPE	SYLLABLE WHERE STRESS FALLS	EXAMPLE
Aguda	*Last* (última)	ca / mi / **né**
Llana	*Next-to-last* (penúltima)	**lá** / piz
Esdrújula	*Third-to-last* (antepenúltima)	**quí** / mi / ca
Sobresdrújula	*Fourth-to-last* (anteantepenúltima)	**cóm** / pre / me / lo

b) Rules for Written Accents

Agudas: this type of word only needs a written accent when the word ends in a vowel or *n* or *s*.

Accent required:

amó   viví   vivís   francés   caimán

No accent required:

amar   vivir   español   ciudad   Jerez

Llanas: this type of word only needs a written accent when the word ends in a consonant other than *n* or *s*.

Accent required:

carácter   imbécil   lápiz   túnel   versátil

No accent required:

hablo   acento   necesita   consonante   franceses
margen   lunes   examen   estudiaron   bailas

Esdrújulas and sobresdrújulas: these types of words always require an accent mark.

Esdrújulas: carátula   estúpido   luciérnaga
Sobresdrújulas: vendámoselo   démoselas   pongámonoslas

c) Special Cases

(1) Adverbs Ending in *-mente*

Adverbs formed from an adjective + *mente* require an accent when their original adjective had one.

	rápido	is the adjective form of the adverb	rápidamente
	fácil	is the adjective form of the adverb	fácilmente
BUT:	lento	is the adjective form of the adverb	lentamente

(2) Monosyllables

Monosyllables (words consisting of only one syllable) must be left **without** a written accent mark. There is only one part of the word that can be stressed, thus no accent is needed.

a   al   ti   la   le   lo   di   da   me   fui   fue   dio   Dios

Some monosyllables are homonyms (words with the same spelling or pronunciation but with different meanings). One of the two will have an accent mark to distinguish it from the other.

el *the*	**mas** *but*	**se** [pron.]	**te** *you, yourself*
él *he*	**más** *more*	**sé** *I know*	**té** *tea*
de *of, from*	**mi** *my*	**tu** *your*	**si** *if*
dé[7] *give*	**mí** *me*	**tú** *you*	**sí** *yes, itself, oneself*

Me preguntó <u>el</u> nombre <u>de mi</u> profesora.
She asked me the name of my professor.

¿A ti[8] <u>te</u> lo dijo?   *Did she tell you?*
<u>Sí</u>, a <u>mí</u> me lo dijo.   *Yes, she told me.*

¿<u>Tú</u> también necesitas que te <u>dé</u> la llave?
Do you also need me to give you the key?

No <u>sé</u> <u>si</u> <u>él</u> quiere <u>más té</u>.
I don't know if he wants more tea.

El problema en <u>sí</u> no es tan grave.
The problem in itself isn't so serious.

(3) Non-Monosyllabic Homonyms

Although they are not monosyllables, the following words also require accent marks to distinguish them as homonyms.

a. *Aun*[9] vs. *Aún*

b. *Solo* vs. *Sólo*

c. Demonstrative Pronouns

d. Exclamative and Interrogative Pronouns or Adverbs

---

7. When the verb *dar* is conjugated in the imperative and has a pronoun attached, it loses the accent: *dele.* It is no longer a homonym of the preposition in this situation. Of course, it regains the accent when a second pronoun is added, due to the fact that we must maintain the stress on the verb and the new word is an *esdrújula: démelo.*

8. Beware of the temptation to place an accent over *ti*, just because *mí* has one: *ti* is not a homonym, as is *mí.*

9. Although *aun* is a monosyllable, we have placed it outside of the category because when it takes an accent, *aún*, its diphthong splits into two syllables.

(a) *Aun* vs. *Aún*

The word *aún* requires an accent when it means "still" *(todavía)*; however, when it means "even," it has no accent mark *(aun)*.

Aun de día hace frío.	*Even during the day it is cold.*
Aún no hemos llegado.	*We still have not arrived.*

(b) *Solo* vs. *Sólo*

The word *sólo* requires an accent when it is an adverb and means "only" or can be replaced by *solamente; solo* has no accent mark when it is an adjective meaning "alone."

Vivo solo.	*I live alone.*
Sólo tengo cuatro.	*I only have four.*

(c) Demonstrative Pronouns

In contrast with the demonstrative **adjective** forms, the demonstrative **pronoun** forms require an accent.

ése, ésa, ésos, ésas

éste, ésta, éstos, éstas

aquél, aquélla, aquéllos, aquéllas

Mira ese perro. [adj.]	*Look at that dog.*
Éste es mío. [pron.]	*This one is mine.*

The neutral form of the pronouns *eso, esto,* and *aquello* have no adjective equivalent and thus do not require an accent.

Mira eso. [neutral pron.]	*Look at that.*

(d) Exclamative and Interrogative Pronouns or Adverbs

Exclamative and **interrogative** adjectives, pronouns, or adverbs take an accent. In exclamations and interrogations, there is not always an interrogative or exclamative pronoun or adverb. You might, for example, ask: *¿Me dijiste la verdad?* or exclaim: *¡Bien dicho!* None of these words has an accent. You might also exclaim: *¡Que tengas buen día!* Here the *que* is a conjunction, not a pronoun or adjective, and has no accent.

Some examples of exclamative pronouns and adverbs are as follows.

¡Qué día!	*What a day!*
¡Cómo trabajas!	*How you work!*
¡Cuánto comes!	*How much you eat! (i.e., You eat a lot!)*

Some examples of interrogative adjectives, pronouns, and adverbs are in the chart below.

INTERROGATIVE[10] (ACCENT MARK)		NON INTERROGATIVE (NO ACCENT MARK)
Direct Discourse[11]	Indirect Discourse	
¿Qué? = *What?*		**Que** = *That, which, who*
¿Qué quieres? *What do you want?*	**No sabía qué hacer.** *I did not know what to do.*	**Quiero que estudies.** *I want you to study.* (literally: *I want that you study.*) [conjunction] **El libro que quiero es azul.** *The book that I want is blue.* [relative pronoun]
¿Por qué? = *Why?*		**Porque** = *Because*
¿Por qué llamaste? *Why did you call?*	**No sé por qué llamó.** *I do not know why he called.*	**Llamé porque quise.** *I called because I wanted to.*
¿Cómo? = *How?*		**Como** = *Like*
¿Cómo llegó? *How did she get here?*	**No sé cómo llegó.** *I do not know how she got here.*	**Trabaja como yo.** *He works like me.*
¿Cuánto? = *How much/many?*		**Cuanto** = *As much/many as*
¿Cuántos libros tienes? *How many books do you have?*	**No sé cuántos tengo.** *I do not know how many I have.*	**Te di cuantos pude.** *I gave you as many as I could.*
¿Dónde? = *Where?*		**Donde** = *Where, in which*
¿Dónde está? *Where is it?*	**Me dijo dónde estaba.** *He told me where it was.*	**Es la casa donde me crié.** *It is the house in which I grew up.*
¿Cuándo? = *When?*		**Cuando** = *When*
¿Cuándo llega? *When does it arrive?*	**Me dijo cuándo venía.** *She told me when she was coming.*	**Lo vi cuando entró.** *I saw him when he came in.*
¿Quién? = *Who(m)?*		**Quien** = *Who(m), he who*
¿Quién es? *Who is it?*	**Me dijo quién era.** *He told me who it was.*	**Ése es el hombre con quien llegó.** *That is the man with whom she arrived.*

10. **Interrogative vs. non interrogative.** This distinguishes words that are used in questions, whether directly stated or indirectly related, from words that are not interrogative at all, such as conjunctions, relative pronouns, and adverbial phrases.

11. **Direct vs. indirect discourse.** This distinguishes questions that are asked directly (e.g., What is your name?) from reported questions (e.g., He asked me what my name was.).

Que

Please note that the "non interrogative" column for *Que* contains conjunctions and relative pronouns that frequently have no translation into English, whereas the columns to the left, "interrogative", contain interrogative words that will always be stated in English. Notice the translation of the following sentences.

Quiero <u>que</u> estudies.	*I want you to study.*
El libro <u>que</u> quiero es azul.	*The book (that) I want is blue.*

Por qué vs. *porque* • *Cómo* vs. *como* • *Cuánto* vs. *cuanto*

It is not difficult to remember when these words require an accent mark because of the difference in meaning of the two.

por qué = *why*	**cómo** = *how*	**cuánto** = *how much/many*
porque = *because*	**como** = *as, like*	**cuanto** = *as much/many*

Dónde vs. *donde*

Whereas in most cases you can see that the translations of the accented and unaccented words are different, in the case of *dónde* and *donde* there is not always a difference. It would help perhaps to think of the unaccented word as a relative pronoun that requires an antecedent, or a noun prior to it and to which it refers.

Es la <u>casa donde</u> me crié.	*It is the <u>house in which</u> I grew up.*
	OR: *It is the <u>house</u> I grew up in.*

The interrogative *dónde*, whether in direct or in indirect discourse, never has an antecedent.

¿<u>Dónde</u> está?	*<u>Where</u> is she?*
No sé <u>dónde</u> está.	*I do not know <u>where</u> she is.*

Cuándo vs. *cuando*

With these two words, the distinction is perhaps even harder to make; for there to be an accent mark, there must be an explicit or implicit question involved. The non-interrogative "when" might be replaced by "at the time" without much change in meaning, whereas the interrogative could be replaced by "at what time." Compare the following sentences.

No sé cuándo se fue.	*I do not know when (at what time) she left.*
Lloramos cuando se fue.	*We cried when (at the time) she left.*

Frequently in indirect discourse in English, there is a greater stress on the word when it is interrogative in nature than when it is not; compare the following, reading them out loud.

Te vi <u>cuando</u> entraste.	*I saw you <u>when</u> you came in.*
No sé <u>cuándo</u> entraste.	*I don't know <u>when</u> you came in.*

Quién vs. *quien*

Quién with an accent mark is used whenever there is a question, explicit or implicit. *Quien* without an accent mark is not interrogative. It is a relative pronoun, usually preceded by a noun (which is its antecedent). It may be used with no antecedent at the beginning of a sentence also. In such cases, it means "He who . . . " or "Whoever . . . ".

¿<u>Quién</u> eres?	*<u>Who</u> are you?*
No sé <u>quién</u> eres.	*I don't know <u>who</u> you are.*
El hombre con <u>quien</u> habla es espía.	*The man with <u>whom</u> she is talking is a spy.*
<u>Quien</u> busca encuentra.	*<u>He who</u> seeks shall find.*

APPENDIX II

Práctica

Chapter 2

Nouns and Noun Determiners

A. NOUNS AND THEIR EQUIVALENTS

1. Introduction

   a) **Definition**

   b) **Noun Equivalents**

   c) **Noun Companions**

2. Nouns—Gender and Number

   a) **Gender**

   b) **Number**

3. Personal A

B. NOUN DETERMINERS

1. Articles

   a) **Definite Articles**

   b) **Indefinite Articles**

2. Adjectives

A. NOUNS AND THEIR EQUIVALENTS

1. Introduction

a) Definition

Nouns: words that can take on the grammatical function of the subject of a verb.

> **Esa <u>estudiante</u> sabe mucho de gramática.**
> *That student knows a lot about grammar.*

b) Noun Equivalents

Other words that can have the basic function of the subject of a verb are pronouns, infinitives, and any nominalized word (word converted into a noun).

Pronouns: words that replace nouns but have the same gender and number as the noun to which they refer.

<u>Ellas</u> me lo dijeron.	*They told me.*
<u>Éste</u> es el mío.	*This one is mine.*
<u>El mío</u> habla mejor que el tuyo.	*Mine speaks better than yours.*
<u>El que</u> vino ayer fue Juan.	*The one who came yesterday was Juan.*
Esa casa es <u>la mía</u>.	*That house is mine.*
<u>Ésa</u> es la mía.	*That one is mine.*

Infinitives (See *Chapter 6, Part 8* on the use of the infinitive and the present participle.)

> **<u>Caminar</u> es bueno para la salud.**
> *To walk (Walking) is good for one's health.*

> **Me gusta <u>cantar</u>.**
> *I like to sing. (Singing is pleasing to me.)*

Nominalized forms:

> **<u>El azul</u> del Mediterráneo siempre me sorprende.**
> *The blue of the Mediterranean always surprises me.*

> **<u>La mejor</u> siempre gana.**
> *The best one always wins.*

c) Noun Companions

Articles and adjectives are words that accompany and modify nouns. They agree with the noun they modify.

> **<u>La</u> casa blanca. <u>Las</u> casas rojas.**   *The white house. The red houses.*

<u>El</u> árbol. <u>Los</u> árboles.	*The tree. The trees.*
<u>Una</u> mesa. <u>Un</u> libro.	*A table. A book.*
<u>Esa</u> casa. <u>Esas</u> casas.	*That house. Those houses.*
<u>Este</u> libro. <u>Estos</u> libros.	*This book. These books.*
<u>Nuestra</u> casa. <u>Vuestras</u> ideas.	*Our house. Your ideas.*
<u>Mis</u> libros. <u>Tus</u> cuadernos.	*My books. Your notebooks.*
Una niña <u>bonita</u>.	*A pretty girl.*

Prepositions are words that relate a noun or its equivalent to another noun, to the verb, or to the rest of the sentence.

Estoy <u>en</u> mi oficina.	*I am in my office.*
Llegó una carta <u>para</u> ella.	*A letter arrived for her.*
Después <u>de</u> estudiar, saldremos <u>a</u> cenar.	*After studying, we will go out to eat dinner.*

2. Nouns—Gender and Number

a) **Gender** *(Género)*

All Spanish nouns are either masculine or feminine.

Most nouns ending in *-o, -l,* and *-r* are **masculine.**

el libro *book*	**el barril** *barrel*	**el actor** *actor*

EXCEPTIONS:

la foto *photo*	**la capital** *capital*	**la moral** *morals*
la mano *hand*	**la cárcel** *jail*	**la piel** *skin*
la moto *motorcycle*	**la catedral** *cathedral*	**la sal** *salt*
la radio *radio*	**la miel** *honey*	**la señal** *sign, signal*

Most nouns ending in *-a, -d, -ción, -sión, -umbre,* and *-z* are **feminine.**

la casa *house*	**la libertad** *liberty*
la costumbre *custom, habit*	**la luz** *light*
la condición *condition*	**la decisión** *decision*

EXCEPTIONS:

el día *day*	**el arroz** *rice*
el tranvía *streetcar*	**el lápiz** *pencil*
	el maíz *corn*
el ataúd *coffin*	**el matiz** *shade of color*
el césped *lawn*	**el pez** *fish*
el huésped *guest*	

el clima *climate*	**el sistema** *system*
el crucigrama *crossword puzzle*	**el telegrama** *telegram*
el drama *drama*	**el tema** *theme, topic*
el fantasma *ghost*	
el idioma *language*	**el mapa** *map*
el panorama *panorama*	**el cometa** *comet*
el poema *poem*	**el planeta** *planet*
el problema *problem*	**el poeta** *poet*
el programa *program*	

Languages, days of the week, mountains, rivers, and oceans are **masculine.**

el español *Spanish*   **el lunes** *Monday*   **los Pirineos** *Pyrenees*

Letters of the alphabet are **feminine.**

la a *a*   **la hache** *h*   **la ere** *r*

Infinitives are **masculine** when nominalized.

el amanecer *dawn*   **el poder** *power*

Many Spanish nouns referring to humans and animals occur in pairs, sometimes similar in form, sometimes not, but gender is always distinguished.

el hombre *man*	↔	**la mujer** *woman*
el actor *actor*	↔	**la actriz** *actress*
el rey *king*	↔	**la reina** *queen*
el toro *bull*	↔	**la vaca** *cow*

Some Spanish nouns referring to humans are identical in form—only the modifier shows the gender.

el/la estudiante *student*	**el/la demócrata** *democrat*
el/la joven *young man/woman*	**el/la ciclista** *cyclist*
el/la modelo *model*	**el/la comunista** *communist*
el/la turista *tourist*	**el/la pianista** *pianist*
el/la atleta *athlete*	**el/la guía** *guide*
el/la juez *judge*	

Some nouns can change meaning with a change in gender.

el policía *policeman*	BUT	**la policía** *policewoman/the police*
el guía *guide (e.g., tour guide)*	BUT	**la guía** *guide (woman)/guidebook*
el papa *pope*	BUT	**la papa** *potato*
el cura *priest*	BUT	**la cura** *cure*

Some nouns exist only in one gender, but serve for both sexes. The following examples can refer to women as well as to men.

Mi tía es <u>un ángel</u>.

My aunt is an angel.

Esa niña es <u>un amor</u>.

That little girl is a sweetheart.

These examples can refer to men as well as to women.

Mi padre es <u>una persona</u> encantadora.

My father is a charming person.

Ese hombre fue <u>una víctima</u> de la sociedad.

That man was a victim of society.

b) **Number** *(Número)*

Nouns ending in a vowel add *-s* to form the plural.

casa *house*	→	**casas** *houses*

Nouns ending in a consonant, in *-y*, and some ending in a stressed vowel add *-es* to form the plural.

amor *love*	→	**amores** *loves*
ley *law*	→	**leyes** *laws*
rubí *ruby*	→	**rubíes** *rubies*
francés *Frenchman*	→	**franceses**[1] *Frenchmen*
el examen *exam*	→	**los exámenes**[1] *exams*

Nouns ending in *-z* have plurals in *-ces*.

lápiz	→	**lápices**

Nouns ending in an unstressed vowel with final *-s* do not change for the plural.

el lunes	→	**los lunes**
el tocadiscos	→	**los tocadiscos**
la crisis	→	**las crisis**

---

1. Notice the accent on *francés* and *exámenes*: so that the stress may remain on the same syllable as in the singular, a plural may acquire or lose a written accent.

3. Personal A

In Spanish, direct object nouns referring to human beings are preceded by the personal *a*.

Vi el libro en tu casa.	*I saw the book in your house.*
Vi a Carmen en la clase.	*I saw Carmen in class.*
Conozco esa novela.	*I am familiar with that novel.*
Conozco al tío de Juan.	*I know Juan's uncle.*

If the persons referred to are not specific, omit the personal *a*.

Buscan secretarias bilingües.	*They are looking for bilingual secretaries.*
Busco a mi secretario.	*I am looking for my secretary.*

With the verb *tener*, do not use the personal *a* if *tener* means "to have" or "to possess."

Tengo cuatro tíos.	*I have four uncles.*

If it means "to keep" or "to hold," use the personal *a*:

Tenemos a mi padre en el hospital.	*We have my father in the hospital.*

Because the pronouns *alguien, nadie,* and *quien* refer to persons, they are preceded by the personal *a* when they function as direct objects.

Oí a alguien llorando.	*I heard someone crying.*
No conozco a nadie aquí.	*I do not know anyone here.*
¿A quién viste?	*Whom did you see?*

Direct object pronouns *(lo, la, los,* and *las)* are never accompanied by the personal *a* although they may refer to persons. The pronoun form used would be the stressed form.

Lo vi a él ayer.	*I saw him yesterday.*
La llamé a ella anoche.	*I called her last night.*
A ellos no los entiendo nunca.	*I never understand them.*
Las regañé a ellas ayer.	*I scolded them yesterday.*

(Notice that these are examples of repetitive object pronouns, used for emphasis or clarification. If there is no doubt as to reference, the only required pronoun in the four sentences above is the unstressed *lo, la, los,* or *las*.)

APPENDIX II
Práctica

B. NOUN DETERMINERS

Noun determiners are the words that accompany and modify nouns.

1. Articles

a) Definite Articles

DEFINITE ARTICLES		
	Singular	**Plural**
Masculine	el	los
Feminine	la	las

Definite articles agree with the noun they accompany. The only exception is that *la* is changed to *el* when a feminine noun starts with a stressed *a* or *ha*.

el agua *water*	**el aula** *classroom*
el alma *soul*	**el ave** *bird*
el ama de casa *housewife*	**el hacha** *axe*
el águila *eagle*	**el hambre** *hunger*

In the plural, this is no longer necessary, since there is no hiatus.

las aguas, las almas, las amas de casa, etc.

Feminine nouns beginning with an unstressed *a* or *ha* use *la*.

la abeja, la harina

Definite articles have two functions in Spanish—they may refer to a **specific** item or a group of **specific** items.

La conferencia le gustó al público.   *The audience liked the speech.*

They may refer to a **generalized** concept (English uses no article here).

Las conferencias de ese tipo son muy buenas para la gente, porque aumentan los conocimientos humanos.

Speeches of that type are very good for people, because they increase human knowledge.

Subject: subject nouns must be accompanied by a determiner of some kind. As a rule, sentences in Spanish do not begin with unaccompanied subject nouns.

La gente es así.	*People are like that.*
El amor es eterno.	*Love is eternal.*
Me gustan las películas* de horror.	*I like horror movies.*

*Películas here is the subject in Spanish, although in English it is the object.

Titles: use the definite article when speaking **about,** not **to,** someone you address with a title *(señor, señora, señorita, profesor, profesora, doctor, doctora).*

> **La** señora Gómez le explicó a **la** profesora Ruiz por qué su hijo había faltado.
> *Mrs. Gómez explained to Professor Ruiz why her son had missed class.*

EXCEPTIONS: *don, doña, san, santo, santa.*

> **Don** Jesús Gamboa es un ranchero muy conocido de esta región.
> *Don Jesús Gamboa is a very well known rancher of this region.*

When addressing someone directly, no article is used.

> **"Profesora Ruiz, perdone la ausencia de mi hijo: estuvo enfermo".**
> *"Professor Ruiz, forgive my son's absence: he was ill."*

> **"No se preocupe, Señora Gómez, le ayudaré a repasar".**
> *"Do not worry, Mrs. Gómez, I will help him review."*

Languages: the definite article is used before the names of languages, except when the name of the language follows *en* or the verb *hablar.*

Escribe **el** español con facilidad.	*She writes Spanish easily.*
Hablo español.	*I speak Spanish.*
Me lo dijo **en** español.	*She told me that in Spanish.*

Omit the article after *de* when two nouns are used, one to modify the other.

mi profesora **de** español	*my Spanish professor*
el libro **de** ruso	*the Russian book*

With *aprender, entender, comprender, enseñar, leer,* and other verbs relating to activities with language, the article is optional.

Aprendí (el) español a los seis años.	*I learned Spanish when I was six.*
Mi madre **enseña** (el) inglés.	*My mother teaches English.*

The article is necessary if an adverb is used between the verb and the name of the language.

> **Aprendí** **fácilmente** el español cuando tenía seis años.
> *I learned Spanish easily when I was six.*

Possessives vs. articles: with parts of the body, articles of clothing, and anything that pertains to the person in situations where there could be no ambiguity, the possessive is not necessary; a definite article is most frequently used.

El estudiante levantó la mano.	*The student raised his hand.*

In sentences where the part of the body, article of clothing, etc., is the direct object of the verb, and the indirect object indicates the possessor, an article is used instead of a possessive.

El dentista me arrancó <u>el</u> diente.	*The dentist pulled out my tooth.*
Nos admiró <u>el</u> uniforme.	*He admired our uniform.*

With reflexive verbs, the definite article is used with parts of the body and articles of clothing.

Me lavé <u>las</u> manos.	*I washed my hands.*
Se quitaron <u>el</u> abrigo.	*They took off their coats.*

In most cases, the definite article accompanies a prepositional object.

Lo llevaron <u>a la cárcel</u>.	*They took him to jail.*
Salimos <u>de la iglesia</u> a esa hora.	*We left the church at that time.*
Estaban <u>en el salón</u>.	*They were in the room.*

When *casa*, *clase*, or *misa* are objects of *a*, *de*, or *en*, omit the article.

Voy <u>a clase</u> a las ocho.	*I go to class at eight.*
Saldremos <u>de misa</u> a las once.	*We will leave church at eleven.*
No está <u>en casa</u> ahora.	*She is not at home now.*

With days of the week, always use the article, even after *hasta* and *para*.

<u>El lunes</u> tenemos una prueba.	*On Monday we have a test.*
¡<u>Hasta el lunes</u>!	*See you on Monday!*
Esta tarea es <u>para el viernes</u>.	*This assignment is for Friday.*

EXCEPTION: with *ser*, except when the sentence translates into English with **on**.

Hoy <u>es</u> miércoles.	*Today is Wednesday.*
La prueba <u>es el</u> lunes.	*The test is <u>on</u> Monday.*

APPENDIX II
Práctica

b) Indefinite Articles

INDEFINITE ARTICLES		
	Singular	**Plural**
Masculine	un	unos
Feminine	una	unas

Indefinite articles agree with the noun they accompany. The same exception applies for feminine indefinites as for definite articles. *Una* is changed to *un* when a feminine noun starts with a stressed *a* or *ha*.

¡Tengo <u>un</u> <u>ha</u>mbre!   *I am so hungry! (I have such a hunger!)*

The indefinite article is used much more in English than in Spanish, where, in most cases, it has more the meaning of the number "one." In the plural, *unos* and *unas* mean "some."

Omit the indefinite article after *ser* when an unmodified noun referring to profession, religion, nationality, or marital status is used.

Es estudiante. *She is a student.*   **Es mexicana.** *She is (a) Mexican.*

Soy católico. *I am (a) Catholic.*   **Eres soltero.** *You are a bachelor.*

If the noun is modified, use the article.

Es <u>una</u> estudiante muy aplicada.   *She is a very hardworking student.*

Soy <u>un</u> católico practicante.   *I am a practicing Catholic.*

Es <u>una</u> mexicana famosa.   *She is a famous Mexican.*

Omit the indefinite article before or after *cierto, cien, mil, otro, medio, semejante, tal,* and *¡qué…!*

Había <u>cierta</u> duda en su voz.   *There was a certain (some) doubt in her voice.*

Hay <u>cien</u> invitados.   *There are a hundred guests.*

Necesito <u>mil</u> dólares.   *I need a thousand dollars.*

¿Puede darme <u>otro</u> ejemplo?   *Can you give me another example?*

Pesa cinco kilos y <u>medio</u>.   *It weighs five and a half kilos.*

¿Puedes creer <u>semejante</u> mentira?   *Can you believe such a lie?*

Nunca dije <u>tal</u> cosa.   *I never said such a thing.*

¡<u>Qué</u> problema!   *What a problem!*

Omit the indefinite article in negative sentences after *haber* used impersonally and *tener.*

<u>No hay</u> respuesta.	*There is no answer.*
<u>No tiene</u> coche.	*He has no car.*

If you use the singular article, it has the meaning of the number "one."

No tiene <u>un</u> coche —tiene dos.	*He does not have one car—he has two.*
No tengo ni <u>un</u> centavo.	*I do not have a single cent.*

Omit the indefinite article after *sin.*

Salió <u>sin</u> abrigo.	*She went out without a coat.*

Omit the indefinite article after *con* when the object is being referred to as a type of object.

Escriban <u>con</u> pluma, por favor.	*Please write with a pen.*

If the object is specific or the number "one" is present, use the article.

Pudo hacerlo con <u>una</u> mano.	*He was able to do it with one hand.*

2. Adjectives

a) Demonstrative Adjectives

DEMONSTRATIVE ADJECTIVES[2]		
	Singular	**Plural**
Masculine	este	estos
Feminine	esta	estas
Masculine	ese	esos
Feminine	esa	esas
Masculine	aquel	aquellos
Feminine	aquella	aquellas

este = *this,* **ese** = *that* (near you), **aquel** = *that* (over there, far from you)

---

2. See *Chapter 3, Section C* for demonstrative pronouns (*éste, ése, esto, eso,* etc.).

These adjectives precede the noun and agree with it. Remember that in their adjective form they have no accent, whereas in their pronoun form they do. If it is difficult for you to remember which is which, it might help to remember that the adjective is always accompanied by a noun, but the pronoun never is (the pronoun subsumes the noun, replacing it).

<u>Este</u> libro es mío, y ése [pron.] es tuyo.	*This book is mine, and that one is yours.*
Dame <u>esa</u> libreta, por favor.	*Give me that notebook, please.*
¿Recuerdas <u>aquellos</u> días?	*Do you remember those days?*

APPENDIX II
Práctica

b) Possessive Adjectives[3]

"SHORT" POSSESSIVE ADJECTIVES		
	Singular	**Plural**
1st-person singular	mi	mis
2nd-person singular	tu	tus
3rd-person singular	su	sus
1st-person plural	nuestro, nuestra	nuestros, nuestras
2nd-person plural	vuestro, vuestra	vuestros, vuestras
3rd-person plural	su	sus

Possessive adjectives agree in gender and in number with the thing possessed, **not** with the possessor.

No tengo <u>mis</u> libros hoy.	*I do not have my books today.*
Me gustan <u>vuestras</u> ideas.	*I like your ideas.*
<u>Sus</u> manos siempre están limpias.	*His hands are always clean.*
Ellos me regalaron <u>su</u> coche.	*They gave me their car.*

---

3. See *Chapter 3, Section C* for possessive pronouns (*el mío, el tuyo,* etc.).

"LONG" POSSESSIVE ADJECTIVES		
	Singular	**Plural**
1st-person singular	mío, mía	míos, mías
2nd-person singular	tuyo, tuya	tuyos, tuyas
3rd-person singular	suyo, suya	suyos, suyas
1st-person plural	nuestro, nuestra	nuestros, nuestras
2nd-person plural	vuestro, vuestra	vuestros, vuestras
3rd-person plural	suyo, suya	suyos, suyas

Long possessive adjectives are used when the possessive follows the noun, where the English would use "of" . . .

> **Es una amiga <u>mía</u>.**   *She is a friend of mine.*

and after the verb *ser.*

> **Este libro es <u>mío</u>.**   *This book is mine.*
>
> **Esta caja es <u>mía</u>.**   *This box is mine.*

APPENDIX II

Práctica

c) Forms of Descriptive Adjectives

Descriptive adjectives are those that modify nouns, such as *rojo, viejo,* etc.

Adjectives ending in *-o* change to *-a* for the feminine.

> **un libro viej<u>o</u>, una casa viej<u>a</u>**

Adjectives ending in a consonant, *-e,* or *-ista* do not generally change for gender.

> **un hombre <u>joven</u>/una mujer <u>joven</u>**
>
> **un ojo <u>triste</u>/una mirada <u>triste</u>**
>
> **un vestido <u>azul</u>/una camisa <u>azul</u>**
>
> **un país <u>comunista</u>/una idea <u>comunista</u>**

EXCEPTIONS: adjectives referring to nationality ending in a consonant **do** change for gender.

> **español, español<u>a</u>, españoles, español<u>as</u>**
>
> **alemán, aleman<u>a</u>, alemanes, aleman<u>as</u>**
>
> **francés, francesa, franceses, frances<u>as</u>**
>
> **inglés, inglesa, ingleses, ingles<u>as</u>**

Adjectives with short and long forms:

Bueno and *malo* drop the final *-o* before a singular masculine noun.

   un <u>buen</u> libro/un libro <u>bueno</u>   el <u>mal</u> tiempo/el niño <u>malo</u>

Grande becomes *gran* before a singular noun of either gender.

   un <u>gran</u> evento   una <u>gran</u> amiga

Santo becomes *San* before any masculine name, unless it begins with *To-* or *Do-*.

   <u>San</u> Juan de la Cruz/<u>San</u> Nicolás   <u>Santo</u> Tomás/<u>Santo</u> Domingo

Adjectives ending in a consonant add *-es* for the plural, and accents may be added or deleted to maintain the stress on the same syllable as the singular.

   <u>joven, jóvenes</u>

APPENDIX II

Práctica

d) Position of Descriptive Adjectives

Descriptive adjectives usually FOLLOW the noun they modify;[4] as a rule, they serve the purpose of restricting which person, thing, or place is being referred to.

Viene a hablarnos un profesor <u>famoso</u>.

A famous professor is coming to talk to us.

Me gusta la casa <u>verde</u>.

I like the green house.

In the sentences above, a contrast is being established between the mentioned nouns and others that do not have the same quality indicated in the adjective: A famous professor is coming, not an unknown one; I like the green house, not the white one or the others.

Descriptive adjectives will PRECEDE the noun if this noun indicates someone or something that is already identified, known, or otherwise restricted. When adjectives precede the noun, their function is explicative, not restrictive. They add to the already identified thing or person, describe it, color it, decorate it, or define it, with innate or inherent characteristics or traits. Often, the adjective itself is already associated with the noun.

This is the case, for example, with proper nouns, but also with nouns describing things or relations of which we only have one (a nose, a navel; a mother, a father, a husband, a wife…).

---

4. Notice that this is not the case with quantitative adjectives, which usually **precede** the noun: *el **primer** día de clases, tenemos **varias** posibilidades, existen **algunos** casos diferentes…*

el <u>extravagante</u> Dalí	(Salvador Dalí was extravagant by definition)
el <u>elegante</u> Museo del Prado	(elegance is an inherent quality of the museum)
la <u>conocida</u> profesora Sainz	(her fame precedes her)
la <u>simbólica</u> torta de manzanas	(apple pie is symbolic in the United States)
tu <u>pequeño</u> ombligo	(smallness is an inherent quality of your navel)
su <u>gigantesca</u> nariz[5]	(gigantic is a characteristic of his nose)
mi <u>hermosa</u> madre	(my mother is innately beautiful)

A common noun that refers to a specific person, place, or thing would also fit in the category described above.

nuestra <u>adorada</u> maestra

our adored teacher (we know her name)

el <u>utilísimo</u> manual

the very useful manual (we know it by title)

los <u>impresionantes</u> avances de la tecnología moderna

the impressive advances of modern technology (*de la tecnología moderna* clearly specifies the progress to which we are referring)

If an identified or proper noun is followed by an adjective, the implication is that there are two or more such things or people.

el Museo del Prado <u>moderno</u>

the modern Museo del Prado (either the museum was renovated, or there are two parts to the museum, one modern, one not)

tus ojos <u>verdes</u>

your green eyes (your eyes change colors, either naturally or with contact lenses)

When an adjective is used to describe an inherent quality of something, it may have poetic or oratorial overtones, especially when it is universally redundant.

La <u>blanca</u> nieve cubría los montes…

The white snow covered the hills… (snow is inherently white; this construction is poetic)

Adjectives of nationality **always FOLLOW** the noun.

Esa novela es de un autor <u>argentino</u>.

That novel is by an Argentine author.

---

5. If you want to describe something already identified as big or large, avoid using *gran*, which, when placed before the noun, means "great"; other possibilities: *gigantesco, enorme, voluminoso…*

Ten common descriptive adjectives change meaning depending on their location.

	BEFORE THE NOUN	AFTER THE NOUN
ALTO	el <u>alto</u> funcionario *the high official*	el funcionario <u>alto</u> *the tall official*
ANTIGUO	el <u>antiguo</u> contrato *the old (former, not current)* *contract*	la mesa <u>antigua</u> *the old (not new)* *table*
CIERTO	<u>cierto</u> tono *certain tone (indeterminate)*	una declaración <u>cierta</u> *a true statement*
GRANDE	un <u>gran</u> hombre *a great man*	un hombre <u>grande</u> *a big man*
NUEVO	el <u>nuevo</u> contrato *the new (latest) contract*	un coche <u>nuevo</u> *a (brand-) new car*
POBRE	el <u>pobre</u> hombre *the poor (unfortunate) man*	un hombre <u>pobre</u> *a poor (not rich) man*
RARO	la <u>rara</u> habilidad *the rare ability*	una voz <u>rara</u> *a strange voice*
SIMPLE	un <u>simple</u> adiós *just a simple good-bye* *(nothing more)*	un hombre <u>simple</u> *a simpleton*
TRISTE	una <u>triste</u> manzana *just one humble,* *insignificant apple*	una empleada <u>triste</u> *a sad employee*
VIEJO	un <u>viejo</u> amigo *an old (longtime) friend*	un amigo <u>viejo</u> *an old (aged) friend*

When these special adjectives are used with nouns referring to specific, already identified, people, things, or places, they lose some of their variety of meaning.

mi <u>viejo</u> padre

my old father (obviously not former or longtime)

las <u>pobres</u> obreras de esa fábrica

the poor workers of that factory (they may be pitiful or penniless, or both)

Fixed order: some adjectives are fixed in certain expressions by sheer usage.

idea <u>fija</u> *set idea*	la <u>pura</u> verdad *the basic truth*
sentido <u>común</u> *common sense*	<u>libre</u> albedrío *free will*
Semana <u>Santa</u> *Holy Week*	<u>alta</u> fidelidad *high fidelity*

Bueno and malo: two special adjectives.

These two adjectives can follow the rule; when after the noun, there is a restriction of the noun it modifies.

Los estudiantes <u>buenos</u> terminarán primero.

The good students will finish first. (We clarify which students will finish first by placing the adjective after the noun.)

When these adjectives precede the noun, the noun is already identified, and the contrast being established is between it and other nouns.

Hace un <u>buen</u> guacamole, pero sus enchiladas son divinas.

She makes a good guacamole, but her enchiladas are divine. (The contrast here is between guacamole and enchiladas.)

In many cases, these adjectives exist in ready-made expressions.

<u>buena</u> suerte *good luck*	<u>mala</u> suerte *bad luck*
un <u>buen</u> día *one day, unexpectedly*	un <u>mal</u> dormir *a sleepless night*
de <u>buena</u> familia *from a good family*	<u>malos</u> pensamientos *evil thoughts*

Some nouns have been formed incorporating the adjective.

la hierbabuena *spearmint*	el malhumor *ill temper*
la buenaventura *good fortune*	el malparto *miscarriage*

Ultimately, the dictionary is the best place to check special usage of common adjectives.

APPENDIX II
Práctica

e) Comparisons

(1) Comparisons of Inequality

(a) With **Adverbs, Adjectives,** and **Nouns**

"a"	más/menos	adverb adjective noun	que	"b"

Marta comprende <u>más</u> fácilmente <u>que</u> yo.
Marta understands more easily than I.

Esa novela es <u>más</u> larga <u>que</u> ésta.
That novel is longer than this one.

José tiene <u>menos</u> dinero <u>que</u> yo.
José has less money than I do.

(b) With a **Numerical Expression,** Use *De* Instead of *Que*

Hay <u>más de diez</u> sillas aquí.
There are more than ten chairs here.

Nos quedan <u>menos de veinte</u> minutos.
We have less than twenty minutes left.

Te di <u>más de la mitad</u>.
I gave you more than half.

Conocí a <u>menos de diez</u> personas nuevas.
I met fewer than ten new people.

No invitó a <u>más de treinta</u> personas.
He did not invite more than thirty people.

Special use of *más que:* in negative sentences, *más que* is the equivalent of "only" in English, or some other exclusive type expression, and is not comparative in meaning.

No tengo <u>más que</u> tres pesos.
I have <u>only</u> three dollars.

No invitó <u>más que</u> a tres personas.
She invited <u>only</u> three people.

Nunca come <u>más que</u> fruta.
He eats <u>only</u> fruit. (He never eats anything but fruit, anything other than fruit.)

Nunca viaja <u>más que</u> a España.

She only travels to Spain. (She never travels to any other place than Spain, nowhere but to Spain.)

Irregular comparatives:

mejor(es) *better, best*	**mayor**(es) *older, oldest*
peor(es) *worse, worst*	**menor**(es) *younger, youngest*

(*Más bueno* and *más malo* are used only occasionally, when the emphasis is on character traits of people, especially in idiomatic expressions. *Más viejo* and *más joven* are often interchangeable with *mayor* and *menor.*)

Mi clase es mejor que la tuya.

My class is better than yours.

Yo canto peor que tú.

I sing worse than you do.

Yo soy mayor que tú. Yo soy más viejo que tú.

I am older than you.

Tú eres menor que yo. Tú eres más joven que yo.

You are younger than I.

(c) With a **Verb** or Clause as Second Part of Comparison

With a noun in the first part:

más/menos	noun [masc. sing.] noun [fem. sing.] noun [masc. pl.] noun [fem. pl.]	**del que** **de la que** **de los que** **de las que**	clause

Planté más <u>maíz</u> <u>del que</u> coseché.

I planted more corn than I harvested.

Hay menos <u>nieve</u> <u>de la que</u> esperábamos.

There was less snow than we expected.

Recibió más <u>regalos</u> <u>de los que</u> dio.

He received more gifts than he gave.

Vendió menos <u>flores</u> <u>de las que</u> había comprado.

She sold fewer flowers than she had bought.

Without a noun in the first part of the comparison, use the neuter form *de lo que*.

> **Nevó más <u>de lo que</u> esperábamos.**
> *It snowed more than we expected.*

> **Fue más interesante <u>de lo que</u> creíamos.**
> *It was more interesting than we thought.*

(2) Comparisons of Equality

a. **Tanto(-as, -os, -as)... Como**

With a noun, use the variable *tanto(-a, -os, -as)... como*, in agreement with the noun.

> **Tengo <u>tantos problemas como</u> tú.**
> *I have as many problems as you do.*

b. **Tanto Como**

Alone as an adverb, use the invariable *tanto como*.

> **Ella no come <u>tanto como</u> yo.**
> *She does not eat as much as I do.*

c. **Tan... Como**

With an adverb or an adjective, use *tan... como*.

> **Ese coche está <u>tan brillante como</u> el nuestro.**
> *That car is as shiny as ours.*

> **Ellos hablan <u>tan bien como</u> tú.**
> *They speak as well as you do.*

APPENDIX II

Práctica

f) Superlatives

The superlative in Spanish is formed with an **article** + *más/menos* + *de* (if a group is being indicated).

Iris es <u>la más lista de</u> la clase.	*Iris is the smartest of the class.*
Esas flores son <u>las más rojas de</u> todas.	*Those flowers are the reddest of all.*
Mi tío es <u>el menos presumido de</u> todos.	*My uncle is the least conceited of all.*
Julio es <u>el más alto</u>.	*Julio is the tallest.*
Este coche es <u>el menos caro</u>.	*This car is the least expensive.*

El más grande and *el más pequeño* become *el mayor* and *el menor* when referring to age.

Jorge es <u>el mayor</u> y Juan es <u>el menor</u>.

Jorge is the oldest and Juan is the youngest.

Chapter 3

Pronouns

A. PERSONAL PRONOUNS

The usage of pronouns is closely linked to the type of verb with which they are found.

I. Definitions

a) Intransitive Verbs

Intransitive verbs have only a subject.[1] They have no direct or indirect object.

Llegué. *I arrived.*	**Salieron.** *They went out.*

When these verbs have complements, they are complements of place, of destination, of origin, of time, etc., but **never** object complements.

Llegué a casa temprano.	*I got home early.*
Voy a clase a las ocho.	*I go to class at eight.*
Volvimos del museo a las cuatro.	*We returned from the museum at four.*
Llegaron por la avenida.	*They arrived by the avenue.*

b) Transitive Verbs

Transitive verbs can have a subject and a direct and/or indirect object.

(1) With Subject and Direct Object

Estudié la lección.	*I studied the lesson.*
[subj.: **yo**; d.o.: **la lección**]	
Vimos la película.	*We saw the movie.*
[subj.: **nosotros**; d.o.: **la película**]	
Vi a[2] tu hermana.	*I saw your sister.*
[subj.: **yo**; d.o.: **tu hermana**]	

(2) With Subject, Direct Object, and Indirect Object

Le regalamos las flores a[3] mi mamá.
We gave the flowers to my mother.
    [subj.: **nosotros**; d.o.: **las flores**; i.o.: **mi mamá**]

¿Le diste la carta al cartero?
Did you give the letter to the mailman?
    [subj.: **tú**; d.o.: **la carta**; i.o.: **el cartero**]

Les dio la niña[4] a los padres adoptivos.
She gave the child to the adoptive parents.
    [subj.: **ella**; d.o.: **la niña**; i.o: **los padres**]

---

1. The subject pronoun in Spanish is used mostly for emphasis or clarification.
2. Personal *a* used with a human or personified direct object.
3. Preposition *a* used to introduce an indirect object.
4. In case of possible ambiguity, the personal *a*, usually required before the human direct object *la niña*, is eliminated. Here, there is an indirect object *(los padres)* introduced by the preposition *a*. If the personal *a* were used before *la niña*, it wouldn't be clear who is being given to whom.

(3) With Subject and Indirect Object Only

There are special verbs in Spanish that are sometimes called "flip" verbs because they are most frequently the opposite of English in construction, the subject in English being the indirect object in Spanish, and the object in English being the subject in Spanish. The verb *gustar* is used generally as model of this type of verb. (See *Chapter 6, Section 9* on *gustar*-type verbs.)

Me gusta esta clase.	Spanish—subj.: **esta clase**; i.o.: **a mí**
I like this class.	English—subj.: *I*; d.o.: *this class*
Le caes bien a mi hermano.	Spanish—subj.: **tú**; i.o.: **a mi hermano**
My brother likes you.	English—subj.: *My brother*; d.o.: *you*
Nos encanta Madrid.	Spanish—subj.: **Madrid**; i.o.: **a nosotros**
We love Madrid.	English—subj.: *We*; d.o.: *Madrid*

2. Subject Pronouns

SUBJECT PRONOUNS		
Person	**Singular**	**Plural**
1st	yo	nosotros
2nd	tú	vosotros
3rd	él/ella/usted*	ellos/ellas/ustedes*

* *Usted* is used to speak to a person you do not know well, particularly in Latin America.

* *Ustedes* is the plural of *tú* or *usted* in Latin America, but in Spain, it is only the plural of *usted*; *vosotros* is the plural of *tú*.

The subject pronoun in Spanish is not used except when emphasis, clarity, or contrast is needed; in English, this emphasis is marked with stress in the voice.

Tengo cuatro hermanos.	*I have four brothers.*
¿Cuántos hermanos tienes?	*How many brothers do you have?*
Tengo tres hermanos.	*I have three brothers.*
¿Quién hizo esto?	*Who did this?*
Lo hice <u>yo</u>.	<u>*I*</u> *did it.*
<u>Nosotros</u> llevamos la ensalada, y <u>tú</u> el pan.	<u>*We*</u> *will take the salad, and <u>you</u> the bread.*

Using *usted* as a subject pronoun conveys an idea of formality or courtesy, rather than emphasis or contrast.

¿Desea usted algo más?	*Would you like something else?*
Usted conoce a mi prima, ¿verdad?	*You know my cousin, don't you?*

The third person subject pronouns *él, ella, ellos,* and *ellas*[5] refer only to persons, never to things. There is no subject pronoun for "it" (or its plural "they") in Spanish.

Esa mesa es de madera.	*That table is made of wood.*
Es de madera.	*It is made of wood.*
Me gusta[6] **esa película.**	*I like that movie.*
Me gusta mucho.	*I like it a lot.*
Se venden[7] **muchos autos ahora.**	*Many cars are sold now.*
Se venden rápido.	*They are sold quickly.*

APPENDIX II
Práctica

3. Direct Object Pronouns

a) Formation and Usage

DIRECT OBJECT PRONOUNS		
Person	**Singular**	**Plural**
1st	me	nos
2nd	te	os
3rd	lo/la	los/las

Direct object pronouns receive the direct action of the verb.

Me ven.	*They see me.*
Te conocen.	*They know you.*
Nos escuchan.	*They listen to us.*
Os entiendo.	*I understand you.*
Lo vi ayer.	*I saw him/you (usted) yesterday.*
Las conozco bien.	*I know them/you (ustedes) well.*

---

5. These pronouns cannot be used as subjects when they refer to things; however, they can be used as prepositional objects referring to things: **¿Y esos tomates? ¿Qué vas a preparar con ellos?** *And those tomatoes? What are you going to prepare with them?*
6. For *gustar* and similar verbs, the subject in English is the indirect object in Spanish, and the object in English is the subject in Spanish.
7. With the impersonal *se* construction with inanimate objects, the inanimate object functions as the subject of the verb. This translates frequently as the passive voice in English.

In most of Spain, but not in most of Latin America, *le(s)* is used instead of *lo(s)* for male human beings.

No <u>lo</u> conozco. (Latin America)

No <u>le</u> conozco. (Spain)

Os is used only in Spain, for the plural of *te*.

	Latin America *(I saw you.)*	**Spain** *(I saw you.)*
Singular	Te vi.	Te vi.
Plural	Los vi (a ustedes).	Os vi.

The direct object pronoun replacing an inanimate object will reflect the gender and number of the noun it replaces.

Miro la televisión. ¿Tú <u>la</u> miras?   *I watch TV. Do you watch it?*

APPENDIX II

Práctica

b) *Lo*—The Neuter (Invariable) Pronoun

The neuter *lo* refers to an idea or situation that is not specific enough to be either masculine or feminine.

Nos queda poco tiempo.   *We have little time left.*

Sí, ya <u>lo</u> sé.   *Yes, I know it.*

Lo is used as a complement to replace adjectives, pronouns, or nouns with *ser*, *estar*, and *parecer;* notice that in English the equivalent of *lo* in most cases is merely represented by emphasis on the verb when spoken.

—**Creo que ella es muy lista.**   *I think she is very clever.*

—**Yo no creo que <u>lo</u> sea.**   *I do not think she is.*

—**Esa mujer es la tía de Juan.**   *That woman is Juan's aunt.*

—**Sé que no <u>lo</u> es porque**   *I know she is not because*
conozco a su tía.   *I know his aunt.*

—**¿Estas llaves son tuyas?**   *Are these keys yours?*

—**No, no <u>lo</u> son.**   *No, they are not.*

—**¿Estás frustrada?**   *Are you frustrated?*

—**Sí, <u>lo</u> estoy.**   *Yes, I am.*

—**Pareces loca.**   *You are acting crazy.*

—**Quizá <u>lo</u> parezca, pero no <u>lo</u> estoy.**   *Maybe I look that way, but I am not.*

4. Indirect Object Pronouns

INDIRECT OBJECT PRONOUNS		
Person	Singular	Plural
1st	me	nos
2nd	te	os
3rd	le*	les*

*When combined with *lo(s)* or *la(s)*, *le(s)* becomes *se*.

Le dio la manzana a la maestra.   →   **Se** la dio.
He gave the apple to the teacher.   *He gave it to her.*

Les regaló el coche.   →   **Se** lo regaló.
She gave them the car.   *She gave it to them.*

The indirect object is used to indicate the person(s) receiving the direct object or to indicate the person or thing that is affected in some way by the action of the verb.

Me regaló sus guantes.   *He gave me his gloves.*

¿**Te** dijo su secreto?   *Did she tell you her secret?*

Les mandó la carta.   *She sent them the letter.*

There are many possible translations into English of indirect objects in Spanish, with a variety of prepositions used in the English version.

Le hiciste la tarea.   *You did the homework <u>for</u> him.*

Les quitó la llave.   *He took the key <u>away from</u> them.*

Nos pidió ese favor.   *He asked that favor <u>of</u> us.*

Verbs commonly used with indirect objects may be flip verbs (see *Chapter 6, Section 9* on *gustar*) or other verbs that may change meaning if used with a direct object.

No **le** creo.   No **lo** creo.

I do not believe him (or her).   *I do not believe it.* (what he is saying)

i.e., he is lying.   He may be telling what he believes to
            be the truth, but I think the truth is
            different: i.e., he is not lying.

¿**Le** pagaste?   ¿**La** pagaste?

Did you pay him (or her)?   *Did you pay it?* (e.g., **la cuenta**)

Le gané.   **Lo** gané.

I beat him (or her) [at a game].   *I won it.*

Le pegué duro.   **Lo** pegamos.

I hit him (or her) hard.   *We glued it.*

Le di en la cara.	**Me lo** dio.
I hit him (or her) in the face.	*He gave it to me.*
Le robaron.	**Lo** robaron.
They robbed him (or her).	*They stole it.*
Le extraña que hagas eso.	**Lo** extraña mucho.
It surprises him (her) that you do that.	*She misses him a lot.*

5. Required Repetitive Object Pronouns

The following object pronouns must be used, however redundant it may sound.

a) Direct Object Pronouns

Direct object pronouns must be used when the object noun precedes rather than follows the verb . . .

La salida la encontrará a su derecha.	*You will find the exit to the right.*
A todos los niños los felicitó.	*He congratulated all of the children.*
A ella no **la** vi.	*I did not see her.*

and whenever the pronoun *todo (toda, todos, todas)* is used as a direct object.

Lo vendieron **todo**.	*They sold it all.*
La cantaron **toda**. (la canción)	*They sang it all.*
Nos invitaron a **todos**.	*They invited all of us.*

b) Indirect Object Pronouns

These are almost always used redundantly even though their referent appears in the clause.

Le dije **a Maira** que venías.	*I told Maira you were coming.*
Les regalé eso **a los niños**.	*I gave that to the children.*
Le caes bien **a mi hermano**.	*My brother likes you.*
Le caes bien **a él**.	*He likes you.*
Le caes bien.	*He likes you.*
Les hace falta **a sus padres**.	*Her parents miss her.*
Les hace falta **a ellos**.	*They miss her.*
Les hace falta.	*They miss her.*

6. Order of Object Pronouns When Combined

ORDER OF OBJECT PRONOUNS WHEN COMBINED			
#1	#2	#3	#4
se	2nd-person	1st-person	3rd-person
se	te os	me nos	lo(s) la(s) le(s)

Examples:

<u>Se te</u> cayeron los libros.	*You dropped your books.*
<u>Se os</u> dirá cuando sea tiempo.	*You will be told when it is time.*
<u>Se me</u> dijo la verdad.	*I was told the truth.*
<u>Se nos</u> acabaron las ideas.	*We ran out of ideas.*
<u>Se lo</u> expliqué.	*I explained it to him/her.*
<u>Se los</u> regalé.	*I gave them to him /her.*
<u>Se la</u> mandaron.	*They sent it to them.*
<u>Se le</u> olvidó.	*He/She forgot it.*
<u>Te lo</u> dije.	*I told you (so/it).*
<u>Te la</u> regalé.	*I gave it to you.*
<u>Me lo</u> dijeron.	*They told me (so/it).*
<u>Me la</u> enseñaron.	*They showed it to me.*
<u>Nos lo</u> contaste.	*You told us (so/it).*
<u>Nos la</u> enseñaron.	*They showed it to us.*

7. Position of Object Pronouns

Direct and indirect object pronouns must be placed before or after their related verb depending on the form of the verb itself. There is no choice as to position after the verb with the affirmative command. There is no choice as to position before the verb with every other form except the infinitive and the present participle; with these last two, pronouns may be placed before or after the verb phrase, as long as all pronouns relating to the same verb are placed in the same position.

VERB FORM	POSITION OF PRONOUN(S)	EXAMPLES
conjugated verb	before	**<u>La</u> vi ayer.** *I saw her yesterday.*
compound tense	before auxiliary *(haber)*	**Nunca <u>la</u> he visto.** *I have never seen her.*
infinitive	before auxiliary or after infinitive	**<u>Me la</u> quiero comprar.** **Quiero comprár<u>mela</u>.** *I want to buy it (for myself).*
present participle	before auxiliary or after present participle[8]	**<u>Lo</u> estaba mirando.** **Estaba mirándo<u>lo</u>.** *I was looking at it.*
affirmative command	after[8]	**Míra<u>la</u>. Cómprate<u>los</u>.** *Look at it. Buy them (for yourself.)*
negative command	before	**No <u>la</u> mires.** **No <u>te los</u> compres.** *Do not look at it. Do not buy them.*

The only time there is a choice as to pronoun position is in a verb phrase containing a conjugated verb and an infinitive or present participle. There are some circumstances, however, where this flexibility is lost; in the following cases, the pronoun must always be placed after the infinitive or present participle.

If the infinitive follows a preposition:

Viajaremos para conseguir<u>lo</u>.   *We will travel to get it.*

If a present participle is used adverbially:

Salieron riéndo<u>se</u>.   *They left laughing.*

If an infinitive or present participle follows a command:

Vaya a comprar<u>lo</u>.   *Go and buy it.*
Sigue estudiándo<u>lo</u>.   *Continue studying it.*

APPENDIX II

Práctica

---

8. When pronouns are attached to the end of an infinitive, a present participle, or a command, an accent may be needed to maintain the original stress on the verb: vend<u>e</u>r—vend<u>e</u>rlos—vend<u>é</u>rselos; vendi<u>e</u>ndo—vendi<u>é</u>ndolos; v<u>e</u>nde—v<u>é</u>ndelos.

8. Prepositional Object Pronouns

PREPOSITIONAL OBJECT PRONOUNS		
Person	**Singular**	**Plural**
1st	mí	nosotros
2nd	ti	vosotros
3rd	él/ella	ellos/ellas
formal	usted	ustedes
reflexive	sí	sí

Prepositional object pronouns are used after prepositions.

Lo hizo <u>por mí</u>.	*She did it because of me.*
Puedes contar <u>con nosotros</u>.	*You can count on us.*
Se fue <u>sin ella</u>.	*He left without her.*
Lo guardó <u>para sí</u>.	*He kept it for himself.*
Lo guardó <u>para él</u>.	*She kept it for him.*
Estaba sentado <u>frente a vosotros</u>.	*He was sitting in front of you.*
Corrió <u>tras ella</u>.	*He ran after her.*
Estaba <u>cerca de ti</u>.	*He was close to you.*
No encuentro mi diccionario;	*I cannot find my dictionary;*
ayer trabajé <u>con él</u>.	*yesterday I worked with it.*
La gorra de Roberto es parte de él;	*Roberto's cap is a part of him;*
nunca sale <u>sin ella</u>.	*he never leaves without it.*

The following prepositions take the subject pronoun form for *yo* and *tú*.

entre: Estaba sentado <u>entre tú y yo</u>.
              He was sitting between you and me.

según: <u>Según tú</u>, esto es incorrecto.
              According to you, this is incorrect.

Como, excepto, and *menos* take *yo* and *tú*, unless they are followed by another preposition. Use the pronoun that goes with the last preposition.

como: Mis amigos piensan <u>como yo</u>.
              My friends think like me.
              A mí no me duele <u>como a ti</u>.
              It does not hurt me the way it does you.

excepto: Todos lo vieron <u>excepto yo</u>.

They all saw it except me.

Les dieron a todos <u>excepto a mí</u>.

They gave to everyone but me.

Se lleva bien con todos <u>excepto conmigo</u>.

He gets along with everyone but me.

menos: **Todos <u>menos tú</u> comieron postre.**

They all ate dessert except you.

Hubo carta para todos <u>menos para ti</u>.

There was a letter for everyone but you.

The preposition *con* with *mí, ti,* and *sí* becomes *conmigo, contigo,* and *consigo.*

Ven <u>conmigo</u>.	*Come with me.*
Pensé que estaba <u>contigo</u>.	*I thought he was with you.*
Se lo llevó <u>consigo</u>.	*He took it along (with himself).*

Consigo vs. con *él, ella,* etc.

Consigo is used when the subject of the verb is the same as the object of *con;* in situations where the subject is different from the object of *con,* use the standard third-person prepositional pronoun.

Fuimos al cine con Juan. Fuimos al cine <u>con él</u>.

Quiero bailar con María. Quiero bailar <u>con ella</u>.

Me gusta hablar con mis vecinos. Me gusta hablar <u>con ellos</u>.

Nunca he ido al cine con mis hermanitas. Nunca he ido al cine <u>con ellas</u>.

APPENDIX II

Práctica

B.   *S E*

1. Introduction

The pronoun *se* in Spanish can have different usages, depending on the context in which it is used.

The indirect object pronouns *le* and *les*, when followed by a direct object pronoun such as *lo* or *la*, are transformed into *se*.

Se is also the third-person singular and plural form of the reflexive pronoun.

In its function as a reflexive pronoun, *se* can be used in constructions with a thing as a subject and a person as an indirect object to describe an accidental occurrence. In *Se me olvidó la tarea*, the subject of the verb is *tarea* and the person is the indirect object. In this type of sentence the thing is doing the action to itself (thus the reflexive), and the person appears as an innocent bystander or victim, indirectly affected by the event.

The impersonal usage of *se* is where the action is being done with no subject mentioned—clearly someone is doing it, but it is irrelevant to the context. When you read *Se habla español* on the door of a store, it indicates that Spanish is spoken in that store in case of need. It is irrelevant to state who speaks the language.

OVERVIEW OF USES OF *SE*
1. *Le* or *les* transformed before *lo(s)* or *la(s)* **Le di la flor.** ➜ **Se la di.** *I gave her the flower.* ➜ *I gave it to her.*
2. Third-person reflexive **Ella se levanta temprano.** *She wakes up early.* Third-person reciprocal **Ellos se odian.** *They hate each other.*
3. Irresponsible or accidental **Se me cayó el libro.** *I dropped the book.*
4. Impersonal **Se habla español.** *Spanish is spoken.*

2. Reflexive Pronouns[9]

a) Reflexives

REFLEXIVE PRONOUNS		
Person	**Singular**	**Plural**
1st	me	nos
2nd	te	os
3rd	se	se

A reflexive construction occurs when the subject and the object of a verb are the same person. In some cases, the object of the verb is direct.

Me lavo.   *I wash myself.*

In other cases, the object of the verb is indirect.

Se escribían todos los días.   *They wrote (to) each other every day.*

Certain verbs that refer to daily personal habits are most frequently used in the reflexive construction (see *Chapter 6, Section 10* on reflexive verbs).

bañarse *to bathe (oneself)*   **lavarse** *to wash (oneself)*

despertarse *to wake (oneself) up*   **levantarse** *to get (oneself) up*

These verbs can be used non-reflexively, in a standard transitive construction, with the object different from the subject.

La madre bañó a su bebé.   →   **Lo bañó.**
The mother bathed her baby.   *She bathed him.*

Ella se bañó a las seis.   →   **Se bañó.**
She bathed (herself) at six.   *She bathed (took a bath).*

Possessives change to definite articles with parts of the body or articles of clothing.

Me lavé las manos.   *I washed my hands.*

Me puse el abrigo.   *I put on my coat.*

---

9. See *Chapter 6, Section 10* on commonly used verbs with reflexive pronouns.

To stress or emphasize the reflexive pronouns, the following reflexive prepositional object pronouns are used.

REFLEXIVE PREPOSITIONAL OBJECT PRONOUNS		
Person	**Singular**	**Plural**
1st	mí	nosotros
2nd	ti	vosotros
3rd	sí	sí

Mi abuela ya está viejita. Se habla <u>a sí misma</u> de más en más.	*My grandmother is getting old. She speaks to herself more and more.*

These pronouns are used after other prepositions and in constructions where the verb itself is not reflexive, but the action is.

Lo hago <u>por mí</u>.	*I do it for myself.*
Lo compró <u>para sí</u>.	*She bought it for herself.*
Trajo el paraguas <u>consigo</u>.	*She brought the umbrella (with her).*

b) Reciprocals

The plural pronouns can be used for reciprocal actions as well.

Ellos <u>se</u> conocen bien.	*They know each other well.*

In case of ambiguity, the following may be added.

RECIPROCAL = *each other*		
	Singular	**Plural**
Masculine	el uno al otro	unos a otros
Feminine	la una a la otra	unas a otras

REFLEXIVE = *myself, yourself,* etc.		
Person	**Singular**	**Plural**
1st	a mí mismo(a)	a nosotros(as) mismos(as)
2nd	a ti mismo(a)	a vosotros(as) mismos(as)
3rd	a sí mismo(a)	a sí mismos(as)

<u>**Nos**</u> conocemos <u>el uno al otro</u>.

We know each other. (Reciprocal)

<u>**Nos**</u> conocemos <u>a nosotros mismos</u>.

We know ourselves. (Reflexive—each one of us knows him- or herself.)

APPENDIX II
Práctica

3. *Se me* Construction—Accidental or Irresponsible *Se*

In Spanish there is a structure that is very commonly used when dealing with accidental, chance, or unplanned situations, where something happens that was not intended. This is often the case with such actions as forgetting, dropping, burning, breaking, etc. In such situations, the thing involved in the accident becomes the subject of the verb, and the verb is used in a reflexive format. The person, or victim of the accident, becomes the indirect object of the verb. Therefore, it might appear misleading to name this *se* differently from any other reflexive *se*— the only reason it is invariable is because things are always third-person singular or plural, never first- or second-person, forms that are reserved for humans.

Examples:

Se rompieron mis lentes.

My glasses broke. [subj.: *my glasses*; d.o.: none]

Se rompió tu libro.

Your book broke. [subj.: *your book*; d.o.: none]

<u>**Se me**</u> **rompieron los lentes.**[10] [subj.: **los lentes**; i.o.: **a mí**)

I broke[11] *(accidentally) my glasses.* [subj.: *I*; d.o.: *my glasses*]

<u>**Se me**</u> **rompió tu libro.**

I broke (accidentally) your book. [subj.: *your book*; d.o.: none]

In English, as in Spanish, there are a number of verbs that can be used in such a way that the thing to which the accident occurred is the subject of the verb: things break, fall, tear, close, open, go out (light), wrinkle, get dirty, get wet, go bad, etc.

---

10. The nouns in these sentences that function as subject or indirect object may be placed before or after the verb.
    Se me rompieron los lentes. = Los lentes se me rompieron.
    A Daniel se le olvidó la cita. = Se le olvidó la cita a Daniel.
11. If the action of breaking was done on purpose, the verb and pronouns behave "normally" in Spanish, with the person being the subject of the verb.
    Ese chico me puso tan furioso que le rompí los lentes. (subj.: **yo**; d.o.: **lentes**)
    That kid made me so angry that I broke his glasses.

The difference in structure in Spanish is that to this accidental occurrence can be added the person to whom it happened. Notice that the possessive changes to a definite article when referring to a part of the body or an article of clothing or personal possession.

<u>Se</u> <u>me</u> rompieron los lentes.	*My glasses broke.*
<u>Se</u> <u>te</u> rompieron los lentes.	*Your (**tú**) glasses broke.*
<u>Se</u> <u>le</u> rompieron los lentes.	*His/Her/Your (**Ud.**) glasses broke.*
<u>Se</u> <u>nos</u> rompieron los lentes.	*Our glasses broke.*
<u>Se</u> <u>os</u> rompieron los lentes.	*Your (**Vosotros**) glasses broke.*
<u>Se</u> <u>les</u> rompieron los lentes.	*Their/Your (**Uds.**) glasses broke.*

Notice that *rompieron* is third-person plural because the subject of the verb is plural: *los lentes.* If the subject were singular, the verb would be singular too.

<u>Se</u> <u>te</u> rompió el lente.	*Your lens broke.*

If you wish to state the person to whom the accident happened, remember that the grammatical function of the person is the indirect object, introduced with the preposition *a.*

Se le olvidó la cita <u>al paciente</u>.	*The patient forgot the appointment.*
<u>A Quico</u> se le perdieron los boletos.	*Quico lost the tickets.*
Se le rompió el paraguas <u>a Carmelita</u>.	*Carmelita's umbrella broke.*

If the subject of this type of sentence need not be stated because it has already been mentioned before in the context, remember the basic rule that in Spanish there is no subject pronoun equivalent to "it" in English (or "they" when it is the plural of "it").

¿Qué pasó con tu lente?	*What happened to your lens?*
Se me rompió.	*It broke.*

The following verbs can be used with this construction.

quemársele a uno *to burn*

On purpose: **Quemaron los libros.** *They burned the books.*

Accidental/no victim: **Los libros se quemaron.** *The books burned (up).*

Accidental/with victim: **Se nos quemaron los libros.** *Our books burned (up).*

caérsele a uno *to drop/to fall* (**Dejar caer** is used for the purposeful action, and means, literally, *to let fall.*)

On purpose: **Dejó caer el vaso.** *He dropped the glass.*

Accidental/no victim: **El vaso se cayó.** *The glass fell.*

Accidental/with victim: **Se le cayó el vaso.** *He dropped the glass.*

olvidársele a uno *to forget*

On purpose: **Olvidemos nuestros problemas.** *Let's forget our problems.*

Accidental/no victim: impossible in Spanish.

Accidental/with victim: **Se nos olvidó el libro.** *We forgot the book.*

In Spanish, a variety of unfortunate accidental occurrences can be described with this construction.

Se me cerró la puerta en la mano.	*The door closed on my hand.*
Se nos apagó el fuego.	*The fire went out (on us).*
Se nos fue la electricidad.	*The electricity went out (on us).*
Los temblores no se me van.	*My shaking will not go away.*
Se te arrugó la falda.	*Your skirt got wrinkled.*
Se les ensuciaron los pantalones.	*Their pants got dirty.*
Se me cierran los ojos.	*My eyes are closing.*
El frío no se te va a quitar si no te pones los calcetines.	*The cold you feel is not going to go away if you do not put on your socks. (You will not warm up . . .)*
Siempre se te ocurren las ideas más raras.	*You always come up with the strangest ideas. (They come to your mind unexpectedly.)*
Se nos pasó la hora; ya son las nueve.	*We are running late; it is already nine. (The hour went by us . . . We forgot the time . . .)*
Se me quedaron los libros en casa.	*I left my books at home. (They stayed at home . . .)*
Se te paró el reloj.	*Your watch stopped.*
Se me pararon los pelos.	*I got goosebumps.*
Se le dobló la foto.	*She accidentally folded the picture. (Her picture got folded.)*

Notice that this construction cannot be used with every accident or involuntary action, even if the word "accidentally" or some similar indication of accident is added.

Me robaron el coche.	*They stole my car.*
Leímos el libro equivocado.	*We read the wrong book.*
El gato me saltó encima.	*The cat jumped on me.*
Nos castigaron. (OR: **Se nos castigó.** [impersonal *se*])	*We were punished.*
Mi coche chocó.	*My car crashed.*

APPENDIX II
Práctica

4. Impersonal *Se*

a) Introduction

The impersonal *se* is used for actions with no specific subject. These sentences correspond to the English passive voice or the impersonal "they, you, people," or "one."

> **En México <u>se toma</u> una siesta después de la comida.**
> *In Mexico, they take a nap after lunch.*

> **No entiendo por qué <u>se dicen</u> tantas mentiras.**
> *I do not understand why people tell so many lies.*

> **No <u>se debe</u> llevar mucho cuando <u>se viaja</u>.**
> *One should not take much when one travels.*

There are other ways of expressing impersonal sentences in Spanish.

> **En España usan el "vosotros" como plural de "tú".**
> *In Spain they use "vosotros" as the plural of "tú."*

> **En época de sequía la gente come lo que haya.**
> *In times of drought, people eat whatever there is.*

> **Uno nunca sabe lo que el futuro puede traer.**
> *One never knows what the future might bring.*

However, the most common way of expressing impersonal situations is with the impersonal *se.* The structure of sentences with this *se* changes depending on whether the focus is on human beings or inanimate objects.

b) Impersonal *Se* with Inanimate Objects

When referring to inanimate objects, the inanimate object functions grammatically as the subject of the verb (i.e., the verb agrees in number with the inanimate object[s]).

<u>Se</u> habla español.	*Spanish is spoken.*
<u>Se</u> hablan muchas lenguas en Suiza.	*Many languages are spoken in Switzerland.*

If the subject of the verb has been stated previously in the context, and you wish to replace it with a pronoun, remember that there is no subject pronoun for inanimate objects (it/they).

<u>Se</u> habla.	*It is spoken.*
<u>Se</u> hablan.	*They are spoken.*

¿Cómo <u>se</u> dice eso?	*How do you say that?*
¿Cómo <u>se</u> dice?	*How do you say it?*
¿Cómo <u>se</u> prepara ese platillo?	*How do you prepare that dish?*
<u>Se</u> prepara con huevos y leche.	*You prepare it with eggs and milk.*

c) Impersonal *Se* with Persons

When an impersonal sentence talks about a human being and not an inanimate object, the grammatical function of the person is that of the **direct object** of the verb, and there is no agreement; the personal *a* is used to differentiate from the reflexive. The verb remains invariable in person and number.

Se castigó <u>al</u> criminal.	*The criminal was punished.*

(If you were to use *el* instead of *al*, the structure would be reflexive: *The criminal punished himself.*)

If the human direct object is plural, the verb is not affected.

Se torturaba a los disidentes.	*The dissidents were tortured.*

The person may be replaced by an indirect object[12] pronoun.

Se <u>le</u> castigó.	*He was punished.*
Se <u>les</u> torturaba.	*They were tortured.*

This construction avoids the confusion with reflexive constructions.
Reflexive:

Se castigaron.	*They punished themselves (or each other).*
Se mataron.	*They killed themselves (or each other).*

Impersonal:

Se <u>les</u> castigó.	*They were punished.*
Se <u>les</u> mató.	*They were killed.*

In rare cases where the persons are being perceived as a category, and not as specific individuals, they are treated in this construction as if they were things.

Se buscan empleados.	*Help needed. Now hiring.* (Literally: *Employees are being sought.*)

Notice that no article is used with *empleados,* since they are nonspecific.

---

12. In some dialects, the direct object pronoun is used for animals, and *la(s)* for women.

d) Impersonal *Se* with Both Human and Inanimate Objects

In such sentences, the person is the **indirect object** of the verb, and the inanimate object continues to function as the grammatical subject of the verb.

No se me dio una copia.	*I was not given a copy.*
No se nos anunciaron los cambios.	*The changes were not announced to us.*
Se les envió una invitación a los padres.	*The parents were sent an invitation.* (OR: *An invitation was sent to the parents.*)

Notice that in the third example, *les* is a repetitive indirect object pronoun.

e) Impersonal Reflexive Construction—*Uno*

It is not possible to use both the reflexive and the impersonal *se* together. Use *se* as a reflexive pronoun and *uno* as an impersonal pronoun. Notice the variations of position in the following sentences.

<u>Uno se</u> levanta temprano en el ejército.

<u>Se</u> levanta <u>uno</u> temprano en el ejército.

One gets up early in the army.

<u>Uno se</u> broncea rápido con ese sol.

Con ese sol <u>se</u> broncea <u>uno</u> rápido.

With that sun, one tans quickly.

APPENDIX II

Práctica

C. DEMONSTRATIVE AND POSSESSIVE PRONOUNS

1. Demonstrative Pronouns

In their form, these are identical to demonstrative adjectives, except that, to distinguish them, an accent is added on the stressed syllable.

DEMONSTRATIVE PRONOUNS		
	Singular	**Plural**
Masculine	éste	éstos
Feminine	ésta	éstas
Masculine	ése	ésos
Feminine	ésa	ésas
Masculine	aquél	aquéllos
Feminine	aquélla	aquéllas

éste = *this one*
ése = *that one* (near you)
aquél = *that one* (over there, far from you)

Examples:

Esta mesa es más grande que <u>ésa</u>.	*This table is larger than that one.*
¿Qué asiento prefieres?	*Which seat do you prefer?*
Me gusta más <u>éste</u>.	*I like this one better.*
¿Desea Ud. este pastel?	*Do you want this cake?*
No, deme <u>aquél</u>, el de chocolate.	*No, give me that one, the chocolate one.*

When there is no noun as referent for the pronoun, the neutral pronoun is used. Since there is no equivalent in adjective form, there is no need for the accent.

NEUTRAL DEMONSTRATIVE PRONOUNS	
esto	*this*
eso	*that*
aquello	*that*

Examples:

<u>Esto</u> es riquísimo.	*This is delicious.*
¿De quién es <u>eso</u>?	*Whose is that?*
<u>Aquello</u> fue aburrido.	*That was boring.*

2. Possessive Pronouns

Possessive pronouns are formed with the "long" form of the adjective, with an added definite article that agrees with the possessed item, not with the possessor.

POSSESSIVE PRONOUNS	
mine	**el mío, la mía, los míos, las mías**
yours *(tú)*	**el tuyo, la tuya, los tuyos, las tuyas**
ours	**el nuestro, la nuestra, los nuestros, las nuestras**
yours *(vosotros)*	**el vuestro, la vuestra, los vuestros, las vuestras**
yours *(Ud./Uds.)* his hers its theirs	**el suyo, la suya, los suyos, las suyas**

Examples:

Mi mochila pesa más que <u>la tuya</u>.	*My knapsack weighs more than yours.*
—**¿Cuál es mi café?**	*Which is my coffee?*
—**Éste es el suyo.**	*This one is yours.*
—**Mis abuelos están en Florida.**	*My grandparents are in Florida.*
—**¿Y <u>los vuestros</u>?**	*And yours?*
—<u>**Los nuestros**</u> **están en California.**	*Ours are in California.*

With *ser* the article is omitted.

Esa llave es <u>mía</u>.	*That key is mine.*

The article is used when there is a choice between items.

—**¿Cuáles son tus llaves?**	*Which are your keys?*
—**Éstas son <u>las mías</u> y ésas son <u>las tuyas</u>.**	*These are mine and those are yours.*

The preposition *de* can be used to clarify possessors of the *suyo* types.

—**¿Cuál es mi café?**	*Which is my coffee?*
—**Éste es el <u>de usted</u>,**	*This one is yours,*
este otro es el <u>de él</u>,	*this other one is his,*

ése es el <u>de ella</u>,	*that one is hers,*
ése es el <u>de vosotros</u>, y	*that one is yours* (familiar plural in Spain), and
ése es el <u>de ustedes</u>.	*that one is yours* (plural in Latin America, formal plural in Spain).

When the possessed item is not specific, but general (my things, my part, etc.), the neutral form *lo* is used instead of the article.

Quiero <u>lo mío</u> y nada más.	*I want what is mine, and nothing else.*

APPENDIX II
Práctica

D. INTERROGATIVES

¿Qué?	*What? (before a noun—Which?)*
¿Cuál?	*Which? (before **ser**—What?)*
¿Cuánto(a)(s)?	*How much? How many?*
¿Quién?	*Who?*
¿Dónde?	*Where?*
¿Cómo?	*How?*
¿Por qué?	*Why?*
¿Cuándo?	*When?*

¿Qué? vs. *¿Cuál?* with *Ser*

¿Qué? + ser asks for a definition.

¿Cuál? + ser asks for a choice, and the answer is a noun, pronoun, etc.

—¿<u>Qué es</u> "La Bamba"?	*What is "La Bamba"?*
—Es un baile folklórico mexicano que se ha hecho famoso hoy día con una película del mismo título.	*It is a Mexican folkloric dance which has become famous nowadays with a movie of the same title.*
—¿<u>Cuál es</u> tu apellido?	*What is your last name?*
—Gómez.	*Gómez.*
¿<u>Cuál es</u> la diferencia entre los dos bailes?	*What is the difference between the two dances?*
—¿<u>Cuál es</u> el tuyo?	*Which one is yours?*
—Éste.	*This one.*

¿Cuál fue el problema?	*What was the problem?*
¿Cuál era la fecha?	*What was the date?*
¿Cuál es tu número de teléfono?	*What is your phone number?*

When a noun follows the interrogative instead of the verb, *que* is preferred.

¿Qué color te gusta más?	*What color do you prefer?*
¿Cuál es tu color favorito?	*Which is your favorite color?*

Who has a singular and a plural form in Spanish: *¿Quién? ¿Quiénes?*

¿Quién te dijo eso?	*Who told you that?*
¿Quiénes fueron a la fiesta?	*Who (all) went to the party?*

Whose is translated with the preposition *de* preceding *¿quién(es)?*

¿De quién es esto?	*Whose is this?*

In Spanish, the preposition must always precede the interrogative.

¿De dónde eres?	*Where are you from?*
¿Para qué sirve esto?	*What is this for?*
¿Con cuál lo escribiste?	*Which one did you write it with?*

The translation into Spanish of questions starting with "How?" will vary depending on whether a verb or an adjective or adverb follows the interrogative.

How + verb = *¿Cómo?*

¿Cómo estás?	*How are you?*
¿Cómo lo hiciste?	*How did you do it?*
¿Cómo llegaron?	*How did they get here?*

Be aware of the following questions:

¿Cómo te llamas?	*What is your name?*
¿Cómo es?	*What is he/she/it like?*

How + adjective or adverb

Never use *¿cómo?* to translate "how?" followed by an adjective or adverb.

In Mexico, "How tall is he?" is translated as *¿Qué tan alto es?*, and in the Caribbean as *¿Cuán alto es?*, but in many other Spanish-speaking countries, neither of these forms is used. This type of question must be reformulated using a noun instead of the adjective or adverb by saying, for example, "What is his height?" If you learn the last type of reformulated question, you'll be best equipped for communicating this question in any Spanish-speaking country.

HOW + Adjective or Adverb QUESTION	NOUN EQUIVALENT	SPANISH QUESTION	LITERAL MEANING
How tall is he?	height = **estatura**	**¿Qué estatura tiene?**	*What height does he have?*
		¿Cuánto mide de estatura?	*What does he measure in height?*
How important is it?	importance = **importancia**	**¿Qué importancia tiene?**	*What importance does it have?*
		¿Cuál es su importancia?	*What is its importance?*
How far is it?	distance = **distancia**	**¿A qué distancia queda?**	*At what distance is it?*
How big is it?	size = **tamaño**	**¿De qué tamaño es?**	*What size is it?*
How old is she?	age = **edad**	**¿Qué edad tiene?**	*What age does she have?*
How fast do you run?	speed = **velocidad**	**¿A qué velocidad corres?**	*At what speed do you run?*
How often do you see him?	frequency = **frecuencia**	**¿Con qué frecuencia lo ves?**	*With what frequency do you see him?*

These questions may also be asked as follows:

¿Es muy alto? ¿Cómo es de alto?   **¿Es de nuestra edad?**

¿Es muy importante?   **¿Corres muy rápido?**

¿Queda muy lejos?   **¿Lo ves a menudo/frecuentemente?**

¿Es muy grande? ¿Cómo es de grande?

How much/many = ¿Cuánto(a)(s)…?

<u>**¿Cuánto**</u> **dinero tienes?**   *How much money do you have?*

<u>**¿Cuántos**</u> **huevos compraste?**   *How many eggs did you buy?*

APPENDIX II

Práctica

E. EXCLAMATIVES

¡Qué! + noun, adjective, or adverb	*What (a)(an) . . . ! How . . . !*
¡Cómo! + verb	*(How) . . . !*
¡Cuánto! + noun or verb	*How much . . . !*
¡Cuántos(as)! + noun	*How many . . . !*
¡Quién! + verb	*Who . . . !*

¡Qué! + noun

Please notice in the following examples that Spanish does not use an article in this construction as English does when the noun is singular.

¡Qué alivio!	*What a relief!*
¡Qué problema!	*What a problem!*
¡Qué lío!	*What a mess!*
¡Qué nubes!	*What clouds!*

In some cases, the Spanish noun translates into an adjective in English, with a variety of constructions.

¡Qué asco!	*Ugh! Gross! How revolting!*
¡Qué calor (hace)!	*It is so hot!*
¡Qué frío (hace)!	*It is so cold!*
¡Qué cansancio (tengo)!	*I am so tired!*
¡Qué hambre (tengo)!	*I am so hungry!*

¡Qué! + modified noun

If the adjective precedes the noun:

¡Qué buena idea!	*What a good idea!*
¡Qué lindos ojos!	*What beautiful eyes!*

If the adjective follows the noun, it must be preceded by *más* or *tan*.

¡Qué libro más (tan) interesante!	*What an interesting book!*
¡Qué final más (tan) sorprendente!	*What a surprising end!*

¡Qué! + adjective

¡Qué interesante!	*How interesting!*

Some of these exclamations are very idiomatic, geographically or historically marked, and translate very differently depending on the context or the period.

¡Qué rico! This exclamation can be used in many situations. Essentially, it is a positive comment on practically anything, and means something like "How nice!" If referring to food, it could mean "Mmm! Delicious!".

Other similar expressions are as follows.

¡Qué bueno!	*Good! Great!*
¡Qué chévere!,[13] ¡Qué padre!,[14]	*Wow! (other equivalents: Cool! Excellent!*
¡Qué guay!,[15] ¡Qué bestial![16]	*Awesome! Rad!)*

***¡Qué!* + adverb**

¡Qué rápido acabaste!	*You finished so fast! How quickly you finished! That was fast!*
¡Qué bien bailas!	*How well you dance! You dance so well! You are such a good dancer!*
¡Qué mal me siento!	*I feel so poorly!*

***¡Cómo!* + verb**

¡Cómo gritan!	*How they scream!*
¡Cómo te miraban!	*How they looked at you!*

***¡Cuánto!* + verb**

¡Cuánto lo siento!	*I am so sorry!*
¡Cuánto me gusta este pan!	*I like this bread so much!*
¡Cuánto gastan!	*They spend so much!*
¡Cuánto quisiera ser así!	*How I wish I could be like that!*

***¡Cuánto(a)!* + noun**

¡Cuánta paciencia tienes!	*How patient you are! You are so patient!*
¡Cuánto vino producen!	*They produce so much wine!*

***¡Cuántos(as)!* + noun**

¡Cuántos amigos tienes!	*You have so many friends!*
¡Cuántas islas hay en el Caribe!	*There are so many islands in the Caribbean!*

***¡Quién!* + verb**

¡Quién pudiera bailar como ella!	*If only I could dance the way she does!*

APPENDIX II
Práctica

---

13. The adjective *chévere* is used in Puerto Rico and other Caribbean countries.
14. The adjective *padre* is used in Mexico.
15. The adjective *guay* is used in Spain.
16. The adjective *bestial* is used in Bolivia, Ecuador, and other countries.

F. INDEFINITES AND NEGATIVES

INDEFINITE PRONOUNS	
Affirmative	**Negative**
alguien *someone*	**nadie** *nobody, no one, not anyone*
alguno(a) *someone, anyone, one*	**ninguno(a)** *no one, none, neither (of two)*
algunos *some* **unos** *some*	**ninguno** *nobody, no one, none, not any, not anyone*
algo *something*	**nada** *nothing, not anything*
cualquiera *anybody, any*	**nadie** *nobody, no one, not anyone*

Examples:

<u>Alguien</u> te llamó.   *Someone called you.*

No conozco a <u>nadie</u> aquí.   *I do not know anyone here.*

—¿Quieres <u>algo</u> de beber?   *Do you want something to drink?*
—No, no quiero <u>nada</u>, gracias.   *No, I do not want anything, thank you.*

—No sé de dónde es.   *I do not know where he is from.*
—¿Lo sabrá <u>alguno</u> de tus abuelos?   *Would one of your grandparents know?*
—No, <u>ninguno</u> de ellos lo sabe.   *No, none of them knows.*

<u>Cualquiera</u> podría cantar mejor.   *Anybody could sing better.*

INDEFINITE ADJECTIVES	
Affirmative	**Negative**
algún *some* **todo** *all of*	**ningún*** *not any, no*

*This is never plural.

Examples:

<u>Algún</u> libro tendrá eso.   *Some book will have that.*
<u>Algunas</u> manzanas son agrias.   *Some apples are bitter.*
Aquí no hay <u>ningún</u> niño.   *There is no little boy here.*
<u>Toda</u> la clase aplaudió.   *All of the class applauded.* (NOTE: Do not use *de*.)
No regó <u>ninguna</u> flor.   *He did not water any flowers.*

INDEFINITE ADVERBIALS	
Affirmative	**Negative**
también *also*	**tampoco** *neither, not . . . either*
en alguna parte *somewhere*	**en ninguna parte** *nowhere, not anywhere*
de algún modo *somehow*	**de ningún modo** *no way, by no means*
alguna vez *ever, at some (any) time* **algunas veces** *sometimes* **una vez** *once* **algún día** *some day, ever* **siempre** *always*	**nunca** *never, not . . . ever*

Examples:

—Tú <u>también</u> lo hiciste.   *You did it too.*

—Yo no lo hice. ¿Y tú?   *I did not do it. Did you?*

—Yo <u>tampoco</u> lo hice.   *I did not do it either.*

—¿Dónde estará mi libro? No lo encuentro <u>en ninguna parte</u>.   *Where is my book? I cannot find it anywhere.*

—Tiene que estar <u>en alguna parte</u>.   *It has to be somewhere.*

—No puedo convencerlo <u>de ningún modo</u>.   *I cannot convince him at all.*

—<u>De algún modo</u> lo convencerás.   *Somehow you will convince him.*

—Cantó <u>una vez</u> en Buenos Aires.   *She sang in Buenos Aires once.*

—Yo <u>nunca</u> la oí cantar.   *I never heard her sing.*

—<u>Algún día</u> comprenderás.   *Some day you will understand.*

—No comprenderé <u>nunca</u>.   *I will never understand.*

—<u>Siempre</u> cometes el mismo error.   *You always make the same mistake.*

—Y tú <u>nunca</u> cometes errores....   *And you never make mistakes . . . .*

In questions, *alguna vez* and *algún día* mean "ever," the first for the standard meaning of "ever," the second for a distant future.

—¿Has ido a España <u>alguna vez</u>?   *Have you ever been to Spain?*

—No, <u>nunca</u> he ido a España.   *No, I have never been to Spain.*

—¿Irás a España <u>algún día</u>?   *Will you ever go to Spain?*

If the negative precedes the verb, it is used alone; if it follows the verb, *no* or *ni* must precede the verb.

<u>Nadie</u> te llamó.   *No one called you.*
<u>No</u> te llamó <u>nadie</u>.

<u>Nada</u> le gusta.   *He does not like anything.*
<u>No</u> le gusta <u>nada</u>.

<u>Nunca</u> lo vi.   *I never saw it.*
<u>No</u> lo vi <u>nunca</u>.

<u>Tampoco</u> lo vi.   *I did not see it either.*
<u>No</u> lo vi <u>tampoco</u>.

Multiple negatives are frequent in Spanish.

<u>Nunca</u> entiendes <u>nada</u>.   *You never understand anything.*
<u>Nunca</u> le digas <u>nada</u> a <u>nadie</u>. *Never tell anything to anyone.*

Ningún (**Ninguna**) is used for emphatic negatives.

No tengo interés.   *I have no interest. I am not interested.*
No tengo <u>ningún</u> interés.   *I have no interest whatsoever. I am not interested at all.*

NOTE: "Any," "anything," and "anyone" in English can be either negative or indefinite and translate differently into Spanish depending on the usage.

NEGATIVE	INDEFINITE
No veo <u>ninguno</u>. *I do not see <u>any</u>.*	**Podríamos usar <u>cualquiera</u>.** *We could use <u>any</u>.*
No quiero <u>nada</u>. *I do not want <u>anything</u>.*	**<u>Cualquier cosa</u> serviría.** *<u>Anything</u> would work.*
No traigas a <u>nadie</u>. *Do not bring <u>anyone</u>.*	**<u>Cualquiera</u> podría hacer eso.** *<u>Anyone</u> could do that.*

APPENDIX II
Práctica

G. RELATIVE PRONOUNS

1. Formation and Usage

RELATIVE PRONOUNS
que *(invariable)*
el que (los que, la que, las que)
el cual (los cuales, la cual, las cuales)
lo que *(invariable)*
lo cual *(invariable)*
quien (quienes)
cuyo (cuyos, cuya, cuyas)
donde *(invariable)*

A relative pronoun refers to a noun (its antecedent) from the main clause and introduces a subordinate clause: a relative or adjectival clause. It joins two references to the same noun.

1. **El estudiante se especializa en español.** *The student is a Spanish major.*

2. **El estudiante vino a verme.** *The student came to see me.*

1 + 2. **El estudiante <u>que</u> vino a verme se especializa en español.** *The student who came to see me is a Spanish major.*

In English, the relative pronoun is often not expressed.

The house we saw yesterday is too big.

In Spanish, however, the relative pronoun cannot be omitted.

La casa <u>que</u> vimos ayer es demasiado grande.

The relative pronoun follows its antecedent immediately; only a few structures, such as prepositions, can come between them.

Ésa es la <u>finca</u> <u>frente a</u> <u>la cual</u> vivimos. *That is the farm in front of which we live.*

The antecedent *(finca)* and its relative pronoun *(la cual)* are separated by the preposition *frente a.*

A relative pronoun may hold the same variety of grammatical functions in a sentence that a noun can; it can thus be the subject, direct object, or indirect object of the verb of the relative clause or the object of the preposition that precedes it.

La autora <u>que</u> nos habló ayer es famosa en Chile.

The author who spoke to us yesterday is famous in Chile.

Function of **<u>que</u>**: subject of **habló**

El perro <u>que</u> vimos es de los vecinos.

The dog (that) we saw is the neighbors'.

Function of <u>que</u>: direct object of **vimos**

El hombre a<u>l que</u> le preguntamos no sabía la respuesta.

The man (whom) we asked did not know the answer.

Function of <u>el que</u>: indirect object of **preguntamos**

La ventana al lado de <u>la cual</u> trabajo no cierra bien.

The window next to which I work does not close well.

Function of <u>la cual</u>: object of the preposition **al lado de**

There is often a variety of pronouns you may use depending on the grammatical structure of the sentence. To simplify your task in learning to use these pronouns, we will be presenting here a reduced set of options that are always grammatically correct.

ANTECEDENT = ONE NOUN	NO PREPOSITION	PREPOSITION
	que	el cual/el que*
ANTECEDENT = CLAUSE	lo que/lo cual	
the one . . .	el que	
what	lo que	
whose	cuyo	

*A, de, en, and *con* may take *que* alone when the antecedent is an inanimate object.

NOTE: *El que* and *el cual* agree with their antecedent; *cuyo* agrees with the noun that follows it.

2. Relative Pronouns Without a Preposition

Que can always be used, whether the antecedent is an inanimate object or a human being. (*Quien* is <u>never</u> correct in this type of sentence.)

La casa <u>que</u> tengo en Ithaca es vieja. (a thing)

The house (that) I have in Ithaca is old.

El amigo <u>que</u> vive en Ithaca es viejo. (a person)

The friend who lives in Ithaca is old.

3. Relative Pronouns with a Preposition

El cual/el que [17]

The forms *el/la cual, los/las cuales, el/la que,* and *los/las que* can always be used. (NOTE: Always place the preposition before the relative pronoun.)

La compañía para <u>la cual/la que</u> trabajo es americana.

The company for which I work (I work for) is American.

La mujer para <u>la cual/la que</u> trabajo es americana.

The woman for whom I work (I work for) is American.

Exceptional prepositions: the following prepositions may[18] be used with *que* alone when the antecedent is an inanimate object (not human): *a, de, en, con.*

La iglesia <u>a que</u> voy está en el centro.

The church I go to is downtown.

El libro <u>de que</u> me habló parece interesante.

The book he talked to me about seems interesting.

La silla <u>en que</u> me senté estaba pegajosa.

The chair in which I sat was sticky.

El lápiz <u>con que</u> escribo se me rompió.

The pencil with which I write broke.

4. Additional Uses

Lo que/Lo cual (invariable)

If the antecedent is an entire clause, both *lo que* and *lo cual* are possible.

El examen fue difícil, <u>lo que/lo cual</u> nos sorprendió.

The exam was hard, which surprised us.

El que[19]

When used with *ser,* this pronoun means "the one, the one who, the one (that), the one (which)."

Margarita es <u>la que</u> me regaló estas flores.

Margarita is the one who gave me these flowers.

Ese libro es <u>el que</u> me gusta.

That book is the one (that) I like.

---

17. There is dialectal variation; in many areas, *el que* is preferred to *el cual.*
18. They can also be used with *el que* or *el cual.*
19. *El que* followed by the subjunctive means "whoever" or "whomever."
    Regálaselo al que quieras. *Give it to whomever you want.*
    La que le gane a Sánchez se hará famosa. *Whoever beats Sánchez will become famous.*

Esas mujeres, <u>las que</u> están vestidas de traje (y no las otras), son abogadas.[20]

Those women, the ones wearing suits (not the other ones), are lawyers.

Mi coche, <u>el que</u> está en el garaje, es un Ford.

My car, the one that is in the garage, is a Ford. (I have another one)

<u>La que</u> me gustó fue la verde.

The one (table) I liked was the green one.

<u>Los que</u> no tenían eran los azules.

The ones they did not have were the blue ones.

<u>La que</u> me cae bien es Nilda.

The one I like is Nilda.

In structures such as these, *quien* is only required if the sentence is a proverb.

<u>Quien</u> bien te quiera te hará llorar.

Whoever loves you a lot will make you cry.

Lo que

When used without an antecedent at the beginning of a sentence, *lo que* means "what."

<u>Lo que</u> no entiendo es por qué lo hicieron. Eso es <u>lo que</u> me molesta.

What I do not understand is why they did it. That is what bothers me.

<u>Lo que</u> dijiste no es verdad.

What you said is not true.

<u>Lo que</u> me gustó fue la mesa.

What I liked was the table.

NOTE: *Lo que* followed by the subjunctive means "whatever."

Haré <u>lo que</u> digas.

I will do whatever you say.

Cuyo

This relative pronoun means "whose" and agrees as an adjective would with the noun that follows it, not with its antecedent.

Tenemos un perro <u>cuyos</u> ojos siempre parecen tristes.

We have a dog whose eyes always seem sad.

---

20. If you were to use *la que* instead of *que* in the following sentence, it would translate as "the one who" and would sound—in most cases—absurd:

Mi madre, <u>que</u> vive en México, nunca viaja. *My mother, who lives in Mexico, never travels.*

NOTE: The interrogative "Whose?" is translated into Spanish with *¿De quién(es)?* (notice the accent mark).

> **¿De quién es este libro?** (direct discourse)
> *Whose book is this?*
> **No me dijo de quién era el libro.** (indirect discourse)
> *He did not tell me whose book it was.*

Donde

Donde means "where" and is invariable.

> **Prefiero las oficinas <u>donde</u> entra mucha luz del día.**
> *I prefer offices where there is a lot of daylight.*

NOTE: The interrogative "Where?" is translated into Spanish with *¿Dónde?*, with an accent mark.

> **¿Dónde están los niños?**
> *Where are the children?*

Remember that the interrogative in indirect discourse can be distinguished from the relative pronoun because of the absence of an antecedent.

> **Quería saber dónde estabas.**
> *He wanted to know where you were.*

Who

"Who" in a question translates as *quién*, but in a relative clause it is *que*.
Questions:

> **¿<u>Quién</u> te dio eso?** (direct discourse)
> *<u>Who</u> gave you that?*

> **No sé <u>quién</u> lo hizo.** (indirect discourse)
> *I do not know <u>who</u> did it.*

Please be aware of the danger of translating "who" with *quien* in relative clauses, especially when there is no preposition before it. *Quien* is never required to translate the relative "who" or "whom."

Que translates "who" when there is no preposition.

> **El candidato <u>que</u> copie perderá.** (NEVER use *quien* here.)
> *The candidate <u>who</u> copies will lose.*

El cual or *el que* are always possible with prepositions.

> **La estudiante con <u>la cual</u> llegaste es nueva.** (also: con <u>la que</u> , con <u>quien</u>)
> *The student with whom you arrived is new.*

What

"What" in a question translates as *qué*, but in a relative clause it is *lo que*.

Questions:

> **¿Qué dijo?** (direct discourse)
>
> *What did he say?*

> **No sé qué hacer.** (indirect discourse)
>
> *I do not know what to do.*

Relative clause:

> **Eso es lo que me gusta.**
>
> *That is what I like.*
>
> (antecedent = *that*)

> **Lo que hizo fue horrible.**
>
> *What he did was horrible.*
>
> (relative clause without an antecedent)

Chapter 4

Prepositions and Conjunctions

A. PREPOSITIONS

1. **Function of Prepositions**

2. **Verbs Used Without Prepositions**

3. **Individual Prepositions**

   a) *A*   d) *En*
   b) *Con*   e) *Para*
   c) *De*   f) *Por*

4. **List of Expressions with Prepositions (English–Spanish)**

5. **Review of Prepositional Phrases**

B. RELATED ADVERBS AND PREPOSITIONS

C. CONJUNCTIONS

1. **Usage**

2. **Conjunctions of Coordination**

3. **Conjunctions of Subordination**

A. PREPOSITIONS

I. Function of Prepositions

A preposition relates a noun or its equivalent to another noun, to the verb, or to the rest of the sentence.

With **nouns:**

Salí <u>con Ana</u>.	*I went out with Ana.*
Esta comida es <u>para mi perro</u>.	*This food is for my dog.*

With **pronouns:**

Vete <u>con ellos</u>.	*Go with them.*
Entremos <u>en ésta</u>.	*Let's go into this one.* (e.g., tienda)
Vamos <u>en el mío</u>.	*Let's go in mine.* (e.g., coche)
¿Esta tortilla es <u>para alguien</u>?	*Is this tortilla for someone?*
No, no es <u>para nadie</u>.	*No, it is not for anyone.*
<u>¿Con quién</u> saliste?	*Whom did you go out with?*
Ése es el hombre <u>con el cual</u> llegó.	*That is the man she arrived with.*

With **infinitives:**

Terminé rápido <u>para salir</u>.	*I finished quickly so as to go out.*

In **combination:** prepositions may be grouped to form a single prepositional expression.

debajo de	Se escondió <u>debajo de</u> la mesa. *He hid under the table.*
delante de	Ella se sienta <u>delante de</u> mí. *She sits in front of me.*
dentro de	La pluma está <u>dentro de</u> mi chequera. *The pen is inside of my checkbook.*
detrás de	Yo me siento <u>detrás de</u> ella. *I sit behind her.*
encima de	Pon las llaves <u>encima de</u> mi mochila. *Put the keys on top of my knapsack.*
enfrente de	Está <u>enfrente de</u> usted. *It is in front of you.*
frente a	La casa <u>frente a</u> la nuestra se vendió. *The house in front of ours was sold.*

fuera de	Eso está <u>fuera de</u> mi alcance.
	That is out of my reach.
para con	Su actitud <u>para con</u>migo ha cambiado.
	His attitude towards me has changed.
por delante de	El desfile pasa <u>por delante de</u> la casa.
	The parade passes in front of the house.
por encima de	El avión voló <u>por encima de</u> mi casa.
	The plane flew over my house.

2. Verbs Used Without Prepositions

The following verbs are transitive in Spanish, and the thing you are waiting for, looking for, etc., is the direct object of the verb.

agradecer	**Te agradezco la ayuda.**
to be grateful for	*I am grateful to you **for** your help.*
buscar	**¿Qué buscas?**
to look for	**Estoy buscando mis llaves, pero no las encuentro.**
	*What are you looking **for**?*
	*I am looking **for** my keys, but I cannot find them.*
esperar	**Esos niños siempre esperan el autobús en la esquina.**
to wait for	*Those children always wait **for** the bus on the corner.*
pedir + thing	**Siempre me piden dinero cuando no tengo.**
to ask for (something)	*They always ask me **for** money when I do not have any.* (See also *preguntar por* + person.)
pensar + inf.	**Pensamos ir a Sudamérica el verano entrante.**
to plan on	*We are planning **on** going to South America next summer.*
	(See also *pensar en* and *pensar de.*)

3. Individual Prepositions

a) *A*

(1) Usage

A	
Usage	**Examples**
To introduce the indirect object	**Se lo dio <u>a</u> Jorge.** *He gave it to Jorge.*
To indicate direction towards something or some place, after a verb of movement (**ir, venir, bajar, subir, dirigirse, acercarse...**)	**Fueron <u>a</u> la cabaña.** *They went to the cabin.* **Subieron <u>al</u> tren.** *They got onto the train.*
To indicate the time at which something happens	**Me levanté <u>a</u> las ocho.** *I got up at eight.*
To indicate the period of time after which something happened	**Se divorciaron <u>a</u> los dos años.** *They divorced after two years.*
To indicate the distance at which something is	**Mi auto está <u>a</u> una cuadra.** *My car is one block away.*
Al + infinitive: To indicate simultaneous actions	**<u>Al</u> entrar, lo vi.** *When I went in, I saw it.*

(2) Personal *A*

PERSONAL *A*	
Usage	**Examples**
To introduce a human or personified direct object	**Veo <u>a</u> Juan.** *I see Juan.* **Veo <u>a</u> mi perro.** *I see my dog.*
With indefinite pronouns **alguien, nadie, alguno, ninguno, cualquiera,** when referring to humans	**No veo <u>a</u> nadie.** *I do not see anyone.*
Omission	**Examples**
After **tener**	**Tengo una hermana.** *I have a sister.*
With indefinite direct objects	**Buscan secretarias.** *They are looking for secretaries.*

(3) Prepositional Phrases with *A*

| a caballo | Llegaron <u>a caballo</u>. *They arrived on horseback.* |
| a causa de | No pudimos ir <u>a causa de</u> la tormenta. *We were unable to go because of the storm.* |

	because + conjugated verb = **porque**:
	No pudimos ir <u>porque</u> había una tormenta.
	We were unable to go because there was a storm.
a eso de	**Llegaron <u>a eso de</u> las tres.**
	They arrived at about (around) three.
	(NOTE: *A eso de* is used only with time, not with space: *It is about two miles away.* = **Está a unas dos millas.**)
a fondo	**Quiero que estudies esto más <u>a fondo</u>.**
	I want you to study this more in depth.
a fuerza de	<u>**A fuerza de**</u> **trabajar día y noche, lo terminé.**
	By (dint of) working day and night, I finished it.
a la vez	**No puedo hacer dos cosas <u>a la vez</u>.**
	I cannot do two things at the same time.
al menos	**Nos quedan <u>al menos</u> dos horas.**
	We have at least two hours left.
a lo mejor	**¿Qué es eso? No sé; <u>a lo mejor</u> es el viento.**
	What is that? I do not know; maybe it is the wind.
a mano	**Lo hice <u>a mano</u>.**
	I did it by hand.
a menudo	**Visito a mi abuela <u>a menudo</u>.**
	I visit my grandmother frequently (often).
a ojo	**No tengo cinta métrica; tendré que calcular la distancia <u>a ojo</u>.**
	I do not have a measuring tape; I will have to calculate the distance by eye (roughly, guessing).
a pesar de	**Me gusta jugar en la nieve <u>a pesar del</u> frío.**
	I like to play in the snow in spite of the cold.
a pie	**Prefiero ir <u>a pie</u> por el ejercicio.**
	I would rather go on foot (walking) for the exercise.
a tiempo	**¡Por fin llegaste <u>a tiempo</u>!**
	You finally arrived on time!
a veces	<u>**A veces**</u> **no sé qué decir.**
	Sometimes I do not know what to say.

(4) Verbs with A[1]

acostumbrarse a + inf.	**Me acostumbré a levantarme temprano.** *I got used to getting up early.*
aprender a + inf.	**Quiero aprender a patinar.** *I want to learn how to skate.*
apresurarse a + inf.	**Se apresuró a esconder el regalo.** *She hurried to hide the present.*
asistir a + noun (not inf.)	**Asistieron a clase ayer.** *They attended class yesterday.*
atreverse a + inf.	**Se atrevió a hablar.** *He dared to speak.*
ayudar a + inf.	**Me ayudaron a pintar la casa.** *They helped me paint the house.*
comenzar a + inf.	**Comencé a estudiar inglés a los cinco años.** *I began to study English at the age of five.*
detenerse a + inf.	**Los turistas se detuvieron a admirar la estatua.** *The tourists stopped to admire the statue.*
empezar a + inf.	**Los pájaros empiezan a cantar al amanecer.** *The birds begin to sing at dawn.*
enseñar a + inf.	**¿Quién te enseñó a cantar así?** *Who taught you to sing like that?*
invitar a + inf.	**Te invito a ir al cine.** *I invite you to go to the movies.*
ir a + inf.	**Vamos a comer a las ocho.** *We are going to eat at eight.*
negarse a + inf.	**La víctima se negó a identificar al criminal.** *The victim refused to identify the criminal.*
ponerse a + inf.	**De repente, se puso a gritar.** *Suddenly, he began to scream.*
resignarse a + inf.	**Tendrás que resignarte a ganar menos dinero.** *You will have to resign yourself to earning less money.*
volver a + inf.	**Tu amigo volvió a llamar.** *Your friend called again.*

---

1. Some verbs, like *aprender,* use *a* only to link to a following infinitive; others, like *acostumbrarse,* use *a* with any direct object including an infinitive; still others, like *asistir,* govern *a,* but do not take infinitives.

b) *Con*

(1) Usage

CON	
Usage	**Examples**
To express accompaniment	**Vengan <u>con</u> nosotros al cine.** *Come with us to the movies.*
Followed by a noun in adverbial expressions	**Lo hicieron <u>con</u> coraje.** *They did it with anger (angrily).* **Lo visitamos <u>con</u> frecuencia.** *We visit him frequently.*
To describe people by something accompanying them	**El hombre <u>con</u> la guitarra se llama José.** *The man with the guitar is named José.*
Followed by an instrument or tool	**Tendremos que cortarlo <u>con</u> el serrucho.** *We will have to cut it with the saw.*

(2) Prepositional Phrases with *Con*

con respecto a — No sé qué hacer <u>con respecto a</u> mi abuela.
I do not know what to do regarding my grandmother.

con tal (de) que — Te ayudaré <u>con tal (de) que</u> me pagues.
I will help you provided that you pay me.

(3) Verbs with *Con*

casarse con — Se casó con su novio en Las Vegas.
She married her fiancé in Las Vegas.

encontrarse con — Me encontré con mis amigos en el centro.
I met my friends downtown.

enojarse con — Creo que se enojó conmigo.
I think she got mad at me.

meterse con — No te metas con esa pandilla.
Do not get involved (mixed up) with that gang.

quedarse con — Se quedó con mi libro.
She kept my book.

soñar con — Anoche soñé contigo.
Last night I dreamed about you.

c) *De*

(1) Usage

DE	
Usage	**Examples**
Possession	**El suéter <u>de</u> María es lindo.** *María's sweater is pretty.*
Origin, nationality	**Jorge es <u>de</u> Colombia.** *Jorge is from Colombia.*
Material something is made of	**La mesa es <u>de</u> madera.** *The table is (made of) wood.*
With noun complements functioning as adjectives	**Me encanta la clase <u>de</u> español.** *I love Spanish class.*
Followed by a noun, to describe condition or state	**<u>De</u> niña, me dormía fácilmente.** *As a child, I fell asleep easily.*
With **estar** to signify "acting as"	**Están <u>de</u> directoras este semestre.** *This semester they are working (acting) as directors.*
With **estar** in typical expressions: **de pie, de rodillas, de luto, de acuerdo con, de buen humor, de mal humor, a favor de, en contra de, de huelga, de vacaciones, de viaje, de visita, de vuelta, de regreso**	**No estoy <u>de</u> acuerdo contigo.** *I do not agree with you.* **Los obreros están <u>de</u> huelga.** *The workers are on strike.*
To indicate the place of something or someone	**La farmacia <u>de</u> la esquina cerró.** *The corner drugstore closed.* **Conozco a la gente <u>del</u> barrio.** *I know the people of the neighborhood.*
To describe people by something physical or worn	**El hombre <u>del</u> bigote.** *The man with the mustache.* **La mujer <u>de</u> ojos azules.** *The woman with blue eyes.*

(2) Prepositional Phrases with *De*

de buena/mala gana   Lo hizo <u>de buena gana</u>.
                                    He did it willingly.

de esta manera   Mira, se hace <u>de esta manera</u>.
                                    Look, this is the way you do it.

de modo que	Habló rápido <u>de modo que</u> no la interrumpieran.
	She spoke quickly so that they would not interrupt her.
	<u>De modo que</u> no me vas a decir tu secreto, ¿eh?
	So, you are not going to tell me your secret, are you?
de nuevo	El vecino se estacionó <u>de nuevo</u> en nuestra entrada.
	The neighbor parked in our entrance again.
de pie	He estado <u>de pie</u> todo el día.
	I have been standing all day long.
de repente	<u>De repente</u> empezó a llover a cántaros.
	Suddenly it started pouring.
de veras	<u>De veras</u> que no sé la respuesta.
	I really do not know the answer.
de vez en cuando	<u>De vez en cuando</u> me gusta viajar.
	Once in a while I like to travel.

(3) Verbs with *De*

acabar de + inf.	Acabo de comer. *I just ate.*
	Acababa de comer. *I had just eaten.*
	Acabé de comer. *I finished eating.*
acordarse de	Me acordé de ponerme el reloj.
	I remembered to put on my watch.
alegrarse de	Me alegro de verte.
	I am glad to see you.
arrepentirse de	Se arrepintió de haberse burlado de ella.
	He regretted having made fun of her.
avergonzarse de	Me avergüenzo de mis estupideces.
	I am ashamed of my stupidities.
burlarse de	¡No se burlen de él!
	Do not make fun of him!
darse cuenta de	Me di cuenta de mi error.
	I realized my mistake.
dejar de	Dejen de molestar al perro.
	Stop bothering the dog.

depender de	¿Cuál es la verdad? Depende de quién habla. *Which is the truth? It depends on who is speaking.*
despedirse de	Nos despedimos de nuestros padres en el aeropuerto. *We said good-bye to our parents at the airport.*
enamorarse de	Se enamoró de ella. *He fell in love with her.*
enterarse de	¿Te enteraste de las noticias? *Did you hear (find out about) the news?*
estar enamorado(a) de	Estamos enamorados de la misma chica. *We are in love with the same girl.*
irse de + place	Se fueron de la universidad ayer. *They left the university yesterday.*
olvidarse de	No te olvides de sacar la basura. *Do not forget to take out the garbage.*
pensar de	¿Qué piensas de este libro? *What do you think about this book?* (i.e., Do you like it?)
quejarse de	Se quejaron del trabajo. *They complained about the work.*
reírse de	Nunca se ríen de mis chistes. *They never laugh at my jokes.*
terminar de + inf.	Terminé de preparar la cena. *I finished preparing dinner.*
tratar de + inf.	Trataron de ayudarme, pero no pudieron. *They tried to help me, but could not.*
tratarse de	—Me gustó esa película. —¿De qué se trata? —Se trata de una familia durante la segunda guerra mundial. *I liked that movie.* *What is it about?* *It is about a family during the Second World War.*

d) *En*

(1) Usage

EN	
Usage	**Examples**
To indicate where something takes place or is located	**Estábamos <u>en</u> la playa.** *We were at the beach.*
Signifiying "in, inside"	**Ese cuaderno está <u>en</u> mi mochila.** *That notebook is in my knapsack.*
Signifying "on, on top of"	**Tu libro está <u>en</u> mi escritorio.** *Your book is on my desk.*
With time expressions—months, years, and other expressions of time (but not days of the week: **Lo haré el lunes.** *I will do it on Monday.*)	**La visité <u>en</u> enero.** *I visited her in January.* **No quería verlo <u>en</u> ese momento.** *I did not want to see him at that moment.*
With ordinal numbers followed by the infinitive	**Fue el primero <u>en</u> irse.** *He was the first to leave.*

(2) Prepositional Phrases with *En*

en cambio	Yo no hablaba su idioma; ellos, <u>en cambio</u>, sí hablaban inglés. *I did not speak their language; they, however, did speak English.*
en cuanto	Llámame <u>en cuanto</u> llegues a casa, por favor. *Call me as soon as you get home, please.*
en cuanto a	<u>En cuanto a</u> la comida india, no sé mucho. *In regard to Indian food, I do not know much.*
en frente de	Se sentó <u>en frente de</u> mí en el cine. *She sat in front of me at the movies.*
en seguida	Vendrá <u>en seguida</u> (OR: enseguida). *He will come right away (immediately).*
en vez de	<u>En vez de</u> llorar, deberíamos reír. *Instead of crying, we should laugh.*

(3) Verbs with *En*

Some of these may take the infinitive, others not.

consentir en	**Ella nunca consentirá en casarse contigo.** *She will never consent to marrying you.*
consistir en	**¿En qué consiste este programa?** *What does this program consist of?*
convenir en	**Convinimos en encontrarnos a las diez.** *We agreed to meet at ten.*
convertirse en	**Estas semillas pronto se convertirán en plantitas.** *These seeds will soon become little plants.*
empeñarse en	**Se empeñó en pagarme lo que me debía.** *He insisted on paying me what he owed me.*
entrar en	**Entró en la clase corriendo.** *He entered the classroom running.*
especializarse en	**Ella se especializa en ingeniería.** *She is majoring in engineering.*
fijarse en	**No me había fijado en sus ojos.** *I had not noticed his eyes.*
influir en	**La enseñanza influye en nuestras decisiones.** *Education influences our decisions.*
insistir en	**Insistimos en pagar.** *We insist on paying.*
pensar en	**Pienso en ti a menudo.** *I often think of you.*
tardar en	**Tardaron mucho en contestar.** *They took a long time to answer.*

APPENDIX II

Práctica

e) *Para*

(1) Usage

PARA	
Usage	**Examples**
Destination	**Lo escribí para la profesora de historia.** *I wrote it for the history professor.*
Purpose	**Lo hice para ti.** *I did it for you. (e.g., to give it to you)* **Fue a la tienda para comprar pan.** *He went to the store to (so as to) buy bread.* **¿Para qué sirve esto?** *What is this for?* **Es un buen libro para leer.** *It is a good book to read.* **Necesita una mesa para estudiar.** *He needs a table to study.*
Destination in time, deadline	**Lo terminaré para las diez.** *I will finish it by ten.*
Destination in space	**Salimos para Europa.** *We left for Europe.* **Ven para acá.** *Come over here.*
Comparison with the "norm"	**Para extranjero, habla muy bien.** *For (Considering he is) a foreigner, he speaks very well.*
To indicate the employer	**Ella trabaja para el gobierno.** *She works for the government.*
With **estar,** meaning "to be about to," in Spain	**¿Estabais para salir?** *Were you about to leave?*

(2) Prepositional Phrases with *Para*

no estar para bromas — <u>No estoy para bromas</u> hoy.
I am not in the mood for jokes today.

no ser para tanto — ¡No llores! <u>No es para tanto</u>.
Do not cry! It is not that bad.

para siempre — Pensé que la conferencia duraría <u>para siempre</u>.
I thought the lecture would last forever.

f) *Por*

(1) Usage

POR	
Usage	**Examples**
To introduce the agent of the passive voice	**Esa novela fue escrita por Cervantes.** *That novel was written by Cervantes.*
Reason	**Lo hice por ti.** *I did it because of you.*
Cause	**Por comer tanto, le dio dolor de estómago.** *He got a stomachache from eating so much.* **No fuimos por la lluvia.** *We did not go because of the rain.*
Through time	**Trabajó por dos horas.** *She worked for two hours.*
Through space	**Pasamos por el parque.** *We went through the park.* **Los vi por aquí.** *I saw them somewhere around here.*
Means of communication	**Te llamaron por teléfono.** *They called you on the phone.*
Means of transportation	**Lo mandaron por avión.** *They sent it airmail.*
Exchange	**Te daré un dólar por tu ayuda.** *I will give you a dollar (in exchange) for your help.*
Indicating substitution (instead of)	**Ella trabajó por mí porque estaba enfermo.** *She worked for (instead of) me, because I was ill.*
With verbs of movement, introducing a noun, signifying "to get" or "to fetch"	**Fue a la tienda por pan.** *He went to the store for (to fetch) bread.*
With **estar**, meaning "to be about to" (in Latin America) or "to be in favor of"	**Estamos por salir.** *We are about to leave.* **Yo estoy por la libertad de expresión.** *I am in favor of freedom of speech.*
With **quedar**, followed by the infinitive, meaning "yet to be done"	**Me quedan dos tareas por hacer.** *I have two assignments (yet) to be done.*

(2) Prepositional Phrases with *Por*

por eso   Llueve. <u>Por eso</u> llevo el paraguas.
                           It is raining. That is why I am taking my umbrella.

por fin	<u>Por fin</u> me dieron trabajo. *They finally gave me work.*
por lo general	<u>Por lo general</u> estudio de noche. *As a rule, I study at night.*
por lo menos	Me dijo que tardaría <u>por lo menos</u> una hora. *He told me that it would take him at least an hour.*
por otra parte	No me gusta el clima aquí. <u>Por otra parte</u>, sí me gusta el pueblo. *I do not like the climate here. On the other hand, I do like the town.*
por poco	¡<u>Por poco</u> me caigo! *I almost fell!*
por… que + subjuntive	<u>Por más que</u> trate, no puedo alzarlo. *However much I try, I cannot lift it.* _<u>Por más</u> sed <u>que</u> tenga, no bebe._ *However thirsty she may be, she will not drink.* <u>Por</u> alto <u>que</u> sea, no alcanzo el techo. *However tall I may be, I cannot reach the roof.*
por supuesto	—¿Te gustaría ir al cine conmigo? —¡<u>Por supuesto</u>! *Would you like to go to the movies with me?* *Of course!*

(3) Verbs with *Por*

esforzarse por	Ella se esfuerza por darles lo mejor a sus hijos. *She makes an effort to give her children the best.*
interesarse por	Me intereso por tu futuro. *I am interested in your future.*
preguntar por + person	Llamó Carlos y preguntó por ti. *Carlos called and asked for you.*
preocuparse por	No te preocupes por mí. *Do not worry about me.*
tomar por	Lo tomaron por idiota. *They took him for an idiot.*

APPENDIX II

Práctica

4. List of Expressions with Prepositions (English–Spanish)

EXPRESSIONS WITH PREPOSITIONS			
English	**Spanish**	**English**	**Spanish**
again	**de nuevo**	*not to exaggerate*	**no ser para tanto**
almost	**por poco**	*of course*	**por supuesto**
as soon as	**en cuanto**	*often*	**a menudo**
at about, around (time)	**a eso de**	*on foot*	**a pie**
at least	**al menos, por lo menos**	*on horseback*	**a caballo**
at the same time	**a la vez**	*on the other hand*	**por otra parte**
because of	**a causa de**	*on time*	**a tiempo**
because of that	**por eso**	*once in a while*	**de vez en cuando**
by dint of	**a fuerza de**	*provided that*	**con tal (de) que**
finally	**por fin**	*really*	**de veras**
forever	**para siempre**	*regarding*	**con respecto a**
however much . . .	**por. . . que. . . + subj.**	*sometimes*	**a veces**
immediately	**en seguida; enseguida**	*standing*	**de pie**
in depth	**a fondo**	*suddenly*	**de repente**
in exchange, however	**en cambio**	*that is why*	**por eso**
in front of	**en frente de**	*to agree to*	**convenir en**
in general, as a rule	**por lo general**	*to ask a question*	**hacer una pregunta**
in regard to	**en cuanto a**	*to ask for someone*	**preguntar por alguien**
in spite of	**a pesar de**	*to ask for something*	**pedir algo**
in such a way that	**de modo que**	*to be about, deal with* (e.g., a story)	**tratarse de**
that way	**de esa manera**	*to be ashamed of*	**estar avergonzado de**
instead of	**en vez de**	*to be glad that*	**alegrarse de**
maybe	**a lo mejor**	*to be in love with*	**estar enamorado de**
not to be up for jokes	**no estar para bromas**	*to get used to*	**acostumbrarse a**

EXPRESSIONS WITH PREPOSITIONS

English	Spanish	English	Spanish
to begin to	comenzar a, empezar a, ponerse a	to laugh at	reírse de
to complain about	quejarse de	to learn to	aprender a
to consent to	consentir en	to look for	buscar (no prep.)
to consist of	consistir en	to major (specialize) in	especializarse en
to dare to	atreverse a	to make an effort to	esforzarse por
to delay in doing	tardar en	to make fun of	burlarse de
to depend on	depender de	to marry, get married to	casarse con
to do again	volver a	to meet	conocer, encontrarse con
to fall in love with	enamorarse de	to notice	fijarse en
to feel ashamed of	avergonzarse de	to plan (to do something)	pensar (no prep.)
to find out about	enterarse de	to realize	darse cuenta de
to finish	terminar de	to refuse to	negarse a
to fire someone	despedir a alguien	to remember	acordarse de
to forget about	olvidarse de, olvidar (no prep.), olvidársele a uno	to repent, regret	arrepentirse de
to get angry with	enojarse con	to say good-bye to	despedirse de
to have just (done)	acabar de	to stop to (do something)	detenerse a
to help to	ayudar a	to take for	tomar por
to hurry to	apresurarse a	to teach to	enseñar a
to influence	influir en	to thank (someone) for	agradecer (no prep.)
to insist on	empeñarse en, insistir en	to think about	pensar en, pensar de
to intend to (do something)	pensar (no prep.)	to try to	tratar de
to interest oneself in, become interested in	interesarse por	to wait for	esperar (no prep.)
to invite to	invitar a	to worry about	preocuparse por
to keep	quedarse con	willingly/unwillingly	de buena/mala gana

5. Review of Prepositional Phrases

por	(más) + *adj./adv.* + que	**a**	lo mejor	**de**	pie
de	buena/mala gana	**por**	lo menos	**por**	poco
en	cambio	**al**	menos	**de**	repente
en	cuanto	**por**	más + *noun* + que	**en**	seguida
por	eso	**por**	más que	**para**	siempre
de	esta manera	**a**	menudo	**por**	supuesto
por	fin	**de**	modo que	**con**	tal (de) que
a	fondo	**de**	nuevo	**a**	tiempo
a	la vez	**por**	otra parte	**a**	veces
por	lo general	**a**	pie	**de**	veras

no estar	**para**	bromas
no ser	**para**	tanto

de	vez	**en**	cuando

a	causa	**de**
a	eso	**de**
a	fuerza	**de**
a	pesar	**de**
con	respecto	**a**
en	cuanto	**a**
en	frente	**de**
en	vez	**de**

acabar *(+ inf.)*	**de**	depender	**de**	olvidar	**Ø**
acordarse	**de**	despedirse	**de**	olvidarse	**de**
acostumbrarse	**a**	detenerse *(+ inf.)*	**a**	pedir *(+ thing)*	**Ø**
agradecer	**Ø**	empeñarse	**en**	pensar	**en**
alegrarse	**de**	empezar *(+ inf.)*	**a**	pensar *(+ inf.)*	**Ø**
aprender *(+ inf.)*	**a**	enamorarse	**de**	pensar *(opinion)*	**de**
apresurarse *(+ inf.)*	**a**	encontrarse	**con**	ponerse *(+ inf.)*	**a**
arrepentirse	**de**	enojarse	**con**	preguntar *(+ person)*	**por**
atreverse *(+ inf.)*	**a**	enseñar *(+ inf.)*	**a**	preocuparse	**por**
avergonzarse	**de**	enterarse	**de**	quedar *(+ inf.)*	**por**
ayudar *(+ inf.)*	**a**	esforzarse	**por**	quedarse	**con**
burlarse	**de**	especializarse	**en**	quejarse	**de**
buscar *(+ thing)*	**Ø**	esperar	**Ø**	reírse	**de**
casarse	**con**	estar enamorado	**de**	resignarse	**a**
comenzar *(+ inf.)*	**a**	fijarse	**en**	soñar	**con**
consentir	**en**	influir	**en**	tardar	**en**
consistir	**en**	insistir	**en**	terminar	**de**
convenir	**en**	interesarse	**por**	tomar	**por**
convertirse	**en**	invitar *(+ inf.)*	**a**	tratar *(+ inf.)*	**de**
darse cuenta	**de**	irse	**de**	tratarse	**de**
dejar *(to let, leave)*	**Ø**	meterse	**con**	volver *(+ inf.)*	**a**
dejar *(to stop) (+ inf.)*	**de**	negarse *(+ inf.)*	**a**		

APPENDIX II

Práctica

B. RELATED ADVERBS AND PREPOSITIONS

RELATED ADVERBS AND PREPOSITIONS			
Adverb	**Example**	**Preposition**	**Example**
abajo *below, downstairs*	**Los niños están abajo, en la cocina.** *The children are downstairs, in the kitchen.*	**bajo** *below, under (not physically underneath)*	**Nos sentamos bajo los árboles.** *We sat under the trees. (not underneath their roots, however)*
(a)delante *in front, ahead*	**Sigan adelante.** *Continue ahead.*	**delante de** *in front of, ahead of*	**Ella se sienta delante de mí.** *She sits in front of me.*
(a)dentro *inside*	**Prefiero trabajar adentro.** *I prefer to work inside.*	**dentro de** *inside*	**Mi cuaderno está dentro de la gaveta.** *My notebook is inside the drawer.*
(a)fuera *outside*	**Vamos afuera a jugar.** *Let's go outside to play.*	**fuera de** *out(side) of*	**Estaba fuera de nuestro alcance.** *It was out of our reach.*
alrededor *around*	**Miraron alrededor, pero no vieron nada.** *They looked around, but did not see anything.*	**alrededor de** *around*	**Corrimos alrededor de la casa.** *We ran around the house.*
atrás *behind, back*	**¿Dónde están los niños? Están atrás, jugando a la pelota.** *Where are the children? They are in the back, playing ball.*	**detrás de, tras** *behind, after*	**Venían detrás de nosotros.** *They were coming behind us.* **Venían tras nosotros.** *They were coming after (pursuing) us.*
cerca *near, nearby*	**Viven cerca.** *They live nearby.*	**cerca de** *near, close to*	**Ese árbol está muy cerca de la casa.** *That tree is very close to the house.*
debajo *below, underneath*	**Lo pusieron debajo.** *They put it underneath.*	**debajo de** *below, under(neath)*	**El perro duerme debajo de la casa.** *The dog sleeps underneath the house.*
encima *on top*	**Cayó encima.** *It fell on top.*	**encima de** *on top of, above*	**Ponga la fruta encima de las latas de conserva.** *Put the fruit on top of the cans.*
enfrente *facing, in front, across the street*	**La casa de enfrente es linda.** *The house across the street is pretty.*	**enfrente de, frente a** *in front of, facing*	**Hay tres árboles frente a la casa.** *There are three trees in front of the house.*
lejos *far away*	**¿Vives lejos?** *Do you live far away?*	**lejos de** *far from*	**No está muy lejos de la casa.** *It is not very far from the house.*

C. CONJUNCTIONS

1. Usage

A conjunction is a word that is used to join two parts of speech. This union may be of equal parts, or the second half of the union may be subordinated to the first. If the union is one of two equal parts, conjunctions of coordination are used; if the second part is subordinated to the first, conjunctions of subordination are used.

2. Conjunctions of Coordination

Conjunctions of coordination join any two parts of speech: nouns, adjectives, adverbs, pronouns, etc., or two clauses of equal value.

CONJUNCTIONS	
Spanish	**English**
y/e	*and*
o/u	*or*
pero	*but*
sino	*but rather*
ni... ni	*neither . . . nor*

Y becomes *e* before words beginning with *i* or *hi*.

España e Italia se encuentran en el sur de Europa.

Spain and Italy are in the south of Europe.

O becomes *u* before words beginning with *o* or *ho*.

No importa que sea mujer u hombre.

It does not matter whether it is a man or a woman.

Pero is used to indicate something contrary to what precedes it.

Sé que hace frío, pero yo tengo calor.

I know it is cold but I am hot.

No hace calor, pero yo estoy sudando.

It is not hot but I am sweating.

Sino is used after a negative to indicate alternate (rather, instead).

No fue Marta sino Juana la que me lo dijo.

It was not Marta but (rather) Juana who told me.

Sino becomes the conjunction *sino que* before a conjugated verb.

No me lo vendió <u>sino que</u> me lo regaló.

She did not sell it to me, but rather gave it to me.

No sólo… sino también is translated as *not only … but also.*

<u>No sólo</u> trajeron flores, <u>sino también</u> una botella de vino.

They not only brought flowers, but a bottle of wine too.

3. Conjunctions of Subordination

Conjunctions of subordination introduce a subordinate clause. *Que* is the most common conjunction of subordination.

Veo <u>que</u> estás cansada. *I see (that) you are tired.*

In English, the conjunction "that" may be omitted, but in Spanish it must be stated.

Dice <u>que</u> viene. *He says he is coming.*

Most prepositions combined with *que* become conjunctions to introduce clauses instead of nouns or their equivalent. This is usually the case when the subject of the main verb and the subject of the subordinate are different.

Te llamé <u>para</u> darte las últimas noticias. (infinitive equal to noun)

I called you to give you the latest news.

Te llamé <u>para que</u> supieras que estoy pensando en ti.

I called you so (that) you would know (that) I am thinking about you.

Chapter 5

Verbs I

FORMATION

1. Indicative Mood

   a) Present Indicative

   b) Past Tenses of the Indicative

   c) Future

2. Conditional Mood

   a) Present Conditional

   b) Conditional Perfect

3. Subjunctive Mood

   a) Present Subjunctive

   b) Imperfect Subjunctive

   c) Present Perfect Subjunctive

   d) Pluperfect Subjunctive

4. Imperative Mood

   a) Direct Commands

   b) Indirect Commands

5. Infinitive

   a) Present Infinitive

   b) Perfect Infinitive

6. Participle

   a) Present Participle

   b) Past Participle

FORMATION

I. Indicative Mood

a) Present Indicative

(1) Regular Verbs

	-ar Hablar	-er Comer	-ir Vivir
yo	hablo	como	vivo
tú	hablas	comes	vives
él, ella, usted	habla	come	vive
nosotros	hablamos	comemos	vivimos
vosotros	habláis	coméis	vivís
ellos, ellas, ustedes	hablan	comen	viven

(2) Stem-Changing Verbs

	-ar Cerrar	-er Perder	-ir Sentir
	cierro	pierdo	siento
	cierras	pierdes	sientes
	cierra	pierde	siente
	cerramos	perdemos	sentimos
	cerráis	perdéis	sentís
	cierran	pierden	sienten

Other verbs with this change:

-ar	-er	-ir
comenzar	defender	mentir
empezar	encender	preferir
negar	entender	
pensar	querer	

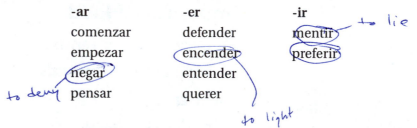

$$\boxed{e \rightarrow i}$$

Pedir

pido
pides
pide
pedimos
pedís
piden

estoy consiguiendo

Other verbs with this change: *conseguir, impedir, seguir, elegir, repetir, servir*

estoy siguiendo

$$\boxed{o \rightarrow ue}$$

-ar	-er	-ir
Contar	**Volver**	**Dormir**
cuento	vuelvo	duermo
cuentas	vuelves	duermes
cuenta	vuelve	duerme
contamos	volvemos	dormimos
contáis	volvéis	dormís
cuentan	vuelven	duermen

hacer un esfuerzo
to make an effort
esforzarse

Other verbs with this change:

regresar

-ar	-er	-ir
costar	devolver	morir
encontrar	llover	
mostrar	mover	
probar	poder	
recordar		

tratar - to treat the west
to get up in the morning
tratar - to try

usar
to try (food)

Other verbs with this change, with some variation:

Oler	Jugar
huelo	juego
hueles	juegas
huele	juega
olemos	jugamos
oléis	jugáis
huelen	juegan

(3) Spelling-Changing Verbs

Spelling changes are made with the purpose of maintaining the same sound throughout the verb; for example, a verb with an infinitive ending in *-ger* or *-gir* (not the "hard" *g* of "go") will have a *j* in the conjugation in front of an *a* or an *o*. If the *g* were maintained, the sound would become hard.

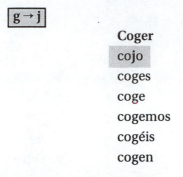

g → j

Coger
cojo
coges
coge
cogemos
cogéis
cogen

Other verbs with this change:

-er	-ir
escoger	corregir
proteger	dirigir
	elegir
	exigir
	fingir

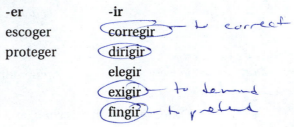

(handwritten annotations: corregir — to correct; exigir — to demand; fingir — to pretend)

gu → g

Distinguir
distingo
distingues
distingue
distinguimos
distinguís
distinguen

Other verbs with this change: *seguir, conseguir*

c → zc
Before o

Parecer
parezco
pareces
parece
parecemos
parecéis
parecen

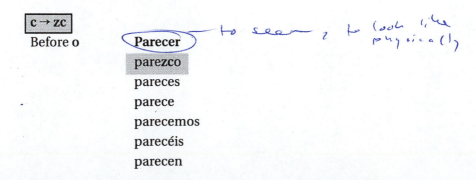

(handwritten annotation: to seem, to look like physically)

Other verbs with this change:

	-er	**-ir**
	agradecer	conducir
	aparecer	introducir
	conocer	producir
	merecer	traducir
	obedecer	
	ofrecer	
	permanecer	
	reconocer	

(handwritten annotations: twin → ; to show up; to deserve / merit; offer; queda; obey; recognize; conducir – manejar; introducir – to introduce; traducir – translate*)*

c → z

Before o   **Convencer**

convenzo

convences

convence

convencemos

convencéis

convencen

Other verbs with this change: *vencer, torcer, ejercer, mecer*

(handwritten annotations: twist; to feed; exercise?; rock/swing*)*

(4) Classified Irregular Verbs

	i → í	**u → ú**
	Enviar	**Continuar**
	envío	continúo
	envías	continúas
	envía	continúa
	enviamos	continuamos
	enviáis	continuáis
	envían	continúan

Other verbs with this change:

	-iar	**-uar**
	confiar	acentuar
	criar	actuar
	guiar	graduar

(handwritten annotations: to trust; to raise; manejar; acentuar → to accentuate; graduar → graduate*)*

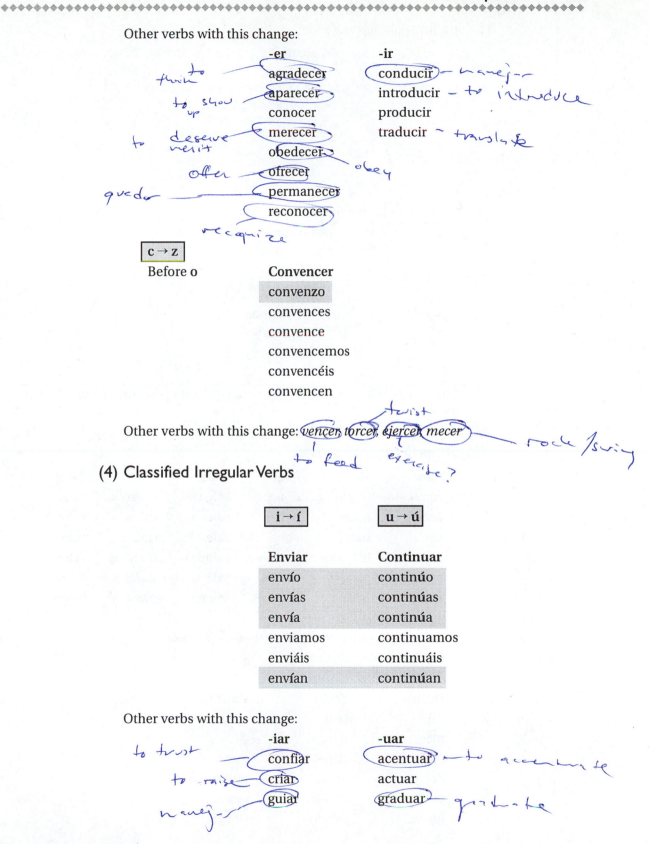

Reunir is similar:

Reunir

reúno

reúnes

reúne

reunimos

reunís

reúnen

$$ui \rightarrow uy$$

Concluir

concluyo

concluyes

concluye

concluimos

concluís

concluyen

Other verbs with this change: *construir, distribuir, contribuir, huir, destruir, incluir*

(5) Other Irregular Verbs

to be worth

Caer	Hacer	Poner*	Salir	Traer°	Valer
caigo	hago	pongo	salgo	traigo	valgo
caes	haces	pones	sales	traes	vales
cae	hace	pone	sale	trae	vale
caemos	hacemos	ponemos	salimos	traemos	valemos
caéis	hacéis	ponéis	salís	traéis	valéis
caen	hacen	ponen	salen	traen	valen

* Like *poner: componer, disponer, proponer, suponer*

° Like *traer: atraer, distraer*

Decir	Tener	Venir
digo	tengo	vengo
dices	tienes	vienes
dice	tiene	viene
decimos	tenemos	venimos
decís	tenéis	venís
dicen	tienen	vienen

Like *decir:* desdecir, maldecir
Like *tener:* atenerse, contener, detener, mantener, obtener, sostener
Like *venir:* convenir, prevenir

Dar	Estar	Haber*	Ir
doy	estoy	he	voy
das	estás	has	vas
da	está	ha	va
damos	estamos	hemos	vamos
dais	estáis	habéis	vais
dan	están	han	van

Oír	Saber	Ser	Ver
oigo	sé	soy	veo
oyes	sabes	eres	ves
oye	sabe	es	ve
oímos	sabemos	somos	vemos
oís	sabéis	sois	veis
oyen	saben	son	ven

Haber has a special third-person singular form: *hay* for "there is, there are."

b) Past Tenses of the Indicative

(1) Imperfect Indicative

Regular:

-ar	-er	-ir
Hablar	**Comer**	**Vivir**
hablaba	comía	vivía
hablabas	comías	vivías
hablaba	comía	vivía
hablábamos	comíamos	vivíamos
hablabais	comíais	vivíais
hablaban	comían	vivían

Irregular:

Ir	Ser	Ver
iba	era	veía
ibas	eras	veías
iba	era	veía
íbamos	éramos	veíamos
ibais	erais	veíais
iban	eran	veían

APPENDIX II

Práctica

(2) Preterite

Regular:

-ar	-er	-ir
Hablar	**Comer**	**Vivir**
hablé	comí	viví
hablaste	comiste	viviste
habló	comió	vivió
hablamos	comimos	vivimos
hablasteis	comisteis	vivisteis
hablaron	comieron	vivieron

PRETERITE TENSE (Irregular Stems with "u")		
Infinitive	**Stem**	**Endings**
andar	anduv-	
caber	cup-	-e
estar	estuv-	-iste
haber	hub-	-o
poder	pud-	-imos
poner	pus-	-isteis
saber	sup-	-ieron
tener	tuv-	

PRETERITE TENSE (Irregular Stems with "i")	
Infinitive	Stem
hacer*	hic-
querer	quis-
venir	vin-

Hacer has a third-person spelling change to *hizo*.

Dar has -*ir* endings.

di
diste
dio
dimos
disteis
dieron

Ir and *ser* are identical in the preterite.

fui
fuiste
fue
fuimos
fuisteis
fueron

Irregular: stem change in *j* (including all verbs in -*ducir*):

Decir	Producir	Traer
dije	produje	traje
dijiste	produjiste	trajiste
dijo	produjo	trajo
dijimos	produjimos	trajimos
dijisteis	produjisteis	trajisteis
dijeron	produjeron	trajeron

All *-ir* verbs with stem changes in the present show a stem change in the third-person singular and plural of the preterite.

e → i			o → u
Pedir	**Reír**	**Sentir**	**Dormir**
pedí	reí	sentí	dormí
pediste	reíste	sentiste	dormiste
pidió	rió	sintió	durmió
pedimos	reímos	sentimos	dormimos
pedisteis	reísteis	sentisteis	dormisteis
pidieron	rieron	sintieron	durmieron

Spelling changes:

i → y				
Caer	**Creer**	**Leer**	**Oír**	**Concluir***
caí	creí	leí	oí	concluí
caíste	creíste	leíste	oíste	concluiste
cayó	creyó	leyó	oyó	concluyó
caímos	creímos	leímos	oímos	concluimos
caísteis	creísteis	leísteis	oísteis	concluisteis
cayeron	creyeron	leyeron	oyeron	concluyeron

*Applies to verbs ending in *-uir* with the same spelling change in the present tense.

c → qu	g → gu	z → c
Buscar	**Llegar**	**Alcanzar**
busqué	llegué	alcancé
buscaste	llegaste	alcanzaste
buscó	llegó	alcanzó
buscamos	llegamos	alcanzamos
buscasteis	llegasteis	alcanzasteis
buscaron	llegaron	alcanzaron

Other verbs with this change:

-car	-gar	-zar
explicar	apagar *to turn off*	almorzar
sacar *to take / to take out*	colgar *to hang*	comenzar
tocar *take / play / touch / turn*	entregar *to turn in*	empezar
	jugar	
	negar *deny*	
	pagar	

APPENDIX II
Práctica

(3) Present Perfect Indicative

The present perfect indicative is formed with the present indicative of the auxiliar *haber* + a past participle always ending in *-o.*

he	
has	
ha	(hablado)
hemos	
habéis	
han	

APPENDIX II
Práctica

(4) Pluperfect Indicative

The pluperfect indicative is formed with the imperfect indicative of the auxiliary *haber* + a past participle always ending in *-o.*

había	
habías	
había	(hablado)
habíamos	
habíais	
habían	

APPENDIX II
Práctica

c) Future

(1) Simple future

The future tense is formed with the infinitive plus endings that are identical for all verbs.

Infinitive +	-é
	-ás
	-á
	-emos
	-éis
	-án

-ar	-er	-ir
Hablar	**Comer**	**Vivir**
hablaré	comeré	viviré
hablarás	comerás	vivirás
hablará	comerá	vivirá
hablaremos	comeremos	viviremos
hablaréis	comeréis	viviréis
hablarán	comerán	vivirán

FUTURE TENSE (IRREGULAR STEMS)			
Infinitive	**Stem**	**Infinitive**	**Stem**
caber	cabr-	**querer**	querr-
decir	dir-	**saber**	sabr-
haber	habr-	**salir**	saldr-
hacer	har-	**tener**	tendr-
poder	podr-	**valer**	valdr-
poner	pondr-	**venir**	vendr-

Verbs derived from these have the same irregularity: *desdecir, deshacer, suponer, mantener,* etc.

APPENDIX II
Práctica

(2) Future Perfect

The future perfect tense is formed with the future of the auxiliary *haber* + a past participle always ending in *-o*.

habré	
habrás	
habrá	(hablado)
habremos	
habréis	
habrán	

APPENDIX II
Práctica

2. Conditional Mood

a) Present Conditional

The present conditional is formed with the infinitive plus endings that are identical for all verbs.

		-ía
		-ías
Infinitive	**+**	-ía
		-íamos
		-íais
		-ían

-ar	-er	-ir
Hablar	**Comer**	**Vivir**
hablaría	comería	viviría
hablarías	comerías	vivirías
hablaría	comería	viviría
hablaríamos	comeríamos	viviríamos
hablaríais	comeríais	viviríais
hablarían	comerían	vivirían

CONDITIONAL TENSE (IRREGULAR STEMS)			
Infinitive	Stem	Infinitive	Stem
caber	cabr-	querer	querr-
decir	dir-	saber	sabr-
haber	habr-	salir	saldr-
hacer	har-	tener	tendr-
poder	podr-	valer	valdr-
poner	pondr-	venir	vendr-

Verbs derived from these have the same irregularity: *desdecir, deshacer, suponer, mantener,* etc.

b) Conditional Perfect

The conditional perfect is formed with the present conditional of the auxiliary *haber* + a past participle always ending in *-o*.

habría	
habrías	
habría	(hablado)
habríamos	
habríais	
habrían	

3. Subjunctive Mood

a) Present Subjunctive

(1) Regular Verbs

The present subjunctive is formed by dropping the *o* of the first-person singular present indicative and adding the "opposite" vowel endings: *e* for *-ar* verbs and *a* for *-ir/-er* verbs.

	-ar	-er	-ir
	Hablar	**Comer**	**Vivir**
yo	hable	coma	viva
tú	hables	comas	vivas
él, ella, usted	hable	coma	viva
nosotros	hablemos	comamos	vivamos
vosotros	habléis	comáis	viváis
ellos, ellas, ustedes	hablen	coman	vivan

(2) Stem-Changing Verbs

If the verb is stem-changing in the present indicative, the present subjunctive will show the same changes.

Cerrar	Perder	Contar	Volver
cierre	pierda	cuente	vuelva
cierres	pierdas	cuentes	vuelvas
cierre	pierda	cuente	vuelva
cerremos	perdamos	contemos	volvamos
cerréis	perdáis	contéis	volváis
cierren	pierdan	cuenten	vuelvan

Exceptions: The first- and second-person plural forms or stem-changing *-ir* verbs. The *e* of the stem changes to *i*, and the *o* of the stem changes to *u*.

Pedir	Sentir	Dormir
pida	sienta	duerma
pidas	sientas	duermas
pida	sienta	duerma
pidamos	sintamos	durmamos
pidáis	sintáis	durmáis
pidan	sientan	duerman

(3) Irregular Verbs

If the verb is irregular in the present indicative, the present subjunctive will show the same irregularities.

Decir	Oír	Tener
diga	oiga	tenga
digas	oigas	tengas
diga	oiga	tenga
digamos	oigamos	tengamos
digáis	oigáis	tengáis
digan	oigan	tengan

Enviar	Continuar	Reunir
envíe	continúe	reúna
envíes	continúes	reúnas
envíe	continúe	reúna
enviemos	continuemos	reunamos
enviéis	continuéis	reunáis
envíen	continúen	reúnan

Parecer	Conducir	Concluir
parezca	conduzca	concluya
parezcas	conduzcas	concluyas
parezca	conduzca	concluya
parezcamos	conduzcamos	concluyamos
parezcáis	conduzcáis	concluyáis
parezcan	conduzcan	concluyan

The following verbs also maintain the irregularity throughout all persons:

PRESENT SUBJUNCTIVE (IRREGULAR STEMS)			
Infinitive	1st Person	Infinitive	1st Person
caber	quepa	salir	salga
caer	caiga	traer	traiga
hacer	haga	valer	valga
poner	ponga	venir	venga

Even *dar, estar, haber, ir, saber* and *ser,* all of which have a first-person singular present indicative that does not end with *-o,* remain regular in their endings.

Dar[1]	Estar	Haber
dé	esté	haya
des	estés	hayas
dé	esté	haya
demos	estemos	hayamos
deis	estéis	hayáis
den	estén	hayan

Ir	Saber	Ser
vaya	scpa	sea
vayas	sepas	seas
vaya	sepa	sea
vayamos	sepamos	seamos
vayáis	sepáis	seáis
vayan	sepan	sean

If the verb has spelling changes in the present indicative, the present subjunctive will show the same irregularities.

g → j		gu → g

Coger	Dirigir	Distinguir
coja	dirija	distinga
cojas	dirijas	distingas
coja	dirija	distinga
cojamos	dirijamos	distingamos
cojáis	dirijáis	distingáis
cojan	dirijan	distingan

c → z	c → qu	g → gu	z → c

Convencer	Buscar	Llegar	Alcanzar
convenza	busque	llegue	alcance
convenzas	busques	llegues	alcances
convenza	busque	llegue	alcance
convenzamos	busquemos	lleguemos	alcancemos
convenzáis	busquéis	lleguéis	alcancéis
convenzan	busquen	lleguen	alcancen

---

1. The first- and third-person singular forms of *dar* have an accent to differentiate them from the preposition *de.*

All verbs ending in:

-*ger* are like *coger* (g → j)   -*car* are like *buscar* (c → qu)

-*gir* are like *dirigir* (g → j)   -*gar* are like *llegar* (g → gu)

-*guir* are like *distinguir* (gu → g)   -*zar* are like *alcanzar* (z → c)

Most verbs ending in -*cer* and -*cir* and all verbs ending in -*ducir* are like *parecer* (c → z).

APPENDIX II
Práctica

b) Imperfect Subjunctive

The imperfect tense of all verbs without exception is formed by dropping -*ron* from the third-person plural preterite and adding -*ra, -ras, -ra, ´-ramos, -rais, -ran* or -*se, -ses, -se, ´-semos, -seis, -sen*. In most of Latin America, the -*ra* forms predominate.

	-ar Hablar	-er Comer	-ir Vivir
yo	hablara	comiera	viviera
tú	hablaras	comieras	vivieras
él, ella, usted	hablara	comiera	viviera
nosotros	habláramos	comiéramos	viviéramos
vosotros	hablarais	comierais	vivierais
ellos, ellas, ustedes	hablaran	comieran	vivieran

OR:

yo	hablase	comiese	viviese
tú	hablases	comieses	vivieses
él, ella, usted	hablase	comiese	viviese
nosotros	hablásemos	comiésemos	viviésemos
vosotros	hablaseis	comieseis	vivieseis
ellos, ellas, ustedes	hablasen	comiesen	viviesen

All verbs irregular in the preterite show the same irregularities in the imperfect subjunctive.

IMPERFECT SUBJUNCTIVE (IRREGULAR STEMS)			
Infinitive	**1st Person**	**Infinitive**	**1st Person**
andar	anduviera	**poder**	pudiera
caber	cupiera	**poner**	pusiera
caer	cayera	**poseer**	poseyera
concluir	concluyera	**preferir**	prefiriera
conducir	condujera	**producir**	produjera
dar	diera	**querer**	quisiera
decir	dijera	**reír**	riera
dormir	durmiera	**saber**	supiera
estar	estuviera	**seguir**	siguiera
haber	hubiera	**sentir**	sintiera
ir	fuera	**ser**	fuera
leer	leyera	**tener**	tuviera
oír	oyera	**traer**	trajera
pedir	pidiera	**venir**	viniera

c) Present Perfect Subjunctive

The present perfect subjunctive is formed with the present subjunctive of the auxiliary *haber* + a past participle always ending in *-o*.

haya	
hayas	
haya	(hablado)
hayamos	
hayáis	
hayan	

d) Pluperfect Subjunctive

The pluperfect subjunctive is formed with the imperfect subjunctive of the auxiliary *haber* + a past participle always ending in *-o*.

> **hubiera**
> **hubieras**
> **hubiera**
> **hubiéramos**   (hablado)
> **hubierais**
> **hubieran**

OR:

> **hubiese**
> **hubieses**
> **hubiese**
> **hubiésemos**   (hablado)
> **hubieseis**
> **hubiesen**

APPENDIX II
Práctica

4. Imperative Mood

a) Direct Commands

(1) *Tú*

Affirmative commands are formed with the third-person singular of the present indicative.

Examples: **habla, come, vive, cierra, abre**

Eight exceptions:

TÚ IMPERATIVE (IRREGULAR AFFIRMATIVE FORMS)			
Infinitive	**Form**	**Infinitive**	**Form**
decir	di	**salir**	sal
hacer	haz	**ser**	sé
ir	ve	**tener**	ten
poner	pon	**venir**	ven

Object pronouns are attached to the ending of the affirmative imperative, and a written accent is added when it is necessary to maintain stress on the same syllable of the stem.

háblame	*talk to me*
ciérrala	*close it* (**la** = **la puerta**)
ábrelo	*open it* (**lo** = **el sobre**)
dímelo	*tell it to me* (**lo** = **el secreto**)
hazlo	*do it* (**lo** = **el trabajo**)
vete	*go away* (**irse** is reflexive)
póntelo	*put it on* (**lo** = **el abrigo**; **ponerse** is reflexive)

Negative commands are formed with the second-person singular of the present subjunctive.

Examples: **no hables, no comas, no vivas, no cierres, no abras**

Those irregular in the affirmative are regular in the negative.

TÚ IMPERATIVE (NEGATIVE FORMS)			
Infinitive	**Form**	**Infinitive**	**Form**
decir	no digas	**salir**	no salgas
hacer	no hagas	**ser**	no seas
ir	no vayas	**tener**	no tengas
poner	no pongas	**venir**	no vengas

Pronouns are placed before the imperative in the negative.

no me hables	*do not talk to me*
no la cierres	*do not close it*
no lo abras	*do not open it*
no me lo digas	*do not tell it to me*
no lo hagas	*do not do it*
no te vayas	*do not go away*
no te lo pongas	*do not put it on*

(2) *Usted/Ustedes*

The imperative of *usted/ustedes* is formed with the third-person singular and plural of the present subjunctive, for both the affirmative and the negative.

hable	**coma**	**viva**	**cierre**	**abra**
hablen	**coman**	**vivan**	**cierren**	**abran**

no hable	**no hablen**

The command may be followed by the pronoun to be more formal and polite.

Hable usted con la gerencia.   *Speak with the management.*
Pidan ustedes lo que deseen.   *Order whatever you wish.*

Examples of affirmative *usted/ustedes* imperatives with pronouns:

USTED(ES) IMPERATIVES (AFFIRMATIVE FORMS)		
Usted	**Ustedes**	**Translation**
hábleme	háblenme	*talk to me*
ciérrela	ciérrenla	*close it*
ábralo	ábranlo	*open it*
dígamelo	díganmelo	*tell it to me*
hágalo	háganlo	*do it*
váyase	váyanse	*go away*
póngaselo	pónganselo	*put it on*

Examples of negative *usted/ustedes* imperatives with pronouns:

USTED(ES) IMPERATIVES (NEGATIVE FORMS)		
Usted	**Ustedes**	**Translation**
no me hable	no me hablen	*do not talk to me*
no la cierre	no la cierren	*do not close it*
no lo abra	no lo abran	*do not open it*
no me lo diga	no me lo digan	*do not tell it to me*
no lo haga	no lo hagan	*do not do it*
no se vaya	no se vayan	*do not go away*
no se lo ponga	no se lo pongan	*do not put it on*

(3) *Vosotros*

The affirmative is formed with the infinitive, minus the *r*, plus *d.*

hablad	**cerrad**	**abrid**
decid	**haced**	**id**

Examples of affirmative *vosotros* imperatives with pronouns:

habladme	*talk to me*
cerradla	*close it*
abridlo	*open it*
decídmelo	*tell it to me*

With the reflexive pronoun *os,* the *d* of the ending is dropped. (The only exception is *ir: idos.*)

levantaos	*get up*
callaos	*be quiet*
laváoslas	*wash them* (**las = las manos**)
ponéoslo	*put it on* (**lo = el abrigo**)

The negative *vosotros* imperative is formed with the second-person plural of the present subjunctive.

no me habléis	*do not talk to me*
no la cerréis	*do not close it*
no me lo digáis	*do not tell it to me*
no lo hagáis	*do not do it*
no os vayáis	*do not go away*
no os lo pongáis	*do not put it on*

(4) *Nosotros*

Affirmative commands are formed with the first-person plural of the present subjunctive.

hablemos	**digamos**
comamos	**hagamos**
abramos	**pongamos**

Exception: *Ir* and *irse* in the affirmative imperative become *vamos* and *vámonos.*

With pronouns:

hablémosle	*let's talk to him*
cerrémosla	*let's close it* (**la = la puerta**)
abrámoslo	*let's open it* (**lo = el sobre**)
hagámoslo	*let's do it* (**lo = el trabajo**)

With *nos* and *se*, drop the final *s* of the verb.

digámoselo	*let's tell it to him* (**lo** = **el secreto**)
levantémonos	*let's get up*
callémonos	*let's be quiet*
lavémonoslas	*let's wash them* (**las** = **las manos**)
pongámonoslo	*let's put it on* (**lo** = **el abrigo**)

In the negative imperative, pronouns precede the verb.

no le hablemos	*let's not talk to him*
no la cerremos	*let's not close it*
no lo hagamos	*let's not do it*
no nos levantemos	*let's not get up*
no nos las lavemos	*let's not wash them*

b) Indirect Commands

When a command is being given to one person, but meant to be carried out by another, *que* + the present subjunctive third-person singular or plural is used.

Que venga.	*Let him come. Have him come. Tell him to come.*
Que lo haga Regina.	*Let Regina do it. Have her do it. Tell her to do it.*
Que pague Elena.	*Let Elena pay. Have her pay. Tell her to pay.*

5. Infinitive

a) Present Infinitive

This is the standard form used as identification of any verb.

hablar *to speak*   **comer** *to eat*   **vivir** *to live*

b) Perfect Infinitive

This is formed with the infinitive of the auxiliary *haber* + the past participle of the verb.

haber hablado *to have spoken*   **haber comido** *to have eaten*

6. Participle

a) Present Participle

Regular present participles are formed with -*ando* and -*iendo.*

> **hablar: hablando**   **comer: comiendo**   **vivir: viviendo**

Stem-changing verbs ending in -*ir* have stem changes: $e \rightarrow i, o \rightarrow u.$

> **sentir: sintiendo**   **pedir: pidiendo**   **dormir: durmiendo**

The ending -*iendo* becomes -*yendo* when added to a stem that ends in a vowel.

> **concluir: concluyendo**   **leer: leyendo**
>
> **caer: cayendo**   **oír: oyendo**

Other irregular present participles:

> **decir: diciendo**   **poder: pudiendo**
>
> **ir: yendo**   **venir: viniendo**

b) Past Participle

Regular past participles are formed by adding -*ado* and -*ido* to the stem of the infinitive.

> **hablar: hablado**   **comer: comido**   **vivir: vivido**

IRREGULAR PAST PARTICIPLES			
Infinitive	**Past Participle**	**Infinitive**	**Past Participle**
abrir	abierto	**morir**	muerto
cubrir	cubierto	**poner**	puesto
decir	dicho	**resolver**	resuelto
escribir	escrito	**volver**	vuelto
hacer	hecho		

Verbs derived from the above infinitives have the same irregularity: *descubrir, devolver,* and *suponer* are examples. There are many more such verbs, such as *recubrir, encubrir, desdecir, envolver, revolver, reescribir, rehacer, deshacer, posponer, anteponer, deponer, reponer* . . . .

Some verbs have two past participles: one regular used in compound tenses with *haber* and one irregular used as an adjective.

he bendecido	*I have blessed*
bendito (un lugar bendito)	*holy, blessed*
he freído	*I have fried*
frito (papas fritas)	*fried*
he maldecido	*I have cursed*
maldito (maldito examen)	*cursed*
he prendido	*I have arrested*
preso (un hombre preso)	*prisoner*
he soltado	*I have released*
suelto (pelo suelto)	*loose*
he imprimido	*I have printed*
impreso (la palabra impresa)	*the printed word*

APPENDIX II

Práctica

Chapter 6

Verbs II

USAGE

131

USAGE

1. Uses of the Present Indicative

The present indicative in Spanish is equivalent to the present or present progressive in English.

Hablo español.	*I speak Spanish.*
Viven en España.	*They are living in Spain.*

In the interrogative, it is equivalent to the English "do" or "does" + a verb.

¿Hablas español?	*Do you speak Spanish?*

In addition to this, it can be translated as:

¿Lo compro?	*Shall I buy it? Should I buy it?*

With *si* meaning "if":

<u>**Si**</u> **lo hace Iris, le pago.**	*If Iris does it, I will pay her.*

With *si* meaning "whether," the future is used in Spanish.

No sé <u>**si**</u> **lloverá.**	*I do not know if (whether) it will rain.*

For polite commands:

Nos da la cuenta, por favor.	*Give us the check, please.*

Acabar + *de* in the present means "to have just."

Acabo de comer.	*I just ate.*

The present progressive in Spanish, formed with the present indicative of *estar* + a present participle, is used to express ongoing actions in the present, as in English.

Estamos estudiando.	*We are studying.*

Never use the present progressive in Spanish to refer to the future.

Josefina se va mañana a las diez.	*Josefina is leaving tomorrow at ten.*

Other auxiliary verbs used occasionally in the progressive are *andar, ir,* and *seguir.*

Anda buscando a su perro.	*He is looking for his dog. He is going around looking for his dog.*
Poco a poco vamos comprendiendo.	*We are understanding little by little.*
Siguen durmiendo.	*They are still sleeping. They continue sleeping.*

2. Preterite vs. Imperfect

a) Introduction

The preterite and the imperfect are two aspects of the past tense of the indicative; each one is used following specific criteria. Any verb can be conjugated in either of the two, and it depends on the **context** in which the verb is used whether you use one or the other. If the context demands the imperfect and you use the preterite instead, at best you may be creating a very funny sentence. It is wise to try to reduce the chances of making such mistakes. There are several ways of explaining the difference between the two aspects. These are three of the most popular:

♦ Action vs. state
♦ Beginning–middle–end
♦ Diachronic vs. synchronic

b) Action vs. State

(1) Definitions

A verb of **action** may be best defined as one that denotes movement or change, such as *caminar, correr,* and *viajar.* Even *quedarse* (to stay) must be considered a verb of action because it is the contrary of a verb of action—*irse* (to leave).

A verb of **state** is one that denotes no movement or change, such as *ser, estar, parecer,* and *querer.*

(2) Verbs of Action: Preterite Is the Rule, Imperfect Is the Exception

Once you have determined that you are dealing with a verb of action, you must visualize the perspective or focus given the verb within its specific context. If the action is being perceived as **beginning** or **ending** at a specified point, or as a **completed** act within the context, you must use the preterite.

If the speaker or narrator is focusing on the **middle** of the action, seeing it as **habitual, interrupted, descriptive/photographic,** or **"future,"** you must put it in the imperfect.

Many times in English this difference can be seen as the one between "walked" and "was walking" or "used to walk," but this is not always the case.

Compare the following sentences:

1. **Celia <u>caminó</u> toda la tarde.** *Celia walked all afternoon.*
   In sentence #1, the act of walking is perceived as **complete,** with no reference to habit, interruption by another act, or presence of any other simultaneous acts. **However long it may have lasted,** it must be in the preterite.

2. **Celia <u>caminaba</u> todas las tardes por una hora.** *Celia used to walk (OR: would walk) in the afternoons for one hour.* (habitual)

In sentence #2, the act of walking is perceived as **habitual** and must be in the imperfect. However, if there were in the sentence an indication of the number of times the act was done, this would no longer be considered as habitual, but **repetitive.** Repetitive actions take the preterite: *Caminé tres veces hasta la tienda.* If there is an indication in the sentence of **how long the habit lasted,** this specification of limits of time takes precedence over the habitual aspect, and the verb must be in the preterite: *Por tres años **acompañé** a Celia a la escuela todos los días.*

3. **Cuando la vi, Celia <u>caminaba</u> hacia su casa.** *When I saw her, Celia was walking towards her house.* (interrupted)

In sentence #3, the act of walking is perceived in the **middle,** giving the reader no visualization of a beginning or an end, only the point at which the act of "seeing" (*vi*) made contact with the act of walking, or **interrupted** it. Notice that when we say "interrupted" it does not mean that the act stopped, only that another action intervened when the first one was in progress. For **interrupted** actions, you must use the imperfect.

4. **Cuando la vi, Celia <u>caminaba</u> con su perro y su amiga. El perro <u>corría</u> de un lado a otro y <u>olía</u> todo lo que estaba en el camino. La amiga <u>platicaba</u> incesantemente mientras Celia <u>escuchaba</u>, distante.** *When I saw her, Celia was walking with her dog and her friend. The dog was running here and there and smelling everything along the way. The friend was chatting incessantly while Celia listened, lost in thought.* (descriptive, simultaneous, photographic acts)

In sentence #4, the various acts of Celia, the dog, and the friend are seen as occurring **simultaneously.** At the moment when the eyes of the narrator catch the scene, these acts are taking place all at once. These acts are called **descriptive** in many grammar books. They may also be seen as **photographic** in the sense that the onlooker could have taken a picture at the instant his eyes caught the scene, and the photograph would have shown all of the actions taking place at once: Celia taking a stride forward, the dog running to the side with his nose to the ground, the friend with her mouth open, speaking, and Celia's gaze blank, distant. This type of action takes the imperfect. In other words, the preterite can be conceived as a snapshot; the imperfect as a moving picture.

5. **Me sentía triste porque mi mejor amiga se <u>casaba</u> ese fin de semana.**
   I felt sad because my best friend was getting married that weekend. (The friend had not yet gotten married when this feeling was expressed— future in relation to the rest of the narration in the past.)

   In sentence #5, the action of getting married has not yet occurred in relation to the context in the past. The imperfect serves as future in the past here.

In indirect discourse (see *Chapter 6, Section 11*), the imperfect is used to shift the present to the past.

DIRECT DISCOURSE	INDIRECT DISCOURSE
Me caso mañana. *I am getting married tomorrow.*	**Marta me dijo que se <u>casaba</u> el día siguiente.** *Marta told me that she was getting married the following day.*

The same logic applies to the near future form *ir a* + an infinitive. When shifted to the past, this expression is always in the imperfect.

PRESENT	PAST
Esta noche voy a cenar con mis amigos. *Tonight I am going to have dinner with my friends.*	**Esa noche <u>iba</u> a cenar con mis amigos.** *That night I was going to have dinner with my friends.*

With a verb of **action,** follow the steps indicated below, so as to decide, by process of elimination, which tense to use.

> 1. Be certain that you are dealing with a verb of action.
> 2. Ask yourself if it is one of the following:
>   a) habitual?
>   b) interrupted?
>   c) photographic?
>   d) future in the past?
>
> If the answer is "yes" to any of the above, use the imperfect.
> If the answer is "no" to all of the above, use the preterite.

(3) Verbs of State: Imperfect Is the Rule, Preterite Is the Exception

If the verb you are dealing with is a **verb of state** (*ser, estar, haber, tener, parecer, etc.*), you will follow a different set of rules to determine whether to use imperfect or preterite. As a basic rule, use the imperfect every time you have a **verb of state,** with the exception of contexts where there is a clear indication of **change, reaction,** or **implied action,** or if there is a **specified limitation of time,** in which cases you must use the preterite.

IMPERFECT	PRETERITE
No implication of change, reaction or action, or time limitation	**To indicate a sudden change, a reaction, or time limitation**
Eran las dos de la tarde. *It was two o'clock.*	**De repente, fueron las dos de la tarde.** *Suddenly, it was two o'clock in the afternoon.* (Here, the expression **de repente** is altering the standard way of seeing time.)
Jorge tenía catorce años. *Jorge was fourteen years old.*	**Jorge cumplió catorce años ese día.** *Jorge turned fourteen that day.* (Notice you do not use **tener.**)
Mi madre creía en Dios. *My mother believed in God.*	**En ese instante creyó en Dios.** *In that instant, he believed in God.* (Sudden conversion)
Hacía mucho frío ayer. *It was very cold yesterday.*	**Todo ese invierno hizo mucho frío.** *All that winter it was very cold.* (This sentence is almost identical to the one to the left. The only difference is in the way the narrator wishes to perceive the cold, as in progress or lasting a specific amount of time.)
Había diez sillas en la clase. *There were ten chairs in the classroom.* (Notice that these are objects, not events.)	**Hubo una tormenta, una huelga, una pelea, un incendio...** *There was a storm, a strike, a fight, a fire...* (Events or actions)
Estaba en España cuando oí la noticia. *I was in Spain when I heard the news.*	**Estuve en España por dos años.** *I was in Spain for two years.* (Time limit: **dos años**)

Verbs that change meaning when used in the preterite:

SABER
♦ Imperfect—to know
   Sabía español cuando era niño. *He knew Spanish as a child.*
♦ Preterite—to find out
   Supo que ella había muerto. *He found out that she had died.*

CONOCER

- ♦ Imperfect—to know

  Conocíamos a los Gómez. *We knew the Gomezes.*
- ♦ Preterite—to meet

  Conocí a Marta en la fiesta. *I met Marta at the party.*

PODER

- ♦ Imperfect—to be able, can

  Podían trabajar juntos. *They could work together.*
- ♦ Preterite—affirmative: to succeed, be able, manage; negative: to fail

  Después de mucho esfuerzo, pudieron abrir la ventana. *After a lot of effort, they succeeded in opening the window.*

  No pudieron salir. *They could not (failed to) get out.*

QUERER

- ♦ Imperfect—to want

  Queríamos viajar. *We wanted to travel.*
- ♦ Preterite—affirmative: to attempt, try; negative: to refuse to

  Quiso escapar, pero no pudo. *He tried to escape, but failed.*

  No quiso ayudarme. *He would not help me.* (He refused to.)

TENER QUE

- ♦ Imperfect—obligation not necessarily fulfilled

  Tenía que trabajar, pero fui al cine. *I had to work, but went to the movies.*
- ♦ Preterite—fulfilled obligation

  Tuve que trabajar anoche. *I had to work last night (and did).*

ACABAR DE

- ♦ Imperfect—to have just done something

  Acababa de comer cuando llegaste. *I had just eaten when you arrived.*
- ♦ Preterite—to finish

  Acabé de comer y me fui. *I finished eating and left.*

The verb *ser* is a special case when used in the following type of sentence:

SER + time expression + RELATIVE PRONOUN + VERB

Fue la última vez que lo vi. *It was the last time I saw him.*

Era la primera vez que lo veía. *It was the first time I saw him.*

What determines the tense of the verb *ser* in these sentences is the tense of the second verb.

The sentence in the imperfect would in most likelihood be found at the **beginning** or in the **middle** of a context describing that first time of seeing someone, when the description of the encounter is still in progress. The sentence in the preterite would be at the **end** of the narrative, closing the description of the first encounter.

c) Beginning–Middle–End

Another way of perceiving the preterite and the imperfect is by means of the three concepts of **beginning**, **middle**, and **end**. The preterite would be used for actions seen at their origin or at their end, or as begun and ended in the past; the imperfect is used for actions perceived in the middle, or in process, with no vision of beginning or end.

(1) Preterite: Beginning and/or End

Beginning	|—————— - - - - - -

Empecé a trabajar a las tres. *I started to work at three.*

End	- - - - - - ——————|

Trabajé hasta las cuatro de la tarde. *I worked until four in the afternoon.*

Estuve en México hasta la edad de veinte años. *I was in Mexico until the age of twenty.*

Beginning and end	|——————|

Trabajé desde las tres hasta las cuatro. *I worked from three to four.*

Estuve en España por dos meses. *I was in Spain for two months.*

There are times when the distance between beginning and end is reduced to the extent that it is invisible. All that can be perceived is a point in time at which something occurred. The act is not seen as in process.

Ayer **comí** en un restaurante mexicano. *Yesterday I ate in a Mexican restaurant.*

Me levanté, **me vestí** y **me fui** a clase. *I got up, got dressed, and left for class.*

(2) Imperfect: Middle

Middle	- - - - - - —————— - - - - - -

> **Cuando entré, las dos <u>hablaban</u> de sus clases.** *When I entered, both were speaking about their classes.* (I don't know when they began speaking; they were in the process of speaking when I entered.)
>
> **<u>Tenía</u> veinticinco años cuando fui a Barcelona.** *I was twenty-five years old when I went to Barcelona.* (It is not stated when I began to be twenty-five, only that it was during that year in which I was twenty-five.)

In summary, since the imperfect is used only to refer to the middle of events, with no concern as to their beginning or end, and the preterite is used to focus specifically on the beginning or end of an event, or to encompass the entirety of the occurrence of the event from beginning to end, we can safely state the following general rule: Use the preterite every time except to refer to the middle of events.

MORE ABOUT THE IMPERFECT

There is a certain parallelism between the imperfect tense and the present tense. Remember that the **present** tense is used for the following:

1. To refer to something that is happening at the present moment, at the moment of speaking
   Lee una novela. *He reads (is reading) a novel.*
2. To refer to a customary event
   Siempre me despierto al amanecer. *I always wake up at dawn.*
3. To indicate futurity
   Dice que sale en una hora. *He says he is leaving in an hour.*

The **imperfect** is used for these three types of reference, recalling them from the past:

1. What was happening in the past
   <u>Leía</u> una novela. *He read (was reading) a novel.*
2. What was customary in the past
   Siempre me <u>despertaba</u> al amanecer. *I always woke up (used to wake up, would wake up) at dawn.*
3. What was going to happen
   Dijo que <u>salía</u> en una hora. *He said he was leaving in an hour.*

---

d) Diachronic vs. Synchronic

Yet another way of perceiving the difference between the preterite and the imperfect is one that relates to narration. If we were to say that a story is basically formed by actions that advance the plot and descriptions that add color, we could visualize the diagram of a story with two sets of lines: one horizontal, along which the actions that advance the plot, one after the other, successively, are located (diachronic); and along it, vertical lines along which descriptive portions are formed, not advancing in time, but immobile, forming a sort of painting or visual framework in which the other actions will occur (synchronic). Depending on the type of novel or story, you may have mostly a horizontal line, or a short horizontal line, indicating that little really happened in the plot, but many vertical lines, indicating a great deal of description. Thus, a summary of a story would be **preterite**; a typical love story could be seen like this: They met, they fell in love, he met her parents, he gave her an engagement ring, they got married, they had children, they lived happily ever after. On the other hand, the weather when they met, or what the scenery was when he gave her the engagement ring, or what everyone was doing in church while she walked up the aisle would be in the **imperfect.**

The following diagram plots out the verbs of the paragraph below. Notice that the <u>horizontals</u> are in the **preterite** (diachronic) and the <u>verticals</u> are in the **imperfect** (synchronic); numbers identify the preterite, letters the imperfect.

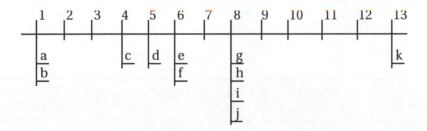

Esta mañana cuando me <u>desperté</u> [1], el sol <u>brillaba</u> [a] y los pájaros <u>cantaban</u> [b]. Me <u>levanté</u> [2] y me <u>bañé</u> [3]. <u>Fui</u> [4] a la cocina donde ya <u>comían</u> [c] mis hermanos y me <u>preparé</u> [5] el desayuno. <u>Parecía</u> [d] un día normal.

En camino al trabajo, <u>ocurrió</u> [6] algo muy extraño. En la carretera, que a esa hora de la mañana por lo general <u>estaba</u> [e] vacía, <u>había</u> [f] una fila de carros larguísima. Cuando <u>llegué</u> [7] por fin hacia el frente de la fila, <u>pude</u> [8] ver que un carro de policía <u>estaba</u> [g] estacionado al lado de la carretera, y que dos policías <u>paraban</u> [h] cada carro y <u>miraban</u> [i] dentro del carro, como buscando a alguien o algo. Un motociclista <u>iba</u> [j] delante de mí, y cuando le <u>tocó</u> [9] a él pasar la inspección, el policía le <u>pidió</u> [10] que se quitara el casco para mostrarle la cara. Al llegar yo, me <u>quité</u> [11] las gafas de sol, y <u>pasé</u> [12] sin problema. Pero me <u>asusté</u> [13] mucho al ver que uno de los policías <u>tenía</u> [k] un rifle.

This morning when I woke up, the sun was shining and the birds were singing. I got up and bathed. I went to the kitchen where my brothers were already eating and prepared myself breakfast. It seemed to be a normal day.

On the way to work, something very strange happened. On the road, which at that time in the morning was usually empty, there was a very long line of cars. When I finally arrived at the front of the line, I was able to see that a police car was parked on the side of the road, and that two police officers were stopping each car and looking inside the car, as if they were looking for someone or something. A motorcyclist was (going) ahead of me, and when it was his turn to pass inspection, the police officer asked him to take off his helmet to show him his face. When I arrived, I took off my sunglasses, and passed with no problem. But I became very frightened when I saw that one of the police officers had a rifle.

APPENDIX II

Práctica

3. Compound Tenses

a) Introduction

In the table that follows, the verbs in bold are what we call "compound tenses," because they are formed of more than one part. Notice that for the progressive form, *estar* is used with the **present participle.** For the perfect forms, *haber* is used as auxiliary with the **past participle.** Progressive perfect forms combine *estar* in the perfect form (auxiliary *haber* + the past participle of *estar*) and the present participle of the verb being conjugated.

	MOOD	TENSE	NONPROGRESSIVE	PROGRESSIVE
S	Indicative	Present	camino	**estoy caminando**
I	Indicative	Future	caminaré	**estaré caminando**
M	Indicative	Imperfect	caminaba	**estaba caminando**
P	Indicative	Preterite	caminé	**estuve caminando**
L	Conditional	Present	caminaría	**estaría caminando**
E	Subjunctive	Present	camine	**esté caminando**
	Subjunctive	Imperfect	caminara	**estuviera caminando**
P				
E	Indicative	Present Perfect	**he caminado**	**he estado caminando**
R	Indicative	Future Perfect	**habré caminado**	**habré estado caminando**
F	Indicative	Pluperfect	**había caminado**	**había estado caminando**
E	Conditional	Perfect	**habría caminado**	**habría estado caminando**
C	Subjunctive	Present Perfect	**haya caminado**	**haya estado caminando**
T	Subjunctive	Pluperfect	**hubiera caminado**	**hubiera estado caminando**

b) Perfect Tenses

As a rule, perfect tenses are used to focus on the completion of an action in relation to a moment, present or past.

PERFECT TENSES			
Formation	Auxiliary **Haber**	**+**	Past Participle
Example	**Hemos**		**llegado.**
Translation	*We have*		*arrived.*

(1) Present Perfect Indicative

This tense refers to completed events in relation to the present.

> **Hemos regresado** del museo. *We have returned from the museum.*
>
> **Todavía no he terminado** el libro. *I still have not finished the book.*

(2) Future Perfect

This tense refers to a future event that will have been completed by a specific time or after another event in the future.

> **Habremos terminado** para las cinco. *We will have finished by five.*

The future perfect can also be found in contexts expressing probability, for probably completed actions in the past.

> **¿Adónde crees que fue Roberto?** *Where do you think Roberto went?*
>
> **No sé. Habrá ido** a la tienda. *I do not know. I guess he went to the store.*

(3) Past Perfect (Pluperfect) Indicative

This tense refers to an event prior to another one in the past.

> **Ya había terminado** de comer cuando llamaste.
>
> *I had already finished eating when you called.*

(4) Conditional Perfect

This tense refers to an event that is the future in relation to another event in the past.

> **Me dijeron que habrían terminado** para el viernes pasado.
>
> *They told me they would have finished by last Friday.*

This form can also be found in probability structures, referring to an action in the past prior to another one in the past.

> **¿Por qué piensas que esa estudiante se aburría en clase el semestre pasado?** *Why do you think that student was bored in class last semester?*
>
> **No sé. Ya <u>habría leído</u> los mismos libros para otra clase.** *I do not know. Maybe she had already read the same books for another class.*

(5) Present Perfect Subjunctive

This tense describes an event that is completed in relation to the present.

> **Me sorprende que <u>haya llegado</u> tarde.**
>
> *It surprises me that he arrived late.*

(6) Pluperfect Subjunctive

This tense describes an event that was completed before another in the past.

> **Nos sorprendió que <u>hubiera cenado</u> antes de venir.**
>
> *It surprised us that he had eaten before coming.*

c) Simple Progressive Tenses

(1) Introduction

The progressive is used to express an ongoing action.

PROGRESSIVE TENSES			
Formation	Auxiliary **Estar**	**+**	Present Participle
Example	**Estamos**		**estudiando.**
Translation	We are		*studying.*

Exception: *Ir* and *venir* are NEVER used in the progressive in Spanish.

We are going to Spain.	**Vamos a España.**
She is coming to dinner.	**Viene a cenar.**

In Spanish, the progressive is NEVER used for states or conditions.

She was wearing a leather jacket.	**Llevaba una chaqueta de cuero.**
I am wearing shoes.	**Tengo zapatos puestos.**
I am sitting. (position)	**Estoy sentado.**
Two chairs were missing.	**Faltaban dos sillas.**
Your undershirt is showing.	**Se te ve la camiseta.**

(2) Present Progressive

This tense is formed with the present of *estar* and refers to ongoing actions in the present.

> <u>Estoy trabajando</u> en este momento y no podré ayudarte.
>
> *I am working at this moment and will not be able to help you.*

> Pronto comeremos; <u>están preparando</u> la cena.
>
> *We will eat soon; they are preparing dinner.*

The present progressive is NEVER used in Spanish to refer to the future, as it often is in English.

> *We are doing it tomorrow.*   →   **Lo vamos a hacer mañana.**

(3) Future Progressive

This tense is formed with the future of *estar* and refers to ongoing actions in the future.

> **Mañana, domingo, a las siete de la tarde, Asunción <u>estará cenando</u>. Lo sé porque siempre hace lo mismo.**
>
> *Tomorrow, Sunday, at seven in the evening, Asunción will be eating dinner. I know it because she always does the same thing.*

The future progressive is also used to express probability in the present.

> **¿Qué hace Regina?**   *What is Regina doing?*
>
> **No lo sé. <u>Estará estudiando</u>.**   *I do not know. She must be studying.*

(4) Past Progressive

This tense is formed with the imperfect or preterite of *estar* and refers to an ongoing or finished action in the past.

> <u>Estaba trabajando</u> cuando me llamaste.
>
> *I was working when you called.*

> <u>Estuve trabajando</u> toda la mañana.
>
> *I was working all morning.*

The past progressive can NEVER be used to refer to a future of the past.

> *It was going to rain.*   →   **Iba a llover.**

(5) Conditional Present Progressive

This tense, formed with the present conditional of *estar,* refers to an ongoing action that is future in the past, a backshift from the section on future progresssive (above).

Cecilia me dijo que el día siguiente, domingo, a las siete de la tarde, Susana <u>estaría cenando</u>. Añadió que lo sabía porque siempre hacía lo mismo.

Cecilia told me that the next day, Sunday, at seven in the evening, Susana would be eating dinner. She added that she knew it because she always did the same thing.

The conditional progressive is also used to express probability for an ongoing action in the past.

—¿Por qué no vino Georgina a clase ayer?

—Quién sabe. <u>Estaría durmiendo</u>.

Why did Georgina not come to class yesterday?

Who knows. Maybe she was sleeping.

(6) Subjunctive Present Progressive

This tense is formed with the present subjunctive of *estar* and refers to an ongoing action in the present, colored by the subjunctive.

Dudo que mis hijos <u>estén comiendo</u> lo suficiente.

I doubt that my children are eating enough.

(7) Subjunctive Imperfect Progressive

This tense is formed with the imperfect subjunctive of *estar* and refers to an ongoing action in the past, colored by the subjunctive.

No podía creer que <u>estuvieran peleando</u> todavía.

I could not believe they were still fighting.

d) Perfect Progressive Tenses

(1) Introduction

This combination serves to focus on the completion of an ongoing action in relation to another moment, present, past, or future.

PERFECT PROGRESSIVE TENSES				
Formation	Auxiliary **Haber**	**+**	Past Participle **Estar**	**+**	Present Participle Main Verb
Example	**Hemos**		**estado**		**corriendo.**
Translation	*We have*		*been*		*running.*

(2) Indicative Present Perfect Progressive

Mi madre <u>ha estado llamándome</u> todos los días.

My mother has been calling me every day.

(3) Indicative Future Perfect Progressive

Para cuando llegue, <u>habré estado manejando</u> durante doce horas sin parar.

By the time I get there, I will have been driving for twelve hours nonstop.

This form can also serve for probability, when referring to a completed ongoing action in the past.

—¿Por qué está tan cansada Zelmira?

—No sé. <u>Habrá estado trabajando</u> toda la noche.

Why is Zelmira so tired?

I do not know. She was probably working all night.

(4) Indicative Pluperfect Progressive

Cuando por fin me dejaron entrar, <u>había estado esperando</u> tres horas.

When they finally let me in, I had been waiting for three hours.

(5) Conditional Perfect Progressive

La policía <u>habría estado vigilando</u> la casa si se lo hubieras pedido.

The police would have been watching the house if you had asked them.

This form can also be used for probability, when referring to a completed ongoing action in the past prior to another.

—¿Por qué crees que tardó tanto en abrir la puerta?

—<u>Habría estado escondiendo</u> las pruebas.

Why do you think he took so long to open the door?

He must have been hiding the evidence.

(6) Subjunctive Present Perfect Progressive

Use in subordinate clauses when the main verb is in the present set and to refer to a completed ongoing action in the past.

Dudo que <u>haya estado haciendo</u> lo que decía.

I doubt that he was doing what he said.

(7) Subjunctive Pluperfect Progressive

Use in subordinate clauses to refer to a completed ongoing action in a moment in the past prior to another one also in the past.

Me sorprendió que no <u>hubiera estado durmiendo</u> a esa hora.

It surprised me that he had not been sleeping at that time.

Práctica

APPENDIX II

4. Ways of Expressing the Future

The future in Spanish can be expressed with the simple future.

Mañana <u>iremos</u> al cine. *Tomorrow we will go to the movies.*

It can also be expressed with the present of *ir + a +* an infinitive.

Mañana <u>vamos a ir</u> al cine. *Tomorrow we are going to go to the movies.*

It can also be expressed with the present tense.

Mañana <u>vamos</u> al cine. *Tomorrow we are going to the movies.*

NOTE: The future cannot be expressed in Spanish with the progressive, as it can in English.

APPENDIX II
Práctica

5. Conditional

a) Introduction

The conditional is used to express the following:

- ♦ Courtesy
- ♦ Hypothetical situations
- ♦ Future of the past
- ♦ Probability in the past

b) Courtesy: Conditional of Modal Auxiliaries

This is merely a softening of the indicative, as in English; the difference between *can you* and *could you, must not* and *should not, I want* and *I would like*, etc.

¿<u>Podría</u> Ud. ayudarme, por favor? *Could you help me, please?*

No <u>deberías</u> decir eso. *You should not say that.*

The verb *querer* can be used in the same fashion, but is most frequently used in the imperfect subjunctive to express courtesy.

<u>Quisiera</u> que me ayudaras. *I would like you to help me.*

c) Hypothetical Situations with or Without Condition Expressed with *Si* (See *Chapter 6, Section 7* on *si* clauses.)

En esa situación, yo <u>tendría</u> mucho miedo.
In that situation, I would be very frightened.

Yo en tu lugar no le <u>pagaría</u> por grosero.
In your place, I would not pay him, because he was rude.

Si pudiera, me <u>compraría</u> ese coche.
If I could, I would buy that car.

d) Future of the Past (See *Chapter 6, Section 11* on indirect discourse.)

Dijo que <u>irían</u> al cine hoy.   *He said they would go to the movies today.*

e) Probability in the Past (See *Chapter 6, Section 6* on probability.)

¿Dónde <u>estaría</u> Juan?   *I wonder where Juan was.*
¿Adónde <u>habría</u> ido?   *I wonder where he had gone.*

6. Probability

English has many ways of expressing probability. Here is a list of some of the many possibilities of expressing doubt with the question "Who is it?":

I wonder who it is.

Who can it be?

Who in the world is it?

Who do you suppose it is?

Who do you think it is?

Spanish uses a variation of tenses to express probability.

The **future** is used to express probability in the present.

¿Quién <u>será</u>? (All of the variations of the English above would be translated like this.)

The **future progressive** form is frequently used with verbs of action.

¿Qué <u>estarán haciendo</u>?   *I wonder what they are doing.*

The **future perfect** is used to express the preterite or the present perfect.

<u>Habrá ido</u> al cine. *He probably went to the movies.*
I guess he went to the movies.
He has probably gone to the movies.
I suppose he went… etc.

The **conditional present** is used to express the imperfect aspect of the past.

<u>Estaría</u> en el cine. *He probably was at the movies.*
He must have been at the movies.
I guess he was… etc.

The **conditional progressive** form is used for verbs of action.

<u>Estaría bañándose.</u> *He was probably bathing.*

The **conditional perfect** is used to express the pluperfect.

<u>Habría salido</u> temprano. *He probably had gone out early.*
He must have gone out early.
I guess he went out… etc.

The following parallel columns show how probability is expressed in Spanish. On the left, the sentences are formed with the adverb *probablemente* and the standard form of the verb, whereas the column to the right gives you the altered verb tense that expresses probability without the need for the adverb.

STANDARD	PROBABILITY	TRANSLATION
Probablemente **está** en casa.	**Estará** en casa.	*He must be home.*
Probablemente **está bañándose.**	**Estará bañándose.**	*He must be bathing.*
Probablemente **estaba** en casa.	**Estaría** en casa.	*He must have been home.*
Probablemente **estaba comiendo.**	**Estaría comiendo.**	*He must have been eating.*
Probablemente **murió.**	**Habrá muerto.**	*He must have died.*
Probablemente lo **ha visto.**	Lo **habrá visto.**	*He must have seen it.*
Probablemente **había regresado.**	**Habría regresado.**	*He must have returned.*

In English, the first sentence above could also be: "He's probably at home, I guess he's at home, I suppose he's at home," etc. Each sentence above could thus have a variety of translations in English.

APPENDIX II
Práctica

7. Subjunctive

a) Introduction

The subjunctive is used mainly in subordinate clauses and in some independent clauses introduced by *ojalá, quizá(s),* and *tal vez*.

There are three types of subordinate clauses in which the subjunctive might be necessary:

♦   Nominal
♦   Adjectival
♦   Adverbial

Each type of clause will have its own set of rules to determine whether or not you need to use the subjunctive. It is therefore necessary to be able to recognize the three types.

b) Nominal Clauses

(1) Definition and Usage

Definition: A nominal clause is one that has the same function as a noun would (i.e., it may be the subject of the main verb or its direct object).

Quiero <u>pan</u>.	*I want bread.*
Quiero <u>que me ayudes</u>.	*I want you to help me.*

Both *pan* and *que me ayudes* have the same function in the sentence, that of direct object of the main verb; *que me ayudes* is called a **nominal clause** because it behaves like a noun. In the sentence *Me gusta que canten* the subordinate clause is the subject of the main verb.

Use of the subjunctive: What determines whether or not you need to use the subjunctive in the nominal clause is the **verb** of the main clause. If this verb indicates emotion, doubt, desire, approval, feeling, volition, influence, etc., the verb of the nominal clause will have to be in the subjunctive.

Me encanta que <u>vengan</u>.	*I am delighted that they are coming.*
Dudo que ellos <u>puedan</u> hacerlo.	*I doubt that they can do it.*
Quiero que me <u>des</u> pan.	*I want you to give me bread.*
Me gusta que <u>participen</u> tanto.	*I like them to participate so much.*

Parecer, creer, and *pensar* take the subjunctive only if in the negative or the interrogative when there is doubt in the mind of the speaker. Also, *parecer* followed by an adjective takes the subjunctive.

Parece que <u>va</u> a llover.	*It seems it is going to rain.*
<u>No</u> parece que <u>vaya</u> a llover.	*It does not seem that it is going to rain.*

Parece <u>increíble</u> que <u>hagan</u> eso.	*It seems incredible that they do that.*
Creo que <u>puede</u> hacerlo.	*I believe he can do it.*
<u>No</u> creo que <u>pueda</u> hacerlo.	*I do not believe he can do it.*
Pienso que <u>vendrá</u>.	*I think he will come.*
<u>No</u> pienso que <u>venga</u>.	*I do not think he will come.*

Sentir will change meaning if followed by the subjunctive.

| Siento que <u>voy</u> a estornudar. | *I feel I am going to sneeze.* |
| Siento que <u>estés</u> enferma. | *I am sorry that you are ill.* |

(2) Subjunctive After Expressions of Emotion

If the main clause contains a verb or an expression of emotion, this affects the verb of the subordinate clause; whether it is true or not that the action of the subordinate occurred or will occur, the subjunctive must be used.

<u>Estás</u> aquí.	*You are here.*
Sé que <u>estás</u> aquí.	*I know you are here.*
Me alegro que <u>estés</u> aquí.	*I am glad you are here.*

Following is a list of commonly used verbs of emotion:

esperar	*to hope*	Espero que puedas venir.
		I hope you can come.
lamentar	*to regret*	Lamento que esté enferma.
		I regret that she is ill.
sentir	*to be sorry,* *regret*	Siento que no puedas ir.
		I am sorry you cannot go.
temer	*to fear*	Temo que sea muy tarde.
		I fear it is too late.
tener miedo	*to be afraid*	Tengo miedo que haya una tormenta.
		I am afraid there will be a storm.

Reflexive verbs:

alegrarse de	*to be happy,* *glad*	Me alegro que se encuentre mejor.
		I am glad he is feeling better.
avergonzarse de	*to be ashamed*	Se avergüenza de que su padre beba.
		He is ashamed that his father drinks.

Flip verbs:

encantarle a uno	*to delight, "love"* (not romantic)	**Me encanta que jueguen.** *I am delighted that they play.* **Nos encantaría que vinieran.** *We would love you to come.*
enojarle a uno	*to anger, to make angry, be angry*	**Nos enoja que nos griten.** *It angers us that they yell at us.* *We are angry that they yell at us.*
gustarle a uno	*to please, like*	**Le gusta que ganen.** *It pleases him that they win.* *He likes them to win.*
molestarle a uno	*to annoy, be annoyed*	**¿Te molesta que haga ruido?** *Does it annoy you that I make noise?*
sorprenderle a uno	*to surprise, be surprised*	**Les sorprende que podamos hacerlo.** *They are surprised that we can do it.*

Use of the infinitive in the subordinate clause: For verbs of emotion, if the subject is the same in both clauses, use an **infinitive** in the subordinate clause.

Sentimos no <u>poder</u> ir a la fiesta.	*We are sorry we cannot go to the party.*
Quiero <u>dar</u>te un regalo.	*I want to give you a present.*
Me encantó <u>bailar</u> contigo.	*I loved dancing with you.*
Me gustó <u>visitar</u> a mis abuelos.	*I enjoyed visiting my grandparents.*

(3) Subjunctive After Expressions of Volition and Influence

If the main clause contains a verb or an expression of volition or influence, the subjunctive must be used in the subordinate clause.

Quiero que <u>cantes</u> conmigo.	*I want you to sing with me.*

Commonly used verbs of volition:

desear	*to want*	**¿Desea que le traiga algo de beber?** *Do you want me to bring you something to drink?*
empeñarse en	*to insist*	**Se empeña en que la respeten.** *She insists that they respect her.*
insistir en	*to insist on*	**Insistieron en que les pagáramos.** *They insisted on our paying them.*

necesitar	*to need*	**Necesito que me escuches.** *I need you to listen to me.*
oponerse a	*to object to*	**Se oponía a que le abrieran la maleta.** *He objected to their opening his suitcase.*
preferir	*to prefer*	**Prefiero que me hables en español.** *I prefer that you speak to me in Spanish.*
querer	*to want*	**Queremos que llegue la primavera.** *We want spring to arrive.*

Use of the infinitive in the subordinate clause: For verbs of volition, if the subject is the same in both clauses, use an **infinitive** in the subordinate clause.

Deseamos <u>ir</u> solos.	*We want to go alone.*
Se empeña en <u>gritar</u>.	*He insists on yelling.*
Insisto en <u>llamar</u> primero.	*I insist on calling first.*
Necesitas <u>estudiar</u>.	*You need to study.*
Me opongo a <u>votar</u> por él.	*I refuse (object) to vote for him.*
Prefieren <u>viajar</u> en barco.	*They prefer to travel by ship.*
Quiero <u>darte</u> un regalo.	*I want to give you a present.*

Verbs of communication such as *decir, escribir,* and *telefonear* may be followed by the indicative or the subjunctive; if they are used with the subjunctive, they imply a command.

Dijo que quería irse.	*He said he wanted to leave.*
Me dijo que me fuera.	*He told me to leave.*

Commonly used verbs of influence with a direct object:

dejar*	*to let, allow*	**Dejé que él pagara.** *I let him pay.*
hacer*	*to make*	**Hizo que limpiaran su cuarto.** *He made them clean their room.*
invitar a*	*to invite*	**La invito a que cene con nosotros.** *I invite you to eat dinner with us.*
obligar a*	*to force*	**Los obliga a que bailen.** *He forces them to dance.*

*****Dejar, hacer, invitar a, obligar a, exigir, impedir, prohibir, recomendar, mandar,* and *permitir* are commonly used with the infinitive, even if there is a change of subject, and with a direct or indirect object pronoun: **Le dejé pagar. Las hizo limpiar su cuarto. Te mandó callarte. Le permiten regresar tarde.** (See *Chapter 6, Section 8* on the infinitive.)

Commonly used verbs of influence with an indirect object:

aconsejar	*to advise*	**Le aconsejo que se calle.**
		I advise you to be quiet.
advertir	*to warn*	**Les advierto que estudien.**
		I warn you to study.
convencer	*to convince*	**¿Te convencieron que hablaras?**
		Did they convince you to speak?
exigir	*to demand*	**Exigen que cerremos la puerta.**
		They demand that we close the door.
impedir*	*to prevent*	**Impidieron que fuera al baile.**
		They prevented her from going to the dance.
mandar*	*to order*	**Mandó que te callaras.**
		He ordered you to be quiet.
pedir	*to ask*	**Nos pide que lleguemos temprano.**
		He asks us to arrive early.
permitir*	*to allow*	**Permiten que regrese tarde.**
		They allow him to return late.
persuadir a	*to persuade*	**Me persuadieron a que cantara.**
		They persuaded me to sing.
prohibir*	*to forbid*	**Te prohíbo que salgas con ellos.**
		I forbid you from going out with them.
recomendar*	*to recommend*	**Nos recomiendan que tomemos aspirina.**
		They recommend that we take aspirin.
rogar	*to beg*	**Le ruego que me disculpe.**
		I beg you to forgive me.
sugerir	*to suggest*	**Sugieren que comamos aquí.**
		They suggest that we eat here.

Impersonal expressions:

bastar	*to be enough*	**Basta que me lo pidas.**
		It is enough that you ask me for it.

*Please refer to footnote on page 153.

convenir	*to be suitable, a good idea*	**Conviene que lleguen temprano.** *It is a good idea that you arrive early.*
importar	*to matter*	**No importa que no tengas dinero.** *It does not matter that you do not have money.*
más valer	*to be better*	**Más vale que me pague pronto.** *He had better pay me soon.*

(4) Subjunctive After Expressions of Doubt and Negation of Reality

If the main clause contains a verb or an expression of doubt, or a negation of reality, the subjunctive must be used in the subordinate clause.

Dudo que pueda hacerlo.   *I doubt that he can do it.*
Niega que lo haya visto.   *She denies that he saw it.*

Commonly used verbs of doubt and negation of reality:

dudar	*to doubt*	**Dudo que venga esta noche.** *I doubt that he will come tonight.*
negar	*to deny*	**Negó que fuera verdad.** *He denied that it was true.*
puede ser	*it may be*	**Puede ser que llueva hoy.** *It may be that it will rain today.*
no creer	*not to believe*	**No creo que sepa la verdad.** *I do not believe that he knows the truth.*
no decir	*not to say*	**No digo que seas culpable.** *I do not say that you are guilty.*
no pensar	*not to think*	**No piensa que tú le creas.** *He does not think you believe him.*
no ser	*not to be*	**No es que no quiera, es que no puedo.** *It is not that I do not want to, it is that I cannot.*
no significar	*not to mean*	**Eso no significa que no te quiera.** *That does not mean that he does not love you.*

(5) Subjunctive After Impersonal Expressions with *Ser*

If the main clause contains an impersonal expression with *ser* + an adjective or a noun, and the adjective or noun denotes anything but truth or certainty, the subjunctive must be used in the subordinate clause.

Indicative:

Es verdad que se **fue** temprano.　　*It is true that he left early.*

Es cierto que **hace** frío.　　*It is true that it is cold.*

Subjunctive:

Es posible que **pueda** hacerlo.　　*It is possible that he can do it.*

No es cierto que lo **haya visto**.　　*It is not true that he saw it.*

Commonly used impersonal expressions taking the subjunctive:

(ser) bueno	*(to be) good*	**Es bueno que sepas hacerlo sola.** *It is good you know how to do it alone.*
malo	*bad*	**Fue malo que se lo dijeras.** *It was bad for you to tell him.*
mejor	*better*	**Es mejor que nos vayamos temprano.** *It is better that we leave early.*
curioso	*curious, odd*	**Es curioso que no haya correo.** *It is odd that there is no mail.*
extraño	*strange*	**Fue extraño que no me saludara.** *It was strange that he did not greet me.*
fantástico	*fantastic*	**Es fantástico que puedas venir.** *It is fantastic that you can come.*
raro	*strange, odd*	**Es raro que no haga frío.** *It is strange that it is not cold.*
triste	*sad*	**Es triste que se vayan.** *It is sad that you are leaving.*
deseable	*desirable*	**Es deseable que pague al contado.** *It is desirable that you pay cash.*

importante	*important*	**Es importante que lo aprendan.** *It is important that they learn it.*
necesario	*necessary*	**Es necesario que estudies más.** *It is necessary that you study more.*
difícil	*unlikely*	**Es difícil que haga calor en invierno.** *It is unlikely to be (that it be) hot in winter.*
fácil	*likely*	**Es fácil que venga hoy.** *It is likely that he will come today.*
imposible	*impossible*	**Es imposible que se lo haya dicho.** *It is impossible that she told him.*
posible	*possible*	**Es posible que se hayan ido.** *It is possible that they left.*
probable	*probable*	**Es probable que no lo sepa.** *It is probable that he does not know it.*
(una) lástima	*a pity*	**Es una lástima que esté lloviendo.** *It is a pity that it is raining.*
(una) maravilla	*a wonder*	**Es una maravilla que comprenda.** *It is a wonder that he understands.*
(una) pena	*a pity*	**Es una pena que no puedas venir.** *It is a pity that you cannot come.*

Notice that these expressions parallel the categories of verbs of emotion, volition, influence, and doubt or uncertainty. All impersonal expressions take the subjunctive, except those that denote absolute certainty:

Es evidente, obvio, cierto, claro, etc....

c) Adjectival Clauses

(1) Definition

An adjectival clause is one that modifies a noun as an adjective would.

Quiero leer una novela <u>divertida</u>.

I want to read a fun novel.

Quiero leer una novela <u>que me haga reír</u>.

I want to read a novel that will make me laugh.

(2) Usage

Notice that *que* in this sentence is a **relative pronoun** and not a conjunction, as is the case in nominal clauses. The **antecedent** of the relative pronoun in this sentence is *novela*. To determine whether or not to use the subjunctive in an adjectival or relative clause, you must find the antecedent and see whether, within the context of the main clause, it is existent or not. You will only use the subjunctive if the antecedent is inexistent, or if its existence is unknown or uncertain.

Tengo una casa que <u>tiene</u> dos pisos.

I have a house that has two floors.

Quiero una casa que <u>tenga</u> dos pisos.

I want a house that has two floors.

Notice that in the first sentence, the fact that I have the house means that the house exists, and thus you must use the indicative in the subordinate clause, but in the second sentence, the house I want has not been found, and I do not know if it exists. For this reason, the verb of the subordinate must be in the **subjunctive.** Compare the following sentences:

Conozco a una mujer que <u>es</u> ingeniera.

I know a woman who is an engineer. (existent)

No conozco a nadie que <u>sea</u> brasileño.

I do not know anyone who is Brazilian. (existence unknown)

Hay alguien aquí que <u>está fumando</u> una pipa.

There is someone here who is smoking a pipe. (existent)

¿Hay alguien aquí que <u>sea</u> doctor?

Is there someone here who is a doctor? (existence unknown)

Lo que is followed by the subjunctive when the implied antecedent is totally unknown and the implication is "whatever it might be." If the antecedent is known by the speaker, the indicative is used.

Haré lo que me digas.

I shall do what (whatever) you tell me to do.

Haré lo que me dijiste.

I shall do (specifically) what you told me to do.

APPENDIX II
Práctica

d) Adverbial Clauses

(1) Definition

An adverbial clause is one that modifies the verb in the main clause in the same manner as an adverb would, by indicating how, when, for what purposes, and under what circumstances the action of the main clause takes place.

Salió <u>rápidamente</u>.	*He left quickly.*
Salió <u>tan pronto como pudo</u>.	*He left as soon as he could.*

(2) Usage

Use of the subjunctive: The primary rule to determine whether the subjunctive is used is that, if the action of the subordinate clause has not been accomplished at the time indicated in the main verb, the subjunctive is used. This rule permits us to subdivide conjunctions into two categories, according to the meaning of the conjunction; some conjunctions, such as *para que* and *antes de que*, will always introduce an action that has not yet taken place at the time of the main clause.

Lo hago para que tú no tengas que hacerlo.

I am doing it so that you will not have to.

Vino antes de que lo llamáramos.

He came before we called him.

Other conjunctions, such as *cuando,* can refer to situations that already occurred or that have not yet occurred. If they refer to a situation that already took place, the verb of the subordinate will be in the indicative; if not, it will be in the subjunctive.

Mi perro viene cuando lo llamo.

My dog comes when I call him.

Mi perro vendrá cuando lo llame.

My dog will come when I call him.

ALWAYS SUBJUNCTIVE	OCCASIONALLY SUBJUNCTIVE
para que	cuando
a fin de que	apenas
a menos que	en cuanto
salvo que	tan pronto como
a no ser que	aunque
antes de que	a pesar de que
con tal de que	después de que
sin que	mientras
en caso de que	hasta que

Conjunctions that change into prepositions plus an infinitive when the subject is the same for both verbs:

Obligatory:

antes de que	→ **antes de**	**Antes de salir, me puse el abrigo.** *Before going out, I put on my coat.*
para que	→ **para**	**Para preparar esto, necesitas dos huevos.** *To prepare this, you need two eggs.*
sin que	→ **sin**	**Se fue sin despedirse.** *He left without saying good-bye.*
después de que	→ **después de**	**Después de cenar, jugaron a la baraja.** *After eating dinner, they played cards.*

Optional:

hasta que	→ **hasta**	**No se irá hasta haberse acabado la comida.** OR: **No se irá hasta que se acabe la comida.** *He will not leave until he has finished his food.*

The following conjunctions **always** take the subjunctive (or the infinitive if the subject is the same for both the main verb and the subordinate, in some cases):

CONJUNCTION	MEANING	EXAMPLES
para que **a fin de que**	*so that*	Subjunctive: **Preparé la comida para que la <u>comieras</u>.** *I prepared the food so that you would eat it.* Infinitive (same subject for both verbs): **para que → para** **a fin de que → a fin de** **Se vistió para <u>salir</u>.** *He got dressed to go out.* **Estudia a fin de <u>mejorarte</u>.** *Study to improve yourself.*
a menos que **salvo que** **a no ser que**	*unless*	Subjunctive: **Iremos al parque a menos que <u>llueva</u>.** *We will go to the park unless it rains.*
antes de que	*before*	Subjunctive: **Lo preparé todo antes de que <u>llegaran</u> los invitados.** *I prepared everything before the guests arrived.* Infinitive: **antes de que → antes de** **Se despidió antes de <u>irse</u>.** *He said good-bye before leaving.*
con tal que **con tal de que**	*provided (that)*	Subjunctive: **Prepararé la comida con tal de que tú <u>laves</u> los platos.** *I will prepare the food provided you wash the dishes.* Infinitive: **con tal de que → con tal de** **Iré al cine con tal de <u>poder</u> ir con ustedes.** *I will go to the movies provided I can go with you.*
sin que	*without*	Subjunctive: **Salí sin que ellos me <u>oyeran</u>.** *I left without their hearing me.* Infinitive: **sin que → sin** **Salí sin <u>hacer</u> ruido.** *I left without making any noise.*
en caso de que	*in case (that)*	Subjunctive: **Traje abrigo en caso de que <u>hiciera</u> frío.** *I brought a coat in case it was cold.*

The following conjunctions only take the subjunctive when the situation referred to has not been experienced or if there is an implication of futurity in the main clause:

CONJUNCTION	MEANING	EXAMPLES
cuando	*when*	Subjunctive: **Vendré cuando <u>pueda</u>.** *I will come when I can. (whenever that might be)* Indicative: **Vino cuando <u>pudo</u>.** *He came when he could.*
apenas **en cuanto** **tan pronto como**	*as soon as*	Subjunctive: **Vendré en cuanto <u>pueda</u>.** *I will come as soon as I can.* Indicative: **Vino en cuanto <u>pudo</u>.** *He came as soon as he could.*
aunque **a pesar de que** **aun cuando**	*even if (subj.)* *although (indic.)*	Subjunctive: **Vendrá aunque no lo <u>invites</u>.** *He will come even if you do not invite him.* Indicative: **Vino aunque no lo <u>invitaste</u>.** *He came although you did not invite him.*
después de que	*after*	Subjunctive: **Llegaré después de que tú te <u>hayas ido</u>.** *I will arrive after you have left.* Indicative: **Llegó después de que tú te <u>fuiste</u>.** *He arrived after you had left.* Infinitive: **Llamó después de <u>irse</u>.** *He called after leaving.*
mientras	*provided (that), as long as (subj.)* *while (indic.)*	Subjunctive: **Mientras no <u>digas</u> la verdad, no te escucharé.** *As long as you do not tell the truth, I will not listen to you.* Infinitive: **Yo miraba la televisión mientras ella <u>trabajaba</u>.** *I watched TV while she worked.*

CONJUNCTION	MEANING	EXAMPLES
hasta que	*until*	Subjunctive: **No me iré hasta que me <u>digas</u> tu secreto.** *I will not leave until you tell me your secret.* Indicative: **No me fui hasta que me <u>dijo</u> su secreto.** *I did not leave until he told me his secret.* Infinitive: **No me iré hasta <u>saber</u> la verdad.** *I will not leave until I know the truth.*

Práctica · APPENDIX II

e) Sequence of Tenses

(1) Introduction

The relationship between the action of the main clause and that of the subordinate clause will determine which tenses you may use. We will present three perspectives, the first more generally applicable than the other two, which relate to specific formats only.

♦ Chronological relativity
♦ Aspect relativity
♦ Tense relativity

(2) Chronological Relativity

The first perspective we will present is the one that uses one basic concept for all combinations: the relativity of occurrence of the actions in the sentence.

The first question would be: What is the tense of the verb of the main clause? There are two general subdivisions of tenses for the verb of the main clause:

♦ The **present set** (present, present perfect, future, or imperative)
♦ The **past set** (imperfect, preterite, pluperfect, conditional present, or conditional perfect)

The next question is: When did the action of the subordinate clause occur in relation to the action of the verb of the main clause? After it? At the same time? Before it? Before another action in the past? We will call the four relationships as follows:

♦ Subsequent
♦ Simultaneous
♦ Prior
♦ Prior to prior

The last question is: Which tense of the subjunctive must be used? There are four tenses of the subjunctive:

♦ Present
♦ Present perfect
♦ Imperfect
♦ Pluperfect

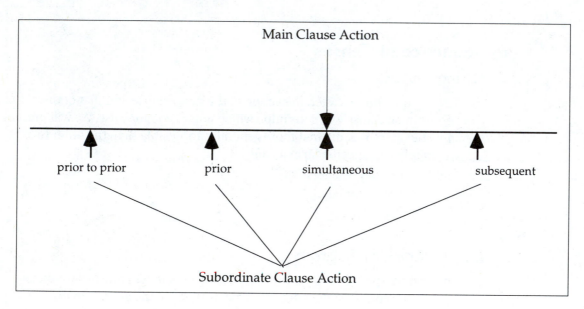

The following table indicates which tense could be used for each situation:

MAIN VERB TENSE	CHRONOLOGICAL RELATIVITY OF SUBORDINATE TO MAIN	SUBORDINATE CLAUSE: TENSES OF THE SUBJUNCTIVE	EXAMPLES	REF. #
Present set	1. Subsequent OR 2. Simultaneous	a. Present	Dudo que llueva mañana.	1a
			Dudo que esté enfermo.	2a
	3. Prior	b. Present perfect	Dudo que ya haya comido.	3b
		c. Imperfect	Dudo que estuviera verde.	3c
	4. Prior to another prior action	d. Pluperfect	Me sorprende que no hubiera llamado antes de venir.	4d
Past set	1. Subsequent OR 2. Simultaneous	c. Imperfect	Dudaba que se acabara pronto la conferencia.	1c
			Dudaba que estuviera enfermo.	2c
	3. Prior	d. Pluperfect	Dudaba que hubiera dicho esa mentira.	3d

Please note that the present and present perfect subjunctive cannot be used in sentences where the main clause is in the past set.

Explanation and further contextualization of the examples in the table:

1a. **Dudo que <u>llueva</u> mañana.** *I doubt (now) that it <u>will rain</u> tomorrow.*
The act of raining is subsequent to the moment of doubt; my doubt is formulating itself now, the rain has not yet occurred.

2a. **Dudo que <u>esté</u> enfermo.** *I doubt (now) that he <u>is</u> ill (now).*
The illness is simultaneous to the moment of doubt.

3b. **Dudo que ya <u>haya comido</u>.** *I doubt (now) that he <u>has eaten</u> (or ate) already.*
My doubt relates to his having eaten already. Has he already eaten? Did he eat already? I doubt it.

3c. **Dudo que <u>estuviera</u> verde.** *I doubt (now) that it <u>was</u> green (yesterday).*
I was just told that the apple I ate yesterday was green and that is what caused my stomach trouble. I doubt now that the apple was green (or unripe). I think my stomach trouble was due to something else.

4d. **Me sorprende que no <u>hubiera llamado</u> antes de venir.** *I am surprised that he <u>had not called</u> before he came.*

Yesterday, David came to visit me. He did not call before coming. Now that I think about it, it surprises me that he had not called before coming yesterday.

1c. **Dudaba que se <u>acabara</u> pronto la conferencia.** *I doubted that the lecture <u>would end</u> soon.*

The end of the lecture is subsequent to my doubt. I was doubting about the eventual ending of the lecture happening soon.

2c. **Dudaba que <u>estuviera</u> enfermo.** *I doubted that he <u>was</u> ill.*

I was at a party, and a friend of mine arrived and told me that my roommate could not come because he was sick. I doubted at that moment that my roommate was sick at that moment. The two actions are simultaneous.

3d. **Dudaba que <u>hubiera dicho</u> esa mentira.** *I doubted that he <u>had told</u> that lie.*

I was told yesterday that my younger brother had lied about his age a few days before. When I was told this, I doubted it. His alleged lie was prior to my doubt.

More examples:

1a. Subsequent to a main verb in the present set:

No quiero que <u>vayas</u> al cine. *I do not want you to go to the movies.*

Dile a Natalia que me <u>llame</u>. *Tell Natalia to call me.*

Nunca te lo he dicho para que no te <u>enojes</u>. *I have never told you so you would not get angry.*

2a. Simultaneous to a main verb in the present set:

Me sorprende que la manzana ya <u>esté</u> madura. *I am surprised the apple is already ripe.*

Encontraré una casa que <u>tenga</u> invernadero. *I will find a house that will have a greenhouse.*

3b. Prior to a main verb in the present set:

¿Conoces a alguien que <u>haya viajado</u> a Chile? *Do you know someone who has travelled to Chile?*

Me iré cuando <u>haya terminado</u>. *I shall leave when I have finished.*

Llámala, a menos que ya lo <u>hayas hecho</u>. *Call her, unless you have already done so.*

3c. Prior to a main verb in the present set:

Es extraño que no <u>supiera</u>. *It is strange that she did not know.*

Me sorprende que no <u>pudiera</u> hacerlo. *It surprises me that he was not able to do it.*

4d. Prior to another action prior to a main verb in the present set:

Carlota vino a cenar a casa anoche. *Carlota came to dinner last night.*

Antes de venir, había llamado para averiguar si podía traer algo. *Before coming, she had called to find out whether she could bring something.*

Me sorprende que <u>hubiera llamado</u> antes de venir ayer. *It surprises me that she had called before coming yesterday.*

Los empleados se quejan de que los patrones nunca les <u>hubieran pedido</u> su opinión antes de cambiar esa regla. *The employees complain that the bosses never asked their opinion before changing that rule.*

Lamentamos que no <u>hubieran recibido</u> nuestro mensaje antes de salir de viaje. *We are sorry that they had not received our message before they left on their trip.*

La adivina sabe el pasado de Raúl sin que nadie se lo <u>hubiera contado</u> antes. *The soothsayer knows Raúl's past without anyone having told her before.*

1c. Subsequent to a main clause in the past set:

Dudaba que mi hermana <u>viniera</u> a visitarme para Navidad. *I doubted that my sister would come to visit me for Christmas.*

Mi hermana me lo dio en caso de que lo <u>necesitara</u> más tarde. *My sister gave it to me in case I needed it later.*

Querían una compañía de seguros que <u>cumpliera</u> en caso de accidente. *They wanted an insurance company that would pay its part in case of an accident.*

Preferiría que te <u>fueras</u>. *I would prefer that you leave.*

2c. Simultaneous to a main clause in the past set:

Me encantó que <u>llegaran</u> a tiempo. *I was delighted that they arrived on time.*

La artista lo pintó sin que nadie la <u>viera</u>. *The artist painted it without anyone seeing her.*

No había nada allí que le <u>gustara</u>. *There was nothing there that she liked.*

3d. Prior to a main verb in the past set:

Dudaba que Miguel <u>hubiera dicho</u> esa mentira. *I doubted that Miguel had told that lie. (I doubted, yesterday when I was told, that he had told the lie the week before….)*

Salió corriendo en caso de que no le <u>hubieran quitado</u> la pistola al ladrón. *He ran out in case they had not taken the gun away from the thief.*

Buscaban una casa a la que ya le <u>hubieran hecho</u> todas las reparaciones necesarias. *They were looking for a house that would have already had all the necessary repairs.*

Se habían hablado sin que nadie los <u>hubiera presentado</u>. *They had talked to each other without anyone having introduced them.*

Los bomberos habrían llegado antes de que la casa se <u>hubiera quemado</u> si ese accidente no hubiera ocurrido en la carretera. *The firemen would have arrived before the house had burned down if that accident had not happened on the highway.*

(3) Aspect Relativity

The second perspective we will present elaborates on the distinction between the use of the imperfect and present perfect subjunctive when the main clause is in the **present set** (3b and 3c from the preceding table).

Aspect: Perfective (completed) and inchoative (beginning) vs. ongoing and habitual[1]

Use the **present perfect subjunctive** when the action of the verb of the subordinate clause is **perfective** or **inchoative** in aspect; this means that the action is perceived as completed (perfected, in grammatical terms) or beginning (inchoative) in the past. In many cases, it is the meaning of the verb itself that will determine the aspect ("to begin" is often inchoative, though it can be perceived as progressive or ongoing in "I was beginning…").

Perfective:

Es extraño que Luis no <u>haya venido</u> a clase. *It is strange that Luis did not come to class.*

¿Has conocido a alguien que <u>haya viajado</u> a Chile? *Have you met anyone who has travelled to Chile?*

Me iré cuando <u>haya terminado</u>. *I shall leave when I have finished.*

Llámala, a menos que ya lo <u>hayas hecho</u>. *Call her, unless you have already done so.*

Inchoative:

Dudo que el vuelo <u>haya salido</u> a tiempo. *I doubt that the flight left on time.* (focus on the beginning of the flight)

Me sorprende que todavía no <u>hayan empezado</u> a leer la novela. *I am surprised that you still have not begun to read the novel.*

Use the **imperfect subjunctive** when the action of the verb of the subordinate clause is **imperfective** in aspect; this means that the action is perceived as ongoing or stative in the past, or habitual.

---

1. This is the same difference that applies to preterite and imperfect in the indicative (see *Chapter 6, Section 2* "Preterite vs. Imperfect").

Ongoing or stative:

Jorge dice que <u>era</u> gordo de niño. Dudo que <u>fuera</u> gordo. *Jorge says he used to be fat as a child. I doubt that he was fat.*

Estaban jugando cuando entré. Me sorprende que <u>estuvieran</u> jugando. *They were playing when I entered. It suprises me that they were playing.*

Habitual:

Nunca he conocido a nadie que <u>cantara</u> así de niño. *I have never met anyone who used to sing that way as a child.*

Se avergüenza de que sus padres nunca <u>pagaran</u> impuestos. *She is ashamed that her parents never used to pay taxes.*

(4) Tense Relativity from Indicative to Subjunctive

This explanation runs parallel to the previous two explanations, but might be more palatable to some.

(a) Main Clause in the **Present Set**

Notice the conversion of each of the tenses of the indicative in the sentences on the left of the chart below, through the filter of the main clause *Dudo…*, for example, into the appropriate subjunctive in the new subordinate clause.

INDICATIVE	MAIN CLAUSE	SUBJUNCTIVE
Irá al cine.	Dudo	que vaya al cine.
Va al cine.	Dudo	que vaya al cine.
Iba al cine.	Dudo	que fuera al cine.
Fue al cine.	Dudo	que haya ido/fuera al cine.
Ha ido al cine.	Dudo	que haya ido al cine.
Habrá ido al cine.	Dudo	que haya ido al cine.
Había ido al cine.	Dudo	que hubiera ido al cine.

The above sentences translate as follows:

I doubt that he will go to the movies.
goes/is going
used to go/was going
went
has gone
will have gone
had gone

Table of tense conversions with **dudo:**

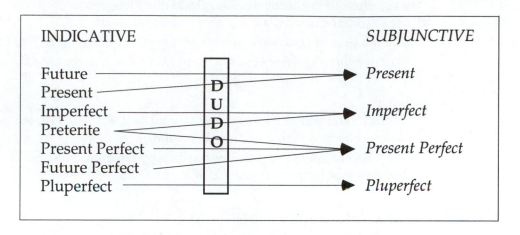

INDICATIVE   *SUBJUNCTIVE*

Future — *Present*
Present
Imperfect — *Imperfect*
Preterite
Present Perfect — *Present Perfect*
Future Perfect
Pluperfect — *Pluperfect*

(b) Main Clause in the **Past Set**

INDICATIVE	MAIN CLAUSE	SUBJUNCTIVE
Irá al cine.		
Va al cine.	Dudaba	que fuera al cine.
Iba al cine.		
Fue al cine.		
Fue al cine.		
Ha ido al cine.	Dudaba	que hubiera ido al cine.
Habrá ido al cine.		
Había ido al cine.		

The above sentences translate as follows:

> *I doubted that he*   *would go*   *to the movies.*
>   *went/was going*
>   *used to go*
>   *went*
> *I doubted that he*   *went/had gone*   *to the movies.*
>   *had gone*
>   *would have gone*
>   *had gone*

Table of tense conversions with **dudaba:**

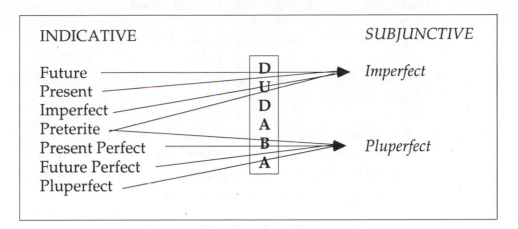

f) If (Si) Clauses

(1) Sequence of Tenses

In Spanish, sentences that contain a clause with *si* (if) or the implication of a condition follow a rigid construction pattern that must always be followed. Memorize the following three types of sentences and remember that they are essentially unchanging:

SI CLAUSE		MAIN CLAUSE
1. Indicative	↔	Indicative or Imperative
2. Imperfect Subjunctive	↔	Present Conditional
3. Pluperfect Subjunctive	↔	Past (Perfect) Conditional or Pluperfect Subjunctive

Sentence type #1 refers to situations that are possible. For example, one could say:

1a. **Si llueve, me llevo el paraguas.** *If it rains, I take my umbrella.*

1b. **Si llueve, llévate el paraguas.** *If it rains, take your umbrella.*

1c. **Si llovía, me llevaba el paraguas.** *If it rained, I used to take my umbrella.*

Notice that in each case we are speaking about the possibility of it raining. Just about any tense of the indicative can be used, and usually the same tense is used for both clauses. In the main clause (the one that does not begin with *si*), you can also find the imperative (sentence type 1b).

The future does not occur in conditional if clauses; it does occur when *si* means "whether" *(No sé si lloverá o no.).*

Sentence types 2 and 3 refer to situations that are contrary to the truth. Type 2 refers to a situation contrary to the present truth. For example:

    2a. **Si estuviera lloviendo, no saldría.**
       If it were raining (now), I would not go out.

    2b. **Si fuera rico, me compraría un coche deportivo.**
       If I were rich (now), I would buy myself a sports car.

Sentence type 3 refers to a situation contrary to past reality:

    3a. **Si hubiera estudiado más, habría/hubiera pasado el examen.**
       If I had studied more (last week), I would have passed the exam.

There exists one other type of cause-effect relationship, not depicted in the above table, and that is when a situation in the past affects the present:

       Si no hubiera llovido anoche, hoy todo estaría seco.
       If it had not rained last night, everything would be dry today.

All of these sentences can be inverted in order of clauses, beginning with the main clause instead of the *si* clause.

(2) *Como Si* (As If)

The expression *como si* is always followed by the subjunctive—either the imperfect subjunctive to speak of an action simultaneous with the main verb, or the pluperfect subjunctive to speak of an action prior to the main verb.

    Habla como si te <u>conociera</u>.
    He speaks as if he knew you.

    Te saluda como si te <u>hubiera visto</u> antes.
    He greets you as if he had seen you before.

APPENDIX II

Práctica

g) *Ojalá*

Sentences with *ojalá* can be translated into English as either "I hope" or "I wish." When you **hope** something, it is because you do not know what the reality of the situation is. Consider the following sentences:

1. *I hope that it will not rain tomorrow.* (hope for the future)
2. *I hope that it is not raining.* (hope for the present)
3. *I hope that our team won.* (hope for the past)

In these sentences, the speaker does not know: 1. whether it will rain, 2. whether it is raining, or 3. whether the team won or lost.

On the other hand, when you **wish** something, it is contrary to the actual reality. Consider the following sentences:

4. *I wish it were not raining.* (It is in fact raining; wish for the present)
5. *I wish our team had won.* (Actually, they lost; wish for the past)

To translate this difference in Spanish, you use *ojalá* with different tenses of the subjunctive.

Present subjunctive—hope for the future and the present:

Ojalá que no llueva mañana.	*I hope it will not rain tomorrow.*
Ojalá que no esté lloviendo.	*I hope it is not raining.*

Present perfect subjunctive—hope for the past:

Ojalá que nuestro equipo haya ganado.	*I hope our team won.*

Imperfect subjunctive—wish for the present and the future:

Ojalá que no estuviera lloviendo.	*I wish it were not raining.*
Ojalá que pudiera venir mañana.	*I wish he could come tomorrow.*

Pluperfect subjunctive—wish for the past:

Ojalá que nuestro equipo hubiera ganado.	*I wish our team had won.*

APPENDIX II
Práctica

h) Expressions of Leave-Taking

In English, when saying good-bye to someone, the imperative is often used in expressions of well-wishing: "Have a good day," "Have a good time," "Have fun," "Get well," etc.… In Spanish, it is not the custom to always express such feelings unless you know the person well, and even then, a simple *adiós, chau, nos vemos,* and *hasta luego* are more common in most cases. However, if you do wish to express any of the following, you cannot use the imperative for them in Spanish.

For someone whom you address as:

Tú:

Que[2] te vaya bien.	*May it go well for you.*
Que pases buen día.	*Have a good day.*
Que pases un buen fin de semana.	*Have a good weekend.*
Que la/lo pases bien.	*Have a good one.*
Que te diviertas.	*Have fun.*
Que te alivies.	*Get well.*
Que te mejores.	*Get better (Get well).*
Que Dios te acompañe.	*May God accompany you.* (for someone leaving on a trip)

Usted:	Ustedes:
Que le vaya bien.	Que les vaya bien.
Que pase buen día.	Que pasen buen día.
Que pase un buen fin de semana.	Que pasen un buen fin de semana.
Que la/lo pase bien.	Que la/lo pasen bien.
Que se divierta.	Que se diviertan.
Que se alivie.	Que se alivien.
Que se mejore.	Que se mejoren.
Que Dios lo/la acompañe.	Que Dios los/las acompañe.

Notice that these verbs are of different constructions.

In a standard construction, with a subject and a direct object, the verb agrees with the person being addressed.

Verb	Direct object	Example
pasar	buen día	Que **pasen** buen día. *May* <u>*you*</u> *have a good day.*
	un buen fin de semana	Que **pases** un buen fin de semana. *May* <u>*you*</u> *have a good day.*
	lo/la bien	Que lo **paséis** bien. *May* <u>*you*</u> *have a good one.*

---

2. Notice that this *que* does not have an accent mark, even if you choose to place the expression in an exclamation. This is because it is not an exclamative *que,* but the conjunction.

With reflexive verbs, when the same word serves as both subject and object, the verb agrees with the person being addressed.

Verb	Reflexive pronoun	Example
divertir	te, se, os	**Que te diviertas.** *Have fun.*
aliviar	te, se, os	**Que os aliviéis.** *Get well.*
mejorar	te, se, os	**Que se mejoren.** *May they get well.*

With flip verbs, with a subject and an indirect object, the verb itself remains invariable, because the subject is impersonal: *irle bien a uno.*

Verb	Indirect object	Example
ir	te, le, les, os	**Que te vaya bien.** *May it go well for you.*

With *Dios* as the subject and the person being addressed as the direct object:

Verb	Indirect object	Example
acompañar	te, lo(s), la(s), os	**Que Dios los acompañe.** *May He (God) accompany them* (los).

APPENDIX II
Práctica

8. Infinitive and Present Participle

a) Infinitive

(1) Present Infinitive

The **infinitive** functions like a **noun** in Spanish, and like a noun, it can be the subject or object of a verb, or object of a preposition. In English, the present participle is frequently used in these roles.

The infinitive as a subject (sometimes preceded by the article *el*):

<u>Caminar</u> es bueno para la salud.
Walking is healthy.

Me gusta <u>comer</u> helado.
I like eating (to eat) ice cream.

Nos encanta <u>ver</u> esas películas.
We love seeing those movies.

El <u>trabajar</u> tanto en la computadora le dañó los ojos.
Working so much on the computer harmed his eyes.

The infinitive as a direct object:

Quiero <u>aprender</u> el español.	*I want to learn Spanish.*
No sé <u>hacer</u> eso.	*I do not know how to do that.*
Pienso <u>comprar</u> ese coche.	*I am planning on buying that car.*
Debemos <u>estudiar</u> la lección.	*We must study the lesson.*
Decidimos <u>ir</u> al cine.	*We decided to go to the movies.*
¿Desea <u>comprar</u> algo?	*Do you wish to buy something?*
Logré <u>convencerla</u>.	*I succeeded in convincing her.*
Parece <u>estar</u> triste.	*He seems to be sad.*

Verbs used with a direct object pronoun and the infinitive (*dejar, hacer*):

No *lo* dejan <u>jugar</u>.	*They do not let him play.*
Lo hizo <u>recitar</u> el poema.	*She made him recite the poem.*

Verbs used with an indirect object pronoun and the infinitive (*permitir, aconsejar, impedir, prohibir, recomendar, rogar*):

No *le* permiten <u>salir</u>.	*They do not let him go out.*
Les aconsejo <u>llegar</u> temprano.	*I advise you to arrive early.*
Le impidieron <u>hablar</u>.	*They prevented him from speaking.*
Les prohíbe <u>beber</u> cerveza.	*He forbids their drinking beer.*
Le recomiendo <u>ver</u> esa película.	*I recommend that you see that movie.*
Les ruego <u>escucharme</u>.	*I beg you to listen to me.*

Verbs of perception are used with a direct object and an infinitive (*ver, oír*):

La *vi* <u>llegar</u> hace una hora.	*I saw her arrive an hour ago.*
Los *oí* <u>cantar</u> anoche.	*I heard them sing (singing) last night.*

The infinitive as an object of a preposition:

Se fue *sin* <u>despedirse</u>.	*He left without saying good-bye.*
Lo hice *para* <u>ayudarte</u>.	*I did it to help you.*
Eso te pasa *por* <u>comer</u> tanto.	*That happens to you for eating so much.*
Antes de <u>salir</u>, siempre desayuna.	*Before going out, he always eats breakfast.*
Estoy cansada *de* <u>estudiar</u>.	*I am tired of studying.*

The infinitive after *que* (*hay que, tener que, algo que, nada que, poco que*):

Hay que <u>tener</u> confianza.	*It is necessary to have confidence.*
Tienes que <u>venir</u> conmigo.	*You have to come with me.*
No tiene *nada que* <u>hacer</u>.	*He does not have anything to do.*
Tenemos *poco que* <u>hacer</u>.	*We have little to do.*

The infinitive after *de* with *fácil, difícil, posible,* and *imposible*:

Ese sonido es difícil *de* pronunciar.

That sound is difficult to pronounce.

In the above sentence, the subject of the verb *ser* is *sonido.* However, if the infinitive itself is to be the subject of *ser,* the preposition *de* must be omitted.

Es difícil pronunciar ese sonido.

It is difficult to pronounce that sound.

The same construction is used with *fácil, posible,* and *imposible.*

The infinitive after *al*:

The construction *al* + **infinitive** is used for an action that occurs at the same time as the main verb:

Al entrar, los saludaron a todos.

When they entered (Upon entering), they greeted everyone.

Al pedirles el favor, se arrepintió.

When he asked them for the favor, he regretted (doing) it.

The infinitive in advertising, signs, commands, questions:

No fumar.	*No smoking.*
Prohibido tirar basura.	*No littering.*
¿Por qué engordar? Con nuestro	*Why get fat? With our system,*
sistema puede usted reducir	*you can lose weight effortlessly.*
de peso sin ningún esfuerzo.	

The infinitive with a passive meaning after *oír, ver, mirar, escuchar, dejar, mandar, hacer*:

Lo he oído decir.	*I have heard it (being) said.*
Hice copiar las pruebas.	*I had the tests copied.*
Mandé comprar sellos.	*I ordered stamps to be bought.*

(2) Perfect Infinitive

The perfect infinitive (formed with the auxiliary *haber* in the infinitive, plus the past participle of the main verb) is used to express an action that occurred before the action of the main verb, when the subject is the same for both.

Debes haberlos dejado en el coche.	*You must have left them in the car.*
Creo habérselo dicho.	*I think I told him that.*
Se fue sin haber comido nada.	*He left without having eaten anything.*
Se cansó de la película después de haberla visto tres veces.	*He got tired of the movie after having seen it three times.*

b) Present Participle

The **present participle,** when not used with auxiliaries such as *estar,* functions in Spanish like an **adverb** and refers to an action occurring at the same time as or prior to the main action, indicating manner, cause, or condition.

Manner:	**Entró <u>gritando</u>.**
	He entered yelling.
Cause:	**<u>Siendo</u> persona sencilla, nunca pensó que otros no fueran honrados.**
	Being a simple person, he never thought that others would not be honest.
Condition:	**<u>Estando</u> los padres en casa, él no llamará.**
	With the parents at home, he will not call.

In Spanish, the present participle may be used to indicate simultaneity of two actions.

Preparó la cena <u>escuchando</u> el radio.

He prepared dinner while he listened to the radio.

As a rule, the present participle follows the main verb. However, in cases where it describes a cause or condition related to the main verb, it may be placed before.

<u>Explicándoselo</u> claramente de antemano, no habrá ambigüedad.

By explaining it clearly to them in advance, there will be no ambiguity.

In English the present participle can be used as an adjective. In these cases, Spanish uses:

1. an adjective (**not** formed with the present participle form):

an *<u>interesting</u> person*	**una persona <u>interesante</u>**
a *<u>growing</u> interest*	**un interés <u>creciente</u>**
the *<u>existing</u> problems*	**los problemas <u>existentes</u>**

2. *de* + noun or infinitive:

<u>writing</u> paper	**papel <u>de escribir</u>**
<u>growing</u> pains	**dolores <u>de crecimiento</u>**

3. a clause:

She saw a bird <u>singing</u>.	**Vio un pájaro <u>que cantaba</u>.**
She's a <u>growing</u> child.	**Es una niña <u>que está creciendo</u>.**

4. a preposition:

    the book <u>containing</u> pictures   el libro <u>con</u> fotos de España
    of Spain

    those things <u>belonging</u> to her   lo <u>de</u> ella

5. a past participle for postures and other conditions:

    standing = **parado**   *boring* = **aburrido**
    sitting = **sentado**   *amusing* = **divertido**
    lying down = **acostado**   *entertaining* = **entretenido**

In idiomatic expressions, the present participle of some verbs of motion indicates location:

Mi cuarto se encuentra <u>entrando</u>   *My room is to the left of the*
a la izquierda.   *entrance.*

Esa tienda está <u>pasando</u> el museo.   *That store is beyond the museum.*

In summary, never use the present participle form in Spanish as if it were a **noun** (i.e., as subject, object, or object of preposition) or as an **adjective**. In Spanish, it only functions as an **adverb**.

9. Verbs Like *Gustar*

a) Formation

The verb *gustar* ("to like") behaves differently in Spanish than it does in English. What in English is the subject of the verb, in Spanish is the **indirect object,** and the direct object of the English sentence is the **subject** of the Spanish sentence.

Me gustan las películas mexicanas.   *I like Mexican movies.*

In the Spanish sentence, *me* is the **indirect object** of the verb, and *las películas mexicanas* is the **subject.** (Notice the agreement of the verb with the plural of its subject.) To illustrate more clearly the fact that *me* is the indirect object, notice that if you wished to give emphasis to the person, you would add *a mí* to the basic sentence (and **not** *yo*).

<u>A mí</u> **me gustan las películas**   *I like Mexican movies.*
mexicanas.

For further emphasis on this structure, look at the **subject,** *películas mexicanas.* If you wished to replace the subject with a pronoun, it would be impossible. The rule is that **a thing that is a subject cannot be replaced by a pronoun,** because subject pronouns always refer to people. If you wished to not repeat the noun, because, for example, you already mentioned it in the context preceding the sentence, you would simply omit it.

> **Me gustan.** *I like them.*

One last means of emphasizing this construction is to see what happens when the question is asked: "Who likes Mexican movies?" In English the answer is "<u>I</u> (do)." Observe what happens in Spanish:

> —¿**A quién le gustan las películas mexicanas?** *Who likes Mexican movies?*
>
> —**<u>A mí</u>.** *I do.*

You would **never** answer *yo* to this question, because the person is the indirect object, not the subject of the verb.

b) Verbs Similar to *Gustar*

There is a group of verbs that behave the same way *gustar* does.

caer bien/mal	*to like/to dislike*
encantar	*to "love"* (as on bumper stickers)
faltar	*to lack*
hacer falta	*to miss; to need*
quedar	*to have remaining, left*
sobrar	*to have in excess, left over*

Some of these verbs have other uses and meanings, for example, *caer* and *caerse* mean "to fall, fall down," and *faltar* can mean "to be absent." Also, the verb *quedarse* used reflexively means "to stay, remain." Thus, depending on the grammatical construction you give the sentence, its meaning can change dramatically.

Caer bien(mal) (to like/dislike [a person])

Mis amigos <u>me caen bien</u>.	*I like my friends.*
Creo que <u>les caigo bien</u> a tus padres.[3]	*I think your parents like me.*
El novio de mi hermana <u>me cae mal</u>.	*I do not like my sister's boyfriend.*
OR: El novio de mi hermana no <u>me cae bien</u>.	

---

3. The majority of these verbs is used exclusively in the third-person singular or plural, but those that may have a person as subject can be used in any person. The two most common verbs of this category are *caer bien* and *hacer falta.*
  I miss you. = **Me haces falta.** *She likes me.* = **Le caigo bien.**
  Given the meaning of *gustar* in certain dialects, it is best to avoid using it with human beings as the subject of the verb, or to make certain it is being used with its true meaning.

Gustar is used with things or with people perceived as professionals, such as professors, presidents, etc. When you use *gustar* with these, you mean that you respect their work, not necessarily that you like them personally.

<u>Me gusta</u> mi profesor de historia. Es excelente, y siempre viene preparado.
I like my history professor. He is excellent and he always comes prepared.

<u>Me cae bien</u> mi profesor de historia. Es muy simpático.
I like my history professor. He is very nice.

If you use the verb *gustar* with an individual whose relationship to you is other than professional, the implication is that you are attracted to that person.

Me gusta Silvia.   *I am attracted to Silvia.*

Caer bien/mal with food:

<u>Le cayó</u> muy <u>mal</u> la cena.   *Dinner disagreed with her.*

Encantar   (to love, as in "I love New York.")

Bumper-sticker "love" is different from sentimental love. Once you understand its meaning, you can use it, as bumper stickers do, with almost anything **except sentimental love.**

<u>Me encanta</u> Nueva York, me encantan los perros, los bebés, etc.
I (just) love NY, dogs, babies, etc.…   I ♥ NY…

Sentimental love is expressed with *querer.*

Te quiero. Te quiero mucho.   *I love you. I love you a lot.*
(Te amo is more passionate, more intense than *te quiero.)*

Quiero mucho a mis padres,   *I love my parents, my dog…*
a mi perro…

Faltar   (to lack)

A esta baraja le faltan dos cartas.
This deck of cards lacks (is missing) two cards.

Hacer falta   (to miss [a person], to need [a thing])

Me haces falta.   *I miss you.*
Te hace falta un abrigo.   *You need a coat.*

Quedar   (to have left)

Nos quedan cinco minutos.   *We have five minutes left.*

Sobrar   (to have left over, in excess)

Les sobró mucha comida.   *They had a lot of food left over.*

There are other verbs that are used in the same type of construction, but these behave essentially the way the English does, and are not used in exactly the opposite type of construction. These other verbs are:

bastarle a uno *to be sufficient*	**parecerle a uno** *to seem*
convenirle a uno *to be convenient*	**pasarle a uno** *to happen*
dolerle a uno[4] *to hurt*	**sentarle bien a uno** *to suit*
importarle a uno *to matter*	**sucederle a uno** *to happen*
interesarle a uno *to interest*	**tocarle a uno** *to be one's turn*

Examples:

Me <u>bastan</u> cinco minutos.	*Five minutes are sufficient for me.*
Esa hora no nos <u>conviene</u>.	*That time is not convenient for us.*
¿Te <u>duele</u> la pierna?	*Does your leg hurt?*
No nos <u>importa</u> si llueve.	*It does not matter to us if it rains.*
Me <u>interesaría</u> participar.	*It would interest me to participate.*
Eso me <u>parece</u> increíble.	*That seems incredible to me.*
Siempre me <u>pasan</u> cosas así.	*Things like that always happen to me.*
El azul te <u>sienta</u> bien.	*Blue suits you.*
¿Qué te <u>sucedió</u>?	*What happened to you?*
A mí me <u>toca</u> jugar.	*It is my turn to play.*

c) Articles

Remember to use the definite article in Spanish with *gustar, caer bien,* and *encantar* when their subject is general in nature. (See *Chapter 2, Section B.*)

Me gusta <u>el</u> chocolate semi-amargo.	*I like semisweet chocolate.*
Me caen bien <u>los</u> hijos de Juana.	*I like Juana's sons.*
Me encantan <u>las</u> playas.	*I love beaches.*

d) Position of Subject

With *faltar, sobrar,* and *quedar,* **always** place the subject **after** the verb.

Te falta <u>un ejercicio</u>.	*You are missing an exercise.*
Nos sobró <u>comida</u>.	*We had food left over.*

Some verbs can have other meanings if used in different grammatical constructions.

convenir en *(to agree to)*	<u>Convinimos</u> en encontrarnos en la plaza a las dos.
	We agreed to meet in the plaza at two o'clock.

---

4. The subject of *doler* can only be a body part: **Me duele la pierna.** *My leg hurts.* If you want to say "That shoe hurts," you need the verb *lastimar*: **Ese zapato me lastima.** The translation of "hurt" with animate objects is *hacer daño*: **¿Te hizo daño?** *Did he hurt you?*

importar + d.o. *(to import)*	**Los EE.UU. <u>importan</u> automóviles del Japón.** *The U.S. imports cars from Japan.*
interesarse por/en *(to be interested in)*	**Ella <u>se interesa</u> en la política.** *She is interested in politics.*
parecerse a *(to look like)*	**Tú <u>te pareces a</u> tu mamá.** *You look like your mother.*
pasar + d.o. *(to pass)*	**Pasa la sal, por favor.** *Pass the salt, please.*
sentar/sentarse *(to seat/to sit)*	**La mamá <u>sentó</u> al niño en la silla.** *The mother sat the child on the chair.* **<u>Te sentaste</u> en mi silla.** *You sat on my chair.*
tocar *(to touch* or *to play* [a musical instrument])	**Los turistas lo <u>tocaban</u> todo.** *The tourists touched everything.* **<u>Tocamos</u> la guitarra.** *We play the guitar.*

APPENDIX II
Práctica

10. Reflexive Verbs

Grammatically speaking, the reflexive construction implies that the subject of the verb receives the action of the verb as well. In other words, the subject and the object are the same.

Nonreflexive	<u>**Miro**</u> **el cielo.** subject= **yo**; object= **el cielo**	*I look at the sky.*
Reflexive	*Me* <u>**miro**</u> **en el espejo.** subject = object = **yo**	*I look at myself in the mirror.*

In many cases Spanish uses a reflexive when no evident reflexivity appears to exist in the English translation. This is why we perceive this lesson as a lexical rather than grammatical one, and offer a list which may serve as a memory aid.

Notice that in Spanish, the reflexive almost always indicates a change of state or the beginning of an action. Consider the differences between the following sentences:

Me <u>dormí</u> a las siete.	I <u>fell asleep</u> at seven.
<u>Dormí</u> siete horas.	I <u>slept</u> seven hours.
<u>Estaba dormido</u>.	I <u>was asleep</u>.
Me <u>estaba durmiendo</u> cuando llamaste.	I <u>was falling asleep</u> when you called.
Se <u>sentó</u> frente a nosotros.	He <u>sat down</u> in front of us.
<u>Está sentado</u> frente a nosotros.	He <u>is sitting</u> in front of us.
Me <u>enamoré</u> de él.	I <u>fell in love</u> with him.
<u>Estoy enamorada</u> de él.	I <u>am in love</u> with him.

Change of emotional state, or emotional reaction to something:

aburrirse *to get bored*	**divertirse** *to have fun*
alegrarse *to rejoice, be glad*	**enojarse** *to become or be angry*
asustarse *to become or be frightened*	**enorgullecerse** *to feel or be proud*
avergonzarse *to be ashamed, embarrassed*	**entristecerse** *to become or be sad*
calmarse *to calm down*	**preocuparse** *to worry*

Change of physical state:

acostarse *to lie down*	**moverse** *to move* (physically)
despertarse *to wake up*	**mudarse** *to move* (residences)
dormirse *to fall asleep*	**secarse** *to dry off, dry out*
levantarse *to get up*	**sentarse** *to sit down*
mojarse *to get wet*	**volverse** *to turn around*

Change of mental state or level of consciousness or memory:

acordarse *to remember*	**equivocarse** *to be mistaken*
darse cuenta *to realize*	**fijarse** *to notice*
enterarse *to find out*	**olvidarse** *to forget*

Verbs with more than one usage:

Some verbs may be used in the reflexive construction or not. The basic meaning of the verb may change depending on the construction used.

Los soldados <u>**marcharon**</u> **por una hora.**	*The soldiers marched for an hour.*
Los invitados *se* <u>**marcharon**</u>**.**	*The guests left.*

Other verbs of this type are:

bajar *to go down*	**bajarse** *to get down from, get off*
caer *to fall*	**caerse** *to fall down*
despedir *to fire (a person)*	**despedirse de** *to say good-bye to*
dormir *to sleep*	**dormirse** *to fall asleep*
ir *to go (somewhere)*	**irse** *to leave*

Reflexive pronouns are also used in situations where the subject is somehow affected by the action of the verb; with verbs of consumption, such as eating and drinking, the implication in the reflexive is one of enjoyment or thoroughness of the consumption.

<u>Comí</u> a las cuatro.	*I ate at four.*
¿*Te* <u>comiste</u> todo el desayuno?	*Did you eat all of your breakfast?*

Other verbs of this type:

aprender *to learn*	**aprenderse** *to learn (thoroughly, by heart)*
beber *to drink*	**beberse** *to drink (up, totally)*
saber *to know*	**saberse** *to know (thoroughly, by heart)*
tomar *to drink, eat, take*	**tomarse** *to drink, eat (up, totally)*

The verbs in the nonreflexive form are used with a more general meaning, while in the reflexive they are used with more specific information.

Aprender es fácil.	*It is easy to learn.*
Aprenderse el vocabulario es difícil.	*Learning vocabulary is difficult.*

Obligatory reflexives: These verbs exist exclusively in the reflexive form.

acordarse *to remember*	**jactarse** *to brag, boast*
arrepentirse *to regret, repent*	**quejarse** *to complain*
atreverse *to dare*	**rebelarse** *to rebel*
equivocarse *to make a mistake*	**suicidarse** *to commit suicide*

APPENDIX II
Práctica

On the following pages are lists of verbs that are frequently or always used in the reflexive construction.

REFLEXIVE VERBS (ENGLISH–SPANISH)			
English	**Spanish**	**English**	**Spanish**
address someone	**dirigirse <u>a</u> alguien**	*commit suicide*	**suicidarse**
approach something, get near something or someone	**acercarse <u>a</u> algo o alguien**	*complain about something*	**quejarse <u>de</u> algo**
be angry with someone	**enojarse <u>con</u> alguien**	*dare to do something*	**atreverse <u>a</u> hacer algo**
be ashamed of something	**avergonzarse <u>de</u> algo**	*die*	**morirse**
be called, named	**llamarse**	*dry off, dry out*	**secarse**
be frightened	**asustarse**	*face/confront something or someone*	**encararse <u>con</u>/ enfrentarse <u>a</u> algo o alguien**
be interested in something	**interesarse <u>por</u> algo**	*fall asleep*	**dormirse**
be mistaken, make a mistake	**equivocarse**	*fall behind, be late*	**atrasarse**
be proud	**enorgullecerse**	*fall down*	**caerse**
be quiet, shut up	**callarse**	*fall in love with someone*	**enamorarse <u>de</u> alguien**
become (by physical or metaphysical transformation)	**convertirse <u>en</u> algo**	*feel*	**sentirse**
become (describing mood)	**ponerse** (+ adj.)	*fight with someone*	**pelearse <u>con</u> alguien**
become (describing undesired state [blind, crazy...])	**volverse** (+ adj.)	*find out about something*	**enterarse <u>de</u> algo**
become (through one's efforts [a lawyer, doctor...])	**hacerse** (+ noun)	*forget something*	**olvidarse <u>de</u> algo**
become sad	**entristecerse**	*get ahead*	**adelantarse**
begin to do something	**ponerse <u>a</u> hacer algo**	*get along (not get along) with someone*	**llevarse bien (mal) <u>con</u> alguien**
brush (one's teeth, hair...)	**cepillarse**	*get bored*	**aburrirse**
calm down	**calmarse, tranquilizarse**	*get divorced*	**divorciarse**
comb (one's hair)	**peinarse (el pelo)**	*get down from something, get off (bus, train, tree...)*	**bajarse <u>de</u> algo**

REFLEXIVE VERBS (ENGLISH–SPANISH)

English	Spanish	English	Spanish
get lost	perderse	make an appointment/a date with someone	citarse con alguien
get married to someone	casarse con alguien	make an effort to do something	esforzarse por hacer algo
get onto something, get on (bus, train…)	subirse a algo	make fun of someone	burlarse de alguien
get rid of something	deshacerse de algo	make up one's mind to do something	decidirse a hacer algo
get sick, become ill	enfermarse	meet someone (not for the first time)	encontrarse con alguien
get up	levantarse	miss out on something	perderse algo
get used to something	acostumbrarse a algo	move away from something	alejarse de algo
get well	aliviarse, curarse	move (change residences)	mudarse
get wet	mojarse	move (one's body, objects)	moverse
get worse	empeorarse	notice something	fijarse en algo
graduate	graduarse	object to something	oponerse a algo
have fun	divertirse	prepare to do something	disponerse a hacer algo
improve	mejorarse	put on something (article of clothing)	ponerse algo
insist on doing something	empeñarse en hacer algo	realize something	darse cuenta de algo
interfere with someone	meterse con alguien	rebel	rebelarse
keep something	quedarse con algo	refer to something	referirse a algo
laugh at something or someone	reírse de algo o alguien	refuse to do something	negarse a hacer algo
leave	marcharse, irse	rejoice/be glad about something	alegrarse de algo
lie down, go to bed	acostarse	remember something	acordarse de algo
look like someone or something	parecerse a alguien o algo	repent (about) something	arrepentirse de algo

REFLEXIVE VERBS (ENGLISH–SPANISH)

English	Spanish	English	Spanish
resign oneself to	**resignarse <u>a</u> algo**	*stay*	**quedarse**
rub up against, scrub	**frotarse**	*take off/remove something*	**quitarse algo**
say good-bye to someone	**despedirse <u>de</u> alguien**	*take something away/with oneself*	**llevarse algo**
scratch oneself	**rascarse**	*trust someone*	**fiarse <u>de</u> alguien**
sit down	**sentarse**	*wake up*	**despertarse**
specialize/major in something	**especializarse <u>en</u> algo**	*worry about something*	**preocuparse <u>por</u> algo**

REFLEXIVE VERBS (SPANISH–ENGLISH)

Spanish	English	Spanish	English
aburrirse	*get bored*	**atreverse a hacer algo**	*dare to do something*
acercarse a algo o alguien	*approach something, get near something or someone*	**avergonzarse de algo**	*be ashamed of something*
acordarse de algo	*remember something*	**bajarse de algo**	*get down from something, get off (bus, train, tree…)*
acostarse	*lie down, go to bed*	**burlarse de alguien**	*make fun of someone*
acostumbrarse a algo	*get used to something*	**caerse**	*fall down*
adelantarse	*get ahead*	**callarse**	*be quiet, shut up*
alegrarse de algo	*rejoice/be glad about something*	**calmarse**	*calm down*
alejarse de algo	*move away from something*	**casarse con alguien**	*get married to someone*
aliviarse	*get well*	**cepillarse**	*brush (one's teeth, hair…)*
arrepentirse de algo	*repent (about) something*	**citarse con alguien**	*make an appointment/a date with someone*
asustarse	*be frightened*	**convertirse en algo**	*become (by physical or metaphysical transformation)*
atrasarse	*fall behind, be late*	**curarse**	*get well*

REFLEXIVE VERBS (SPANISH–ENGLISH)

Spanish	English	Spanish	English
darse cuenta de algo	realize something	enterarse de algo	find out about something
decidirse a hacer algo	make up one's mind to do something	entristecerse	become sad
deshacerse de algo	get rid of something	equivocarse	be mistaken, make a mistake
despedirse de alguien	say good-bye to someone	esforzarse por hacer algo	make an effort to do something
despertarse	wake up	especializarse en algo	specialize/major in something
dirigirse a alguien	address someone	fiarse de alguien	trust someone
disponerse a hacer algo	prepare to do something	fijarse en algo	notice something
divertirse	have fun	frotarse	rub up against, scrub
divorciarse	to get divorced	graduarse	graduate
dormirse	fall asleep	hacerse (+ noun)	become (through one's efforts [a lawyer, doctor...])
empeñarse en hacer algo	insist on doing something	interesarse por algo	be interested in something
empeorarse	get worse	irse	leave
enamorarse de alguien	fall in love with someone	lavarse	wash or bathe oneself (or a part of oneself)
encararse con algo o alguien	face/confront something or someone	levantarse	get up
encontrarse con alguien	meet someone (not for the first time)	llamarse	be called, named
enfermarse	get sick, become ill	llevarse algo	take something away/with oneself
enfrentarse a algo o alguien	face/confront something or someone	llevarse bien (mal) con alguien	get along well (not get along) with someone
enojarse con alguien	be angry with someone	marcharse	leave
enorgullecerse	be proud	mejorarse	improve

REFLEXIVE VERBS (SPANISH–ENGLISH)			
Spanish	**English**	**Spanish**	**English**
meterse con alguien	interfere with someone	**quedarse**	stay
mojarse	get wet	**quedarse con algo**	keep something
morirse	die	**quejarse de algo**	complain about something
moverse	move (one's body, objects)	**quitarse algo**	take off/remove something
mudarse	move (change residences)	**rascarse**	scratch oneself
negarse a hacer algo	refuse to do something	**rebelarse**	rebel
olvidarse de algo	forget something	**referirse a algo**	refer to something
oponerse a algo	object to something	**reírse de algo o alguien**	laugh at something or someone
parecerse a alguien o algo	look like someone or something	**resignarse a algo**	resign oneself to
peinarse (el pelo)	comb (one's hair)	**secarse**	dry off, dry out
pelearse con alguien	fight with someone	**sentarse**	sit down
perderse	get lost	**sentirse**	feel
perderse algo	miss out on something	**subirse a algo**	get onto something, get on (bus, train…)
ponerse (+ adj.)	become (describing mood)	**suicidarse**	commit suicide
ponerse a hacer algo	begin to do something	**tranquilizarse**	calm down
ponerse algo	put on something (article of clothing)	**volverse** (+ adj.)	become (describing undesired state [blind, crazy…])
preocuparse por algo	worry about something		

REFLEXIVE VERBS WITH CHARACTERISTIC PROPOSITIONS				
a	**con**	**de**	**en**	**por**
acercarse a	casarse con	acordarse de	convertirse en	esforzarse por
acostumbrarse a	citarse con	alegrarse de	empeñarse en	interesarse por
atreverse a	encararse con	alejarse de	especializarse en	preocuparse por
decidirse a	encontrarse con	arrepentirse de	fijarse en	
dirigirse a	enojarse con	asustarse de		
disponerse a	llevarse bien con	avergonzarse de		
enfrentarse a	meterse con	bajarse de		
negarse a	pelearse con	burlarse de		
oponerse a	quedarse con	darse cuenta de		
parecerse a		deshacerse de		
ponerse a		despedirse de		
referirse a		enamorarse de		
		enterarse de		
		fiarse de		
		olvidarse de		
		quejarse de		
		reírse de		

APPENDIX II

Práctica

11. Indirect Discourse

a) Introduction

Indirect discourse is the relating of oral statements without quoting them directly:

DIRECT DISCOURSE	INDIRECT DISCOURSE	
	Present	**Past**
"Te llamaré mañana". *"I will call you tomorrow."*	**Dice que me llamará mañana.** *He says that he will call me tomorrow.*	**Dijo que me llamaría al día siguiente.** *He said that he would call me the following day.*

Notice the three possible types of changes in indirect discourse:

Verb [will → would]

Person [I → He; you → me]

Time reference [tomorrow → the following day]

As logic indicates, these changes do not always occur, or only some of them might occur. For example, if I am quoting what I just said today about today, there will be no change ("It is cold today." → I am saying it is cold today.). However, when there is a change of person or of time reference between the direct quote and the indirect quote, there will be changes, as in English. If the communication verb is in the past, there is a change in most tenses.

b) Verb-Tense Changes

Present Indicative → Imperfect Indicative
  Lo <u>hago</u>.   Dijo que lo <u>hacía</u>.
  I do it.   *He said he did it.*

Present Subjunctive → Imperfect Subjunctive
  Quiere que <u>vaya</u>.   Dijo que quería que <u>fuera</u>.
  He wants me to go.   *He said he wanted me to go.*

Present Perfect Indicative → Pluperfect Indicative
  Nos <u>han visto</u>.   Dijeron que nos <u>habían visto</u>.
  They have seen us.   *They said they had seen us.*

Present Perfect Subjunctive → Pluperfect Subjunctive
  Dudo que lo <u>hayan visto</u>.   Dijo que dudaba que lo <u>hubieran visto</u>.
  I doubt that they saw it.   *He said that he doubted they had seen it.*

Preterite → Pluperfect Indicative
  Lo <u>vi</u>.   Dijo que lo <u>había visto</u>.
  I saw it.   *He said he had seen it.*

Future → Present Conditional
  <u>Iré</u> mañana.   Dijo que <u>iría</u> al día siguiente.
  I will go tomorrow.   *He said he would go the next day.*

Future Perfect → Perfect Conditional
  Para el lunes <u>habré acabado</u>.   Dijo que para el lunes <u>habría acabado</u>.
  By Monday I will have finished.   *He said that by Monday he would have finished.*

Imperative → Imperfect Subjunctive
  <u>Cómete</u> la fruta.   Me dijo que me <u>comiera</u> la fruta.
  Eat your fruit.   *She told me to eat my fruit.*

c) No Verb-Tense Changes

The following verb tenses never change in indirect discourse, even if the communication verb is in the past (notice, however, changes in **pronouns**):

Imperfect indicative or subjunctive

Pluperfect indicative or subjunctive

Conditional present or perfect

Íbamos a comer.   →   **Dijeron que <u>iban</u> a comer.**
We were going to eat.   *They said they were going to eat.*

Ya <u>habíamos comido</u>.   →   **Contesté que ya <u>habíamos comido</u>.**
We had already eaten.   *I answered that we had already eaten.*

<u>Dudo</u> que me <u>estuvieras</u>   →   **Me dijo que <u>dudaba</u> que le <u>estuviera</u>**
mintiendo.   **mintiendo.**
I doubt that you were lying   *He told me that he doubted that I was*
to me.   *lying to him.*

Si <u>fuera</u> rico, me lo   →   **Pensó que si <u>fuera</u> rico, se lo**
<u>compraría</u>.   **<u>compraría</u>.**
If I were rich, I would buy it.   *He thought that if he were rich, he*
                                           would buy it.

Verb changes in a nutshell (when communication verb is in the past):

Present*	→	Imperfect
Preterite	→	Pluperfect
Future°	→	Conditional
Imperative	→	Imperfect Subjunctive

* Present indicative becomes imperfect indicative, present subjunctive becomes imperfect subjunctive, present perfect indicative becomes pluperfect indicative (i.e., present of auxiliary becomes imperfect of auxiliary), present perfect subjunctive becomes pluperfect subjunctive (i.e., present of auxiliary becomes imperfect of auxiliary).

° Future becomes conditional present, future perfect becomes conditional perfect (i.e., future of auxiliary becomes conditional of auxiliary).

d) Person Changes

Logic rules here, just as it does in English. Any reference to an individual that is altered by a change of a point of view will affect all references to the individual. Read the following transformations carefully.

Direct discourse:

Vamos a visitar a <u>nuestros</u> padres. <u>We</u> are going to visit <u>our</u> parents.

Indirect discourse:

Dijeron que iban a visitar a <u>sus</u> padres. They said <u>they</u> were going to visit <u>their</u> parents.

Direct discourse:

<u>Te</u> di <u>tu</u> libro. I gave <u>you</u> <u>your</u> book.

Indirect discourse:

Ella le dijo que <u>le</u> había dado <u>su</u> libro. She told him <u>she</u> had given <u>him</u> <u>his</u> book.

Direct discourse:

No voy con<u>tigo</u>. I am not going with <u>you</u>.

Indirect discourse:

Ella me dijo que no iba con<u>migo</u>. She told me <u>she</u> was not going with <u>me</u>.

e) Time Changes

In indirect discourse in the past, time expressions will change unless the relation of the statement occurs within the same day. (If I say something today about tomorrow, and you repeat my words before the day is up, there is no change; the same logic applies here as in English.) If the relation of the direct statement is done on a day other than the one on which the statement was made, *yesterday* becomes *the day before* and *tomorrow* becomes *the next day*. In Spanish, some common changes are:

ahora	→	entonces
<u>Ahora</u> sí puedo.		Dijo que <u>entonces</u> sí podía.
Now I can.		*He said that he could then.*

ayer	→	el día anterior
Lo hice <u>ayer</u>.		Confesó que lo había hecho <u>el día anterior</u>.
I did it yesterday.		*He confessed that he had done it the day before.*

anoche	→	la noche anterior
La vi <u>anoche</u>.		Dijo que la había visto <u>la noche anterior</u>.
I saw it last night.		*He said that he had seen it the night before.*
(**La** = **la película**)		

mañana	→	al día siguiente
Iré <u>mañana</u>.		Anunció que iría <u>al día siguiente</u>.
I will go tomorrow.		*He announced that he would go the following day.*

la semana pasada	→	la semana anterior
La vi <u>la semana pasada</u>.		Admitió que la había visto <u>la semana anterior</u>.
I saw her last week.		*He admitted that he had seen her the week before.*

la semana entrante	→	la próxima semana
Te llamaré <u>la semana entrante</u>.		Me prometió que me llamaría <u>la próxima semana</u>.
I will call you next week.		*He promised me he would call me the following week.*

f) Other Changes

(1) Connectives

When the quotations are for questions requiring a yes/no type **answer**, connect them with *si* ("whether, if"). When the quotations are for "yes" and "no" **responses**, use *que* before *sí* or *no*.

Example:

DIRECT DISCOURSE	INDIRECT DISCOURSE
"**¿Quieres ir al cine conmigo?**" "**No.**" *"Do you want to go to the movies with me?"* *"No."*	**Me preguntó si quería ir al cine con él.** **Yo le contesté que no.** *He asked me if I wanted to go to the movies with him.* *I said "no."*

(2) This, That, and the Other

When the speaker changes locations from the moment of direct speech to the moment of reported speech, other things change referentially as well.

"¿Quieres <u>esto</u>?"	→	Me preguntó si quería <u>eso</u>.
"Do you want <u>this</u>?"	→	*He asked me if I wanted <u>that</u>.*

(3) Verbs of Communication

♦ For questions: *preguntar*

♦ For statements: *exclamar, agregar, contestar, responder, insistir, confesar, admitir,* etc.

♦ For requests or commands: *rogar, pedir, suplicar, decir, insistir,* etc.

Chapter 7

Ser, Estar, Haber, Hacer, and Tener

A.   SER VS. ESTAR

I. Overview

The verb "to be" in English can be translated into Spanish in different ways, depending on the context.

Examples of *ser, tener,* and *haber* ("there is/are") with nouns and pronouns:

Ángela <u>es</u> mi amiga.	*Angela is my friend.*
Éste <u>es</u> Javier.	*This is Javier.*
Carmen <u>es</u> profesora.	*Carmen is a professor.*
<u>Es</u> católica.	*She is a Catholic.*
<u>Es</u> soltero.	*He is a bachelor.*
Ese libro <u>es</u> mío.	*That book is mine.*
<u>Fue</u> Gema la que lo hizo.	*It was Gema who did it.*
<u>Tengo</u> veinte años.	*I am twenty years old.*
La niña <u>tiene</u> sed, calor, hambre, etc.	*The little girl is thirsty, hot, hungry, etc.*
<u>Hay</u> un lápiz en la mesa.	*There is a pencil on the table.*
<u>Hay</u> dos sillas en el corredor.	*There are two chairs in the hallway.*

Examples of *hacer* + noun and *estar* + adjective or present participle in descriptions of the weather:

<u>Hace</u> calor hoy.	*It is hot today.*
<u>Hace</u> frío hoy.	*It is cold today.*
<u>Hace</u> viento.	*It is windy.*
<u>Hace</u> buen tiempo.	*The weather is good. (We are having good weather.)*
<u>Hace</u> mal tiempo.	*The weather is bad. (We are having bad weather.)*
<u>Está</u> nublado.	*It is cloudy.*
<u>Está</u> lloviendo, nevando.	*It is raining, snowing.*

Examples of *ser* (characteristic) and *estar* (subject to change) with adjectives:

Jorge <u>es</u> peruano.	*Jorge is Peruvian.*
<u>Es</u> alto, delgado.	*He is tall, slender.*
Rosa <u>está</u> emocionada.	*Rosa is excited.*
Berta <u>está</u> triste.	*Berta is sad.*

Examples of *ser* and *estar* with prepositions:

<u>Soy</u> de Guatemala.	*I am from Guatemala.*
<u>Estoy</u> de pie, de rodillas, de luto, etc.	*I am standing, kneeling, in mourning, etc.*
<u>Estoy</u> por salir.	*I am about to go out.*

Example of *estar* with present participle:

Están *leyendo, cantando.*   *They are reading, singing.*

Example of *ser, estar,* and *haber* with past participles:

Passive—*ser*

Esa novela <u>fue</u> **escrita por Cervantes.**   *That novel was written by Cervantes.*

Resultant condition—*estar* (past participle = adjective):

La novela <u>está</u> *escrita.*   *The novel is written.*

Perfect Tenses—*haber* (to have as an auxiliary verb):

<u>He</u> *escrito,* <u>había</u> *escrito...*   *I have written, I had written…*

2. Different Translations

The study of the different translations of "to be" is broken down into categories of verbs and expressions: *Ser* vs. *estar*; idiomatic expressions with *estar* and *tener*; passive voice with *ser* vs. resultant condition with *estar*; *hacer* with time expressions, etc.

SER	ESTAR
Functions as an equal sign (=) to equate or identify two parts of speech: **Susana** <u>es</u> **doctora.** **Dos y dos** <u>son</u> **cuatro.**	
Telling time: **¿Qué hora** <u>es</u>**?** <u>Son</u> **las tres.**	
Impersonal expressions: <u>Es</u> **importante que lo leas.**	With *bien, claro*: **Está** *bien* **que lo hagan.** **No** <u>está</u> *claro* **lo que quiere.**
DE	
Origin (*¿de dónde?*): **Ana** <u>es</u> **de Madrid.** Material (*¿de qué?*): **La mesa** <u>es</u> **de madera.** Possession (*¿de quién?*): **Ese auto** <u>es</u> **de Pepe.**	Used with expressions of adverbial force which answer the question *¿cómo?*: **Está** *de* **rodillas. Estamos** *de* **vacaciones.** **Los muchachos** <u>están</u> *de* **acuerdo.** Signifying "acting as": <u>Están</u> **de directoras.**
LOCATION	
Events located in space and time: **La fiesta** <u>es</u> **a las ocho.** **El examen** <u>es</u> **en el salón.** *(event)*	Entities in space and time: **Juan** <u>está</u> **en casa.** **El examen** <u>está</u> **en la mesa.** *(the exam papers)*

(This chart is continued on the next page.)

SER	ESTAR
PARA	
Destination in time or place: **Esto <u>es</u> *para* mañana.** **Este regalo <u>es</u> *para* mi hermano.**	Used with the infinitive to signify immediacy in Spain ("to be about to do something") **<u>Estamos</u> *para* salir.**
PREDICATE ADJECTIVES	
Used to indicate the norm, the basic characteristic not subject to change: **Los elefantes <u>son</u> grandes.** **El café de aquí <u>es</u> rico.** First appearance—when the speaker sees something for the first time, and there is no evidence of change: **José <u>es</u> delgado.**	Used for the variation of the norm; describes a state or condition of the subject at a given time (state that may change): **Mi vaso <u>está</u> vacío.** **La casa <u>está</u> sucia.** Reactions (tastes, looks, etc.): **El café <u>está</u> malo hoy.** **José <u>está</u> gordo.** Always used with *enfermo, contento, harto, bien*: **Rosita <u>está</u> enferma.** **<u>Estoy</u> contento.**
ADJECTIVES THAT CHANGE MEANINGS	
Juana <u>es</u> lista. *(clever, smart)* **La clase <u>es</u> aburrida.** *(boring)* **El chico <u>es</u> callado.** *(quiet by nature)*	**Juana <u>está</u> lista.** *(ready)* **Roberto <u>está</u> aburrido.** *(bored)* **El chico <u>está</u> callado.** *(silent, now)*
PAST PARTICIPLE	
Passive voice: **La ventana <u>fue</u> abierta por el conserje.** *(was opened by)*	Resultant condition of an action: **La ventana <u>estaba</u> abierta.** *(was open)*
PRESENT PARTICIPLE	
(Never used with *ser*.)	Used to form the progressive: **<u>Estamos</u> *caminando*.**

APPENDIX II
Práctica

B. PASSIVE VOICE AND RESULTANT CONDITION

The passive voice in Spanish is formed essentially in the same way as in English.

ACTIVE VS. PASSIVE VOICE				
Active	**La tormenta**	**destruyó**		**la casa.**
	subject	verb		direct object
	The storm	*destroyed*		*the house.*
Passive	**La casa**	**fue destruida**	**por**	**la tormenta.**
	subject	verb		agent
	The house	*was destroyed*	*by*	*the storm.*

To change from active to passive voice:

♦ The subject of the active sentence becomes the agent (preceded by *por*) of the passive.

♦ The direct object of the active sentence becomes the subject of the passive sentence.

♦ The verb of the active sentence undergoes the following transformation:

The verb itself becomes a past participle (variable in gender and number with its new subject) and is preceded by the verb *ser* in the same tense and mood of the verb of the original active sentence.

Examples:

ACTIVE PASSIVE

Isabel Allende escribió esa novela. → **Esa novela fue escrita por Isabel Allende.**
Isabel Allende wrote that novel. *That novel was written by Isabel Allende.*

Heinle & Heinle publicará el libro. → **El libro será publicado por Heinle & Heinle.**

Heinle & Heinle will publish the book. *The book will be published by Heinle & Heinle.*

Ella había corregido las tareas. → **Las tareas habían sido corregidas por ella.**
She had corrected the homework. *The homework had been corrected by her.*

The passive voice, very common in English, is rarely used in Spanish. In most cases, an agent is required for the passive voice to be justified in Spanish, and even there, it is preferable to use the active voice. If there is no agent, the impersonal *se* is used instead.

Se habían vendido todos los coches cuando llegué. *All the cars had been sold when I arrived.*

Resultant condition: When what is being focused upon is not the action or who did it, but the result of the action, the verb *estar* is used with the past participle functioning as an adjective.

Passive voice:

Las ventanas fueron abiertas a las ocho.	*The windows were opened at eight.* (Somebody opened them.)

Resultant condition:

Las ventanas están abiertas.	*The windows are open.* (It does not matter who did it.)

APPENDIX II

Práctica

C. EXPRESSIONS WITH *ESTAR* AND *TENER*

1. Expressions with *Estar*

EXPRESSIONS WITH *ESTAR*			
estar a favor de	*to be for, in favor of*	**estar de regreso**	*to be back*
estar ausente[1]	*to be absent*	**estar de rodillas**	*to be kneeling*
estar contento[2]	*to be glad, pleased, happy*	**estar de vacaciones**	*to be on vacation*
estar de acuerdo con	*to agree with*	**estar de viaje**	*to be travelling*
estar de buen (mal) humor	*to be in a good (bad) mood*	**estar de visita**	*to be visiting*
estar de huelga	*to be on strike*	**estar de vuelta**	*to be back*
estar de luto	*to be in mourning*	**estar en contra de**	*to be against*
estar de pie[3]	*to be standing*		

---

1. This expression may only be used with *estar*; "to be late" = *llegar tarde*; "to be on time" = *llegar a tiempo*.
2. This expression may only be used with *estar*.
3. The expression used for "to be sitting" is *estar sentado*, whereas *sentarse* means "to sit down" (the process of changing from the standing to the sitting position).

2. Expressions with *Tener*

Notice that *tener frío* and *tener calor* are used exclusively for people or animals. If you wish to say that an **object** is hot or cold, use *ser* or *estar*.

EXPRESSIONS WITH *TENER*			
tener _____ años	*to be _____ years old*	**tener la culpa**	*to be guilty*
tener calor	*to be hot*	**tener lugar**	*to take place*
tener cuidado	*to be careful*	**tener miedo**	*to be afraid*
tener en cuenta que	*to bear in mind that*	**tener prisa**	*to be in a hurry[4]*
tener éxito	*to be successful, succeed*	**tener razón**	*to be right[5]*
tener frío	*to be cold*	**tener sed**	*to be thirsty*
tener ganas de	*to feel like, desire*	**tener sueño**	*to be sleepy[6]*
tener hambre	*to be hungry*	**tener vergüenza**	*to be ashamed*

APPENDIX II

Práctica

D. TIME EXPRESSIONS

1. Introduction

a) Counting Forward

In Spanish, as in English, time can be perceived in various ways: we can narrate a story from beginning to end, with a series of preterites and imperfects.

Me levanté, me bañé y desayuné. Mientras desayunaba, sonó el teléfono.

I got up, I bathed, and I had breakfast. While I was eating breakfast, the phone rang.

We can state the duration of an action in a variety of ways:

Estudié por cuatro horas. Viví en España por seis meses.

I studied for four hours. I lived in Spain for six months.

---

4. "to hurry up" = *apurarse*
5. "to be wrong" = *estar equivocado*
6. "to have a dream" = *tener un sueño*

b) Counting Backward

However, if we want to say how long something has lasted counting back, as we do in English with "I have been studying for four hours" (counting back from the present) or "I had been studying for four hours when you called" (counting back from a moment in the past—when you called), in Spanish we most frequently use expressions with *hacer que* and *llevar*.

2. Duration

a) Counting Back from the Present

EXPRESSION (INVARIABLE)	AMOUNT OF TIME	EXPRESSION	ACTION VERB FORM (VARIABLE)
Hace (invariable)		**que**	Present tense (**yo, tú,** etc....)

EXPRESSION (VARIABLE)	AMOUNT OF TIME	ACTION VERB FORM (INVARIABLE)
Llevo (Llevas, Lleva, etc....)		1. Affirmative: present participle
		2. **Estar:** Ø (no verb)
		3. Negative: **sin** + infinitive

Affirmative: The sentence "I have been studying for three hours" (implication: and continue to do so) could be translated as:

<u>**Hace**</u> **tres horas** <u>**que estudio**</u>.

OR:

<u>**Llevo**</u> **tres horas** <u>**estudiando**</u>.

Notice where the person is expressed in these two sentences: with *hace…que* the person doing the action is perceived in the second verb (*estudio* [*yo*]), whereas with *llevar* the person is seen in the verb *llevar* itself (*Llevo* [*yo*]) and not in the action verb *estudiando*.

With *estar*: If the main "action" verb is *estar,* the expression with *llevar* would **not** state the verb:

<u>**Hace**</u> **tres horas** <u>**que estamos**</u> **aquí.**

OR:

<u>**Llevamos**</u> **tres horas aquí.**

Never use *estando* in sentences like *Llevamos tres horas aquí.*

Negative: the sentence "We have not slept for two nights" (i.e., the last two nights) could be translated as:

<u>Hace</u> dos noches <u>que no dormimos</u>.

OR:

<u>Llevamos</u> dos noches <u>sin dormir</u>.

In the negative, the sentence with *llevar* does not take the present participle for its second verb, but the **infinitive** preceded by *sin*.

b) Counting Back from a Moment in the Past

EXPRESSION (INVARIABLE)	AMOUNT OF TIME	EXPRESSION	ACTION VERB FORM (VARIABLE)
Hacía (invariable)		**que**	Imperfect tense (**yo, tú,** etc....)

EXPRESSION (VARIABLE)	AMOUNT OF TIME	ACTION VERB FORM (INVARIABLE)
Llevaba (Llevabas, etc....**)**		1. Affirmative: present participle
		2. **Estar:** Ø (no verb)
		3. Negative: **sin** + infinitive

Affirmative: the sentence "I had been studying for three hours" (implication: when something interrupted my work), would be translated as:

<u>Hacía</u> tres horas <u>que estudiaba</u>.

OR:

<u>Llevaba</u> tres horas <u>estudiando</u>.

Here, *hacer* and *llevar* are in the **imperfect,** as is the main verb of the first sentence. In the second sentence, the main verb is still in the **present participle.**

With *estar*: apply the same rule as for *estar* counting back from the present. (See page 204.)

<u>Hacía</u> tres horas <u>que estábamos</u> allá.

OR:

<u>Llevábamos</u> tres horas allá.

Negative: the sentence "We had not gone to the movies for a long time" would translate as follows:

> <u>Hacía</u> mucho tiempo <u>que no íbamos</u> al cine.

> OR:

> <u>Llevábamos</u> mucho tiempo <u>sin ir</u> al cine.

As you see, the same rules apply for the negative in the past as did in the present. The only difference is that the verbs must be kept in the imperfect (all but the infinitive, of course).

3. Ago

Another type of sentence that counts time in reverse relates to finished actions in the past, as opposed to actions that have been going on and continue to go on (duration). In English, this reverse counting uses the expression "ago," as in the example "I did that two hours ago." (as opposed to "I did it at three o'clock."). To translate sentences with "ago," you cannot use *llevar*, only *hace* [present]… *que* + preterite.

> **Hace** tres años <u>que</u> se fue.   *He left three years ago.*

> (OR: Se fue **hace** tres años.)

This same situation shifted into a past context would use the following structure:

> <u>Hacía</u> tres años <u>que</u> se había ido.   *He had left three years before.*

We can also refer to things which "were happening" some time ago. For these actions, Spanish uses the imperfect of the main verb, usually with the progressive form for verbs of action, and nonprogressive for verbs of state.

> **¿Qué estabas haciendo <u>hace</u> dos horas?**

> *What were you doing two hours <u>ago</u>?*

> **Me estaba bañando <u>hace</u> dos horas. (OR: Hace dos horas, me estaba bañando.)**[7]

> *I was bathing two hours <u>ago</u>.*

> **¿Dónde estaba usted <u>hace</u> treinta minutos?**

> Where were you thirty minutes <u>ago</u>?

APPENDIX II

Práctica

---

7. Notice the absence of *que* from the expression.

APPENDIX I

Lexical Variations

A.   TO APPLY = APLICAR/SOLICITAR

aplicar = to apply (e.g., an ointment)

Instrucciones: <u>aplicar</u> la crema a la herida cuatro veces al día.

Instructions: apply the cream to injury four times a day.

solicitar = to apply (for a job)

<u>Solicité</u> el puesto de subgerente.

I applied for the job of assistant manager.

B.   TO ASK = PEDIR/PREGUNTAR/HACER PREGUNTAS

pedir algo (without a preposition) = to ask for something

Me <u>pidieron</u> dinero.

They asked me for money.

pedir que = to ask to

Le <u>pedí</u> que me despertara.

I asked him to wake me up.

preguntar: "¿…?" = to ask: "…?"

Me <u>preguntó</u>, "¿Qué hora es?"

He asked me, "What time is it?"

preguntar si…, qué…, cuándo…, (etc.) = to ask if…, what…, when…, etc.

Le <u>preguntaré</u> si tiene un mapa.

I will ask him if he has a map.

Nos <u>preguntaron</u> qué queríamos.

They asked us what we wanted.

hacer una pregunta = to ask a question

¿Me permite <u>hacerle una pregunta</u>?

May I ask you a question?

C.   TO ATTEND = ASISTIR A/ATENDER*

asistir a = to attend (a class, formal meeting, conference, etc.)

<u>Asistimos</u> a una reunión esta tarde.   *We attended a meeting this afternoon.*

Hoy no <u>asistí</u> a clase.   *Today I did not attend class.*

atender = to assist, serve (a person), pay attention, tend to

¿En qué puedo <u>atenderlo</u>?   *How may I assist you?*

Me <u>atendieron</u> de inmediato.   *They served me immediately.*

<u>Atiéndanme</u>, por favor.   *Pay attention, please.*

<u>Atiende</u> a tus amistades, Gregorio.   *Tend to your friends, Gregorio.*

D.   TO BECOME OR TO GET

alegrarse = to become happy, be glad

<u>Me alegro</u> que puedas venir.   *I am glad you can come.*

callarse = to become quiet, keep silent, shut up

¡<u>Cállate</u>!   *Be quiet!*

calmarse = to become calm, calm down

Al ver a su madre, <u>se calmó</u>.   *When he saw his mother, he calmed down.*

cansarse = to get tired

<u>Me cansé</u> de trabajar.   *I got tired of working.*

empobrecerse = to become poor

<u>Se fueron empobreciendo</u> poco a poco.   *They became poor little by little.*

enfermarse = to get sick

<u>Te</u> vas a <u>enfermar</u> si sales así.   *You are going to get sick if you go out like that.*

enfurecerse = to become furious

Su padre <u>se enfureció</u> al oír las noticias.   *Her father became furious when he heard the news.*

*See also *Section K* on pp. 214–215.

enloquecerse = to go mad, become crazy

 Al perderla, <u>se enloqueció</u>. *When he lost her, he went crazy.*

enojarse = to get angry

 No <u>te enojes</u> conmigo. *Do not get angry with me.*

enriquecerse = to become rich

 Pensaban <u>enriquecerse</u> con eso. *They thought they could get rich with that.*

entristecerse = to become sad

 Me fijé que <u>se entristecieron</u> sus hijos más que él. *I noticed his children became sadder than he did.*

envejecerse = to become old

 Con este producto, nadie <u>se envejece</u>. *With this product, nobody gets old.*

mejorarse = to get better, improve

 ¡Que <u>te mejores</u> pronto! *I hope you get better soon.*

tranquilizarse = to become calm, calm down

 Con esa música, <u>se tranquilizaron</u>. *With that music, they calmed down.*

ponerse (+ **serio**, **pálido**, **triste**, and other <u>adjectives</u> of involuntary and passing psychological or physical states) = to become (serious, pale, sad…)

 <u>Se puso</u> *triste* al oír las noticias. *He became sad upon hearing the news.*

hacerse (+ **abogado**, **médico**, and other <u>nouns</u> of profession) = to become (a lawyer, doctor…)

 Mi hermana <u>se hizo</u> *abogada*. *My sister became a lawyer.*

llegar a ser (+ <u>nouns or adjectives</u> expressing importance or high personal status) = to become (rich, famous...)

 <u>Llegó a ser</u> *famoso*. *He became famous.*

convertirse en = to become or turn into (by physical transformation)

 El vino <u>se convirtió</u> en vinagre. *The wine became (turned into) vinegar.*

E.   TO GO AND TO LEAVE = IR/IRSE/SALIR/ MARCHARSE/DEJAR

ir = to go (<u>towards</u> a specific destination)

Ayer <u>fuimos</u> al museo.	*Yesterday we went to the museum.*

irse = **marcharse** = to leave (direction <u>away from</u> some understood location)

El señor Cárdenas ya <u>se fue</u>.	*Mr. Cárdenas already left.*
El gerente <u>se va</u> a las cinco.	*The manager leaves at five.*
No está; <u>se marchó</u>.	*He is not in; he left.*

salir = to go out

Los niños <u>salieron</u> a jugar.	*The children went out to play.*
Los huéspedes <u>salieron</u> a la playa.	*The guests went out to the beach.*
<u>Saldremos</u> esta noche a las siete.	*We will go out tonight at seven.*

SALIR vs. IRSE = to leave

Salir is used as a synonym for *irse* when the person leaving is also leaving an enclosed area, such as a building. *Irse* is more permanent than *salir,* for example, when a person is at home or in the office and leaves expecting to return, *salir* is used more frequently. At the end of the day, when a person leaves the office until the next day, *irse* would be more common.

In the following sentences *salir* would be preferable.

Elena <u>salió</u> de casa hace una hora.	*Elena left home an hour ago.*
La secretaria <u>salió</u> a almorzar.	*The secretary went out to lunch.*

In sentences like the following you could only use *irse.*

Estábamos en la playa platicando cuando de repente Luis se levantó y <u>se fue</u>.	*We were on the beach chatting when suddenly Luis got up and left.*
Lo siento, pero el gerente ya <u>se fue</u>.	*I am sorry, but the manager has already left.*

Salir is commonly used with travel and with means of transportation. The logic here is that the enclosure from which the traveler departs is his or her country, and for trains, buses, planes and ships, the enclosure is the station, airport or port.

<u>Saldremos</u> para España la semana entrante.	*We will leave for Spain next week.*
El tren <u>sale</u> a las nueve.	*The train leaves at nine.*
Su vuelo <u>sale</u> de Madrid esta tarde.	*Your flight leaves Madrid this afternoon.*

NOTE: The parallel term *salida* is used to indicate the **departure** of a person, flight, etc.

    La <u>salida</u> del vuelo es a las cinco.   *The flight leaves at five.*

dejar [transitive] = to leave something or someone

    <u>Dejé</u> las maletas en el taxi.   *I left the suitcases in the taxi cab.*

    Su hermano la <u>dejó</u> en el aeropuerto.   *Her brother left her at the airport.*

dejar (+ inf.) = to let

    No me <u>dejó</u> *pagar* nada.   *She did not let me pay for anything.*

dejar de (+ inf.) = to stop

    De repente <u>dejaron de</u> *hablar*.   *Suddenly, they stopped talking.*

F.   TO KNOW = SABER/CONOCER

conocer a alguien = to know someone or to meet someone for the first time (make someone's acquaintance) [preterite]

    <u>Conozco</u> a Luis.   *I know Luis.*

    Ayer <u>conocí</u> a Luis.   *Yesterday I met Luis. (See Section H on "to meet.")*

conocer algo = to be familiar with something

    No <u>conozco</u> la ciudad.   *I do not know the city.*

saber algo = to know something

    <u>Saben</u> nuestra dirección.   *They know our address.*

saber hacer algo = to know how to do something

    Ella <u>sabe</u> hablar español.   *She knows how to speak Spanish.*

saber que…, qué…, si…, cuándo…, (etc.) = to know that…, what…, if…, when…, etc.

    <u>Sabíamos</u> que hacía calor.   *We knew that it was hot.*

    No <u>sé</u> qué hacer.   *I do not know what to do.*

    ¿<u>Sabes</u> si llamó?   *Do you know if he called?*

G.   TO LEARN = APRENDER/ENTERARSE DE/SABER

aprender = to acquire knowledge by study or intentionally

<u>Aprendí</u> a nadar.   *I learned how to swim.*

enterarse de = to find out or learn about something accidentally

<u>Se enteró</u> <u>(de)</u> que nos íbamos.   *He found out we were leaving.*

saber [preterite] = to find out or learn about something accidentally (same as *enterarse*)

<u>Supe</u> que estabas enfermo.   *I found out (heard) you were sick.*

H.   TO MEET = CONOCER/ENCONTRARSE CON/ TOPARSE CON/TROPEZAR CON[*]

conocer [preterite] = to meet (make someone's acquaintance)

Lo <u>conocí</u> en la fiesta.   *I met him at the party.*

encontrarse con = to meet (by appointment, by chance)

<u>Me encontré con</u> ella para almorzar.   *I met her for lunch.*

<u>Me encontré con</u> él en el tren.   *I ran into him on the train.*

toparse con = to meet (run into, meet by chance)

<u>Se topó con</u> mi primo en la tienda.   *He met (ran into, met by chance) my cousin at the store.*

tropezar con = to meet (run into, run across, stumble upon)

<u>Tropezó con</u> ellos en el cine.   *He ran into them at the movies.*

*See also *Section P* on pp. 218–219.

I. TO PLAY = JUGAR/TOCAR

jugar = to play a game
　Me gusta <u>jugar</u> al ajedrez.　　　　*I like to play chess.*

tocar = to play an instrument
　Ella <u>toca</u> el piano.　　　　*She plays the piano.*

J. TO PUT = PONER/PONERSE/METER

poner = to put
　<u>Pusimos</u> la llave en la mesa.　　　*We put the key on the table.*

Also means "to set" when used with "table"
　<u>Pongan</u> la mesa.　　　　*Set the table.*

ponerse = to put on
　<u>Me puse</u> el abrigo.　　　　*I put my coat on.*

Also means "to become" when used with an adjective
　<u>Se puso</u> azul.　　　　*He became blue.*

meter = to put in
　¿<u>Metiste</u> el coche en el garage?　　*Did you put the car in the garage?*
　El niño <u>se metió</u> el dedo en la boca.　*The boy put his finger in his mouth.*

K. TO SERVE = SERVIRLE/SERVIRLO*

servirle a alguien = to serve a person; to help
　¿Le <u>sirvo</u> más vino?　　　　*Shall I serve you more wine?*
　¿Le <u>serviste</u> agua a esa persona?　　*Did you serve that person water?*
　¿En qué puedo <u>servirle</u>?　　　*How may I help you?*

*See also *Section C* on p. 209.

servirlo, servirla, servir algo = to serve something

—Ya es hora de <u>servir</u> la comida.	*It is time to serve the meal.*
—¿Dónde está la ensalada?	*Where is the salad?*
—Ya la <u>serví</u>.	*I already served it.*

L.   TO SPEND = GASTAR/PASAR

gastar = to spend money

<u>Gastamos</u> mucho en ese viaje.	*We spent a lot on that trip.*

pasar = to spend time

<u>Pasamos</u> tres semanas allá.	*We spent three weeks there.*

desperdiciar = to waste

No <u>desperdicies</u> dinero.	*Do not waste money.*
No <u>desperdicien</u> mi tiempo.	*Do not waste my time.*

M.   TO TAKE = TOMAR/LLEVAR/LLEVARSE

tomar = to take
llevar = to take (away from speaker, in a specified direction)
llevarse = to take (away from speaker, no specified direction)

tomar algo = to take something, drink, take (a bus, etc.)

<u>Tomó</u> la llave sin decir nada.	*He took the key without saying anything.*
Quiero <u>tomar</u> una cerveza bien fría.	*I want to drink a very cold beer.*
<u>Tome</u> el autobús.	*Take the bus.*
¿Cuánto tiempo <u>tomará</u>?	*How long will it take?*

Toma (Tome usted) is used when you hand someone something ("Here.")

—¿Tienes un lápiz?	*Do you have a pencil?*
—Sí. <u>Toma</u> *(handing out the pencil).*	*Yes. Here.*
—Gracias.	*Thanks.*

llevar a alguien, llevar algo = to take someone or something (somewhere)

<u>Llevamos</u> a mis padres al aeropuerto.	*We took my parents to the airport.*
<u>Llevaremos</u> toallas a la playa.	*We will take towels to the beach.*

llevarse algo = to take something (away, with oneself)

El mesero <u>se llevó</u> mi tenedor.	*The waiter took my fork away.*

apuntar/bajar = to take down

La operadora <u>apuntó</u> el mensaje.	*The operator took down the message.*
El botones <u>bajará</u> su equipaje.	*The bellboy will take (bring) your luggage down.*

subir = to take up

El botones <u>subirá</u> el equipaje.	*The bellboy will take the luggage up.*

admitir/alojar = to take in

Esa casa de huéspedes sólo <u>admite</u> adultos.	*That guesthouse only takes in adults.*

sacar = to take out

<u>Sacaron</u> a los niños a pasear.	*They took the children out for a stroll.*

quitarse = to take off

<u>Se quitó</u> la ropa para bañarse.	*He took off his clothes to bathe.*

tener lugar = to take place

El concierto <u>tendrá lugar</u> esta noche.	*The concert will take place tonight.*

traer = to bring (toward the speaker only)

El mesero nos <u>trajo</u> la comida muy rápido.	*The waiter brought us the food very quickly.*

APPENDIX II
Práctica

N. TO REALIZE = DARSE CUENTA ≠ REALIZAR

darse cuenta = to realize

No <u>me di cuenta</u> de la hora que era.

I did not realize what time it was.

No <u>te das cuenta</u> de las implicaciones de tus actos.

You do not realize the implications of your actions.

realizar = to come true, to carry out

Ahora sí que se me <u>realizará</u> el sueño de viajar a Sudamérica.

*Now my dream to travel to South America will really (**sí**) come true.*

Ese empleado <u>realiza</u> sus funciones con mucha eficacia.

That employee carries out his duties very efficiently.

O. TO THINK = PENSAR/PENSAR EN/PENSAR DE

pensar en = to think about someone or something

Siempre <u>pienso en</u> mi hermano cuando veo ese cuadro.

I always think of my brother when I see that painting.

<u>¿En</u> qué <u>piensas</u>?

What are you thinking about?

pensar de = to think something (opinion) about someone or something—it is only used in direct or indirect interrogatives

¿Qué <u>piensas de</u> este hotel?

What do you think about this hotel?

No quiso decirme lo que <u>pensaba de</u> mi comida.

He did not want to tell me what he thought about my food.

pensar (+ inf.) = to think about doing something (plan on)

—¿Qué <u>piensas</u> *hacer* este verano?

What are you planning on doing this summer?

—<u>Pienso</u> *trabajar* en un restaurante.

I am planning on working in a restaurant.

P.   PEOPLE VS. MACHINES

PEOPLE VS. MACHINES		
	People	**Mechanical Devices**
to run	**correr**	**andar/funcionar**
	Jorge corre. *Jorge runs.*	**Mi coche anda.** *My car runs.*
	People	**Machines and Systems**
to work	**trabajar**	**andar/funcionar**
	Jorge trabaja. *Jorge works.*	**El reloj no funciona.** *The clock is not working.* **Este método funciona.** *This method works.*
	People and Events	**Motors**
to start	**comenzar/empezar**	**poner en marcha/arrancar**
	Empiezo a trabajar a las 7. *I start work at 7 o'clock.* **Comienza a las 8.** *It starts at 8 o'clock.*	**Puse el auto en marcha.** *I started the car.* **Mi coche no arranca.** *My car will not start.*
	People	**Things**
to run out	**salir corriendo**	**acabársele a uno**
	Jorge salió corriendo. *Jorge ran out.*	**Se nos acabó el tiempo.** *We ran out of time.*
	People	**Lights**
to go out	**salir**	**apagarse**
	Jorge salió. *Jorge went out.*	**Se apagó la luz.** *The light went out.*

As a general rule, remember to think about the meaning of the English expression when you have a verb used with a preposition. Following are some other prepositional usages.

To work out:

♦ as in a person doing exercises: **hacer ejercicios**

<u>Hago ejercicios</u> **al levantarme**   *I work out when I get up in the morning.*
por la mañana.

♦ a problem: **resolver un problema**
No pudieron <u>resolver el problema</u>.   *They were unable to work out the problem.*

To run across:

♦ something: **dar con, tropezar con**

<u>Dieron con</u> ese tema tres veces. *They ran across that topic three times.*

♦ literally, a room, a place: **atravesar corriendo**

<u>Atravesó</u> el cuarto <u>corriendo</u>. *He ran across the room.*

To run down:

♦ as in a liquid running down a surface: **escurrir, gotear**

El sudor le <u>goteaba</u> de la cara. *The sweat ran down his face.*

♦ with batteries: **descargarse**

La batería <u>se descargó</u> durante *The battery ran down during the winter.*
el invierno.

♦ with watches: **acabarse la cuerda**

<u>Se le acabó la cuerda</u> al reloj y paró. *The watch ran down and stopped.*

♦ the stairs: **bajar corriendo**

<u>Bajamos</u> las escaleras <u>corriendo</u> *We ran down the stairs to greet her.*
para recibirla.

To run into:

♦ e.g., a tree with your car: **chocar con**

<u>Choqué con</u> el árbol. *I ran into the tree.*

♦ a person by chance: **tropezar con, topar con, encontrarse con***

<u>Tropezamos con</u>/<u>Nos topamos</u> *We ran into her at the library.*
<u>con</u>/ <u>Nos encontramos con</u> ella
en la biblioteca.

To turn out:

♦ a light: **apagar**

<u>Apaga</u> la luz. *Turn out the light.*

♦ things turn out right, wrong, etc…: **las cosas salen bien, mal, etc…**

—¿Cómo <u>salió</u> todo? *How did it turn out?*
—Bien. *Okay.*

APPENDIX II
Práctica

Q.   ACABAR/ACABAR DE/ACABARSE

acabar = to finish

Acabé la tarea.	*I finished the homework.*

acabar de (+ inf.) = to finish doing something

Acabé de *poner* **la mesa.**	*I finished setting the table.*
Cuando <u>acabes de</u> *lavar* **los platos, sécalos y guárdalos.**	*When you finish washing the dishes, dry them and put them away.*

acabar de [present and imperfect indicative] (+ inf.) = to have just (done something)

Present Indicative

Acabo de *comer.*	*I just ate.*

Imperfect Indicative

Acabábamos de *terminar.*	*We had just finished.*

acabarse = to end, finish, use up or eat up [reflexive]; to be no more, run out of ("se" accidental)

Me acabé el pan.	*I ate up all the bread.*
Se acabó el azúcar.	*There is no more sugar.*
Se acabaron los limones.	*There are no more lemons.*
Se nos acabó la leche.	*We have no more (ran out of) milk.*
Se nos acabaron los cacahuates.	*We have no more (ran out of) peanuts.*

(Note the change of the verb in the last two examples.)

R.   DESPEDIR/DESPEDIRSE

despedir = to fire, dismiss

Esa empresa <u>despidió</u> **a veinte empleados.**	*That firm fired twenty employees.*

despedirse = to say good-bye

Nos despedimos en el aeropuerto.	*We said good-bye at the airport.*

S.   TO COME AND TO GO = VENIR/IR/LLEGAR

venir = to come (towards the speaker)

Decidieron <u>venir</u> a vernos.	*They decided to come see us.*
¡<u>Ven</u> acá!	*Come here!*

ir = to go (away from the speaker)

NOTE: In English this is frequently translated as "to come."

<u>Voy</u> a tu casa esta tarde.	*I will go to your house this afternoon.*
¡<u>Voy</u>!	*I am coming!* (literally, in Spanish, "I am going.")

llegar = to arrive, to get someplace; + **tarde, temprano** = to be late, early

Los huéspedes <u>llegaron</u> esta mañana.	*The guests arrived (got here) this morning.*
<u>Llegamos</u> al hotel a las tres.	*We got to the hotel at three.*
<u>Llegaste temprano</u>.	*You are early. (You arrived early.)*
<u>Llegué tarde</u> al trabajo.	*I was late to work.*
Lo siento por <u>haber llegado tarde</u>.	*I am sorry I am late.*

T.   AT = EN/A

En is the usual equivalent of "at" referring to static location in space.

Estoy <u>en</u> casa.	*I am <u>at</u> home.*

A is the usual equivalent of "at" referring to time of day.

La clase es <u>a</u> las diez.	*Class is <u>at</u> ten.*

Other expressions:

<u>at</u> this moment = **<u>en</u> este momento**	<u>at</u> one (the, my) side = **<u>a</u> un (al, a mi) lado**
<u>at</u> times = **<u>a</u> veces**	to throw <u>at</u> = **tirar <u>a</u>, lanzar <u>a</u>**
<u>at</u> (outside) the door = **<u>a</u> la puerta**	to sell <u>at</u> a price = **vender <u>a</u> un precio**
BUT: <u>at</u> (inside) the door = **<u>en</u> la puerta**	to be <u>at</u> the table = **estar <u>a</u> la mesa**

U. BECAUSE = POR/A CAUSA DE/PORQUE

Por and *a causa de* mean "because of" and are used with **nouns.** (*Por* can also have other meanings, such as "on account of," "instead of," etc. Context should indicate the meaning.)

Lo hice <u>por</u> mi hermano.	*I did it because of (on account of, instead of) my brother.*
No salimos <u>a causa de</u> la tormenta.	*We did not go out because of the storm.*

Por is used with **pronouns.**

Vendrán temprano <u>por</u> nosotros.	*They will come early because of us.*
Vendrán temprano <u>por</u> eso.	*They will come early because of that.*

Por can also be used with an **infinitive** [same subject], whereas *a causa de* **cannot.**

Me enfermé <u>por</u> comer tanto.	*I got sick because I ate so much.*

Porque is used **only** with a **conjugated verb.**

No salí <u>porque</u> estaba lloviendo.	*I did not go out because it was raining.*

V. BUT = PERO/SINO/SINO QUE

pero = but (nevertheless)

Tengo suficiente dinero, <u>pero</u> no quiero ir.	*I have enough money, but I do not want to go.*
No tengo suficiente dinero, <u>pero</u> voy a ir.	*I do not have enough money, but I am going to go.*
El nuevo gerente es eficaz, <u>pero</u> antipático.	*The new manager is efficient, but disagreeable.*

sino = but (but rather, but instead), when contrasting with a negative in the first part

No es antipático, <u>sino</u> serio.	*He is not disagreeable, but (rather) serious.*
No fue a la tienda, <u>sino</u> al banco.	*He did not go to the store, but (instead) to the bank.*

sino que = sino followed by a conjugated verb

No se lo vendí, <u>sino que</u> se lo *regalé*.	*I did not sell it to him, but gave it to him (instead).*

W.   EXIT VS. SUCCESS = SALIDA/ÉXITO

éxito = success

   El <u>éxito</u> del hotel depende de la calidad del servicio.   *The success of the hotel depends on the quality of service.*

tener éxito = to be successful

   Si se esmeran, <u>tendrán éxito</u>.   *If you make an effort, you will be successful.*

salida = exit

   ¿Dónde se encuentra la <u>salida</u> de emergencia?   *Where is the emergency exit?*

suceso = event

   Fue un <u>suceso</u> de tal importancia que vinieron los reporteros.   *It was such an important event that the reporters came.*

X.   GUIDE = EL GUÍA/LA GUÍA

el guía = guide (person)

   <u>El guía</u> habló de la estatua.   *The guide spoke about the statue.*

la guía = guide (booklet or female guide)

   Todo está explicado en <u>la guía</u>.   *Everything is explained in the guidebook.*

   <u>La guía</u> hablaba catalán.   *The guide (fem.) spoke Catalan.*

Y.   ORDER = EL ORDEN/LA ORDEN/EL PEDIDO

el orden = order, organization, neatness

**Es esencial que preparen este postre
en el <u>orden</u> indicado.**

*It is essential that you prepare this dessert in
the order indicated.*

**Por favor archíveme estos folletos
en <u>orden</u> alfabético.**

*Please file these brochures in alphabetical
order for me.*

la orden = order, request

Recibirá sus <u>órdenes</u> del supervisor.

*You will receive your orders from the
supervisor.*

¿Puedo tomarles la <u>orden</u> (el <u>pedido</u>)?

May I take your order?

Juan Rodríguez, a sus <u>órdenes</u>.

Juan Rodríguez, at your service.

Z.   TIME = TIEMPO/VEZ/HORA/RATO/DIVERTIRSE

tiempo = time or weather

No tengo <u>tiempo</u> para ayudarte hoy.

I do not have time to help you today.

Hace buen <u>tiempo</u> hoy.

The weather is nice today.

vez = time (countable)

Toma café cuatro <u>veces</u> al día.

He drinks coffee four times a day.

Esta <u>vez</u> yo pago.

This time, I will pay.

hora = time (chronological)

—**¿Qué <u>hora</u> es?**

What time is it?

—**Es <u>hora</u> de irnos.**

It is time to leave.

rato = time, while (**ratito** = a little while)

Hace <u>rato</u> que estoy esperando.

I have been waiting for some time (a while).

divertirse = to have a good time

<u>Nos divertimos</u> mucho en la fiesta ayer.

We had a good time at the party yesterday.

BUT: **Ayer tuvimos buen tiempo.**

Yesterday we had good weather.

AA. WHAT = ¿QUÉ?/¿CUÁL?/¿CÓMO?/LO QUE

¿Qué es… ? = What is…? (asking for a definition)

  ¿Qué es un "cántaro"?   *What is a "cántaro?"*

¿Cuál es…? = What is…? (asking for identification or specification)

  ¿Cuál es la diferencia entre los dos?   *What is the difference between the two?*

¿Qué (+ noun)**…?** = What + noun…? (or Which)

  ¿Qué *libro* leíste anoche?   *What (Which) book did you read last night?*

  ¿Qué *ciudades* visitaste en Sudamérica?   *What cities did you visit in South America?*

  ¿Qué (*comida*) vamos a comer?   *What are we going to eat?*

  ¿Qué (*ropa*) te vas a poner esta noche?   *What are you going to wear tonight?*

¿Cómo? = What? What did you say? (asking for a repetition)

  ¿Cómo?   OR   **¿Cómo dijo?**

Lo que = What (relative pronoun, not used in interrogatives)

  Lo que me gusta de la película es el misterio.   *What I like about the movie is the mystery.*

  No me dijo lo que quería.   *He did not tell me what he wanted.*

APPENDIX II

Práctica

APPENDIX 2

Exercises

Chapter 1 Overview

The following exercises are designed for self-correcting; the answers are located in Appendix 3.

A. SENTENCE COMPONENTS

Ejercicio 1. Identifique las palabras en bastardilla en las frases siguientes.

MODELO: **Me gusta *el* café *negro*.**

> **el:** *artículo definido*; **negro:** *adjetivo calificativo*

1. Después *de* trabajar varias horas *en* la computadora, *se* me cansan los ojos. 2. *Cuando* estudio, me gusta poner música *clásica* en el tocadiscos. 3. *Ayer* fuimos al parque *a* jugar a la pelota con unos *amigos*. 4. *Mi* mamá me llamó *por* teléfono ayer a *las* ocho de la mañana. 5. *Este* libro es más interesante que *ése*. 6. Me gustan *tus* zapatos más que *los míos*. 7. *Algunos* profesores son más estrictos que *otros*. 8. El libro *que* compré ayer me costó *mucho* dinero. 9. Mi hermana me dijo *que* tú eras *un* futbolista famoso. 10. Tengo dos dólares *y* veinte centavos, *pero* no es suficiente para ir al cine.

Ejercicio 2. Haga el análisis gramatical de las siguientes oraciones.

MODELO: **Juan estudia español.**

> **Juan:** *sustantivo propio, sujeto del verbo "estudia"*; **estudia:** *verbo estudiar, 3ª persona singular del presente del indicativo*; **español:** *sustantivo común, masc. sing., objeto directo del verbo "estudia"*

1. Los niños cantaron una canción. 2. Marta me regaló este libro. 3. Estos ejercicios son fáciles.

B. VERB STRUCTURE

Ejercicio. Identifique el modo (MAYÚSCULA) y el tiempo (minúscula) de los verbos en bastardilla.

MODELO: **El niño *llegó cantando* de la escuela; *estaba* contento porque le *habían dado* un premio por *portarse* bien.**

> **llegó:** *INDICATIVO pretérito*; **cantando:** *PARTICIPIO presente*; **estaba:** *INDICATIVO imperfecto*; **habían dado:** *INDICATIVO pluscuamperfecto*; **portarse:** *INFINITIVO*

Estábamos todos en la cocina *preparando* la cena cuando mi hermana *anunció* que tenía buenas noticias—se *había ganado* la lotería. Mi mamá le dijo que *pensara* con mucho cuidado en lo que quería *hacer* con el dinero, porque si no, lo *gastaría* todo y luego se arrepentiría. Pero mi hermana ya lo había planeado todo. "No te *preocupes*, Mami; a ti y a Papi les *daré* la mitad para que la *pongan* en el banco, y el resto lo usaré para comprarme ropa y otras cosas que *necesito*".

C. SENTENCE STRUCTURE

Ejercicio 1. Subraye los verbos conjugados en el texto siguiente.

MODELO: **Ayer mis hermanos y yo nos levantamos temprano.**

> *Ayer mis hermanos y yo nos <u>levantamos</u> temprano.*

Para las vacaciones de Navidad, mi papá, mi hermana y yo íbamos a San Blas, y nos quedábamos en un hotel en la playa. La noche de Navidad, cuando todos los demás estaban celebrando en el hotel, nosotros nos íbamos a un lugar ya seleccionado en la playa oscura y hacíamos un fuego con leña que habíamos recogido el día anterior. Llevábamos comida para cocinar en el fuego, y pasábamos la noche allí, oyendo las olas del mar y mirando las estrellas.

Ejercicio 2. Divida el texto en cláusulas usando una raya (/) y cuente el total de cláusulas.

MODELO: **Tengo una hermana que vive en España.**

> *Tengo una hermana/que vive en España. (2)*

Necesito que me ayudes a preparar la cena. Tendremos cinco invitados a cenar y quiero que todo esté perfecto. ¿Podrías poner la mesa, por favor? Y cuando acabes con eso, ven a la cocina para ayudarme con la comida. Las verduras para la ensalada están lavadas; sólo hay que cortarlas y ponerlas en la ensaladera. Quiero prepararles la receta de pollo que les gustó tanto la última vez que vinieron.

Ejercicio 3. Subraye todas las cláusulas independientes del texto siguiente.

MODELO: **Me desperté a las tres y bajé a hacerme café sin que nadie me oyera.**

> *<u>Me desperté a las tres</u> y bajé a hacerme café sin que nadie me oyera.*

El invierno está casi terminado. Ya no hace frío, y la nieve se ha transformado en lluvia. Pronto tendremos que empezar a preparar el jardín para que podamos plantar las hortalizas. Estoy tan contento que la primavera esté en camino porque me gusta el calor. El invierno aquí es tan triste y gris, y me canso de la ropa pesada que tengo que ponerme.

Ejercicio 4. Subraye todas las cláusulas principales del mismo texto.

MODELO: **Me desperté a las tres y bajé a hacerme café sin que nadie me oyera.**

> *Me desperté a las tres y <u>bajé a hacerme café</u> sin que nadie me oyera.*

El invierno está casi terminado. Ya no hace frío, y la nieve se ha transformado en lluvia. Pronto tendremos que empezar a preparar el jardín para que podamos plantar las hortalizas. Estoy tan contento que la primavera esté en camino porque me gusta el calor. El invierno aquí es tan triste y gris, y me canso de la ropa pesada que tengo que ponerme.

Ejercicio 5. Subraye todas las cláusulas subordinadas del mismo texto.

MODELO: **Me desperté a las tres y bajé a hacerme café sin que nadie me oyera.**

> *Me desperté a las tres y bajé a hacerme café <u>sin que nadie me oyera</u>.*

El invierno está casi terminado. Ya no hace frío, y la nieve se ha transformado en lluvia. Pronto tendremos que empezar a preparar el jardín para que podamos plantar las hortalizas. Estoy tan contento que la primavera esté en camino porque me gusta el calor. El invierno aquí es tan triste y gris, y me canso de la ropa pesada que tengo que ponerme.

Ejercicio 6. Haga el análisis lógico de las frases siguientes.

Modelo: **Quiero que me ayudes a preparar la cena.**

Quiero: *cláusula principal*; **que me ayudes…cena:** *cláusula subordinada nominal, objeto directo de "quiero"*

1. Necesito un libro que describa la revolución mexicana.   2. Te prestaré dinero a condición de que me pagues mañana.   3. Sé que no puedes hablar ahora.

Ejercicio 7. Haga el diagrama de las frases siguientes. (Use los diagramas del capítulo para inspirarse.)

1. Quiero que veas el libro que conseguí sobre la revolución mexicana.   2. Es necesario que los norteamericanos comprendan que estas tierras les pertenecían a los mexicanos originalmente, y que antes eran de los indios que vivieron en ellas por siglos.   3. Me pidió que le comprara pan y le contesté que no tenía dinero.

D. ACCENTS (Syllabification: Consonants)

En los siguientes ejercicios, divida cada palabra en sílabas.

Ejercicio 1. Consonantes sencillas intervocálicas.

raza	meta	visa
callo	fecha	cerro
caballo	metiche	serrano

Ejercicio 2. Dos consonantes intervocálicas.

campo	pantera	ángulo
musgo	fantoche	mantilla
mercado	sincero	cencerro
vibra	hablo	autografiar
retrato	adrenalina	reflorecer
aglomerar	negro	aplastar
reprimir	declive	refresco

Ejercicio 3. Tres o más consonantes intervocálicas.

anglosajón	empresario	constante
estrecho	espléndido	instituto
inspección	instrumento	embrollo
transmitir	resplandor	transcribir

ACCENTS (Syllabification: Vowels)

Ejercicio 1. Hiatos.

recaer	crear	creer
veo	sea	caos
boa	coactar	coexistir
gentío	frío	reí
vestía	etíope	ataúd
raíz	vía	mío
reúnan	continúa	rehúsa

Ejercicio 2. Diptongos.

aviador	aire	bienestar
deleite	miope	oiga
resguardo	causa	fueron
endeudarse	fuimos	diurno
duodeno	Dios	hueso
cariátide	recién	comió
aguántate	acuérdense	cantáis
volvéis	óiganlos	enjáulalo

Ejercicio 3. Triptongos y otras combinaciones.

veían	seáis	caíamos
esquiáis	vivíais	traían
caeríais	oíais	enviéis
creías	actuéis	adquirierais

Ejercicio 4. La "h" intervocálica.

ahora	rehago	ahí
rehíce	prohíben	rehúsa
ahogar	desahogar	ahumado
cacahuate	alcahuete	cohete
rehúyen	sobrehumano	zaherir

Ejercicio 5. Repaso.

divida	las	siguientes
palabras	en	sílabas
luego	vea	cuando
necesitan	acentos	porque
rey	reina	voy
boina	bueno	bien

ACCENTS (Stress)

Ejercicio 1. Indique para cada palabra si es **aguda, llana, esdrújula o sobresdrújula.**

1. camino 2. caminó 3. caminaba 4. caminábamos 5. caminad 6. compra 7. compró 8. compraba 9. comprábamos 10. cómpralo 11. cómpramelo 12. español 13. españoles 14. francés 15. trances 16. encéstalo

Ejercicio 2. Las siguientes palabras son **agudas.** Póngales acento a las que lo necesiten.

1. presto 2. enterrar 3. preparad 4. desperte 5. dividir 6. farol 7. piedad 8. pedi 9. peor 10. caiman 11. cocinar 12. imparcial 13. cajon 14. finlandes 15. trajin 16. temblor 17. cristal 18. riñon

Ejercicio 3. Las siguientes palabras son **llanas.** Póngales acento a las que lo necesiten.

1. lapiz 2. llamas 3. llaman 4. pluma 5. hablaron 6. españoles 7. dioses 8. dia 9. deme 10. españolita 11. peruano 12. consigo 13. traje 14. examen 15. caracter 16. lunes 17. labio 18. infertil

Ejercicio 4. Las siguientes palabras son **esdrújulas** y **sobresdrújulas;** la sílaba tónica (con énfasis) de las palabras de más de una sílaba está subrayada. ¿Necesitan acento?

1. matalo 2. regalamelo 3. callense 4. estupido 5. parpado 6. capitulo 7. projimo 8. bajame 9. animo 10. cascara 11. decada 12. exito 13. pajaro 14. aspero 15. hungaro 16. vinculo 17. maquina 18. pildora

Ejercicio 5. Póngale acento a los adverbios que lo necesiten (la sílaba con énfasis en la parte del adjetivo original está subrayada).

1. rapidamente 2. facilmente 3. lentamente 4. dificilmente 5. piadosamente 6. brillantemente 7. friamente 8. despiadadamente 9. secamente 10. felizmente 11. fijamente 12. calidamente 13. cientificamente 14. misericordiosamente 15. solamente 16. finalmente 17. gravemente 18. proximamente

Ejercicio 6. Las palabras siguientes son **monosílabas;** no hay nada subrayado porque el énfasis es único. Póngales acento si lo necesitan. (Las frases están traducidas por si se necesita.)

1. A él le va bien. *(It's going well for him)* 2. Di que el rey te lo dio. *(Say that the king gave it to you.)* 3. Vio a Dios. *(She saw God.)* 4. El te no me da tos. *(Tea doesn't make me cough.)* 5. No se si se fue. *(I don't know if he left.)* 6. Tu no le des. *(Don't you feed her.)* 7. Tu voz se te va. *(Your voice is going.)* 8. Sin ti no se lo da. *(Without you she won't give it to her.)* 9. No le de la fe. *(Don't give him your faith.)* 10. Yo si se la di. *(I did give it to her.)* 11. A ti te doy lo que hay. *(I give you what there is.)* 12. No hay más miel por mi. *(There is no more honey because of me.)*

Ejercicio 7. Ponga un acento donde se necesite; la sílaba tónica (con énfasis) de las palabras de más de una sílaba está subrayada.

1. Aun los ricos necesitan amor. 2. Los niños aun no han comido. 3. Estoy solo. 4. Solo me siento solo cuando ando mal acompañado. 5. Pasame esa llave, por favor. 6. No quiero esta fruta, prefiero esa. 7. Por eso no quiso ir con nosotros. 8. Me gustaria comprarme ese terreno. 9. ¡Que buena suerte tienes! 10. ¡Como canta!

Ejercicio 8. Ponga un acento sobre los **que** que lo necesiten.

1. Prefiero *que* no llueva. 2. ¿*Que* dijiste? 3. No sé *que* dije. 4. Creo *que* dije *que* preferiría *que* no lloviera. 5. ¡*Que* locura! 6. Dime *que* crees. 7. El día *que* no llueva aquí, no sabremos *que* hacer. 8. Haremos lo *que* ustedes quieran. 9. La última vez *que* vinieron, nos costó mucho decidir *que* cuarto darles. 10. ¡*Que* duerman en el piso!

Ejercicio 9. Llene el blanco con **porque** o **por qué;** traduzca las frases 4 y 5.

1. Te llamé _____ tengo noticias. 2. ¿_____ no me llamaste antes? 3. No te puedo decir _____: ¡es un secreto! 4. El asesino no pudo explicar _____ había matado al policía. 5. El asesino no lo pudo explicar _____ había matado al policía. 6. Yo creo que lo hizo _____ tenía miedo. 7. ¿Tú matarías a alguien simplemente _____ tienes miedo? 8. ¿_____ no? 9. ¡_____ no se debe matar a nadie! 10. No sé _____ se fue. 11. Se fue _____ no le hacías caso.

Ejercicio 10. Póngale acento a **como** si lo necesita; traduzca las frases 4–7.

1. *Como* no tengo hambre, no *como*. 2. ¿*Como* puedes decir eso? 3. Necesitas pensar *como* yo para comprenderme. 4. Dime *como* comes. 5. ¡*Como* comes! 6. ¿*Como como*? 7. *Como como como.* 8. Ella se viste *como* yo. 9. Es un libro *como* los demás. 10. Si baila *como* canta, ha de ser una maravilla.

Ejercicio 11. Póngale acento a **cuanto** si lo necesita.

1. ¿*Cuanto* cuesta este cuarto? 2. No sé *cuanto* cuesta. 3. ¿*Cuantos* hermanos tienes? 4. Me pregunto *cuantos* años tiene esa mujer. 5. Nadie sabe *cuantas* veces se repetirá. 6. Le di *cuanto* dinero tenía al ladrón. 7. No sabe *cuanto* me arrepentí de darle mi dinero. 8. La profesora le dará *cuanta* información tenga.

Ejercicio 12. Póngale acento a **donde** si lo necesita.

1. ¿*Donde* vives? 2. Vivo *donde* viven mis padres. 3. No sé *donde* vive mi amiga. 4. Me dijo *donde* vivía, pero se me olvidó. 5. Apunté su dirección en la libreta *donde* tengo todas las direcciones. 6. Ya no sé *donde* puse la libreta. 7. ¿No estará *donde* siempre la pones?

Ejercicio 13. Póngale acento a **cuando** si lo necesita; traduzca las frases 7 y 8.

1. Llegarán *cuando* estemos en la finca. 2. ¿*Cuando* llegas? 3. No me dijo *cuando* iban a llegar. 4. *Cuando* lleguen, les serviremos cerveza. 5. ¿Nos escondemos *cuando* los veamos llegar? 6. *Cuando* me gradúe, iré al Caribe. 7. ¿... *cuando* te gradúes? 8. ¿*Cuando* te gradúas?

Ejercicio 14. Póngale acento a **quien** si lo necesita.

1. ¿*Quien* se llevó mi paraguas? 2. No sé *quien* se lo llevó. 3. El amigo con *quien* vino Marieta tenía paraguas. 4. ¿Te dijo *quien* era el chico con *quien* estaba? 5. No me dijo con *quien* había venido. 6. Dime con *quien* andas y te diré *quien* eres.

Ejercicio 15. Este ejercicio es un repaso de acentos. Ponga un acento sobre las vocales que lo necesiten; la sílaba con énfasis está subrayada, a menos que sea monosílaba.

ARMANDO: ¿Esta Juan?

MIGUEL: Creo que fue al cine, y no sé cuando va a regresar. ¿Para qué lo quieres?

ARMANDO: Quiero pedirle prestado un libro para mi clase de español.

MIGUEL: ¿Sabes qué libro es?

ARMANDO: Sí. Es uno que tiene la portada negra.

MIGUEL: Yo sé donde lo tiene, pero no estoy seguro si te lo podria prestar.

ARMANDO: A mí me dijo que no lo necesitaba este semestre.

MIGUEL: Si tú te lo llevas, y él lo necesita, yo voy a sentirme muy mal. ¿Por qué no te tomas una taza de té, y esperas a que regrese Juan?

ARMANDO: Bueno. Mientras espero, prestame el libro para mirarlo, por favor.

MIGUEL: Voy a buscarlo. [...] ¿Es este, verdad?

ARMANDO: No, ese no. Es el otro, el de gramatica. Tiene casi la misma portada, pero un título diferente.

MIGUEL: A ver si lo encuentro; esperame. [...] Aquí lo tienes.

ARMANDO: Gracias.

Chapter 2   Nouns and Noun Determiners

A. NOUNS AND THEIR EQUIVALENTS (Introduction)

Ejercicio. Conceptual Questions.

What is a noun? What type of grammatical functions can it have in a sentence? What other types of words can behave this way? Do you know what a "nominalized" word is? Can you think of an example?

NOUNS AND THEIR EQUIVALENTS (Nouns: Gender and Number)

Ejercicio 1. Ponga un artículo definido para indicar si la palabra es masculina o femenina.

MODELO: **libro** → *el libro*

amanecer	amor	arroz	ataúd
auto	barandal	barro	cama
capital	carril	casa	catedral
cárcel	césped	clima	costumbre
crucigrama	día	drama	español
foto	huésped	idioma	juez
lápiz	libertad	lunes	luz
mal	mano	mapa	metal
miel	moral	moto	pez
piel	Pirineos	poder	poema
problema	programa	radar	rama
sal	sapo	señal	sistema
trama	tranvía	vaca	zorro

Ejercicio 2. Escriba el equivalente femenino de las siguientes palabras.

el hombre, el estudiante, el joven, el actor, el modelo, el turista, el rey, el policía, el comunista, el toro

Ejercicio 3. Indique en español la diferencia de significado entre el masculino y el femenino de los siguientes nombres.

el policía/la policía   el papa/la papa

el guía/la guía   el cura/la cura

NOUNS AND THEIR EQUIVALENTS (Personal *A*)

Ejercicio. Llene el blanco con el **a** personal si se necesita.

1. Le gusta mirar _____ la televisión. 2. Vimos _____ nuestros vecinos en el centro. 3. No reconocieron _____ mi hermano. 4. ¿_____ quién viste hoy? 5. ¿_____ qué viste hoy? 6. Estoy buscando _____ mis llaves. 7. Esa compañía busca _____ empleados nuevos. 8. El jefe buscaba _____ su secretaria. 9. Tienen _____ tres gatos. 10. Tiene _____ su hijo en una escuela privada. 11. _____ ellas no las vieron hasta el final. 12. No oímos _____ nadie. 13. ¿Viste _____ alguien? 14. ¿Quieres _____ algo?

B. NOUN DETERMINERS (Articles: Definite Articles)

Ejercicio 1. Póngale a cada nombre el artículo definido correcto (todos son femeninos).

avioneta, atracción, avenida, agua, alarma, alma, ama, águila, aguja, autonomía, aula, avicultura, ave, habitación, habichuela, hacha, hamburguesa, hambre, hartanza, aguas, alarmas, almas, hambres.

Ejercicio 2. Llene el blanco con un artículo definido si se necesita.

1. _____ vida debe disfrutarse. 2. _____ señor Ruiz dice que _____ chocolate es malo para _____ salud, pero _____ doña Luisa sabe que él come _____ chocolate todos los días. 3. "_____ Señorita Guzmán, ¿le gusta _____ chocolate?" 4. Ayer compramos _____ verduras, pero no tenían _____ verduras que tú pediste. 5. _____ inglés es más difícil que _____ español. 6. Hablo _____ español, pero sueño en _____ inglés. 7. Mi clase de _____ español es la más divertida de todas. 8. Aprendí _____ español cuando tenía seis años. 9. A mi padre le costó trabajo aprender _____ español. 10. Salieron temprano de _____ escuela y, como su padre había salido de _____ cárcel ese día, fueron a _____ iglesia a dar gracias. 11. Salimos de _____ clase y fuimos directamente a _____ casa porque teníamos que vestirnos para llegar a _____ misa a tiempo. 12. _____ miércoles vamos a tener una prueba. 13. ¡Hasta _____ jueves! 14. Hoy es _____ viernes.

NOUN DETERMINERS (Articles: Indefinite Articles)

Ejercicio. Llene el blanco con un artículo indefinido si se necesita.

1. Jorge es _____ arquitecto. 2. Carlitos es _____ argentino. 3. Rafael es _____ hombre interesante. 4. Es _____ cantante mexicano. 5. Georgina es _____ protestante muy severa. 6. ¡Qué _____ dilema! 7. ¡Qué _____ lindo día! 8. Esa viejita acaba de cumplir _____ cien años. 9. Vamos a discutir _____ otro tema ahora. 10. Tomaría _____ mil años corregir el daño que se ha hecho. Lo dudo—yo creo que tomaría _____ millón. 11. Dentro de _____ media hora nos iremos. 12. No tengo _____ bicicleta. 13. Ese pobre chico no tiene ni _____ amigo. 14. Se fue sin _____ chaqueta.

NOUN DETERMINERS (Adjectives: Demonstrative Adjectives)

Ejercicio. Traduzca.

1. Are those books new?   2. These apples are for you *(fam. sing.)*.   3. That class does not cover these topics.   4. These students are very good.   5. That man is a friend.   6. Those days are unforgettable.

NOUN DETERMINERS (Adjectives: Possessive Adjectives)

Ejercicio. Traduzca.

1. My cousins are coming today.   2. Did your brother call *(fam. sing.)*?   3. His arm is swollen.   4. Their books are wet.   5. She gave me her ring.   6. She is a friend of mine. 7. This pen is mine.

NOUN DETERMINERS (Adjectives: Forms of Descriptive Adjectives)

Ejercicio. Haga los cambios necesarios para que el adjetivo concuerde con el nombre.

1. la casa (verde)   2. la casa (blanco)   3. la casa (azul)   4. el político (respetable)   5. el político (izquierdista)   6. el político (prometedor)   7. la profesora (severo)   8. la maestra (comunista)   9. los niños (feliz)   10. los vecinos (gritón)

NOUN DETERMINERS (Adjectives: Position of Descriptive Adjectives)

Ejercicio. Reescriba las frases siguientes usando el adjetivo entre paréntesis para modificar el nombre en bastardilla. Puede haber más de una posibilidad.

1. Ese hombre vende *muebles*. (antiguos)   2. La *gente* no siempre es infeliz. (pobre) 3. A esa *millonaria* la persiguen los periodistas. (pobre)   4. Te presento a Guzmán, un *amigo*; hoy es su cumpleaños—cumple dieciocho años. (viejo)   5. Desde que construyeron el *garaje*, ya no usan el viejo. (nuevo)   6. Te presento a mi *vecino*. (nuevo) 7. Mi *esposa* está de viaje. (linda)   8. Cornell es una *universidad*. (grande)   9. Charlie Chaplin fue un *actor*. (grande)   10. En esta tina, el *agua* se abre aquí. (caliente) 11. Subimos a la *torre* de la biblioteca. (alta)   12. Está enamorado de tu *hermana*. (bella) 13. Cruzaron el *río* de las Amazonas. (ancho)   14. Visitaron la *catedral* de Gaudí. (impresionante)   15. Ésta es la *oportunidad* que tendremos. (única)   16. Me gustan las *casas*. (blancas)   17. Las *nubes* flotaban como algodón por el valle. (blancas)   18. Era un cielo extraño: abajo había *nubes* (1), y arriba *nubes* (2). [(1) blancas, (2)negras]   19. Esa película es de un *director*. (español)   20. Se le veía un *aire* de inseguridad. (cierto) 21. Sabían que eran unas *acusaciones*. (ciertas)   22. Tenía la *capacidad* de hacer que todos se sintieran a gusto. (rara)   23. Era un *sonido* que nadie podía identificar. (raro) 24. Te voy a decir la *verdad*. (pura)   25. Es un disco de *fidelidad*. (alta)   26. Querían estar en Sevilla para la *Semana*. (Santa)   27. La mejor solución es usar nuestro *sentido*. (común)

NOUN DETERMINERS (Comparisons)

Ejercicio. Llene el blanco con lo necesario para establecer una comparación. Cada espacio puede necesitar más de una palabra.

1. Beto come más ruidosamente _____ nadie. 2. Sabina es más lista _____ Raúl. 3. Elsa gana menos dinero _____ tú. 4. Hay más _____ veinte árboles aquí. 5. Me diste menos _____ la mitad. 6. Mi bicicleta es mejor _____ la tuya. 7. Hace más frío _____ esperaba. 8. Llovió menos _____ creíamos. 9. Nunca ganaré tanto dinero _____ Héctor. 10. Ese coche es _____ bello como éste. 11. Esa niña grita más _____ las demás. 12. Había menos _____ cinco jugadores en la cancha. 13. Ese examen no fue tan fácil _____ los otros. 14. Compré más servilletas _____ necesitábamos. 15. Hay más servilletas _____ invitados. 16. Tengo menos trabajo _____ esperaba. 17. Elvira trabaja _____ como su hermano, pero no gana _____ dinero como él. Y a mí me parece que él no es _____ listo como ella.

Chapter 3 Pronouns

A. PERSONAL PRONOUNS (Introduction)

Ejercicio. Conceptual Questions.

What is a pronoun? What is its relationship with a noun? What type of grammatical functions can it have in a sentence? What other types of words can behave this way? What different types of pronouns exist?

PERSONAL PRONOUNS (Subject Pronouns)

Ejercicio 1. Decida usted si se necesita pronombre sujeto o no.

1. —¿Cuándo salieron? —[Nosotros/Ø] salimos a las siete. 2. —¿Quién está ahí? —Soy [yo/Ø]. 3. —¿Qué hacen? —[Ellos/Ø] están comiendo. 4. Mis vecinos sacaron la basura, pero [yo/Ø] no me acordé. 5. ¿Tendría [Ud./Ø] tiempo de ayudarme? 6. —¿Por qué no está Luis? —[Él/Ø] está enfermo.

Ejercicio 2. Traduzca, prestando atención al sujeto: ¿necesita pronombre en español? (*you* = **tú**)

1. I bought a book. 2. It is in José's room. 3. We are going to study together this afternoon. 4. You have to start your assignments (*tareas*) for tomorrow. 5. They (your assignments) are long. 6. I know you studied, but I have not finished yet. 7. María is here; she wants to talk to you.

PERSONAL PRONOUNS (Direct Object Pronouns)

Ejercicio 1. Transforme **la comida** en pronombre y reescriba la frase.

1. Traigan la comida. *(mandato)* 2. Quiero guardar la comida. 3. He guardado la comida. 4. Están cocinando la comida. 5. Compramos la comida. 6. No toques la comida. *(mandato)*

Ejercicio 2. Reescriba la frase transformando el objeto directo en pronombre.

1. Veo a mi vecina de esta ventana. 2. Llevé a mis hijas al banco. 3. No conocen a la maestra. 4. Josefina es un poco extraña; nadie entiende a Josefina. 5. Los vecinos miraban a la muchacha mientras barría la calle. 6. El vendedor llamó a la clienta. 7. Oían a la niña cantar. 8. Oían a la niña cantar una canción. 9. Buscaron a la asesina. 10. Encontraron a la doctora. 11. Invitaron a Anita al baile. 12. Extraño a mi madre.

Ejercicio 3. Reescriba la frase transformando el objeto directo en pronombre.

1. Veo a mi vecino de esta ventana. 2. Llevé a mis hijos al banco. 3. No conocen al maestro. 4. Roberto es un poco extraño; nadie entiende a Roberto. 5. Los vecinos miraban al muchacho mientras barría la calle. 6. El vendedor llamó al cliente. 7. Oían al niño cantar. 8. Oían al niño cantar la canción. 9. Buscaron al asesino. 10. Encontraron al doctor. 11. Invitaron a Panchito al baile. 12. Extraño a mi padre.

PERSONAL PRONOUNS (Direct and Indirect Object Pronouns)

Ejercicio 1. Junte las partes para formar frases completas. Reemplace los nombres en bastardilla con el pronombre adecuado.

1. los turistas/miraban/*a los indígenas* 2. el policía/dijo/*al vagabundo*/que se tenía que ir 3. regaló/*sus libros viejos*/*al asilo* 4. mandaron/*el paquete*/*a su familia* 5. el abuelo/contó/*el cuento*/*a sus nietos* 6. hicieron/*la cama*/*a los huéspedes* 7. el padre/quitó/*la llave*/*a su hijo* 8. mi amigo/pidió/*el dinero*/*a su tía*

Ejercicio 2. Traduzca.

1. I beat *him*. 2. I won *it* (the money = *el dinero*). 3. They robbed *him* (his neighbors). 4. They stole *it* (the money = *el dinero*). 5. We believe *him*. 6. We believe *it*. 7. They hit *him*. 8. They glued *it* (the map = *el mapa*). 9. I paid *her*. 10. I paid *it* (the bill = *la cuenta*).

PERSONAL PRONOUNS (Required Repetitive Object Pronouns)

Ejercicio. Llene el blanco con un pronombre repetitivo de objeto directo o indirecto si se necesita.

1. Ayer _____ compré el pan. 2. El pan _lo_ compré ayer. 3. Esta tarde _____ vi a Juan en la tienda. 4. A Juan _lo_ vi en la tienda esta tarde. 5. El correo _____ llegó hace media hora. 6. Hace media hora que _____ llegó el correo. 7. Marta _____ bañó al niño. 8. Al niño Marta _lo_ bañó. 9. Toda la gente _lo_ vio el globo. 10. Anoche _los_ terminé todos. 11. Mañana _____ enviaremos el regalo a Marieta. 12. No _____ digas a Juan el secreto. 13. Nunca _se lo_ cuentes todo a tus amigos. 14. Ese día _nos_ regañaron a todos nosotros. 15. Con esa lluvia _____ crecerán todas las plantas.

PERSONAL PRONOUNS (Order of Pronouns When Combined)

Ejercicio 1. Conteste afirmativamente, transformando las palabras en bastardilla en pronombres, y haciendo los demás cambios necesarios.

1. ¿Te dio *los regalos*? 2. ¿Les enseñaste *la cosecha a los vecinos*? 3. ¿Te contó *la noticia*? 4. ¿Le dijiste *el secreto a Socorro*? 5. ¿Se limpiaron ustedes *las botas*? 6. ¿Os enviaron *la carta*?

Ejercicio 2. Conteste las preguntas siguientes en el afirmativo, reemplazando las palabras en bastardilla con el pronombre adecuado si se necesita pronombre. No use los nombres en bastardilla en sus respuestas. No use pronombre si no se necesita.

1. ¿Están preparando *la cena*? 2. ¿Le pudieron vender *la casa a ese cliente*? 3. ¿Le va a hacer *los mandados a su mamá*? 4. ¿Le has mandado *el libro a Nilda*? 5. ¿*La casa* está pintada? 6. ¿Te gustó *el restaurante*? 7. ¿*Joaquín* le dio *las flores a Marina*? 8. ¿Se habla *español*?

PERSONAL PRONOUNS (Prepositional Object Pronouns)

Ejercicio. Traduzca al español. (*you* = **tú**)

1. This is for you.   2. According to her, it was wrong.   3. They were looking at him.
4. They were looking for him.   5. This is between him and me.   6. Her children are like
her.   7. I am talking about you.   8. Sing with me.   9. I will sing with him.   10. She took it
with her.

B. *SE* (Reflexive Pronouns)

Ejercicio. Traduzca, usando verbos reflexivos. (*you* = **tú**)

1. We noticed his smile.   2. He fell in love with her.   3. We worry about you.   4. They
found out about the accident the next day.   5. I took off my clothes.   6. She stayed there.
7. We complained about the time.   8. He said good-bye to his family.   9. They realized it
was late.   10. They never got used to the weather.   11. He does not dare knock at the door.
12. They look like their mother.

SE (Accidental or Irresponsible *Se*)

Ejercicio 1. Vuelva a escribir estas frases usando el **se** accidental.

1. Olvidamos nuestra cita.   2. Quemé los plátanos.   3. Perdimos nuestras llaves.
4. Mojaron su pelo.   5. Rompiste tu taza.

Ejercicio 2. Traduzca las frases siguientes usando el **se** accidental y el verbo indicado.
(*you* = **tú**)

1. He left his book. (*quedársele a uno*)   2. Our clothes got wet. (*mojársele a uno*)   3. I ran
out of coffee. (*acabársele a uno*)   4. Your papers fell. (*caérsele a uno*)   5. She forgot her
notes. (*olvidársele a uno*)   6. Their plates broke. (*rompérsele a uno*)

Ejercicio 3. Llene el blanco con lo que falta para completar la frase, usando el modelo
como base.

MODELO: **A Marta se __le__ olvidó el libro.**

1. A Jorge se _____ perdió el paraguas.   2. A nosotros se _____ rompió el jarro.   3. A mí se
___ cayó el guante.   4. Se _____ quemaron los frijoles a ti.   5. A los niños se _____ cierran
los ojos.

Ejercicio 4. Conjugue el verbo en la forma correcta del pretérito.

1. Se nos _____ (olvidar) los regalos.   2. A ti se te _____ (olvidar) las llaves.   3. A la niña se
le _____ (bajar) los calcetines.   4. A mí se me _____ (romper) la silla.   5. A los vecinos se
les _____ (ir) la electricidad.

SE (Impersonal *Se*)

Ejercicio 1. Traduzca usando el **se** impersonal.

1. The house was sold. When was it sold?   2. One tans easily in the Caribbean.   3. The employees were fired. Why were they fired?   4. They were not told.   5. You do not say that in public.

Ejercicio 2. Las frases que siguen usan la estructura impersonal; escoja la forma correcta del verbo.

1. En algunas partes del mundo hispano se (toma/toman) una siesta por la tarde.   2. En esa tienda se (habla/hablan) español.   3. A los niños se les (dijo/dijeron) que no salieran de noche.   4. En esa época, se (mataba/mataban) a los criminales.   5. Al presidente se le (recibió/recibieron) con gran aplauso.   6. A los estudiantes se les (mandó/mandaron) la información en verano.   7. Al gerente se le (anunció/anunciaron) los cambios hace mucho.   8. Se (vende/venden) libros.   9. Aquí no se (acepta/aceptan) cheques personales.   10. A la jefa ya se le (dio/dieron) las noticias.

C. DEMONSTRATIVE AND POSSESSIVE PRONOUNS

Ejercicio. Traduzca.

1. That house was more expensive than this one.   2. Which house do you prefer? I liked that one better.   3. Give me that. What? This?   4. My sister is as strong as yours.   5. My parents are coming for graduation. What about yours? (What about = ¿Y…) Mine are not coming.   6. That medicine is his.   7. Which towel is yours? This one is mine and that one is yours.   8. Whose keys are these? These are yours (*formal sing.*), these are his, and these are hers.

D. INTERROGATIVE PRONOUNS

Ejercicio. Traduzca usando los interrogativos. (*you* = **tú**)

1. How did they arrive? 2. How much sugar do you use? 3. Which color do you like? 4. Which one do you want? 5. How far is the store from here? 6. Which one is your name? (on a list) 7. What is your name? 8. How many books did you buy? 9. How often do you go?

E. EXCLAMATIVES

Ejercicio 1. Traduzca usando los exclamativos.

1. What a job! 2. How pretty! 3. What an amusing game! 4. What good coffeee! 5. How fast you run! 6. How the birds sing! 7. We loved her so much! 8. I am so hungry! 9. We visited so many cousins! 10. I wish I could fly the way they do!

Ejercicio 2. Llene los blancos con el exclamativo correcto.

1. ¡_____ agua más fría! 2. ¡_____ se ríen! 3. ¡_____ delicioso! 4. ¡_____ ojos tan verdes tienes! 5. ¡_____ me alegro que puedas venir a la fiesta! 6. ¡_____ hermanos tienes! 7. ¡_____ blanca se ve la nieve! 8. ¡_____ buena película! 9. ¡_____ comen esos niños! 10. ¡_____ suerte!

F.   INDEFINITE AND NEGATIVE PRONOUNS

Ejercicio. Traduzca. (*you* = **tú**)

1. Something fell. 2. Someone spoke. 3. I do not see anyone. 4. Do you need anything? 5. I do not want anything. 6. Maybe one of the neighbors saw him. No, none of them saw him. 7. I went to the movies yesterday. I did too. 8. John could not see. We could not either. 9. Have you ever been to Chile? No, I have not ever been there. Some day I will go. My sister went there once and liked it.   10. I cannot find my keys anywhere. I know they are somewhere in this room.

G. RELATIVE PRONOUNS

Ejercicio 1. Llene el blanco con el pronombre relativo que mejor convenga.

1. Hay momentos en la vida _____ no se olvidarán nunca. 2. La mujer _____ vive ahí es famosa. 3. El libro _____ nosotros compramos era caro. 4. _____ me atrae de la universidad es el ambiente intelectual. 5. Natalia es _____ sabe bailar el merengue. 6. Ésa es la casa en _____ filmaron la película. 7. El actor _____ aparece en esa película es muy arrogante en la vida real. 8. El político _____ fue elegido no era muy popular, _____ sorprendió a muchos extranjeros. 9. Llegó y apagó el radio, _____ estaba a todo volumen. 10. La razón por _____ hice eso fue que sabía que no me iban a dejar en paz. 11. Ésta es la estatua frente a _____ nos besamos por primera vez, ¿te acuerdas? 12. Ése es el pueblo _____ calles son las más limpias. 13. _____ busca, encuentra. 14. _____ me cae bien es Roberto. 15. Esa obra musical es _____ tocaban en la película.

Ejercicio 2. Traduzca.

1. The person who called asked for you. 2. What he gave you was stolen. 3. I do not like what they do. 4. That is the bus I was waiting for. 5. The one who sang that song was Rose.

Chapter 4   Prepositions and Conjunctions

A. PREPOSITIONS (The Function of Prepositions)

Ejercicio.   Conceptual Questions.

What is a preposition? Can you explain its name? What is its relationship with a noun? What is a conjunction? Can you explain its name? What is the difference between a conjunction of coordination and a conjunction of subordination?

PREPOSITIONS (Individual Prepositions)

En los siguientes ejercicios (#1–6), llene los blancos con **a, al, de, del, en, con** o **Ø** (nada), según parezca más lógico.

Ejercicio 1.

1. Asistiré _a_ clase _en_ cuanto me alivie.   2. Comenzaron _a_ cocinar ayer.
3. Creo que _a_ lo mejor se encuentre _a_ Margarita _en_ la ciudad.   4. Decidieron caminar _en_ vez de manejar; nunca llegarán _a_ pie.   5. Dudo que puedan influir _con_ su decisión.   6. El mercado está _a_ dos kilómetros.   7. El programa consiste _en_ varios segmentos; en el primero, se trata _de_ la revolución mexicana.   8. Ella me gana _a_ veces, y se burla _de_ mí.   9. Este bordado está hecho _a_ mano; este otro, _en_ cambio, está hecho _a_ máquina.   10. Fuimos _a_ la tienda _en_ el coche _de_ mi padre _con_ mis cuatro hermanitos.

Ejercicio 2.

1. Iremos al trabajo _a_ pesar de la tormenta.   2. La gente _de_ barrio estaba _de_ mal humor.   3. La mujer _de_ ojos verdes trabaja _en_ la tienda _de_ la esquina.
4. Llegarán _a_ eso de las cinco _con_ tal de que no nieve.   5. Lo mediremos _por_ ojo.
6. Me acosté _a_ las diez _con_ coraje.   7. Me detuve _de_ echarle gasolina al carro.
8. Me enojé _____ ellos porque los dos estaban hablando _a_ la vez.   9. Me gusta montar _a_ caballo _de_ vez en cuando.   10. Me invitaron _a_ cenar _en_ un restaurante que se especializa _en_ comida mexicana.

Ejercicio 3.

1. Nadie se había fijado _____ el cambio que ocurrió desde que se habían quejado _____ su horario.   2. Necesitamos discutir esto más _____ fondo, pero _____ este momento no tengo tiempo.   3. No veo _____ mis amigos _____ estos lentes.   4. Nos pusimos _____ llorar cuando nos enteramos _____ terremoto que hubo _____ Los Ángeles.   5. Nunca se resignará _____ ser menos famoso.   6. Por favor lleguen _____ tiempo (*puntualmente*).
7. Quisiera que se rieran _____ mis chistes, y no _____ mí.   8. _____ cuanto empezó a ir a la escuela, Roberta aprendió _____ defenderse.   9. Sabemos que tardan mucho _____ llegar a su destino.   10. Se casó _____ ella _____ los tres años de ser su novio.

Ejercicio 4.

1. Se enamoró _____ ella cuando le enseñó _____ bailar el tango. 2. Se negó _____ tomarse la píldora. 3. Se quedaron _____ mis libros _____ poesía. 4. Si esos niños no dejan _____ meterse _____ mi hijo, tendré que hablar _____ sus padres. 5. Soñé _____ mi novia. 6. Su hijo le pidió _____ dinero porque pensaba _____ comprarle un regalo a su madre. 7. Subían _____ la montaña _____ frecuencia. 8. Van _____ regalarle un libro _____ Cervantes. 9. Ves a tus padres _____ menudo, y ellos siempre se alegran _____ verte. 10. Volvieron _____ sentarse _____ frente de mí.

Ejercicio 5.

1. Ya empezaron _____ salir las flores. 2. _____ fuerza de hacer tantos ejercicios, bajó de peso. 3. _____ niña, se acostumbró _____ desayunar temprano. 4. _____ repente tuvieron que entrar _____ causa de la tormenta. 5. _____ respecto a ese asunto, parece que lo resolvieron ayer. 6. ¿Me podrían ayudar _____ terminar este trabajo? 7. —¿Qué haces? —Estoy buscando _____ mi libreta _____ direcciones. 8. ¿Te atreverás _____ jugar? 9. Le presté el libro _____ mi amigo _____ buena gana.
10. Estudiamos _____ Miami.

Ejercicio 6.

1. Iremos _____ tal de que no llueva. 2. —Anoche nevó. —¿_____ veras? 3. Mis hijos aprenderán _____ tocar el piano desde muy jóvenes. 4. Pienso _____ ti _____ menudo.
5. ¿Qué piensan tus padres _____ mis amigos? 6. No te olvides _____ traerte las llaves.
7. Nunca dejarán _____ quererte. 8. Pronto se acostumbrarán _____ la comida picante.
9. Decidí ir de compras _____ vez de estudiar. 10. _____ veces es saludable no hacer nada. 11. La tormenta empezó _____ repente. 12. ¿Tú te atreves _____ hablarle?
13. No pudimos ir _____ causa de la lluvia. 14. Mis padres nunca consentirán _____ dejarme ir contigo.

En los siguientes ejercicios (#7–9), llene los blancos con **por, para** o **Ø** [nada], según parezca más lógico.

Ejercicio 7.

1. Fueron al centro _____ visitar el museo. 2. Fueron al mercado _____ verduras.
3. Toma: este regalo es _____ ti. 4. Viajaron _____ toda la isla. 5. Hay _____ lo menos quinientas personas aquí. 6. Prometieron que terminarían toda la construcción en el edificio _____ el semestre entrante. 7. Me gusta pasearme _____ la mañana.
8. Pasaremos _____ casa de tu abuelita en camino al partido. 9. Lo dijeron _____ que sus vecinos lo oyeran _____ que sabían que reaccionarían. 10. _____ fin llegó el cartero.

Ejercicio 8.

1. Buscó _____ la carta en su bolso, pero no la encontró. 2. ¡Cálmate! ¡No es _____ tanto!
3. Necesito medicina _____ curarme. 4. Lo tomaron _____ idiota. 5. Iremos al mercado _____ fruta. 6. Fueron a la tienda _____ comprar lo necesario. 7. Te agradezco _____ la ayuda. 8. No pudieron salir _____ la tormenta. 9. La llamaremos _____ teléfono.
10. Saldrán _____ Madrid en la madrugada.

Ejercicio 9.

1. —¿Quieres bailar? —¡_____ supuesto! 2. No estaba _____ bromas. 3. _____ lo general no me gusta levantarme tarde. 4. _____ más dinero que gane, no es feliz. 5. Tendremos que comprar _____ lo menos cuatro docenas. 6. Le queda un trabajo _____ escribir. 7. Se enfermó _____ comer tanto. 8. _____ llegar al museo, hay que pasar _____ el parque. 9. Acabo de entrar; _____ eso tengo frío. 10. Jorge se esfuerza _____ sacar las mejores notas de la clase.

En los siguientes ejercicios (#10–13), traduzca las oraciones, prestando atención a las preposiciones.

Ejercicio 10.

1. They worry about you. 2. He fell in love with her. 3. It consists of two sections. 4. The decision depends on you. 5. They laughed at him. 6. I dream about you every night. 7. They said goodbye to me. 8. I do not want my ideas to influence your decision. 9. She married my brother. 10. He stopped drinking.

Ejercicio 11.

1. We arrived in Madrid at two. 2. She opposes everything I say. 3. I try to help. 4. I realized my mistake. 5. She thanked me for the favor. 6. We got onto the bus. 7. Their house is five miles away. 8. I met my friends at the restaurant. 9. She studies at the university. 10. They will be the first to leave.

Ejercicio 12.

1. I think about my parents every day. 2. Luisa's book is interesting. 3. I noticed the change. 4. I cannot help you at this moment. 5. They got mad at me because of my mistake. 6. We looked at the clock. 7. He saw his sister. 8. I asked you for money, not for advice. 9. I just ate. 10. They work for me.

Ejercicio 13.

1. I sent it airmail. 2. They went to the store for bread. 3. I have two papers left to write. 4. We will have finished by ten. 5. For a child, he knows a lot. 6. They left for Guatemala yesterday. 7. They are looking for their keys. 8. They talked for three hours. 9. She worries about you. 10. What is this for?

Chapter 5   Verbs I

FORMATION (Indicative Mood: Present Indicative)

Ejercicio 1. Conjugue el verbo en la primera persona singular del presente del indicativo (**yo**).

1. amar 2. cantar 3. comer 4. vivir 5. hablar 6. caminar 7. coser 8. beber 9. abrir 10. imprimir

Ejercicio 2. Conjugue el verbo en la primera persona singular del presente del indicativo (**yo**).

1. cerrar 2. revelar 3. perder 4. mezclar 5. sentir 6. pedir 7. conseguir 8. repetir 9. mentir 10. comenzar 11. comentar 12. defender 13. impedir 14. seguir 15. pensar 16. querer 17. servir 18. elegir

Ejercicio 3. Conjugue el verbo en la tercera persona singular del presente del indicativo (**él, ella**).

1. votar 2. volver 3. doler 4. domar 5. contar 6. cortar 7. acostar 8. poder 9. podar 10. llover 11. llorar 12. recordar 13. recortar 14. oler 15. jugar 16. jurar

Ejercicio 4. Conjugue el verbo en la primera persona singular del presente del indicativo (**yo**).

1. proteger 2. seguir 3. obedecer 4. traducir 5. torcer 6. recoger 7. conseguir 8. agradecer 9. producir 10. convencer

Ejercicio 5. Conjugue el verbo en la segunda persona singular del presente del indicativo (**tú**).

1. enviar 2. continuar 3. confiar 4. reunir 5. criar 6. graduar 7. guiar 8. actuar 9. concluir 10. huir

Ejercicio 6. Conjugue el verbo en la primera y tercera persona singular del presente del indicativo (**yo/él**), y luego en la primera persona plural (**nosotros**).

1. caer 2. hacer 3. poner 4. salir 5. traer 6. valer 7. venir 8. decir 9. tener 10. dar 11. ir 12. ser 13. estar 14. haber 15. oír 16. saber 17. ver

Ejercicio 7. Conjugue el verbo en el indicativo presente de la persona indicada.

1. caminar/yo 2. actuar/tú 3. actuar/nosotros 4. adquirir/yo 5. adquirir/nosotros 6. andar/vosotros 7. aprender/nosotros 8. asir/él 9. avergonzar/ellos 10. avergonzar/nosotros 11. averiguar/yo 12. decir/yo 13. decir/él 14. decir/nosotros 15. buscar/ellos 16. caber/yo 17. caber/ella 18. caer/yo 19. caer/él 20. cerrar/tú 21. cerrar/vosotros 22. coger/yo 23. coger/ellas 24. comenzar/yo 25. comenzar/nosotros 26. contribuir/ella 27. construir/nosotros 28. conducir/yo 29. producir/tú 30. contar/ella

31. sonar/yo 32. recordar/nosotros 33. creer/yo 34. poseer/ellas 35. leer/nosotros
36. cruzar/yo 37. almorzar/tú 38. dar/yo 39. decir/yo 40. contradecir/yo 41. elegir/
yo 42. exigir/tú 43. seguir/yo 44. conseguir/ella 45. perseguir/nosotros 46. dormir/
yo 47. dormir/vosotros 48. enviar/ellos 49. enviar/nosotros 50. escribir/yo 51. estar/
yo 52. forzar/ellos 53. hacer/yo 54. satisfacer/ellos 55. ir/yo 56. ir/ellos 57. jugar/
ella 58. llegar/ellos 59. morir/él 60. mover/tú

61. negar/ellas 62. oír/yo 63. oír/tú 64. oír/nosotros 65. oler/yo 66. oler/ellos
67. parecer/yo 68. pedir/yo 69. pedir/él 70. perder/tú 71. poder/ellos 72. poner/yo
73. querer/ellos 74. reír/yo 75. sonreír/ella 76. reunir/ellos 77. rogar/él 78. tener/yo
79. tener/tú 80. torcer/yo 81. retorcer/él 82. traer/yo 83. valer/yo 84. convencer/yo
85. venir/yo 86. intervenir/ellos 87. ver/nosotros 88. vivir/él 89. volver/ella

FORMATION (Indicative Mood: Past Tenses of the Indicative: Imperfect Indicative)

Ejercicio 1. Conjugue el verbo en el indicativo imperfecto de la persona indicada.
   1. hablar/yo 2. comer/tú 3. vivir/él 4. caminar/nosotros 5. correr/vosotros 6. asir/
   ellas 7. comenzar/yo 8. decir/tú 9. ver/él 10. concluir/nosotros

Ejercicio 2. Conjugue el verbo en el indicativo imperfecto de **yo** y **nosotros.**
   1. ir 2. ser 3. ver 4. pedir 5. cerrar 6. caer 7. andar 8. caber 9. tener 10. hacer
   11. dar 12. dormir 13. reír 14. oír

Ejercicio 3. Conjugue el verbo en el indicativo imperfecto de la persona indicada.
   1. caminar/yo 2. actuar/tú 3. actuar/nosotros 4. adquirir/yo 5. adquirir/nosotros
   6. andar/vosotros 7. aprender/nosotros 8. asir/él 9. avergonzar/ellos 10. avergonzar/
   nosotros 11. averiguar/yo 12. decir/yo 13. decir/él 14. decir/nosotros 15. buscar/
   ellos 16. caber/yo 17. caber/ella 18. caer/yo 19. caer/él 20. cerrar/tú 21. cerrar/
   vosotros 22. coger/yo 23. coger/ellas 24. comenzar/yo 25. comenzar/nosotros
   26. contribuir/ella 27. construir/nosotros 28. conducir/yo 29. producir/tú
   30. contar/ella

31. sonar/yo 32. recordar/nosotros 33. creer/yo 34. poseer/ellas 35. leer/nosotros
36. cruzar/yo 37. almorzar/tú 38. dar/yo 39. decir/yo 40. contradecir/yo 41. elegir/
yo 42. exigir/tú 43. seguir/yo 44. conseguir/ella 45. perseguir/nosotros 46. dormir/
yo 47. dormir/vosotros 48. enviar/ellos 49. enviar/nosotros 50. escribir/yo 51. estar/
yo 52. forzar/ellos 53. hacer/yo 54. satisfacer/ellos 55. ir/yo 56. ir/ellos 57. jugar/
ella 58. llegar/ellos 59. morir/él 60. mover/tú

61. negar/ellas 62. oír/yo 63. oír/tú 64. oír/nosotros 65. oler/yo 66. oler/ellos
67. parecer/yo 68. pedir/yo 69. pedir/él 70. perder/tú 71. poder/ellos 72. poner/yo
73. querer/ellos 74. reír/yo 75. sonreír/ella 76. reunir/ellos 77. rogar/él 78. tener/yo
79. tener/tú 80. torcer/yo 81. retorcer/él 82. traer/yo 83. valer/yo 84. convencer/yo
85. venir/yo 86. intervenir/ellos 87. ver/nosotros 88. vivir/él 89. volver/ella

FORMATION (Indicative Mood: Past Tenses of the Indicative: Preterite)

Ejercicio 1. Conjugue el verbo en el pretérito de la persona indicada.

1. hablar/tú 2. comer/nosotros 3. vivir/ellos 4. caminar/yo 5. andar/tú 6. caber/él
7. estar/nosotros 8. arrestar/nosotros 9. haber/ellos 10. saber/yo 11. poder/tú
12. poner/ella 13. salir/vosotros 14. tener/ellas 15. hacer/yo 16. querer/tú
17. venir/él   *salisteis*

Ejercicio 2. Conjugue el verbo en el pretérito de la persona indicada.

1. dar/nosotros 2. hacer/él 3. ir/yo 4. ser/yo 5. decir/vosotros 6. producir/tú
7. traer/ellas   *dijisteis*

Ejercicio 3. Conjugue el verbo en el pretérito de yo y **él**.

1. sentir 2. pedir 3. reír 4. dormir 5. caer 6. creer 7. leer 8. oír 9. concluir
10. buscar 11. llegar 12. alcanzar 13. explicar 14. almorzar 15. apagar 16. sacar
17. comenzar 18. colgar 19. tocar 20. empezar 21. entregar 22. pagar

Ejercicio 4. Conjugue el verbo en el pretérito de la persona indicada.

1. caminar/yo 2. actuar/tú 3. actuar/nosotros 4. adquirir/yo 5. adquirir/nosotros
6. andar/vosotros 7. aprender/nosotros 8. asir/él 9. avergonzar/ellos 10. avergonzar/
nosotros 11. averiguar/yo 12. decir/yo 13. decir/él 14. decir/nosotros 15. buscar/
ellos 16. caber/yo 17. caber/ella 18. caer/yo 19. caer/él 20. cerrar/tú 21. cerrar/
vosotros 22. coger/yo 23. coger/ellas 24. comenzar/yo 25. comenzar/nosotros
26. contribuir/ella 27. construir/nosotros 28. conducir/yo 29. producir/tú
30. contar/ella

31. sonar/yo 32. recordar/nosotros 33. creer/yo 34. poseer/ellas 35. leer/nosotros
36. cruzar/yo 37. almorzar/tú 38. dar/yo 39. decir/yo 40. contradecir/yo 41. elegir/yo
42. exigir/tú 43. seguir/yo 44. conseguir/ella 45. perseguir/nosotros 46. dormir/yo
47. dormir/vosotros 48. enviar/ellos 49. enviar/nosotros 50. escribir/yo 51. estar/yo
52. forzar/ellos 53. hacer/yo 54. satisfacer/ellos 55. ir/yo 56. ir/ellos 57. jugar/ella
58. llegar/ellos 59. morir/él 60. mover/tú

61. negar/ellas 62. oír/yo 63. oír/tú 64. oír/nosotros 65. oler/yo 66. oler/ellos
67. parecer/yo 68. pedir/yo 69. pedir/él 70. perder/tú 71. poder/ellos 72. poner/yo
73. querer/ellos 74. reír/yo 75. sonreír/ella 76. reunir/ellos 77. rogar/él 78. tener/yo
79. tener/tú 80. torcer/yo 81. retorcer/él 82. traer/yo 83. valer/yo 84. convencer/yo
85. venir/yo 86. intervenir/ellos 87. ver/nosotros 88. vivir/él 89. volver/ella

FORMATION (Indicative Mood: Past Tenses of the Indicative: Present Perfect Indicative)

Ejercicio. Conjugue el verbo en el presente perfecto del indicativo de la persona indicada.

1. caminar/yo 2. actuar/tú 3. adquirir/él 4. andar/nosotros 5. aprender/vosotros
6. asir/ellos 7. avergonzar/yo 8. averiguar/tú 9. buscar/ella 10. caber/nosotros
11. cerrar/vosotros 12. coger/ellas

FORMATION (Indicative Mood: Past Tenses of the Indicative: Pluperfect Indicative)

Ejercicio. Conjugue el verbo en el pluscuamperfecto del indicativo de la persona indicada.

1. caminar/yo 2. actuar/tú 3. adquirir/él 4. andar/nosotros 5. aprender/vosotros
6. asir/ellos 7. avergonzar/yo 8. averiguar/tú 9. buscar/ella 10. caber/nosotros
11. cerrar/vosotros 12. coger/ellas

FORMATION (Indicative Mood: Future: Simple Future)

Ejercicio 1. Conjugue el verbo en el futuro para la persona indicada.

1. caminar/yo 2. actuar/tú 3. adquirir/él 4. andar/nosotros 5. aprender/vosotros
6. asir/ellos 7. avergonzar/yo 8. averiguar/tú 9. buscar/ella 10. cantar/nosotros
11. cerrar/vosotros 12. coger/ellas

Ejercicio 2. Conjugue el verbo en el futuro para la persona indicada.

1. caber/yo 2. decir/tú 3. haber/él 4. hacer/nosotros 5. poder/vosotros 6. poner/
ellos 7. querer/yo 8. saber/tú 9. salir/ella 10. tener/nosotros 11. valer/vosotros
12. venir/ellas

FORMATION (Indicative Mood: Future: Future Perfect)

Ejercicio. Conjugue el verbo en el futuro perfecto para la persona indicada.

1. caminar/yo 2. actuar/tú 3. adquirir/él 4. andar/nosotros 5. aprender/vosotros
6. asir/ellos 7. avergonzar/yo 8. averiguar/tú 9. buscar/ella 10. cantar/nosotros
11. cerrar/vosotros 12. coger/ellas 13. caber/yo 14. poder/tú 15. querer/ella
16. saber/nosotros 17. salir/vosotros 18. tener/ellos 19. valer/ellas 20. venir/yo

FORMATION (Conditional Mood: Present Conditional)

Ejercicio 1. Conjugue el verbo en el condicional presente para la persona indicada.

1. caminar/yo 2. actuar/tú 3. adquirir/él 4. andar/nosotros 5. aprender/vosotros
6. asir/ellos 7. avergonzar/yo 8. averiguar/tú 9. buscar/ella 10. cantar/nosotros
11. cerrar/vosotros 12. coger/ellas

Ejercicio 2. Conjugue el verbo en el condicional presente para la persona indicada.

1. caber/yo   2. decir/tú   3. haber/él   4. hacer/nosotros   5. poder/vosotros   6. poner/ellos   7. querer/yo   8. saber/tú   9. salir/ella   10. tener/nosotros   11. valer/vosotros   12. venir/ellas

FORMATION (Conditional Mood: Conditional Perfect)

Ejercicio. Conjugue el verbo en el condicional perfecto para la persona indicada.

1. caminar/yo   2. actuar/tú   3. adquirir/él   4. andar/nosotros   5. aprender/vosotros   6. asir/ellos   7. avergonzar/yo   8. averiguar/tú   9. buscar/ella   10. cantar/nosotros   11. cerrar/vosotros   12. coger/ellas   13. caber/yo   14. poder/tú   15. querer/ella   16. saber/nosotros   17. salir/vosotros   18. tener/ellos   19. valer/ellas   20. venir/yo

FORMATION (Subjunctive Mood: Present Subjunctive)

Ejercicio 1. Conjugue el verbo en el subjuntivo presente para la persona indicada, usando **que** antes del verbo.

1. caminar/yo   2. hablar/tú   3. estudiar/él   4. cantar/ella   5. bailar/nosotros   6. remar/vosotros   7. amar/ellas   8. preparar/ellos   9. tolerar/usted   10. tararear/ustedes

Ejercicio 2. Conjugue el verbo en el subjuntivo presente para la persona indicada.

1. comer/yo   2. leer/tú   3. ver/él   4. vivir/ella   5. toser/nosotros   6. coser/vosotros   7. correr/ellas   8. partir/ellos   9. beber/usted   10. escribir/ustedes

Ejercicio 3. Conjugue el verbo en el subjuntivo presente para **yo** y **nosotros.**

1. cerrar   2. perder   3. contar   4. volver   5. sentir   6. dormir   7. enviar   8. actuar

Ejercicio 4. Conjugue el verbo en la tercera personal singular del subjuntivo presente.

1. pedir   2. decir   3. oír   4. tener   5. concluir   6. parecer   7. conducir   8. caber   9. caer   10. hacer   11. poner   12. salir   13. traer   14. valer   15. venir

Ejercicio 5. Conjugue el verbo en el subjuntivo presente.

1. dar/yo   2. estar/tú   3. haber/ella   4. ir/nosotros   5. saber/vosotros   6. ser/ellas   7. coger/yo   8. dirigir/tú   9. distinguir/ellas   10. convencer/nosotros   11. buscar/vosotros   12. llegar/yo   13. alcanzar/tú

Ejercicio 6. Repaso del subjuntivo presente.

1. dominar/yo   2. temer/él   3. defender/tú   4. dar/nosotros   5. estar/vosotros   6. haber/ellas   7. ir/yo   8. saber/tú   9. ser/ella   10. coger/nosotros   11. corregir/tú   12. perseguir/vosotros   13. vencer/ella   14. rascar/yo   15. rogar/tú   16. rezar/él   17. entender/ella   18. encontrar/usted   19. devolver/ellos   20. envolver/nosotros   21. confiar/yo   22. criar/nosotros   23. continuar/tú   24. graduar/nosotros   25. poseer/ellas   26. ver/yo   27. subir/ella   28. hacer/ellas   29. dividir/ellos   30. investigar/usted   31. analizar/

ustedes 32. discutir/tú 33. pelear/él 34. llegar/ella 35. querer/nosotros 36. entrar/vosotros 37. salir/ellas 38. repetir/ellos 39. oír/usted 40. volver/ustedes

FORMATION (Subjunctive Mood: Imperfect Subjunctive)

Ejercicio 1. Conjugue el verbo en el imperfecto del subjuntivo.

1. caminar/yo 2. hablar/tú 3. estudiar/él 4. cantar/ella 5. bailar/nosotros 6. remar/vosotros 7. amar/ellas 8. preparar/ellos 9. tolerar/usted 10. tararear/ustedes
11. comer/yo 12. leer/tú 13. ver/él 14. vivir/ella 15. toser/nosotros 16. coser/vosotros 17. correr/ellas 18. partir/ellos 19. beber/usted 20. escribir/ustedes
21. cerrar/yo 22. perder/tú 23. contar/ella 24. volver/nosotros 25. sentir/ellos
26. dormir/ustedes 27. enviar /él 28. actuar /tú

Ejercicio 2. Conjugue el verbo en el imperfecto del subjuntivo.

1. andar/yo 2. caber/tú 3. caer/él 4. concluir/ella 5. conducir/usted 6. dar/nosotros
7. decir/vosotros 8. dormir/ellos 9. estar/ellas 10. haber/ustedes 11. ir/yo 12. leer/tú
13. oír/él 14. pedir/ella 15. poder/usted 16. poner/nosotros 17. poseer/vosotros
18. preferir/ellos 19. producir/ellas 20. querer/ustedes 21. reír/yo 22. saber/tú
23. seguir/él 24. sentir/ella 25. ser/usted 26. ser/nosotros 27. tener/vosotros
28. traer/ellos 29. venir/ellas

FORMATION (Subjunctive Mood: Present Perfect Subjunctive)

Ejercicio. Conjugue el verbo en el presente perfecto del subjuntivo.

1. caminar/yo 2. actuar/tú 3. adquirir/él 4. andar/nosotros 5. aprender/vosotros
6. asir/ellos 7. avergonzar/yo 8. averiguar/tú 9. buscar/ella 10. cantar/nosotros
11. cerrar/vosotros 12. coger/ellas 13. caber/yo 14. poder/tú 15. querer/ella
16. saber/nosotros 17. salir/vosotros 18. tener/ellos 19. valer/ellas 20. venir/yo

FORMATION (Subjunctive Mood: Pluperfect Subjunctive)

Ejercicio. Conjugue el verbo en el pluscuamperfecto del subjuntivo.

1. caminar/yo 2. actuar/tú 3. adquirir/él 4. andar/nosotros 5. aprender/vosotros
6. asir/ellos 7. avergonzar/yo 8. averiguar/tú 9. buscar/ella 10. cantar/nosotros
11. cerrar/vosotros 12. coger/ellas 13. caber/yo 14. poder/tú 15. querer/ella
16. saber/nosotros 17. salir/vosotros 18. tener/ellos 19. valer/ellas 20. venir/yo

FORMATION (Imperative Mood: Direct Commands: *Tú*)

Ejercicio 1. Conjugue en el imperativo de **tú**.

1. hablar 2. comer 3. vivir 4. cerrar 5. abrir 6. saltar 7. escuchar 8. volver 9. pedir
10. conseguir 11. repetir 12. mentir 13. comenzar 14. comentar 15. defender
16. seguir 17. pensar 18. servir 19. elegir 20. votar 21. envolver 22. contar 23. cortar
24. apostar 25. podar 26. llorar 27. recordar 28. recortar 29. oler 30. jugar 31. jurar

32. proteger 33. seguir 34. obedecer 35. traducir 36. producir 37. enviar
38. continuar 39. confiar 40. reunir 41. criar 42. actuar 43. concluir 44. huir 45. caer
46. traer 47. dar 48. oír

Ejercicio 2. Conjugue en el imperativo de **tú.**

1. decir 2. hacer 3. ir 4. poner 5. salir 6. ser 7. tener 8. venir

Ejercicio 3. Conjugue en el imperativo de **tú.**

1. *cantar*, pero no *bailar* 2. *estudiar*, pero no *hablar* en voz alta 3. *beber* mucho, y no *comer* nada artificial 4. *leer* el artículo, pero no *creer* todo lo que dice 5. *volver* a casa, pero no *correr* 6. *descoser* el bolsillo, y no *coser* la bastilla 7. *escribir* una carta, pero no *describir* lo que pasó 8. *contar* lo que debes, y no *descontar* nada 9. *dormir* al bebé, pero no te *dormir* tú 10. *pedir* favores, y no *impedir* que te ayuden 11. *regalar* tu amistad, y no *prestar* nada 12. *buscar* el ungüento, y no te *rascar* la picada 13. *recoger* la basura, pero no *coger* frío

Ejercicio 4. Conjugue en el imperativo de **tú.**

1. *decir* la verdad, y no *decir* mentiras 2. *hacer* la lectura para mañana, pero no *hacer* la tarea 3. *ir* a la tienda, pero no *ir* al correo 4. *poner* tu abrigo aquí, y no *poner* tus zapatos en la mesa 5. *salir* a recoger el periódico, pero no *salir* por esa puerta 6. *ser* bueno, pero no *ser* tonto 7. *tener* hijos, pero no *tener* tantos como ella 8. *venir* a casa, pero no *venir* temprano

FORMATION (Imperative Mood: Direct Commands: *Usted*)

Ejercicio. Conjugue en el imperativo de **usted.**

1. caminar 2. no hablar 3. estudiar 4. no cantar 5. bailar 6. tararear 7. comer 8. no leer 9. vivir 10. no toser 11. correr 12. no beber 13. escribir 14. cerrar 15. no perder 16. contar 17. no volver 18. dormir 19. no pedir favores 20. decir 21. oír 22. no tener miedo 23. conducir con cuidado 24. no caer en la trampa 25. hacer la tarea 26. poner la mesa 27. no salir 28. traer el dinero 29. venir pronto 30. no dar nada 31. ir con ellos 32. no ser ridículo 33. dirigir al grupo 34. buscar el tesoro 35. no llegar tarde

FORMATION (Imperative Mood: Direct Commands: *Vosotros*)

Ejercicio 1. Conjugue en el imperativo de **vosotros.**

1. hablar 2. comer 3. vivir 4. cerrar 5. abrir 6. saltar 7. escuchar 8. volver 9. pedir 10. conseguir 11. repetir 12. mentir 13. comenzar 14. comentar 15. defender 16. seguir 17. pensar 18. servir 19. elegir 20. votar 21. decir 22. hacer 23. ir 24. poner 25. salir 26. ser 27. tener 28. venir

Ejercicio 2. Conjugue en el imperativo de **vosotros.**

1. despertarse 2. levantarse 3. lavarse 4. marcharse 5. acostarse 6. dormirse 7. irse 8. despedirse 9. callarse

Ejercicio 3. Conjugue en el imperativo de **vosotros.**

1. *cantar,* pero no *bailar* 2. *estudiar,* pero no *hablar* en voz alta 3. *beber* mucho, y no *comer* nada artificial 4. *leer* el artículo, pero no *creer* todo lo que dice 5. *volver* a casa, pero no *correr* 6. *descoser* el bolsillo, y no *coser* la bastilla 7. *escribir* una carta, pero no *describir* lo que pasó 8. *contar* lo que debeis, y no *descontar* nada 9. *dormir* al bebé, pero no os *dormir* vosotros 10. *pedir* favores, y no *impedir* que os ayuden 11. *regalar* vuestra amistad, y no *prestar* nada 12. *buscar* el ungüento, y no os *rascar* la picada 13. *recoger* la basura, pero no *coger* frío

Ejercicio 4. Conjugue en el imperativo de **vosotros.**

1. *decir* la verdad, y no *decir* mentiras 2. *hacer* la lectura para mañana, pero no *hacer* la tarea 3. *ir* a la tienda, pero no *ir* al correo 4. *poner* vuestro abrigo aquí, y no *poner* vuestros zapatos en la mesa 5. *salir* a recoger el periódico, pero no *salir* por esa puerta 6. *ser* buenos, pero no *ser* tontos 7. *tener* hijos, pero no *tener* tantos como ellos 8. *venir* a casa, pero no *venir* temprano

FORMATION (Imperative Mood: Direct Commands: *Nosotros*)

Ejercicio 1. Conjugue en el imperativo de **nosotros.**

1. caminar 2. no hablar 3. estudiar 4. no cantar 5. bailar 6. tararear 7. comer 8. no leer 9. vivir 10. no toser 11. correr 12. no beber 13. escribir 14. cerrar 15. no perder 16. contar 17. no volver 18. dormir 19. no pedir favores 20. decir 21. oír 22. no tener miedo 23. conducir con cuidado 24. no caer en la trampa 25. hacer la tarea 26. poner la mesa 27. no salir 28. no dar nada 29. ir con ellos 30. no ser ridículos 31. dirigir al grupo 32. buscar el tesoro 33. no llegar tarde

Ejercicio 2. Conjugue en el imperativo de **nosotros.**

1. despertarlas 2. no levantarse 3. lavarlo 4. marcharse 5. no acostarse 6. dormirse 7. irse 8. no irse

FORMATION (Imperative Mood: Indirect Commands)

Ejercicio. Traduzca usando mandatos indirectos.

1. I do not want to cook; let them cook today. 2. Have the manager call me. 3. If you do not have the money, let Mirta pay. 4. Have them send it to me.

FORMATION (Imperative Mood: Review of the Imperative)

Conteste las preguntas en los siguientes ejercicios (#1–3) usando el imperativo en la persona indicada y transformando los nombres en pronombres cada vez que se pueda.

Ejercicio 1. Use el **imperativo familiar (tú)** en el afirmativo y en el negativo.

1. ¿Les digo el secreto? 2. ¿Hago los mandados? 3. ¿Le vendo los libros? 4. ¿Voy a su casa? 5. ¿Le pongo los zapatos al niño?

Ejercicio 2. Use el **imperativo formal** (**Ud.** o **Uds.**) en el afirmativo y en el negativo.

1. ¿Cantamos la canción? 2. ¿Le digo lo que pasó? 3. ¿Les enviamos las cartas?
4. ¿Vamos al cine?   5. ¿Me quito los zapatos?

Ejercicio 3. Use el imperativo de **nosotros** en el afirmativo y en el negativo.

1. ¿Cantamos las canciones juntos? 2. ¿Vamos al cine? 3. ¿Le damos el dinero? 4. ¿Nos vamos ahora? 5. ¿Nos ponemos el abrigo?

Ejercicio 4. Traduzca la parte en bastardilla usando el mandato indirecto (**Que** + subjunctive).

1. *Have them prepare it.* 2. I don't want to do it. *Let Guillermo do it.*   3. *Have her come see me.* 4. *Have them call me.* 5. If they're hungry, *let them eat.*

FORMATION (Participles: Present Participle)

Ejercicio 1. Indique cuál es el participio presente de los siguientes verbos.

1. hablar 2. comer 3. vivir 4. sentir 5. pedir 6. dormir 7. concluir 8. caer 9. leer
10. oír 11. decir 12. ir 13. venir 14. poder

Ejercicio 2. Indique cuál es el participio presente de los siguientes verbos.

1. caminar 2. actuar 3. andar 4. aprender 5. decir 6. buscar 7. ser 8. cerrar
9. construir 10. conducir 11. producir 12. contar 13. recordar 14. creer 15. almorzar
16. dar 17. elegir 18. seguir 19. hacer 20. jugar

Ejercicio 3. Indique cuál es el participio presente de los siguientes verbos.

1. llegar 2. morir 3. mover 4. negar 5. sonreír 6. oler 7. despedir 8. poner 9. reunir
10. tener 11. traer 12. intervenir 13. ver 14. volver

FORMATION (Participles: Past Participle)

Ejercicio 1. Indique cuál es el participio pasado de los siguientes verbos.

1. hablar 2. comer 3. vivir 4. caminar 5. actuar 6. aprender 7. conducir 8. almorzar
9. dar 10. mover 11. oler 12. venir

Ejercicio 2. Indique cuál es el participio pasado de los siguientes verbos.

1. abrir 2. cubrir 3. decir 4. escribir 5. hacer 6. morir 7. poner 8. resolver 9. volver
10. descubrir 11. devolver 12. suponer

Ejercicio 3. Traduzca.

1. This is holy water. 2. They have blessed the food. 3. I want fried potatoes. 4. He had fried the potatoes. 5. Cursed luck! 6. I have never cursed anyone. 7. She wore her hair loose. 8. They have released the bulls. 9. The printed word is very important. 10. Have you printed your paper?

Chapter 6 Verbs II

USAGE (Preterite vs. Imperfect)

Ejercicio 1. ¿Pretérito o imperfecto? Complete con la forma apropiada del verbo indicado.

El rancho de mi padre

Nunca olvidaré las semanas que (1. pasar/nosotros) en el rancho de mi padre. En esa época yo (2. tener) unos doce o trece años, y mi hermana unos catorce años. En el rancho no (3. haber) ni electricidad ni agua corriente: todo se (4. alumbrar) con velas o linternas, y mi hermana y yo (5. ir) a buscar agua en baldes al ojo de agua cerca de la casa. (6. Cocinar/nosotros) las tortillas y los frijoles con leña. La rutina (7. ser) la siguiente: (8. levantar/nosotros) a las cuatro de la mañana, y mientras una de nosotras (9. salir) a la oscuridad de la madrugada a buscar los caballos, dejándose llevar por el sonido nada más, la otra (10. preparar) el desayuno. (11. Terminar/nosotros) de desayunar, (12. ensillar/nosotros) los caballos, y (13. irse/nosotros) antes de que saliera el sol. Para cuando (14. llegar/nosotros) a donde (15. estar) el ganado, ya el sol (16. haber) salido con todo su poder.

Ejercicio 2. ¿Pretérito o imperfecto? Complete con la forma apropiada del verbo indicado.

Fuego en el monte

Recuerdo la noche del incendio en el rancho. (1. Estar/nosotros) todos dormidos cuando de repente se (2. oír) golpes y gritos en la puerta. Eran los hombres que (3. venir) a decirle a mi padre que (4. haber) fuego en el monte. (5. Vestirse/nosotros) a la carrera y (6. ir/nosotros) corriendo al monte que se (7. ver) desde la casa por el fuego. Una vez frente al fuego, (8. formar/nosotros) entre todos una línea y así (9. empezar) la pelea contra el fuego, que (10. durar) hasta el día siguiente. (11. Agarrar) ramas verdes de árboles para azotar las llamas de fuego y así impedir que avanzaran. (12. Lograr/nosotros) apagar el fuego, y salvar el ganado.

Ejercicio 3. ¿Pretérito o imperfecto? Complete con la forma apropiada del verbo indicado.

Gato

En mi casa, siempre (1. haber/nosotros) sido gente de perros y no de gatos; de hecho, los gatos nos (2. caer) mal, quizá porque les (3. tener/nosotros) algo de miedo y no nos (4. respetar/ellos) como los perros. Pero un día el verano pasado todo eso (5. cambiar). (6. Estar/nosotros) sentados en la terraza tomando café cuando de repente (7. empezar/nosotros) a oír los maullidos insistentes de un gatito perdido. Los maullidos eran tan fuertes que nos (8. imaginar/nosotros) que el gatito estaría atrapado en algún lugar, haciéndose daño. Lo (9. buscar/nosotros) por todos lados, y por fin lo (10. encontrar/

nosotros), debajo de los escalones del frente de la casa. (11. Ser) un gato tan chiquitito que no (12. parecer) posible que esos maullidos salieran de él. (13. Ser) un gatito, y nos (14. tener/él) terror. (15. Estar/él) debajo de los escalones, pero (16. poder/él) salir. (17. Parecer) que su mamá lo (18. haber) abandonado y que no (19. saber) adónde ir. Nos (20. tomar) toda la mañana lograr que saliera de debajo de los escalones para tomar el platito de leche que le (21. ofrecer/nosotros). Muy lentamente se (22. acostumbrar/él) a nosotros y nos (23. adoptar/él). Desde entonces, somos gente de perros y de gatos.

Ejercicio 4. Traduzca el verbo en bastardilla, usando el verbo entre paréntesis. (*you* = **tú**)

1. Yesterday I *met* your brother. (conocer) 2. We *met* at a party. (conocer). 3. I *knew* everyone there. (conocer). 4. When you were an adolescent, *could* you go to parties? (poder) 5. The prisoner *wanted* to get out, but he *knew* it was impossible so he did not even try. (querer/saber) 6. I *wanted* to tear the curtain (and tried), but I *was unable to*. (querer/poder). 7. My sister *did not want* to go with us (refused to), in spite of our insistence. (querer) 8. My sister *did not want* to go with us, but my father made her go. (querer) 9. When did you *find out* about the accident? (saber)

USAGE (Compound Tenses)

Ejercicio. Traduzca.

1. I am writing a letter. 2. They have been working there since last week. 3. I was eating when you arrived. 4. He had been in the sun for three hours. 5. She had been calling for two days. 6. We have eaten. 7. We will have eaten by then *(para entonces)*. 8. I was working on the computer all day yesterday. 9. He said he would have finished. 10. I thought it would be raining by now.

USAGE (Ways of Expressing the Future)

Ejercicio. Traduzca en tres formas distintas.

1. Tomorrow we will eat at a restaurant. 2. This evening we are going to the movies. 3. I will call you this afternoon. 4. What are you doing tonight?

USAGE (Conditional: Courtesy)

Ejercicio. Cambie las oraciones siguientes para que sean más corteses.

1. ¿Puedes ayudarme con esto? 2. ¿Tienes tiempo para ayudarme? 3. No debes hacer eso. 4. Quiero que vengas.

USAGE (Conditional: Future of the Past)

Ejercicio. Cambie las oraciones al pasado.

1. Pienso que llegarán a tiempo. 2. Creo que lo terminarán pronto. 3. Dice que lo hará. 4. Sé que cumplirá con su promesa.

USAGE (Probability)

Ejercicio. Conteste las preguntas expresando conjetura y usando la información entre paréntesis.

1. ¿Por qué salgo mal en todas las pruebas? (no estudiar lo suficiente) 2. ¿Por qué se veía verde ese hombre? (ser marciano) (estar enfermo) (algo asustarlo) 3. ¿Dónde está tu hermano? (estar en el sótano) (ir a la tienda)

USAGE (Subjunctive: Nominal Clauses)

Ejercicio 1. Conjugue el verbo entre paréntesis en el **subjuntivo presente** o el **indicativo** según lo requiera el contexto.

1. Sus padres lo obligan a que (trabajar/él). 2. Creo que (tener/tú) razón. 3. Basta que (pagar/tú) la mitad. 4. Conviene que (salir/nosotros) temprano. 5. ¿Desea usted que le (servir/nosotros) en su habitación? 6. Mi padre se empeña en que yo no (ir) sola. 7. Es bueno que ellos (aprender) a nadar. 8. Es cierto que nosotros lo (ver). 9. Es evidente que tú (comer) demasiado temprano. 10. Es importante que yo la (llevar). 11. Es triste que ellos no (poder) salir de allí. 12. Es una lástima que tus vecinos no te (caer bien). 13. Eso no significa que tu novia no te (querer). 14. Veo que el pájaro no (poder) volar. 15. Insisto en que me (dejar/ustedes) pagar a mí. 16. Lamento que (ser) así. 17. Mi madre siempre me aconseja que (llevar/yo) más dinero del que necesito. 18. Nos encanta que nuestros amigos nos (sorprender) con sus visitas. 19. Te ruego que me (escuchar). 20. Ella siempre lo convence que se (quedar) tarde.

21. Piensan que les (deber/nosotros) dinero. 22. Más vale que ustedes se (levantar) temprano. 23. Le enoja que su hermano siempre (ganar). 24. ¿Necesitas que te (llevar/yo)? 25. El testigo niega que su hijo (ser) culpable. 26. No es que (llover) demasiado—al contrario. 27. No importa que no (querer/ellos); tienen que hacerlo. 28. Sé que me (querer/ella). 29. Los vecinos se quejan de que los niños (gritar) tanto. 30. Puede ser que ella (llegar) temprano. 31. Los adolescentes se avergüenzan de que sus padres los (controlar) en público. 32. Me opongo a que él lo (ver). 33. Estamos seguras que mañana (ir) a llover. 34. Su hermana la persuade a que (hacer/ella) lo que ella quiere. 35. Mi mamá me manda que le (llevar) sus cartas al correo. 36. Les advierto que (callarse/ustedes). 37. Me prohíben que (salir) tarde. 38. Tienen miedo que yo los (denunciar) a la policía. 39. Dice que no (saber/él) nada. 40. Tenemos que impedir que él (pagar) esta vez.

Ejercicio 2. Conjugue el verbo entre paréntesis en el **subjuntivo presente** o el **indicativo** según lo requiera el contexto.

1. Ella cree que él no la (querer). 2. Ella no cree que él la (querer). 3. Su padre le dice que él se (levantar) temprano de niño. (He used to get up early.) 4. Su padre le dice que (levantar se) temprano. (He tells her to get up early.) 5. Recomiendo que (dormir/tú) más. 6. ¿Te pide que (ir/tú) con él? 7. Espero que (poder/ellos) venir a la fiesta. 8. Me molesta que no me (hacer/tú) caso. 9. Me alegro que (ser/tú) feliz. 10. No me gusta que me (gritar/ellos). 11. Parece que (estar/él) triste. 12. No parece que (estar/él) triste. 13. Parece increíble que ellos no lo (saber). 14. Me sorprende que no me (llamar/él). 15. Sugiero que (tomar/tú) vitaminas.

Ejercicio 3. Traduzca.

1. She lets me drive.   2. I hope I can do it.   3. I hope you can do it.   4. I feel it is going to rain.   5. I am sorry it is going to rain.   6. I am sorry I cannot do it.

USAGE (Subjunctive: Adjectival Clauses)

Ejercicio. Complete con el presente del subjuntivo o algún tiempo del indicativo del verbo entre paréntesis, según lo requiera el contexto.

1. Estamos esperando a la mujer que (calcular) nuestros impuestos.   2. Quiero encontrar a una mujer que (saber) hacerlo.   3. ¿Conoces a un hombre que (poder) hacerlo?   4. Yo conozco a un hombre que (poder) hacerlo.   5. No hay nadie que (poder) hacerlo como tú.   6. Hay alguien que (poder) hacerlo.   7. Haz lo que te (decir/yo) ayer.   8. Siempre hace lo que le (decir/ellos), sea lo que sea.   9. Digan lo que (decir/ellos), nunca te abandonaré.

USAGE (Subjunctive: Adverbial Clauses)

Ejercicio 1. Conjugue el verbo entre paréntesis en el **subjuntivo presente** o el **indicativo** según lo requiera el contexto.

1. Ellos llegaron después de que nosotros (salir).   2. Lo hago para que tú no (tener) que hacerlo.   3. Ven a visitarnos tan pronto como (poder/tú).   4. Mañana iremos al parque aunque (llover).   5. Quiero hablar con ella por teléfono antes de que (irse/ella).   6. Me lo dará, a no ser que (arrepentirse/él) primero.   7. Comerá después de que los niños (acostarse).   8. Caminó hasta que no (poder) más.   9. Caminará hasta que no (poder) más.   10. Tendrá el dinero, a menos que no le (pagar/ellos) hoy.   11. Lo haremos cuando (querer/tú).   12. Comí aunque no (tener) hambre.   13. Me gusta mirar por la ventana cuando (llover).   14. Los vemos a ellos sin que ellos nos (ver) a nosotros.   15. Lo haré con tal que no se lo (decir/tú) a los vecinos.

Ejercicio 2. Traduzca. (*you* = **tú**)

1. She will not go unless we go.   2. I will do it as long as (or provided) you do not tell anyone.   3. We will leave as soon as you get dressed.   4. He will insist until she accepts.   5. I do not know anyone who can do that without your explaining how.

USAGE (Subjunctive: Sequence of Tenses)

Ejercicio 1. Combine las dos oraciones, usando la que está entre paréntesis como cláusula principal. Haga las transformaciones necesarias.

1. Mañana llegarán nuestros amigos. (No creo que…)   2. Raúl vive en Suiza. (Parece increíble que…)   3. Los vecinos ya han visto esa película. (Me sorprende que…)   4. Ayer hacía calor. (Dudo que…)   5. Se levantó a las cinco. (Me sorprende que…)   6. Ya habrán terminado a esa hora. (Parece dudoso que…)   7. Mi abuelo ya había muerto cuando llegué. (Lamento que…)   8. Pronto estará lista la cena. (Mi padre dudaba que…)   9. Siempre hace frío en el monte. (Mi tía se quejaba de que…)   10. Tú bailabas el tango a los cinco años. (Era imposible que…)   11. Los perros se escaparon. (Temían que…)   12. Luisa nunca les ha dicho el secreto a sus hijos. (A Roberto le molestaba que…)

13. Habrán regresado para la medianoche. (Me sorprendería mucho que...) 14. Miguel ya había leído esa novela. (Yo tenía miedo que...)

Ejercicio 2. Transforme el verbo de la cláusula subordinada (en bastardilla) para concordar con el nuevo contexto con el verbo principal en el pasado (entre paréntesis).

1. No creo que *puedan* venir. (No creía que...) 2. Parece posible que *haga* calor hoy. (Parecía posible que... ese día) 3. Lamento que no les *guste*. (Lamentaba que...) 4. ¿Conoces a alguien que *sea* de allí? (¿Conocías a alguien que...?) 5. Queremos encontrar una casa que *tenga* piscina. (Queríamos...) 6. Haremos lo que tú *quieras*. (Te dije que haríamos lo que...) 7. Te doy las llaves a fin de que tú *abras*. (Te di las llaves...) 8. Llama antes de que *sea* muy tarde. (Quería llamar antes de que...)

Ejercicio 3. Forme una frase usando la primera como subordinada.

1. Cantaban bien. (Me parecía increíble que...) 2. Ellos caminaron. (Dudo que...) 3. Yo había caminado. (Ellos no creyeron que...) 4. Perdí las llaves. (Ella se quejó de que yo...) 5. Por fin pudimos ver la película. (Me alegro que...) 6. Los perros no habían ladrado en toda la noche. (A él le sorprendió que...)

Ejercicio 4. Conjugue el verbo entre paréntesis en la forma correcta.

1. Nosotros queríamos que ellos nos (llamar) primero. 2. A ella le gustaría que ustedes (ser) más directos. 3. El profesor dijo que no sabía si existía un texto que (explicar) más claramente ese punto. 4. ¿Había alguien que (poder) hacerlo? 5. Nos encantaría que las vacaciones (ser) más largas. 6. Me prometiste que me llamarías tan pronto (poder). 7. Les pedía que se (callar) a fin de que no (despertar) a los niños. 8. Yo no podía creer que ella (cortarse) el pelo la semana anterior.

USAGE (Subjunctive: *Si* Clauses and *Como Si*)

Ejercicio. Conjugue el verbo entre paréntesis en la forma correcta.

1. Ella habría llegado a tiempo si no (haber) una tormenta. 2. Si él tuviera dinero, (comprarse) todos los coches antiguos del mundo. 3. Iría al supermercado si (ser) absolutamente necesario. 4. Si hubiéramos estudiado más, no (tener) tantas dificultades en el examen de ayer. 5. Si tuviera tiempo, te (ayudar/yo). 6. Se abrazaron como si no (verse) en años. 7. Lo trata como si (ser) adulto.

USAGE (Subjunctive: *Ojalá*)

Ejercicio. Traduzca usando **Ojalá.** (*you* = **tú**)

1. I wish we had not gone. 2. I wish you had listened to me. 3. I hope you eat today. 4. I wish he could see me now. 5. I hope they did not do it. 6. I hope we get there on time. 7. I hope they finished. 8. I hope she likes it. 9. I hope they bought it. 10. I wish she could hear me.

USAGE (Subjunctive: Expressions of Leave-Taking)

Ejercicio 1. Traduzca estas expresiones usando la persona indicada.

1. Get well. (*tú*)   2. Have a good weekend. (*tú*)   3. Have a good day. (*Uds.*)   4. Have fun. (*Ud.*)

Ejercicio 2. Despídase de las siguientes personas usando **irle bien a uno.**

1. de un amigo   2. de un profesor   3. de unos amigos (en Latinoamérica)   4. de unos amigos (en España)

Ejercicio 3. Despídase de las mismas personas usando **pasarlo bien.**

1. de un amigo   2. de un profesor   3. de unos amigos (en Latinoamérica)   4. de unos amigos (en España)

USAGE (Infinitive and Present Participle)

Ejercicio 1. Escoja la forma correcta entre paréntesis.

1. (Beber/Bebiendo) agua es muy saludable.   2. No les gusta (cantar/cantando).
3. Pensaban (viajar/viajando) al Caribe este invierno.   4. Se fueron sin (decir/diciendo) nada.   5. Eso es lo que te pasa por (hablar/hablando) tanto.   6. Estoy cansado de (correr/corriendo).   7. Al (salir/saliendo), no se les olvide llevarse el paraguas.   8. El anuncio decía: "No (fumar/fumando)".

Ejercicio 2. Traduzca las oraciones siguientes.

1. That language is difficult to learn.   2. It is difficult to learn that language.   3. That recipe is easy to prepare.   4. It is easy to say the truth.   5. It is possible to live more than ninety years.   6. Some things are impossible to change.

Ejercicio 3. Las frases siguientes tienen participios presentes en inglés. ¿Cuáles usarían un participio presente en español también?

1. That is one of the world's *increasing* problems.   2. What an *interesting* person!   3. She is one of the *leading* experts in that subject.   4. I need to buy some *writing* paper.   5. That psychologist says that all of the problems of adolescence are caused by *growing* pains.
6. I saw the thief *running*.   7. Take a photo of the pitcher *containing* the blue liquid.
8. The court wanted a number of items *belonging* to her.   9. There he was, *standing* in the middle of the room.   10. The movie was *boring*.   11. That is an *amusing* game.
12. I found the cat *lying* on the bed.   13. She was *sitting* in front of me at the movies.
14. This exercise is *entertaining*.   15. Do you have any *drinking* water?

Ejercicio 4. Traduzca al español las frases del Ejercicio 3.

Ejercicio 5. Las frases siguientes tienen algunos de los mismos participios presentes en inglés que las frases del Ejercicio 3. ¿Cuáles usarían un participio presente en español también? ¿Cuál es la diferencia entre los participios del #3 y las del #5? Traduzca las oraciones.

1. Look: they are *increasing* the weight.   2. They were *directing* the traffic to the side.
3. They left *running*.   4. The speaker was *boring* us all.   5. They were just *sitting* down (in the process of taking their seats) when the movie ended.   6. We were *entertaining* ourselves in the kitchen.

Ejercicio 6. Traduzca usando el infinitivo o el participio presente. (*you* = **tú**)

1. They must have eaten.   2. She has to eat more.   3. They were planning on going to the beach.   4. I do not have anything to wear.   5. Put on your coat before leaving.   6. To see those effects, it is necessary to wear special glasses.   7. He was glad to see her.   8. Upon entering, they took off their shoes.   9. My brother had the veterinarian come.   10. Those seeds are hard to plant.   11. That book is easy to read.   12. It is easy to read that book.   13. Seeing is believing.   14. He forbids me to drive.   15. The children love playing in the water. 16. He left without saying a thing.   17. They were sorry after hanging up the phone.   18. They separated without really having gotten to know each other.   19. Do not stop me from moving.   20. My back hurts from having worked so much in the garden.

USAGE (Verbs Like *Gustar*)

Ejercicio 1. Traduzca usando la expresión **caer bien.** (*you* = **tú**)

1. He likes you. 2. I like them. 3. She likes us. 4. They like her. 5. We like him. 6. You like them.

Ejercicio 2. Traduzca las oraciones siguientes, usando los pronombres necesarios para enfatizar lo que está en bastardilla. (Siga usando la expresión **caer bien.**)

1. Nobody likes you. *He* likes me.   2. Yes, but *she* does not like you.   3. *You* like *her,* but s*he* does not like *you.*

Ejercicio 3. Conteste las siguientes preguntas con **A mí** o **Yo**; luego traduzca la pregunta y la respuesta al inglés.

1. ¿A quién le interesa la magia? 2. ¿A quién le toca pagar la cuenta?   3. ¿A quién le gustó la cena? 4. ¿Quién comió más?

Ejercicio 4. Traduzca usando **caer bien, gustar, encantar** o **querer.**

1. I love him. 2. I love my classes. 3. I like your house. 4. I like my neighbors.

Ejercicio 5. Traduzca usando **faltar, hacer falta, quedar** o **sobrar.**

1. They need food. 2. They have two days left. 3. We had time to spare (left over…).
4. I miss you. 5. She is lacking twenty cents.

USAGE (Reflexive Verbs)

Ejercicio 1. Traduzca usando verbos reflexivos. (*you* = **tú**)

1. We got bored at the party. 2. Did you remember the keys? 3. She got used to him very soon. 4. I am glad to see you. 5. He was ashamed of his lie. 6. I got off the bus at the third stop. 7. The other children always made fun of me. 8. You are going to have to confront that problem some day. 9. She realized that she had to say good-bye to me. 10. We must all make an effort to keep the environment clean. 11. How did he find out about that? 12. Do not trust anyone. 13. Notice their eyes when they dance. 14. Where are we going to meet him for lunch? 15. Why did your parents move? 16. What is his name? 17. Please do not leave now. 18. You must not interfere with those children. 19. They stayed with us for the summer. 20. He fought with his father. 21. You look like me. 22. Now he is going to start barking. 23. I feel sad today. 24. I sit here. 25. I felt sad yesterday. 26. I sat here yesterday. 27. I used to feel sad when I heard that song. 28. I used to sit here. 29. He kept my book. 30. Dry yourself well.

Ejercicio 2. Llene el blanco con la preposición correcta, o con Ø si no se necesita preposición.

1. Me enamoré _____ ella hace mucho tiempo. 2. Se casó _____ él en junio. 3. Ella se reía _____ mí. 4. Se quejan _____ todo. 5. No te preocupes _____ mí. 6. Nos parecemos _____ nuestro padre. 7. Se interesa _____ las carreras de caballo. 8. No te fijes _____ los demás. 9. Él se fiaba _____ todos. 10. Nos esforzábamos _____ hablar bajo. 11. Mi madre se empeñaba _____ que limpiara el cuarto todos los días. 12. Por fin se decidieron _____ salir. 13. Se atrevió _____ dirigirse _____ él después de unos minutos. 14. El vino se convirtió _____ vinagre. 15. Él no puede deshacerse _____ nada. 16. ¿Te das cuenta _____ la hora que es? 17. Se curaron _____ los enfermos. 18. Me citaré _____ el dentista mañana. 19. Se arrepintieron _____ haber dicho eso. 20. ¡Aléjate _____ la calle!

USAGE (Indirect Discourse)

Ejercicio. Vuelva a escribir la frase original usando las segundas como nuevo principio. Haga todos los cambios necesarios.

MODELO: **Compró la casa. a. Dice que... b. Dijo que...**

   a. *Dice que compró la casa.* b. *Dijo que había comprado la casa.*

1. Iremos al cine esta noche. a. Dice que… b. Ayer dijo que… c. Esta mañana dijo que… 2. Yo sé hacerlo. a. Ella supone que… b. Ella suponía que… c. Ella supuso que… 3. Yo hice tu trabajo. a. Te digo que… b. Le dije que… c. Me dijo que… 4. Levántate. a. Te pido que… b. Me pidió que… c. Le pedí que… 5. Si pudiera ir ahora, lo haría. a. Dice que… b. Dijo que… 6. ¿Quieres que vayamos la semana entrante? a. Me preguntó esta mañana… b. Me preguntó el mes pasado… c. Sé que me preguntará… 7. Si quieres comer, come. a. Me respondió… b. Te estoy diciendo… 8. Vete. a. Te ruego… b. Me suplicó… c. Insistieron… 9. —¿Sabes qué hora es? —No. a. Siempre me pregunta… y yo siempre le contesto… b. Me preguntó… y yo le contesté… 10. —¿Les gustaría salir a cenar? —¡Sí! a. El domingo por la tarde siempre nos pregunta… y nosotros siempre le gritamos… b. Nos preguntó… y nosotros le gritamos…

Chapter 7 Ser, Estar, Haber, Hacer, and Tener

A. SER VS. ESTAR (etc.)

Ejercicio 1. ¿**Ser** o **estar**? Llene el blanco con el verbo correcto.

1. Ese hombre _____ profesor. 2. _____ importante llegar temprano. 3. Martina _____ de vacaciones. 4. _____ bien que estudien esta noche. 5. Luisa _____ de Guadalajara. 6. ¿Qué hora _____? 7. _____ la una de la tarde. 8. _____ las siete de la mañana. 9. ¿_____ claro lo que tienen que hacer? 10. Los pisos en esa casa _____ de madera. 11. Mis padres _____ de acuerdo con nosotros. 12. Esa mujer _____ de gerente esta semana, hasta que regrese la gerente oficial. 13. ¿Para cuándo _____ la próxima composición? 14. Este libro _____ de Mario. 15. La ceremonia para la graduación siempre _____ en el gimnasio. 16. Mis libros _____ en mi casillero. 17. Su hermano _____ en Princeton. 18. Nosotros _____ en Boston. 19. Tu mochila _____ en el escritorio. 20. La conferencia _____ a las nueve de la mañana. 21. Esta carta _____ para mi papá. 22. El vuelo _____ por salir. 23. Ese puente _____ construido por un arquitecto famoso. 24. Las ventanas _____ cerradas. ¿Quieres que las abra? 25. Bertita _____ aprendiendo a caminar.

Ejercicio 2. ¿**Ser** o **estar**? En las próximas frases, existe flexibilidad en cuanto al uso de **ser** o **estar,** dependiendo del punto de vista del que habla. ¿Es la norma? Entonces se usa **ser.** ¿Es una variación de la norma o una reacción? Entonces se usa **estar.** Decida usted.

1. Liza Minelli _____ delgada. 2. Los cuellos de las jirafas _____ largos. 3. El café de Colombia _____ bueno. 4. Madonna _____ atlética. 5. ¡Qué rico _____ el café esta mañana! 6. Oprah _____ más delgada que hace un año. 7. Mi coche _____ averiado. 8. Su cuarto _____ desordenado hoy —¿qué pasaría? 9. La esposa _____ harta de tener que aguantar sus engaños. 10. El presidente _____ contento con los resultados. 11. —Hola, Quique. ¿_____ bien? (tú) —No, _____ enfermo. (yo) Pero ya _____ mejor que hace una semana. (yo) 12. Esa película _____ aburrida. 13. Mi compañero de cuarto, que por lo general _____ muy platicador, ahora _____ callado. 14. Mi hija _____ más lista que sus amiguitos. 15. Ya es hora de irnos. ¿_____ listos? ¡Vámonos!

Ejercicio 3. ¿**Están** o **hay**? Llene el blanco.

1. _____ veinte estudiantes en esta clase. 2. Los estudiantes _____ sentados cerca de la ventana. 3. _____ mucho trabajo que hacer. 4. Los libros _____ en la biblioteca. 5. _____ libros en la biblioteca. 6. No _____ suficientes fondos para cubrir su cheque. 7. ¿Dónde _____ taxis? 8. Los taxis _____ a dos cuadras de aquí. 9. Ya no _____ tantos árboles como antes. 10. Las leyes que _____ no bastan para controlar el crimen.

Ejercicio 4. Traduzca estas frases usando **ser, estar, tener, haber** o **hacer.**

1. I have been on my knees too long.   2. Is it cold in winter here?   3. The children were thirsty.   4. I do not know why I am sad.   5. It is not that the party is boring, it is that the people are bored.   6. Was your contract signed by the lawyer?   7. How many rooms are there in that building?   8. Where are you from?   9. Is the conference in this building?

B.   PASSIVE VOICE AND RESULTANT CONDITION

Ejercicio.   Complete con el presente de **ser, estar, haber** o **tener.**

1. El pan _____ cortado. ¿Tú comiste?   2. Las cuentas _____ pagadas por el banco.
3. Yo ya _____ visto esa película cuatro veces.   4. Lo _____ todo preparado para los invitados.

D.   TIME EXPRESSIONS: COUNTING BACK

Ejercicio.   Traduzca estas frases de dos formas **si se puede,** usando **hacer** y **llevar.**

1. I have been here for an hour.   2. They had been working for twenty minutes when she came in.   3. We called him a week ago.   4. She had not cut her fingernails for many years.
5. My niece has been learning ballet for three years.   6. She came to visit us two months ago.   7. How long have we been waiting?

Appendix I   Lexical Variations

Traduzca las oraciones de los ejercicios siguientes.

A. TO APPLY

1. She applied for a scholarship.   2. The doctor applied pressure to the wound to stop the bleeding.   3. Apply this ointment three times a day.   4. We will apply for a loan at the bank.   5. The job you applied for no longer exists.

B. TO ASK

1. I want to ask you a favor.   2. I asked him a question.   3. She asked me to take her to town.   4. He asked me, "Are you really sixteen?"   5. We asked him if he had eaten.   6. They asked us why we had called.   7. Do not ask me so many questions.

C. TO ATTEND

1. We attended the lecture in the afternoon.   2. She did not attend class because she was ill.   3. May I assist you?   4. Tend to the guests, please.

D. TO BECOME OR TO GET

1. I am glad it's Friday.   2. The children became quiet.   3. He calmed down after that. 4. They got tired of walking.   5. I got sick during the vacation.   6. They got mad because I did not write.   7. You get old fast in this job.   8. The horse calmed down after the shot (*inyección*).   9. I noticed she had become pale.   10. He became a doctor.   11. She wanted to become a respected citizen.   12. The flower had become a fruit.

E. TO GO AND TO LEAVE

1. We are going to school.   2. She left an hour ago.   3. The cat went outside.   4. They are going out tonight.   5. The nurse went out to lunch.   6. We were playing out in the park, and Luisito got mad and left.   7. At what time does your flight leave?   8. Could you leave me at the corner, please?   9. You will not let me do anything.   10. They stopped screaming.

F. TO KNOW

1. I know you.   2. He met his new wife in Mexico.   3. He does not know the area.   4. He knows my phone number.   5. They know how to skate.   6. We knew it was cold.   7. They did not know what to say.   8. Do you know what time it is?   9. Do you know that hotel? 10. He did not know how to swim.

G. TO LEARN

1. She learned to dance.   2. They found out about our secret.   3. When I found out that you were here, I came immediately.

H. TO MEET

1. She met her in the office. (first acquaintance)   2. Then they decided to meet in the afternoon to discuss the job.   3. Guess who I met on my way to the library.

I.   TO PLAY

1. They played tennis all afternoon.   2. What are you playing?   3. Do you play the guitar?
4. Don't play with your sister's violin.   5. She will be playing the violin tonight.

J.   TO PUT

1. She put her hand on my shoulder.   2. I put on my boots.   3. He put his hand in his jacket.   4. Help me set the table, please.   5. His face became green.   6. Do not put your finger in your brother's eye.

K. TO SERVE

1. Do not serve me so much rice, please.   2. How can I help you?   3. Dinner is usually served at eight. Tonight we will serve it at seven thirty.

L. TO SPEND

1. You spend more money on your children than you do on yourself.   2. I spent three hours on this paper yesterday.   3. She spent some time in jail.   4. It is terrible to waste time and money.

M. TO TAKE

1. What would you like to drink?   2. He took his beer to the table.   3. She took the pencil and left.   4. Can we take you? No, thanks, I will take the bus.   5. This is taking too long.
6. Here. This is yours.   7. We took the camera to the store.   8. They took away our towels.
9. Let me take this down. (write)   10. Do you want me to take your books down?   11. They took the food up to the room.   12. We have to take the garbage out.   13. Do not take off your socks.   4. The exam will take place here.   15. Can I bring a friend to your party?
16. BYOB.

N. TO REALIZE

1. I realize that I cannot realize your dreams in an instant.   2. If you carry out all your duties with responsibility, you can stay.   3. She realized that he was unhappy.   4. He realized his dreams were impossible.

O. TO THINK

1. I cannot stop thinking of you.   2. What were you thinking of?   3. What do you think of me?   4. She refused to tell me what she thought of the workshop.   5. We are planning on visiting our friends next week.

P. PEOPLE VS. MACHINES

1. The children were running.   2. That motor stopped running.   3. They work from nine to five.   4. It does not work like that.   5. When did the movie start?   6. I am going to start the car so it will get warm.   7. The lights went out after ten.   8. He works out every day. 9. We can work it out.   10. I ran out.   11. He ran across his cousin at the museum. 12. The batteries ran down.   13. My watch ran down.   14. He ran down the stairs. 15. They ran into their friends at the bar.   16. He ran into the wall.   17. Turn out the lights. 18. Everything turned out okay.

Q. *ACABAR* PHRASES

1. I finished my work.   2. They finished repairing the bridge in October.   3. He will be finished with the construction by three this afternoon.   4. I just got up.   5. When I got there, they had just eaten.   6. The exam ended at ten.   7. We finished the bread.   8. We ran out of bread.

R. *DESPEDIR* PHRASES

1. They fired me yesterday.   2. I said goodbye to my friends.   3. I fired him.   4. I said goodbye to her.   5. We said goodbye at the door.

S. TO COME AND TO GO

1. When are your parents coming to see us?   2. He went to the movies.   3. I am going to the movies.   4. Can I come with you?   5. Come here, Juanita! I'm coming!   6. They are always late.   7. Do not be late.   8. I am sorry I am late.   9. When did you get here?

T. AT

1. Los niños se quedaron _____ casa.   2. Ellos están _____ Nueva York.   3. La clase es _____ las diez, _____ el edificio de Morrill.   4. Me siento mejor _____ este momento.

5. No sé qué decir _____ veces.   6. Me parece que oí pasos. Creo que hay alguien _____ la puerta.   7. Hay alguien _____ la puerta preguntando por ti.   8. Le gusta tener a su amiga _____ su lado.

U. BECAUSE

1. I went home because of my brother.   2. They had to cancel the trial because of the news.   3. They had to let him leave because of that.   4. She lost her voice because she screamed so much.   5. They did not go out because it was snowing.

V. BUT

1. Estudié el idioma, _____ no me atrevo a hablar.   2. Ese hombre no es mi tío, _____ mi cuñado.   3. No fueron a Puerto Rico, _____ a México.   4. Esta clase es interesante, _____ difícil.   5. No lo compró, _____ se lo regaló su hermana.   6. No hablo el idioma, _____ voy a viajar al país.

W. EXIT VS. SUCCESS

1. If we work hard, we shall be successful.   2. Our success depends on our effort.   3. The exit is to the right.   4. My grandmother liked to go over the events of the day after dinner.

X. GUIDE

1. Our guide at the museum was an old man.   2. The tour guide was from Venezuela.
3. You will find the rules in the guide book.

Y. ORDER

1. Everything had to be placed in a specific order.   2. I did it because I received the order from above.   3. Hello, my name is Julia Ruiz. Hello, Victoria Vargas, at your service.

Z. TIME

1. Do you have time to talk to me?   2. What was the weather like?   3. How many times do I have to tell you?   4. That time it was different.   5. He would not tell me what time it was. 6. I knew it was time to get up.   7. She will be here in a little while.   8. We had a good time. 9. We had good weather.

AA. WHAT

1. What is "cucurucho"?   2. Which one is yours?   3. What countries did you visit?
4. Excuse me? (*polite* "What?")   5. What you do not know will not hurt you.

A
P
P
E
N
D
I
X
2

Answer Key

Chapter 1 Overview

A. SENTENCE COMPONENTS

Ejercicio I.

1. **de**: preposición; **en**: preposición; **se**: pronombre personal reflexivo 2. **cuando**: conjunción; **clásica**: adjetivo calificativo 3. **ayer**: adverbio de tiempo; **a**: preposición; **amigos**: sustantivo o nombre 4. **mi**: adjetivo posesivo; **por**: preposición; **las**: artículo definido 5. **este**: adjetivo demostrativo; **ése**: pronombre demostrativo 6. **tus**: adjetivo posesivo; **los míos**: pronombre posesivo 7. **algunos**: adjetivo indefinido; **otros**: pronombre indefinido 8. **que**: pronombre relativo; **mucho**: adjetivo cuantitativo 9. **que**: conjunción de subordinación; **un**: artículo indefinido 10. **y**: conjunción de coordinación; **pero**: conjunción de coordinación

Ejercicio 2.

1. **Los**: art. def., masc. pl., acompaña el sustantivo "niños"; **niños**: sustantivo común, masc. pl., sujeto del verbo "cantaron"; **cantaron**: verbo "cantar", 3ª pers. plural del pretérito del indicativo; **una**: art. indef., fem. sing., acompaña el sustantivo "canción"; **canción**: sustantivo común, fem. sing., objeto directo de "cantaron" 2. **Marta**: sustantivo propio, sujeto del verbo "regaló"; **me**: pronombre personal, 1ª pers. sing., objeto indirecto del verbo "regaló"; **regaló**: verbo "regalar", 3ª pers. sing. del pretérito del indicativo; **este**: adjetivo demostrativo, masc. sing., modifica el sustantivo "libro"; **libro**: sustantivo común, masc. sing., objeto directo de "regaló" 3. **Estos**: adjetivo demostrativo, masc. pl., modifica el sustantivo "ejercicios"; **ejercicios**: sustantivo común, masc. pl., sujeto del verbo "son"; **son**: verbo "ser", 3ª pers. pl. del presente del indicativo; **fáciles**: adjetivo calificativo, masc. pl., modifica el sustantivo "ejercicios"

B. VERB STRUCTURE

Ejercicio.

estábamos: INDICATIVO imperfecto; **preparando**: PARTICIPIO presente; **anunció**: INDICATIVO pretérito; **había ganado**: INDICATIVO pluscuamperfecto; **pensara**: SUBJUNTIVO imperfecto; **hacer**: INFINITIVO presente; **gastaría**: CONDICIONAL presente; **preocupes**: IMPERATIVO; **daré**: INDICATIVO futuro; **pongan**: SUBJUNTIVO presente; **necesito**: INDICATIVO presente

C. SENTENCE STRUCTURE

Ejercicio I.

Para las vacaciones de Navidad, mi papá, mi hermana y yo íbamos a San Blas, y nos quedábamos en un hotel en la playa. La noche de Navidad, cuando todos los demás estaban celebrando en el hotel, nosotros nos íbamos a un lugar ya seleccionado en la playa oscura y hacíamos un fuego con leña que habíamos recogido el día anterior. Llevábamos comida para cocinar en el fuego, y pasábamos la noche allí, oyendo las olas del mar y mirando las estrellas.

Ejercicio 2.

Necesito/que me ayudes a preparar la cena. (2)   Tendremos cinco invitados a cenar/y quiero/que todo esté perfecto. (3)   ¿Podrías poner la mesa, por favor? (1)   Y cuando acabes con eso,/ven a la cocina para ayudarme con la comida. (2)   Las verduras para la ensalada están lavadas;/sólo hay que cortarlas y ponerlas en la ensaladera. (2)   Quiero prepararles la receta de pollo/que les gustó tanto la última vez/que vinieron. (3)

Ejercicio 3.

El invierno está casi terminado. Ya no hace frío, y la nieve se ha transformado en lluvia. Pronto tendremos que empezar a preparar el jardín para que podamos plantar las hortalizas. Estoy tan contento que la primavera esté en camino porque me gusta el calor. El invierno aquí es tan triste y gris, y me canso de la ropa pesada que tengo que ponerme.

Ejercicio 4.

El invierno está casi terminado. Ya no hace frío, y la nieve se ha transformado en lluvia. Pronto tendremos que empezar a preparar el jardín para que podamos plantar las hortalizas. Estoy tan contento que la primavera esté en camino porque me gusta el calor. El invierno aquí es tan triste y gris, y me canso de la ropa pesada que tengo que ponerme.

Ejercicio 5.

El invierno está casi terminado. Ya no hace frío, y la nieve se ha transformado en lluvia. Pronto tendremos que empezar a preparar el jardín para que podamos plantar las hortalizas. Estoy tan contento que la primavera esté en camino porque me gusta el calor. El invierno aquí es tan triste y gris, y me canso de la ropa pesada que tengo que ponerme.

Ejercicio 6.

1. **Necesito un libro:** cláusula principal; **que describa la revolución mexicana:** cláusula subordinada adjetival, modifica el sustantivo "libro"   2. **Te prestaré dinero:** cláusula principal; **a condición de que me pagues mañana:** cláusula subordinada adverbial, modifica el verbo "prestaré"   3. **Sé:** cláusula principal; **que no puedes hablar ahora:** cláusula subordinada nominal, objeto directo del verbo "sé"

Ejercicio 7.

Diagramas:

1. Quiero que veas el libro que conseguí sobre la revolución mexicana.

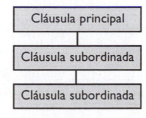

2. Es necesario que los norteamericanos comprendan que estas tierras les pertenecían a los mexicanos originalmente, y que antes eran de los indios que vivieron en ellas por siglos.

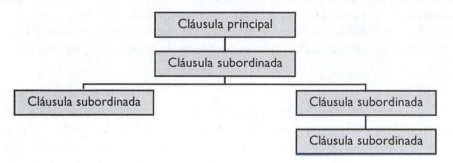

3. Me pidió que le comprara pan y le contesté que no tenía dinero.

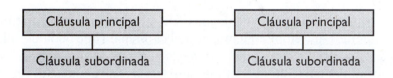

D. ACCENTS (Syllabification: Consonants)

Ejercicio 1.

ra/za	me/ta	vi/sa
ca/llo	fe/cha	ce/rro
ca/ba/llo	me/ti/che	se/rra/no

Ejercicio 2.

cam/po	pan/te/ra	án/gu/lo
mus/go	fan/to/che	man/ti/lla
mer/ca/do	sin/ce/ro	cen/ce/rro
vi/bra	ha/blo	au/to/gra/fiar
re/tra/to	a/dre/na/li/na	re/flo/re/cer
a/glo/me/rar	ne/gro	a/plas/tar
re/pri/mir	de/cli/ve	re/fres/co

Ejercicio 3.

an/glo/sa/jón	em/pre/sa/rio	cons/tan/te
es/tre/cho	es/plén/di/do	ins/ti/tu/to
ins/pec/ción	ins/tru/men/to	em/bro/llo
trans/mi/tir	res/plan/dor	trans/cri/bir

ACCENTS (Syllabification: Vowels)

Ejercicio 1.

re/ca/er	cre/ar	cre/er
ve/o	se/a	ca/os
bo/a	co/ac/tar	co/e/xis/tir
gen/tí/o	frí/o	re/í
ves/tí/a	e/tí/o/pe	a/ta/úd
ra/íz	ví/a	mí/o
re/ú/nan	con/ti/nú/a	re/hú/sa

Ejercicio 2.

a/via/dor	ai/re	bie/nes/tar
de/lei/te	mio/pe	oi/ga
res/guar/do	cau/sa	fue/ron
en/deu/dar/se	fui/mos	diur/no
duo/de/no	/Dios/	hue/so
ca/riá/ti/de	re/cién	co/mió
a/guán/ta/te	a/cuér/den/se	can/táis
vol/véis	ói/gan/los	en/jáu/la/lo

Ejercicio 3.

ve/í/an	se/áis	ca/í/a/mos
es/quiáis	vi/ví/ais	tra/í/an
ca/e/rí/ais	o/í/ais	en/viéis
cre/í/as	ac/tuéis	ad/qui/rie/rais

Ejercicio 4.

a/ho/ra	re/ha/go	a/hí
re/hí/ce	pro/hí/ben	re/hú/sa
a/ho/gar	de/sa/ho/gar	ahu/ma/do
ca/ca/hua/te	al/ca/hue/te	co/he/te
re/hú/yen	so/brehu/ma/no	za/he/rir

Ejercicio 5.

di/vi/da	/las/	si/guien/tes
pa/la/bras	/en/	sí/la/bas
lue/go	ve/a	cuan/do
ne/ce/si/tan	a/cen/tos	por/que
/rey/	rei/na	/voy/
boi/na	bue/no	/bien/

ACCENTS (Stress)

Ejercicio 1.

1. camino (llana) 2. caminó (aguda) 3. caminaba (llana) 4. caminábamos (esdrújula)
5. caminad (aguda) 6. compra (llana) 7. compró (aguda) 8. compraba (llana)
9. comprábamos (esdrújula) 10. cómpralo (esdrújula) 11. cómpramelo (sobresdrújula)
12. español (aguda) 13. españoles (llana) 14. francés (aguda) 15. trances (llana)
16. encéstalo (esdrújula)

Ejercicio 2.

1. prestó 2. enterrar 3. preparad 4. desperté 5. dividir 6. farol 7. piedad 8. pedí
9. peor 10. caimán 11. cocinar 12. imparcial 13. cajón 14. finlandés 15. trajín
16. temblor 17. cristal 18. riñón

Ejercicio 3.

1. lápiz 2. llamas 3. llaman 4. pluma 5. hablaron 6. españoles 7. dioses 8. día 9. deme
10. españolita 11. peruano 12. consigo 13. traje 14. examen 15. carácter 16. lunes
17. labio 18. infértil

Ejercicio 4.

1. mátalo 2. regálamelo 3. cállense 4. estúpido 5. párpado 6. capítulo 7. prójimo
8. bájame 9. ánimo 10. cáscara 11. década 12. éxito 13. pájaro 14. áspero
15. húngaro 16. vínculo 17. máquina 18. píldora

Ejercicio 5.

1. rápidamente 2. fácilmente 3. lentamente 4. difícilmente 5. piadosamente
6. brillantemente 7. fríamente 8. despiadadamente 9. secamente 10. felizmente
11. fijamente 12. cálidamente 13. científicamente 14. misericordiosamente
15. solamente *(Notice that the adverb* solamente *is formed with the adjective* sola, *which has no accent. There is another adverb,* sólo *[only], synonymous with* solamente, *and not to be confused with the adjective* solo *[alone].)* 16. finalmente 17. gravemente
18. próximamente

Ejercicio 6.

1. A él le va bien. 2. Di que el rey te lo dio. 3. Vio a Dios. 4. El té no me da tos. 5. No sé si se fue. 6. Tú no le des. 7. Tu voz se te va. 8. Sin ti no se lo da. 9. No le dé la fe. 10. Yo sí se la di. 11. A ti te doy lo que hay. 12. No hay más miel por mí.

Ejercicio 7.

1. Aun los ricos necesitan amor. 2. Los niños aún no han comido. 3. Estoy solo. 4. Sólo me siento solo cuando ando mal acompañado. 5. Pásame esa llave, por favor. 6. No quiero esta fruta, prefiero ésa. 7. Por eso no quiso ir con nosotros. 8. Me gustaría comprarme ese terreno. 9. ¡Qué buena suerte tienes! 10. ¡Cómo canta!

Ejercicio 8.

1. Prefiero **que** no llueva. 2. ¿**Qué** dijiste? 3. No sé **qué** dije. 4. Creo **que** dije **que** preferiría **que** no lloviera. 5. ¡**Qué** locura! 6. [2 posibilidades] Dime **qué** crees. (Tell me what you believe.) Dime **que** crees. (Tell me that you believe.) 7. El día **que** no llueva aquí, no sabremos **qué** hacer. 8. Haremos lo **que** ustedes quieran. 9. La última vez **que** vinieron, nos costó mucho decidir **qué** cuarto darles. 10. ¡**Que** duerman en el piso!

Ejercicio 9.

1. Te llamé **porque** tengo noticias. 2. ¿**Por qué** no me llamaste antes? 3. No te puedo decir **por qué**: ¡es un secreto! 4. El asesino no pudo explicar **por qué** había matado al policía. *(The murderer was not able to explain **why** he had killed the policeman.)* 5. El asesino no lo pudo explicar **porque** había matado al policía. *(The murderer was not able to explain it **because** he had killed the policeman.)* 6. Yo creo que lo hizo **porque** tenía miedo. 7. ¿Tú matarías a alguien simplemente **porque** tienes miedo? 8. ¿**Por qué** no? 9. ¡**Porque** no se debe matar a nadie! 10. No sé **por qué** se fue. 11. Se fue **porque** no le hacías caso.

Ejercicio 10.

1. **Como** no tengo hambre, no **como**. 2. ¿**Cómo** puedes decir eso? 3. Necesitas pensar **como** yo para comprenderme. 4. Dime **cómo** comes. *(Tell me how you eat.)* 5. ¡**Cómo** comes! *(How you eat! Boy, do you ever eat!)* 6. ¿**Cómo** como? *(How do I eat?)* 7. **Como** como **como**. *(I eat the way I eat.)* 8. Ella se viste **como** yo. 9. Es un libro **como** los demás. 10. Si baila **como** canta, ha de ser una maravilla.

Ejercicio 11.

1. ¿**Cuánto** cuesta este cuarto? 2. No sé **cuánto** cuesta. 3. ¿**Cuántos** hermanos tienes? 4. Me pregunto **cuántos** años tiene esa mujer. 5. Nadie sabe **cuántas** veces se repetirá. 6. Le di **cuanto** dinero tenía al ladrón. 7. No sabe **cuánto** me arrepentí de darle mi dinero. 8. La profesora le dará **cuanta** información tenga.

Ejercicio 12.

1. ¿**Dónde** vives? 2. Vivo **donde** viven mis padres. 3. No sé **dónde** vive mi amiga. 4. Me dijo **dónde** vivía, pero se me olvidó. 5. Apunté su dirección en la libreta **donde** tengo todas las direcciones. 6. Ya no sé **dónde** puse la libreta. 7. ¿No estará **donde** siempre la pones?

Ejercicio 13.

1. Llegarán **cuando** estemos en la finca. 2. ¿**Cuándo** llegas? 3. No me dijo **cuándo** iban a llegar. 4. **Cuando** lleguen, les serviremos cerveza. 5. ¿Nos escondemos **cuando** los veamos llegar? 6. **Cuando** me gradúe, iré al Caribe. 7. ¿**... cuando** te gradúes? *(... when you graduate?)* 8. ¿**Cuándo** te gradúas? *(When do you graduate?)*

Ejercicio 14.

1. ¿**Quién** se llevó mi paraguas?   2. No sé **quién** se lo llevó.   3. El amigo con **quien** vino Marieta tenía paraguas.   4. ¿Te dijo **quién** era el chico con **quien** estaba?   5. No me dijo con **quién** había venido.   6. Dime con **quién** andas y te diré **quién** eres.

Ejercicio 15.

ARMANDO: ¿Está Juan?

MIGUEL: Creo que fue al cine, y no sé cuándo va a regresar. ¿Para qué lo quieres?

ARMANDO: Quiero pedirle prestado un libro para mi clase de español.

MIGUEL: ¿Sabes qué libro es?

ARMANDO: Sí. Es uno que tiene la portada negra.

MIGUEL: Yo sé dónde lo tiene, pero no estoy seguro si te lo podría prestar.

ARMANDO: A mí me dijo que no lo necesitaba este semestre.

MIGUEL: Si tú te lo llevas, y él lo necesita, yo voy a sentirme muy mal. ¿Por qué no te tomas una taza de té, y esperas a que regrese Juan?

ARMANDO: Bueno. Mientras espero, préstame el libro para mirarlo, por favor.

MIGUEL: Voy a buscarlo. [...] ¿Es éste, verdad?

ARMANDO: No, ése no. Es el otro, el de gramática. Tiene casi la misma portada, pero un título diferente.

MIGUEL: A ver si lo encuentro; espérame. [...] Aquí lo tienes.

ARMANDO: Gracias.

Chapter 2   Nouns and Noun Determiners

A. NOUNS AND THEIR EQUIVALENTS (Introduction)

Ejercicio.

A noun is a part of a sentence (a word) which can be the subject of a verb. It can also be a direct or an indirect object, or an object of a preposition. Other words which behave this way are pronouns, infinitives, and any nominalized word. A nominalized word is one which is used as if it were a noun. For example, "red" is an adjective, but in the sentence "The red of those flowers was astonishing," "red" is being used as a noun. In other words, it has been converted from an adjective to a noun, or "nominalized."

NOUNS AND THEIR EQUIVALENTS (Nouns: Gender and Number)

Ejercicio 1.

el amanecer	**el** amor	**el** arroz	**el** ataúd
el auto	**el** barandal	**el** barro	**la** cama
la capital	**el** carril	**la** casa	**la** catedral
la cárcel	**el** césped	**el** clima	**la** costumbre
el crucigrama	**el** día	**el** drama	**el** español
la foto	**el** huésped	**el** idioma	**el** juez
el lápiz	**la** libertad	**el** lunes	**la** luz
el mal	**la** mano	**el** mapa	**el** metal
la miel	**la** moral	**la** moto	**el** pez
la piel	**los** Pirineos	**el** poder	**el** poema
el problema	**el** programa	**el** radar	**la** rama
la sal	**el** sapo	**la** señal	**el** sistema
la trama	**el** tranvía	**la** vaca	**el** zorro

Ejercicio 2.

el hombre—la mujer; el estudiante—la estudiante; el joven—la joven; el actor—la actriz; el modelo—la modelo; el turista—la turista; el rey—la reina; el policía—la policía, el comunista—la comunista; el toro—la vaca

Ejercicio 3.

el policía/la policía: el masculino es el hombre o el individuo; el femenino es el departamento, o una mujer; **el guía/la guía:** el masculino es el hombre que lleva a los turistas de un lugar a otro y les habla de lo que ven; el femenino es un libro con información, o una mujer que hace el papel de dirigir e instruir a los turistas; **el papa/la papa:** el masculino es el de Roma; el femenino es lo que se come; **el cura/la cura:** el masculino es el de la iglesia; el femenino es la solución a una enfermedad

NOUNS AND THEIR EQUIVALENTS (Personal *A*)

Ejercicio.

1. [Ø] 2. a 3. a 4. A 5. [Ø] 6. [Ø] 7. [Ø] 8. a 9. [Ø] 10. a 11. a 12. a 13. a 14. [Ø]

NOUN DETERMINERS (Articles: Definite Articles)

Ejercicio 1.

la avioneta, la atracción, la avenida, el agua, la alarma, el alma, el ama, el águila, la aguja, la autonomía, el aula, la avicultura, el ave, la habitación, la habichuela, el hacha, la hamburguesa, el hambre, la hartanza, las aguas, las alarmas, las almas, las hambres.

Ejercicio 2.

1. **La** vida debe disfrutarse. 2. **El** señor Ruiz dice que el chocolate es malo para **la** salud, pero [Ø] doña Luisa sabe que él come [Ø] chocolate todos los días. 3. "[Ø] Señorita Guzmán, ¿le gusta **el** chocolate?" 4. Ayer compramos [Ø] verduras, pero no tenían **las** verduras que tú pediste. 5. El inglés es más difícil que **el** español. 6. Hablo [Ø] español, pero sueño en [Ø] inglés. 7. Mi clase de [Ø] español es la más divertida de todas. 8. Aprendí [Ø]/**el** español cuando tenía seis años. 9. A mi padre le costó trabajo aprender **el** español. 10. Salieron temprano de **la** escuela y, como su padre había salido de **la** cárcel ese día, fueron a **la** iglesia a dar gracias. 11. Salimos de [Ø] clase y fuimos directamente a [Ø] casa porque teníamos que vestirnos para llegar a [Ø] misa a tiempo. 12. El miércoles vamos a tener una prueba. 13. ¡Hasta **el** jueves! 14. Hoy es [Ø] viernes.

NOUN DETERMINERS (Articles: Indefinite Articles)

Ejercicio.

1. Jorge es [Ø] arquitecto. 2. Carlitos es [Ø] argentino. 3. Rafael es **un** hombre interesante. 4. Es **un** cantante mexicano. 5. Georgina es **una** protestante muy severa. 6. ¡Qué [Ø] dilema! 7. ¡Qué [Ø] lindo día! 8. Esa viejita acaba de cumplir [Ø] cien años. 9. Vamos a discutir [Ø] otro tema ahora. 10. Tomaría [Ø] mil años corregir el daño que se ha hecho. Lo dudo—yo creo que tomaría **un** millón. 11. Dentro de [Ø] media hora nos iremos. 12. No tengo [Ø] bicicleta. 13. Ese pobre chico no tiene ni **un** amigo. 14. Se fue sin [Ø] chaqueta.

NOUN DETERMINERS (Adjectives: Demonstrative Adjectives)

Ejercicio.

1. ¿Son nuevos esos libros? 2. Estas manzanas son para ti. 3. Esa clase no cubre estos tópicos. 4. Estos estudiantes son buenísimos. 5. Ese hombre es un amigo. 6. Aquellos días son inolvidables.

NOUN DETERMINERS (Adjectives: Possessive Adjectives)

Ejercicio.

1. Hoy vienen mis primos.   2. ¿Llamó tu hermano hoy?   3. Su brazo está hinchado.   4. Sus libros están mojados.   5. Me dio su anillo.   6. Es una amiga mía.   7. Esta pluma es mía.

NOUN DETERMINERS (Adjectives: Forms of Descriptive Adjectives)

Ejercicio.

1. la casa verde   2. la casa blanca   3. la casa azul   4. el político respetable   5. el político izquierdista   6. el político prometedor   7. la profesora severa   8. la maestra comunista   9. los niños felices   10. los vecinos gritones

NOUN DETERMINERS (Adjectives: Position of Descriptive Adjectives)

Ejercicio.

1. Ese hombre vende muebles **antiguos.** *(old, not previous)*   2. La gente **pobre** no siempre es infeliz. *(penniless, not unfortunate—the context says so)*   3. A esa **pobre** millonaria la persiguen los periodistas. *(unfortunate; she could not be penniless by definition)*   4. Te presento a Guzmán, un **viejo** amigo; hoy es su cumpleaños—cumple dieciocho años. *(long-time friend; he couldn't be old at 18)*   5. Desde que construyeron el **nuevo** garaje/garaje **nuevo,** ya no usan el viejo. *(before the noun: recent, latest; after the noun, just constructed. In this sentence, either one could be accurate.)*   6. Te presento a mi **nuevo** vecino. *(newest, latest, not newborn)*   7. Mi **linda** esposa está de viaje. *(only one wife: no contrast)*   8. Cornell es una **gran** universidad/universidad **grande.** *(before: great; after: large)*   9. Charlie Chaplin fue un **gran** actor. *(great, not large)*   10. En esta tina, el agua **caliente** se abre aquí. *(contrast with the cold water)*   11. Subimos a la **alta** torre/torre **alta** de la biblioteca. *(before: there is only one tower, and it is high—no contrast. after: there is more than one, and one of them is higher than the rest—contrast)*   12. Está enamorado de tu **bella** hermana/hermana **bella.** *(before: there is only one sister, and she is beautiful—no contrast; after: there are other sisters, but only one beautiful one—contrast)*   13. Cruzaron el **ancho** río de las Amazonas. *(there is only one, and it is wide—no contrast)*   14. Visitaron la **impresionante** catedral de Gaudí. *(only one—no contrast)*   15. Ésta es la **única** oportunidad que tendremos. *(only, not unique)*   16. Me gustan las casas **blancas.** *(contrast with the rest, restrictive)*   17. Las **blancas** nubes flotaban como algodón por el valle. *(no contrast; merely painting an inherent characteristic)*   18. Era un cielo extraño: abajo había nubes **blancas,** y arriba nubes **negras.** *(contrast)*   19. Esa película es de un director **español.** *(nationality always follows its noun)*   20. Se le veía un **cierto** aire de inseguridad. *(indeterminate)*   21. Sabían que eran unas acusaciones **ciertas.** *(true)*   22. Tenía la rara capacidad de hacer que todos se sintieran a gusto. *(rare)*   23. Era un sonido **raro** que nadie podía identificar. *(strange)*   24. Te voy a decir la **pura** verdad. *(fixed order)*   25. Es un disco de **alta** fidelidad. *(fixed order)*   26. Querían estar en Sevilla para la Semana **Santa.** *(fixed order)*   27. La mejor solución es usar nuestro sentido **común.** *(fixed order)*

NOUN DETERMINERS (Comparisons)

Ejercicio.

1. Beto come más ruidosamente **que** nadie.   2. Sabina es más lista **que** Raúl.   3. Elsa gana menos dinero **que** tú.   4. Hay más **de** veinte árboles aquí.   5. Me diste menos **de** la mitad. 6. Mi bicicleta es mejor **que** la tuya.   7. Hace más frío **de lo que** esperaba.   8. Llovió menos **de lo que** creíamos.   9. Nunca ganaré tanto dinero **como** Héctor.   10. Ese coche es **tan** bello como éste.   11. Esa niña grita más **que** las demás.   12. Había menos **de** cinco jugadores en la cancha.   13. Ese examen no fue tan fácil **como** los otros.   14. Compré más servilletas **de las que** necesitábamos.   15. Hay más servilletas **que** invitados. 16. Tengo menos trabajo **del que** esperaba.   17. Elvira trabaja **tanto** como su hermano, pero no gana **tanto** dinero como él. Y a mí me parece que él no es **tan** listo como ella.

Chapter 3 Pronouns

A. PERSONAL PRONOUNS (Introduction)

Ejercicio.

A pronoun is a word which replaces a noun and has the same function as a noun (subject, direct object, object of preposition, indirect object). Its relationship to the noun is that it replaces it, usually to avoid repetition. There are different pronouns: personal, demonstrative, possessive, interrogative, indefinite, negative, and relative.

PERSONAL PRONOUNS (Subject Pronouns)

Ejercicio 1.

1. —¿Cuándo salieron? —Salimos a las siete. 2. —¿Quién está ahí? —Soy yo. 3. —¿Qué hacen? —Están comiendo. 4. Mis vecinos sacaron la basura, pero yo no me acordé. 5. ¿Tendría Ud. tiempo de ayudarme? 6. —¿Por qué no está Luis? —Está enfermo.

Ejercicio 2.

1. Compré un libro. 2. Está en el cuarto de José. 3. Vamos a estudiar juntos esta tarde. 4. Tienes que empezar tus tareas para mañana. 5. Son largas. 6. Sé que tú estudiaste, pero yo no he terminado todavía. 7. María está aquí; quiere hablar contigo.

PERSONAL PRONOUNS (Direct Object Pronouns)

Ejercicio 1.

1. Tráiganla. 2. Quiero guardarla. La quiero guardar. 3. La he guardado. 4. Están cocinándola. La están cocinando. 5. La compramos. 6. No la toques.

Ejercicio 2.

1. La veo de esta ventana. 2. Las llevé al banco. 3. No la conocen. 4. Josefina es un poco extraña; nadie la entiende. 5. Los vecinos la miraban mientras barría la calle. 6. El vendedor la llamó. 7. La oían cantar. 8. La oían cantarla. 9. La buscaron. 10. La encontraron. 11. La invitaron al baile. 12. La extraño.

Ejercicio 3.*

1. Lo veo de esta ventana. 2. Los llevé al banco. 3. No lo conocen. 4. Roberto es un poco extraño; nadie lo entiende. 5. Los vecinos lo miraban mientras barría la calle. 6. El vendedor lo llamó. 7. Lo oían cantar. 8. Lo oían cantarla. 9. Lo buscaron. 10. Lo encontraron. 11. Lo invitaron al baile. 12. Lo extraño.

*Este ejercicio puede hacerse de dos formas: en la versión española, todos los pronombres **lo** serían **le**; ésta es la versión hispanoamericana.

PERSONAL PRONOUNS (Direct and Indirect Object Pronouns)

Ejercicio 1.

1. Los turistas **los** miraban. 2. El policía **le** dijo que se tenía que ir. 3. **Se los** regaló. 4. **Se lo** mandaron. 5. El abuelo **se lo** contó. 6. **Se la** hicieron. 7. El padre **se la** quitó. 8. Mi amigo **se lo** pidió.

Ejercicio 2.

1. **Le** gané. 2. **Lo** gané. 3. **Le** robaron. 4. **Lo** robaron. 5. **Le** creemos. 6. **Lo** creemos. 7. pegaron. 8. **Lo** pegaron. 9. **Le** pagué. 10. **La** pagué.

PERSONAL PRONOUNS (Required Repetitive Object Pronouns)

Ejercicio.

1. Ayer compré el pan. 2. El pan **lo** compré ayer. 3. Esta tarde vi a Juan en la tienda. 4. A Juan **lo** vi en la tienda esta tarde. 5. El correo llegó hace media hora. 6. Hace media hora que llegó el correo. 7. Marta bañó al niño. 8. Al niño Marta **lo** bañó. 9. Toda la gente vio el globo. 10. Anoche **los** terminé todos. 11. Mañana **le** enviaremos el regalo a Marieta. 12. No **le** digas a Juan el secreto. 13. Nunca **se lo** cuentes todo a tus amigos. 14. Ese día **nos** regañaron a todos nosotros. 15. Con esa lluvia crecerán todas las plantas.

PERSONAL PRONOUNS (Order of Pronouns When Combined)

Ejercicio 1.

1. Sí, **me los** dio. 2. Sí, **se la** enseñé. 3. Sí, **me la** contó. 4. Sí, **se lo** dije. 5. Sí, **nos las** limpiamos. 6. Sí, **nos la** enviaron.

Ejercicio 2.

1. Sí, la están preparando. OR: Sí, están preparándola. 2. Sí, se la pudieron vender. OR: Sí, pudieron vendérsela. 3. Sí, se los va a hacer. OR: Sí, va a hacérselos. 4. Sí, se lo he mandado. 5. Sí, está pintada. OR: Sí, lo está. 6. Sí, me gustó. 7. Sí, se las dio. 8. Sí, se habla.

PERSONAL PRONOUNS (Prepositional Object Pronouns)

Ejercicio.

1. Esto es para ti. 2. Según ella, estaba mal. 3. Lo estaban mirando. OR: Estaban mirándolo. 4. Lo estaban buscando. OR: Estaban buscándolo. 5. Esto es entre él y yo. 6. Sus hijos son como ella. 7. Estoy hablando de ti. 8. Canta conmigo. 9. Cantaré con él. 10. Se lo llevó consigo.

B. *SE* (Reflexive Pronouns)

Ejercicio.

1. Nos fijamos en su sonrisa.   2. Se enamoró de ella.   3. Nos preocupamos por ti.   4. Se enteraron del accidente el día siguiente.   5. Me quité la ropa.   6. Se quedó allí (ahí). 7. Nos quejamos (quejábamos) del tiempo (de la hora).   8. Se despidió de su familia. 9. Se dieron cuenta (de) que era tarde.   10. Nunca se acostumbraron al clima.   11. No se atreve a tocar a la puerta.   12. Se parecen a su madre.

SE (Accidental or Irresponsible *Se*)

Ejercicio 1.

1. Se nos olvidó la cita.   2. Se me quemaron los plátanos.   3. Se nos perdieron las llaves. 4. Se les mojó el pelo.   5. Se te rompió la taza.

Ejercicio 2.

1. Se le quedó el libro.   2. Se nos mojó la ropa.   3. Se me acabó el café.   4. Se te cayeron los papeles.   5. Se le olvidaron los apuntes.   6. Se les rompieron los platos.

Ejercicio 3.

1. A Jorge se **le** perdió el paraguas.   2. A nosotros se **nos** rompió el jarro.   3. A mí se **me** cayó el guante.   4. Se **te** quemaron los frijoles a ti.   5. A los niños se **les** cierran los ojos.

Ejercicio 4.

1. Se nos **olvidaron** los regalos. 2. A ti se te **olvidaron** las llaves. 3. A la niña se le **bajaron** los calcetines. 4. A mí se me **rompió** la silla. 5. A los vecinos se les **fue** la electricidad.

SE (Impersonal *Se*)

Ejercicio 1.

1. Se vendió la casa. ¿Cuándo se vendió?   2. Uno se broncea fácilmente en el Caribe. 3. Se despidió a los empleados. ¿Por qué se les despidió?   4. No se les avisó.   5. Eso no se dice en público.

Ejercicio 2.

1. En algunas partes del mundo hispano se **toma** una siesta por la tarde.   2. En esa tienda se **habla** español.   3. A los niños se les **dijo** que no salieran de noche.   4. En esa época, se **mataba** a los criminales.   5. Al presidente se le **recibió** con gran aplauso.   6. A los estudiantes se les **mandó** la información en verano.   7. Al gerente se le **anunciaron** los cambios hace mucho.   8. Se **venden** libros.   9. Aquí no se **aceptan** cheques personales. 10. A la jefa ya se le **dieron** las noticias.

C. DEMONSTRATIVE AND POSSESSIVE PRONOUNS

Ejercicio.

1. Esa casa era más cara que ésta.   2. —¿Qué casa prefieres? —Me gustó más ésa (OR: aquélla).   3. —Dame eso. —¿Qué? ¿Esto?   4. Mi hermana es tan fuerte como la tuya.
5. —Mis padres vienen para la graduación. ¿Y los tuyos? —Los míos no vienen.   6. Esa medicina es suya. (OR: de él)   7. ¿Cuál es tu toalla? Ésta es la mía, y ésa es la tuya.
8. —¿De quién son estas llaves? —Éstas son de usted, éstas son de él y éstas son de ella.

D. INTERROGATIVE PRONOUNS

Ejercicio.

1. ¿Cómo llegaron?   2. ¿Cuánta azúcar usas?   3. ¿Qué color te gusta?   4. ¿Cuál quieres?
5. ¿A qué distancia queda la tienda de aquí?   6. ¿Cuál es tu nombre?   7. ¿Cómo te llamas?
8. ¿Cuántos libros compraste?   9. ¿Con qué frecuencia vas?

E. EXCLAMATIVES

Ejercicio 1.

1. ¡Qué trabajo!   2. ¡Qué lindo (a)(os)(as)! (Instead of *lindo*, other possibilities could be *bonito, precioso, hermoso*, etc.)   3. ¡Qué juego más (tan) divertido!   4. ¡Qué buen café! or: ¡Qué café más (tan) bueno, rico, sabroso...!   5. ¡Qué rápido corres!   6. ¡Cómo cantan los pájaros!   7. ¡Cuánto la queríamos!   8. ¡Cuánta hambre tengo! OR: ¡Qué hambre tengo!
9. ¡Cuántos primos visitamos!   10. ¡Quién pudiera volar como ellos!

Ejercicio 2.

1. ¡**Qué** agua más fría!   2. ¡**Cómo** o **Cuánto** se ríen!   3. ¡**Qué** delicioso!   4. ¡**Qué** ojos tan verdes tienes!   5. ¡**Cuánto** me alegro que puedas venir a la fiesta!   6. ¡**Cuántos** hermanos tienes!   7. ¡**Qué** blanca se ve la nieve!   8. ¡**Qué** buena película!   9. ¡**Cómo** o **Cuánto** comen esos niños!   10. ¡**Qué** suerte!

F. INDEFINITE AND NEGATIVE PRONOUNS

1. Algo se cayó.   2. Alguien habló.   3. No veo a nadie.   4. ¿Necesitas algo?   5. No quiero nada.   6. —Quizá alguno (OR: uno) de los vecinos lo haya visto. —No, ninguno (de ellos) lo vio.   7. —Ayer fui al cine. —Yo también.   8. —Juan no podía ver. —Nosotros tampoco.
9. —¿Has ido a Chile alguna vez? —No, nunca he ido. Algún día iré. Mi hermana fue una vez y le gustó.   10. No puedo encontrar mis llaves en ninguna parte. Sé que están en alguna parte en este cuarto.

G. RELATIVE PRONOUNS

Ejercicio 1.

1. que   2. que   3. que   4. Lo que   5. la que   6. que (OR: la cual)   7. que   8. que/lo que (OR: lo cual)   9. que   10. la cual (OR: la que)   11. la cual   12. cuyas   13. Quien *(proverbio)* 14. El que   15. la que (OR: lo que)

Ejercicio 2.

1. La persona que llamó preguntó por ti. (OR: El/La que llamó preguntó por ti). 2. Lo que te dio era robado. 3. No me gusta lo que hacen. 4. Ése es el autobús que esperaba. 5. La que cantaba esa canción era Rose. (OR: La que cantó esa canción…)

A
P
P
E
N
D
I
X

3

Chapter 4   Prepositions and Conjunctions

A. PREPOSITIONS (The Function of Prepositions)

Ejercicio.

A preposition is a word which introduces a noun or its equivalent. Its name is derived from the Latin—pre- *(before)* position—and explains its function in a sentence: a preposition goes before a noun, thus introducing it. A conjunction joins two parts of speech. Its name is also derived from the Latin—con- *(with)* –junction *(to join)*, or to join together. Conjunctions of coordination join two equal parts of speech (and, or…), whereas conjunctions of subordination join a subordinate (or dependent) clause to its main clause.

PREPOSITIONS (Individual Prepositions)

Ejercicio 1.

1. Asistiré **a** clase **en** cuanto me alivie. 2. Comenzaron **a** cocinar ayer. 3. Creo que **a** lo mejor se encuentre **con** Margarita **en** la ciudad. 4. Decidieron caminar **en** vez de manejar; nunca llegarán **a** pie. 5. Dudo que puedan influir **en** su decisión. 6. El mercado está **a** dos kilómetros. 7. El programa consiste **en** varios segmentos; en el primero, se trata **de** la revolución mexicana. 8. Ella me gana **a** veces, y se burla **de** mí. 9. Este bordado está hecho **a** mano; este otro, **en** cambio, está hecho **a** máquina. 10. Fuimos **a** la tienda **en** el coche **de** mi padre **con** mis cuatro hermanitos.

Ejercicio 2.

1. Iremos al trabajo **a** pesar de la tormenta. 2. La gente **del** barrio estaba **de** mal humor. 3. La mujer **de** ojos verdes trabaja **en** la tienda **de** la esquina. 4. Llegarán **a** eso de las cinco **con** tal de que no nieve. 5. Lo mediremos **a** ojo. 6. Me acosté **a** las diez **con** coraje. 7. Me detuve **a** echarle gasolina al carro. 8. Me enojé **con** ellos porque los dos estaban hablando **a** la vez. 9. Me gusta montar **a** caballo **de** vez en cuando. 10. Me invitaron **a** cenar **en/a** un restaurante que se especializa **en** comida mexicana.

Ejercicio 3.

1. Nadie se había fijado **en** el cambio que ocurrió desde que se habían quejado **de** su horario. 2. Necesitamos discutir esto más **a** fondo, pero **en** este momento no tengo tiempo. 3. No veo **a** mis amigos **con** estos lentes. 4. Nos pusimos **a** llorar cuando nos enteramos **del** terremoto que hubo **en** Los Angeles. 5. Nunca se resignará **a** ser menos famoso. 6. Por favor lleguen **a** tiempo. 7. Quisiera que se rieran **de** mis chistes, y no **de** mí. 8. **En** cuanto empezó a ir a la escuela, Roberta aprendió **a** defenderse. 9. Sabemos que tardan mucho **en** llegar a su destino. 10. Se casó **con** ella **a** los tres años de ser su novio.

Ejercicio 4.

1. Se enamoró **de** ella cuando le enseñó **a** bailar el tango. 2. Se negó **a** tomarse la píldora. 3. Se quedaron **con** mis libros **de** poesía. 4. Si esos niños no dejan **de** meterse **con** mi

hijo, tendré que hablar **con** sus padres.   5. Soñé **con** mi novia.   6. Su hijo le pidió [Ø] dinero porque pensaba [Ø] comprarle un regalo a su madre.   7. Subían **a** la montaña **con** frecuencia.   8. Van **a** regalarle un libro **de** Cervantes.   9. Ves a tus padres **a** menudo, y ellos siempre se alegran **de** verte.   10. Volvieron **a** sentarse **en** frente de mí.

Ejercicio 5.

1. Ya empezaron **a** salir las flores.   2. **A** fuerza de hacer tantos ejercicios, bajó de peso.
3. **De** niña, se acostumbró **a** desayunar temprano.   4. **De** repente tuvieron que entrar **a** causa de la tormenta.   5. **Con** respecto a ese asunto, parece que lo resolvieron ayer.
6. ¿Me podrían ayudar **a** terminar este trabajo?   7. —¿Qué haces? —Estoy buscando [Ø] mi libreta **de** direcciones.   8. ¿Te atreverás **a** jugar?   9. Le presté el libro **a** mi amigo **de** buena gana.   10. Estudiamos **en** Miami.

Ejercicio 6.

1. Iremos **con** tal de que no llueva.   2. —Anoche nevó. —¿**De** veras? 3. Mis hijos aprenderán **a** tocar el piano desde muy jóvenes.   4. Pienso **en** ti **a** menudo.   5. ¿Qué piensan tus padres **de** mis amigos?   6. No te olvides **de** traerte las llaves.   7. Nunca dejarán **de** quererte.   8. Pronto se acostumbrarán **a** la comida picante.   9. Decidí ir de compras **en** vez de estudiar.   10. **A** veces es saludable no hacer nada.   11. La tormenta empezó **de** repente.   12. ¿Tú te atreves **a** hablarle?   13. No pudimos ir **a** causa de la lluvia.
14. Mis padres nunca consentirán **en** dejarme ir contigo.

Ejercicio 7.

1. Fueron al centro **para** visitar el museo.   2. Fueron al mercado **por** verduras.   3. Toma: este regalo es **para** ti.   4. Viajaron **por** toda la isla.   5. Hay **por** lo menos quinientas personas aquí.   6. Prometieron que terminarían toda la construcción en el edificio **para** el semestre entrante.   7. Me gusta pasearme **por** la mañana.   8. Pasaremos **por** casa de tu abuelita en camino al partido.   9. Lo dijeron **para** que sus vecinos lo oyeran **por**que sabían que reaccionarían.   10. **Por** fin llegó el cartero.

Ejercicio 8.

1. Buscó [Ø] la carta en su bolso, pero no la encontró.   2. ¡Cálmate! ¡No es **para** tanto!
3. Necesito medicina **para** curarme. 4. Lo tomaron **por** idiota.   5. Iremos al mercado **por** fruta. 6. Fueron a la tienda **para** comprar lo necesario.   7. Te agradezco [Ø] la ayuda.
8. No pudieron salir **por** la tormenta.   9. La llamaremos **por** teléfono.   10. Saldrán **para** Madrid en la madrugada.

Ejercicio 9.

1. —¿Quieres bailar? — ¡**Por** supuesto!   2. No estaba **para** bromas.   3. **Por** lo general no me gusta levantarme tarde.   4. **Por** más dinero que gane, no es feliz.   5. Tendremos que comprar **por** lo menos cuatro docenas.   6. Le queda un trabajo **por** escribir.   7. Se enfermó **por** comer tanto.   8. **Para** llegar al museo, hay que pasar **por** el parque.
9. Acabo de entrar, **por** eso tengo frío.   10. Jorge se esfuerza **por** sacar las mejores notas de la clase.

Ejercicio 10.

1. Se preocupan por ti. 2. Se enamoró de ella. 3. Consiste en dos secciones. 4. La decisión depende de ti. 5. Se rieron de él. 6. Sueño contigo todas las noches. 7. Se despidieron de mí. 8. No quiero que mis ideas influyan en tu decisión. 9. Se casó con mi hermano. 10. Dejó de beber.

Ejercicio 11.

1. Llegamos a Madrid a las dos. 2. Se opone a todo lo que digo. 3. Trato de ayudar. 4. Me di cuenta de mi error. 5. Me agradeció el favor. 6. Nos subimos al autobús. 7. Su casa está a cinco millas. 8. Me encontré con mis amigos en el restaurante. 9. Estudia en la universidad. 10. Serán los primeros en irse.

Ejercicio 12.

1. Pienso en mis padres todos los días. 2. El libro de Luisa es interesante. 3. Me fijé en el cambio. 4. No puedo ayudarte en este momento. 5. Se enojaron conmigo por mi error. 6. Miramos el reloj. 7. Vio a su hermana. 8. Te pedí dinero, no consejo. 9. Acabo de comer. 10. Trabajan para mí.

Ejercicio 13.

1. Lo envié por correo aéreo. 2. Fueron a la tienda por pan. 3. Me quedan dos trabajos por escribir. 4. Habremos terminado para las diez. 5. Para un niño, sabe mucho. 6. Salieron para Guatemala ayer. 7. Están buscando sus llaves. 8. Hablaron por tres horas. 9. Se preocupa por ti. 10. ¿Para qué es esto?

Chapter 5 Verbs I

FORMATION (Indicative Mood: Present Indicative)

Ejercicio 1.

1. amo 2. canto 3. como 4. vivo 5. hablo 6. camino 7. coso 8. bebo 9. abro
10. imprimo

Ejercicio 2.

1. cierro 2. revelo 3. pierdo 4. mezclo 5. siento 6. pido 7. consigo 8. repito
9. miento 10. comienzo 11. comento 12. defiendo 13. impido 14. sigo 15. pienso
16. quiero 17. sirvo 18. elijo

Ejercicio 3.

1. vota 2. vuelve 3. duele 4. doma 5. cuenta 6. corta 7. acuesta 8. puede 9. poda
10. llueve 11. llora 12. recuerda 13. recorta 14. huele 15. juega 16. jura

Ejercicio 4.

1. protejo 2. sigo 3. obedezco 4. traduzco 5. tuerzo 6. recojo 7. consigo 8. agradezco
9. produzco 10. convenzo

Ejercicio 5.

1. envías 2. continúas 3. confías 4. reúnes 5. crías 6. gradúas 7. guías 8. actúas
9. concluyes 10. huyes

Ejercicio 6.

1. caigo/cae/caemos 2. hago/hace/hacemos 3. pongo/pone/ponemos 4. salgo/sale/
salimos 5. traigo/trae/traemos 6. valgo/vale/valemos 7. vengo/viene/venimos
8. digo/dice/decimos 9. tengo/tiene/tenemos 10. doy/da/damos 11. voy/va/vamos
12. soy/es/somos 13. estoy/está/estamos 14. he/ha/hemos 15. oigo/oye/oímos
16. sé/sabe/sabemos 17. veo/ve/vemos

Ejercicio 7.

1. camino 2. actúas 3. actuamos 4. adquiero 5. adquirimos 6. andáis 7. aprendemos
8. ase 9. avergüenzan 10. avergonzamos 11. averiguo 12. digo 13. dice 14. decimos
15. buscan 16. quepo 17. cabe 18. caigo 19. cae 20. cierras 21. cerráis 22. cojo
23. cogen 24. comienzo 25. comenzamos 26. contribuye 27. construimos
28. conduzco 29. produces 30. cuenta
31. sueno 32. recordamos 33. creo 34. poseen 35. leemos 36. cruzo 37. almuerzas
38. doy 39. digo 40. contradigo 41. elijo 42. exiges 43. sigo 44. consigue
45. perseguimos 46. duermo 47. dormís 48. envían 49. enviamos 50. escribo
51. estoy 52. fuerzan 53. hago 54. satisfacen 55. voy 56. van 57. juega 58. llegan
59. muere 60. mueves

61. niegan 62. oigo 63. oyes 64. oímos 65. huelo 66. huelen 67. parezco 68. pido
69. pide 70. pierdes 71. pueden 72. pongo 73. quieren 74. río 75. sonríe 76. reúnen
77. ruega 78. tengo 79. tienes 80. tuerzo 81. retuerce 82. traigo 83. valgo
84. convenzo 85. vengo 86. intervienen 87. vemos 88. vive 89. vuelve

FORMATION (Indicative Mood: Past Tenses of the Indicative: Imperfect Indicative)

Ejercicio 1.

1. hablaba 2. comías 3. vivía 4. caminábamos 5. corríais 6. asían 7. comenzaba
8. decías 9. veía 10. concluíamos

Ejercicio 2.

1. iba/íbamos 2. era/éramos 3. veía/veíamos 4. pedía/pedíamos 5. cerraba/
cerrábamos 6. caía/caíamos 7. andaba/andábamos 8. cabía/cabíamos 9. tenía/
teníamos 10. hacía/hacíamos 11. daba/dábamos 12. dormía/dormíamos 13. reía/
reíamos 14. oía/oíamos

Ejercicio 3.

1. caminaba 2. actuabas 3. actuábamos 4. adquiría 5. adquiríamos 6. andabais
7. aprendíamos 8. asía 9. avergonzaban 10. avergonzábamos 11. averiguaba
12. decía 13. decía 14. decíamos 15. buscaban 16. cabía 17. cabía 18. caía 19. caía
20. cerrabas 21. cerrabais 22. cogía 23. cogían 24. comenzaba 25. comenzábamos
26. contribuía 27. construíamos 28. conducía 29. producías 30. contaba

31. sonaba 32. recordábamos 33. creía 34. poseían 35. leíamos 36. cruzaba
37. almorzabas 38. daba 39. decía 40. contradecía 41. elegía 42. exigías 43. seguía
44. conseguía 45. perseguíamos 46. dormía 47. dormíais 48. enviaban
49. enviábamos 50. escribía 51. estaba 52. forzaban 53. hacía 54. satisfacían 55. iba
56. iban 57. jugaba 58. llegaban 59. moría 60. movías

61. negaban 62. oía 63. oías 64. oíamos 65. olía 66. olían 67. parecía 68. pedía
69. pedía 70. perdías 71. podían 72. ponía 73. querían 74. reía 75. sonreía
76. reunían 77. rogaba 78. tenía 79. tenías 80. torcía 81. retorcía 82. traía 83. valía
84. convencía 85. venía 86. intervenían 87. veíamos 88. vivía 89. volvía

FORMATION (Indicative Mood: Past Tenses of the Indicative: Preterite)

Ejercicio 1.

1. hablaste 2. comimos 3. vivieron 4. caminé 5. anduviste 6. cupo 7. estuvimos
8. arrestamos 9. hubieron 10. supe 11. pudiste 12. puso 13. salisteis 14. tuvieron
15. hice 16. quisiste 17. vino

Ejercicio 2.

1. dimos 2. hizo 3. fui 4. fui 5. dijisteis 6. produjiste 7. trajeron

Ejercicio 3.

1. sentí/sintió 2. pedí/pidió 3. reí/rió 4. dormí/durmió 5. caí/cayó 6. creí/creyó
7. leí/leyó 8. oí/oyó 9. concluí/concluyó 10. busqué/buscó 11. llegué/llegó
12. alcancé/alcanzó 13. expliqué/explicó 14. almorcé/almorzó 15. apagué/apagó
16. saqué/sacó 17. comencé/comenzó 18. colgué/colgó 19. toqué/tocó 20. empecé/
empezó 21. entregué/entregó 22. pagué/pagó

Ejercicio 4.

1. caminé 2. actuaste 3. actuamos 4. adquirí 5. adquirimos 6. anduvisteis
7. aprendimos 8. asió 9. avergonzaron 10. avergonzamos 11. averigüé 12. dije
13. dijo 14. dijimos 15. buscaron 16. cupe 17. cupo 18. caí 19. cayó 20. cerraste
21. cerrasteis 22. cogí 23. cogieron 24. comencé 25. comenzamos 26. contribuyó
27. construimos 28. conduje 29. produjiste 30. contó

31. soné 32. recordamos 33. creí 34. poseyeron 35. leímos 36. crucé 37. almorzaste
38. di 39. dije 40. contradije 41. elegí 42. exigiste 43. seguí 44. consiguió
45. perseguimos 46. dormí 47. dormisteis 48. enviaron 49. enviamos 50. escribí
51. estuve 52. forzaron 53. hice 54. satisficieron 55. fui 56. fueron 57. jugó
58. llegaron 59. murió 60. moviste

61. negaron 62. oí 63. oíste 64. oímos 65. olí 66. olieron 67. parecí 68. pedí
69. pidió 70. perdiste 71. pudieron 72. puse 73. quisieron 74. reí 75. sonrió
76. reunieron 77. rogó 78. tuve 79. tuviste 80. torcí 81. retorció 82. traje 83. valí
84. convencí 85. vine 86. intervinieron 87. vimos 88. vivió 89. volvió

FORMATION (Indicative Mood: Past Tenses of the Indicative: Present Perfect Indicative)

Ejercicio.

1. he caminado 2. has actuado 3. ha adquirido 4. hemos andado 5. habéis aprendido
6. han asido 7. he avergonzado 8. has averiguado 9. ha buscado 10. hemos cabido
11. habéis cerrado 12. han cogido

FORMATION (Indicative Mood: Past Tenses of the Indicative: Pluperfect Indicative)

Ejercicio.

1. había caminado 2. habías actuado 3. había adquirido 4. habíamos andado
5. habíais aprendido 6. habían asido 7. había avergonzado 8. habías averiguado
9. había buscado 10. habíamos cabido 11. habíais cerrado 12. habían cogido

FORMATION (Indicative Mood: Future: Simple Future)

Ejercicio 1.

1. caminaré 2. actuarás 3. adquirirá 4. andaremos 5. aprenderéis 6. asirán
7. avergonzaré 8. averiguarás 9. buscará 10. cantaremos 11. cerraréis 12. cogerán

Ejercicio 2.

1. cabré 2. dirás 3. habrá 4. haremos 5. podréis 6. pondrán 7. querré 8. sabrás
9. saldrá 10. tendremos 11. valdréis 12. vendrán

FORMATION (Indicative Mood: Future: Future Perfect)

Ejercicio.

1. habré caminado 2. habrás actuado 3. habrá adquirido 4. habremos andado
5. habréis aprendido 6. habrán asido 7. habré avergonzado 8. habrás averiguado
9. habrá buscado 10. habremos cantado 11. habréis cerrado 12. habrán cogido
13. habré cabido 14. habrás podido 15. habrá querido 16. habremos sabido
17. habréis salido 18. habrán tenido 19. habrán valido 20. habré venido

FORMATION (Conditional Mood: Present Conditional)

Ejercicio 1.

1. caminaría 2. actuarías 3. adquiriría 4. andaríamos 5. aprenderíais 6. asirían
7. avergonzaría 8. averiguarías 9. buscaría 10. cantaríamos 11. cerraríais 12. cogerían

Ejercicio 2.

1. cabría 2. dirías 3. habría 4. haríamos 5. podríais 6. pondrían 7. querría 8. sabrías
9. saldría 10. tendríamos 11. valdríais 12. vendrían

FORMATION (Conditional Mood: Conditional Perfect)

Ejercicio.

1. habría caminado 2. habrías actuado 3. habría adquirido 4. habríamos andado
5. habríais aprendido 6. habrían asido 7. habría avergonzado 8. habrías averiguado
9. habría buscado 10. habríamos cantado 11. habríais cerrado 12. habrían cogido
13. habría cabido 14. habrías podido 15. habría querido 16. habríamos sabido
17. habríais salido 18. habrían tenido 19. habrían valido 20. habría venido

FORMATION (Subjunctive Mood: Present Subjunctive)

Ejercicio 1.

1. que camine 2. que hables 3. que estudie 4. que cante 5. que bailemos 6. que
reméis 7. que amen 8. que preparen 9. que tolere 10. que tararen

Ejercicio 2.

1. que coma 2. que leas 3. que vea 4. que viva 5. que tosamos 6. que cosáis 7. que corran 8. que partan 9. que beba 10. que escriban

Ejercicio 3.

1. que cierre/que cerremos 2. que pierda/que perdamos 3. que cuente/que contemos 4. que vuelva/que volvamos 5. que sienta/que sintamos 6. que duerma/que durmamos 7. que envíe/que enviemos 8. que actúe/que actuemos

Ejercicio 4.

1. que pida 2. que diga 3. que oiga 4. que tenga 5. que concluya 6. que parezca 7. que conduzca 8. que quepa 9. que caiga 10. que haga 11. que ponga 12. que salga 13. que traiga 14. que valga 15. que venga

Ejercicio 5.

1. que dé 2. que estés 3. que haya 4. que vayamos 5. que sepáis 6. que sean 7. que coja 8. que dirijas 9. que distingan 10. que convenzamos 11. que busquéis 12. que llegue 13. que alcances

Ejercicio 6.

1. que domine 2. que tema 3. que defiendas 4. que demos 5. que estéis 6. que hayan 7. que vaya 8. que sepas 9. que sea 10. que cojamos 11. que corrijas 12. que persigáis 13. que venza 14. que rasque 15. que ruegues 16. que rece 17. que entienda 18. que encuentre 19. que devuelvan 20. que envolvamos 21. que confíe 22. que criemos 23. que continúes 24. que graduemos 25. que posean 26. que vea 27. que suba 28. que hagan 29. que dividan 30. que investigue 31. que analicen 32. que discutas 33. que pelee 34. que llegue 35. que queramos 36. que entréis 37. que salgan 38. que repitan 39. que oiga 40. que vuelvan

FORMATION (Subjunctive Mood: Imperfect Subjunctive)

Ejercicio 1.

1. que caminara 2. que hablaras 3. que estudiara 4. que cantara 5. que bailáramos 6. que remarais 7. que amaran 8. que prepararan 9. que tolerara 10. que tararearan 11. que comiera 12. que leyeras 13. que viera 14. que viviera 15. que tosiéramos 16. que cosierais 17. que corrieran 18. que partieran 19. que bebiera 20. que escribieran 21. que cerrara 22. que perdieras 23. que contara 24. que volviéramos 25. que sintieran 26. que durmieran 27. que enviara 28. que actuaras

Ejercicio 2.

1. que anduviera 2. que cupieras 3. que cayera 4. que concluyera 5. que condujera 6. que diéramos 7. que dijerais 8. que durmieran 9. que estuvieran 10. que hubieran 11. que fuera 12. que leyeras 13. que oyera 14. que pidiera 15. que pudiera 16. que pusiéramos 17. que poseyerais 18. que prefirieran 19. que produjeran 20. que

quisieran 21. que riera 22. que supieras 23. que siguiera 24. que sintiera 25. que
fuera 26. que fuéramos 27. que tuvierais 28. que trajeran 29. que vinieran

FORMATION (Subjunctive Mood: Present Perfect Subjunctive)

Ejercicio.

1. que haya caminado 2. que hayas actuado 3. que haya adquirido 4. que hayamos
andado 5. que hayáis aprendido 6. que hayan asido 7. que haya avergonzado 8. que
hayas averiguado 9. que haya buscado 10. que hayamos cantado 11. que hayáis
cerrado 12. que hayan cogido 13. que haya cabido 14. que hayas podido 15. que haya
querido 16. que hayamos sabido 17. que hayáis salido 18. que hayan tenido 19. que
hayan valido 20. que haya venido

FORMATION (Subjunctive Mood: Pluperfect Subjunctive)

Ejercicio.

1. que hubiera caminado 2. que hubieras actuado 3. que hubiera adquirido 4. que
hubiéramos andado 5. que hubierais aprendido 6. que hubieran asido 7. que hubiera
avergonzado 8. que hubieras averiguado 9. que hubiera buscado 10. que hubiéramos
cantado 11. que hubierais cerrado 12. que hubieran cogido 13. que hubiera cabido
14. que hubieras podido 15. que hubiera querido 16. que hubiéramos sabido 17. que
hubierais salido 18. que hubieran tenido 19. que hubieran valido 20. que hubiera
venido

FORMATION (Imperative Mood: Direct Commands: *Tú*)

Ejercicio 1.

1. habla 2. come 3. vive 4. cierra 5. abre 6. salta 7. escucha 8. vuelve 9. pide
10. consigue 11. repite 12. miente 13. comienza 14. comenta 15. defiende 16. sigue
17. piensa 18. sirve 19. elige 20. vota 21. envuelve 22. cuenta 23. corta 24. apuesta
25. poda 26. llora 27. recuerda 28. recorta 29. huele 30. juega 31. jura 32. protege
33. sigue 34. obedece 35. traduce 36. produce 37. envía 38. continúa 39. confía
40. reúne 41. cría 42. actúa 43. concluye 44. huye 45. cae 46. trae 47. da 48. oye

Ejercicio 2.

1. di 2. haz 3. ve 4. pon 5. sal 6. sé 7. ten 8. ven

Ejercicio 3.

1. **Canta**, pero no **bailes.** 2. **Estudia**, pero no **hables** en voz alta. 3. **Bebe** mucho, y no
comas nada artificial. 4. **Lee** el artículo, pero no **creas** todo lo que dice. 5. **Vuelve** a casa,
pero no **corras.** 6. **Descose** el bolsillo, y no **cosas** la bastilla. 7. **Escribe** una carta, pero
no **describas** lo que pasó. 8. **Cuenta** lo que debes, y no **descuentes** nada. 9. **Duerme** al
bebé, pero no te **duermas** tú. 10. **Pide** favores, y no **impidas** que te ayuden. 11. **Regala**
tu amistad, y no **prestes** nada. 12. **Busca** el ungüento, y no te **rasques** la picada.
13. **Recoge** la basura, pero no **cojas** frío.

Ejercicio 4.

1. **Di** la verdad, y no **digas** mentiras.   2. **Haz** la lectura para mañana, pero no **hagas** la tarea.   3. **Ve** a la tienda, pero no **vayas** al correo.   4. **Pon** tu abrigo aquí, y no **pongas** tus zapatos en la mesa.   5. **Sal** a recoger el periódico, pero no **salgas** por esa puerta.   6. **Sé** bueno, pero no **seas** tonto.   7. **Ten** hijos, pero no **tengas** tantos como ella.   8. **Ven** a casa, pero no **vengas** temprano.

FORMATION (Imperative Mood: Direct Commands: *Usted*)

Ejercicio.

1. camine 2. no hable 3. estudie 4. no cante 5. baile 6. tararee 7. coma 8. no lea
9. viva 10. no tosa 11. corra 12. no beba 13. escriba 14. cierre 15. no pierda
16. cuente 17. no vuelva 18. duerma 19. no pida favores 20. diga 21. oiga 22. no
tenga miedo 23. conduzca con cuidado 24. no caiga en la trampa 25. haga la tarea
26. ponga la mesa 27. no salga 28. traiga el dinero 29. venga pronto 30. no dé nada
31. vaya con ellos 32. no sea ridículo 33. dirija al grupo 34. busque el tesoro 35. no
llegue tarde

FORMATION (Imperative Mood: Direct Commands: *Vosotros*)

Ejercicio 1.

1. hablad 2. comed 3. vivid 4. cerrad 5. abrid 6. saltad 7. escuchad 8. volved
9. pedid 10. conseguid 11. repetid 12. mentid 13. comenzad 14. comentad
15. defended 16. seguid 17. pensad 18. servid 19. elegid 20. votad 21. decid
22. haced 23. id 24. poned 25. salid 26. sed 27. tened 28. venid

Ejercicio 2.

1. despertaos 2. levantaos 3. lavaos 4. marchaos 5. acostaos 6. dormíos 7. idos
8. despedíos 9. callaos

Ejercicio 3.

1. **Cantad**, pero no **bailéis.**   2. **Estudiad**, pero no **habléis** en voz alta.   3. **Bebed** mucho, y no **comáis** nada artificial.   4. **Leed** el artículo, pero no **creáis** todo lo que dice.   5. **Volved** a casa, pero no **corráis.**   6. **Descosed** el bolsillo, y no **cosáis** la bastilla.   7. **Escribid** una carta, pero no **describáis** lo que pasó.   8. **Contad** lo que debeis, y no **descontéis** nada.
9. **Dormid** al bebé, pero no os **durmáis** vosotros.   10. **Pedid** favores, y no **impidáis** que os ayuden.   11. **Regalad** vuestra amistad, y no **prestéis** nada.   12. **Buscad** el ungüento, y no os **rasquéis** la picada.   13. **Recoged** la basura, pero no **cojáis** frío.

Ejercicio 4.

1. **Decid** la verdad, y no **digáis** mentiras.   2. **Haced** la lectura para mañana, pero no **hagáis** la tarea.   3. **Id** a la tienda, pero no **vayáis** al correo.   4. **Poned** vuestro abrigo aquí, y no **pongáis** vuestros zapatos en la mesa.   5. **Salid** a recoger el periódico, pero no **salgáis** por esa puerta.   6. **Sed** buenos, pero no **seáis** tontos.   7. **Tened** hijos, pero no **tengáis** tantos como ellos.   8. **Venid** a casa, pero no **vengáis** temprano.

FORMATION (Imperative Mood: Direct Commands: *Nosotros*)

Ejercicio 1.

1. caminemos 2. no hablemos 3. estudiemos 4. no cantemos 5. bailemos
6. tarareemos 7. comamos 8. no leamos 9. vivamos 10. no tosamos 11. corramos
12. no bebamos 13. escribamos 14. cerremos 15. no perdamos 16. contemos 17. no
volvamos 18. durmamos 19. no pidamos favores 20. digamos 21. oigamos 22. no
tengamos miedo 23. conduzcamos con cuidado 24. no caigamos en la trampa
25. hagamos la tarea 26. pongamos la mesa 27. no salgamos 28. no demos nada
29. vamos con ellos 30. no seamos ridículos 31. dirijamos al grupo 32. busquemos el
tesoro 33. no lleguemos tarde

Ejercicio 2.

1. despertémoslas 2. no nos levantemos 3. lavémoslo 4. marchémonos 5. no nos
acostemos 6. durmámonos 7. vámonos 8. no nos vayamos

FORMATION (Imperative Mood: Indirect Commands)

Ejercicio.

1. No quiero cocinar; que cocinen ellos hoy. 2. Que me llame el gerente. 3. Si no tienes
el dinero, que pague Mirta. 4. Que me lo manden.

FORMATION (Imperative Mood: Review of the Imperative)

Ejercicio 1.

1. Sí, díselo. No, no se lo digas. (OR: dínoslo, no nos lo digas) 2. Sí, hazlos. No, no los
hagas. 3. Sí, véndeselos. No, no se los vendas. (OR: véndemelos, no me los vendas)
4. Sí, ve. No, no vayas. 5. Sí, pónselos. No, no se los pongas.

Ejercicio 2.

1. Sí, cántenla. No, no la canten. 2. Sí, dígaselo. No, no se lo diga. (OR: dígamelo, no me
lo diga) 3. Sí, envíenselas. No, no se las envíen. (OR: envíennoslas, no nos las envíen)
4. Sí, vayan. No, no vayan. 5. Sí, quíteselos. No, no se los quite.

Ejercicio 3.

1. Sí, cantémoslas juntos. No, no las cantemos juntos. 2. Sí, vamos. No, no vayamos.
3. Sí, démoselo. No, no se lo demos. 4. Sí, vámonos ahora. No, no nos vayamos ahora.
5. Sí, pongámonoslo. No, no nos lo pongamos.

Ejercicio 4.

1. **Que lo preparen.** 2. Yo no quiero hacerlo. **Que lo haga Guillermo.** 3. **Que venga a
verme.** 4. **Que me llamen.** 5. Si tienen hambre, **que coman.**

FORMATION (Participles: Present Participle)

Ejercicio 1.

1. hablando 2. comiendo 3. viviendo 4. sintiendo 5. pidiendo 6. durmiendo
7. concluyendo 8. cayendo 9. leyendo 10. oyendo 11. diciendo 12. yendo
13. viniendo 14. pudiendo

Ejercicio 2.

1. caminando 2. actuando 3. andando 4. aprendiendo 5. diciendo 6. buscando
7. siendo 8. cerrando 9. construyendo 10. conduciendo 11. produciendo
12. contando 13. recordando 14. creyendo 15. almorzando 16. dando 17. eligiendo
18. siguiendo 19. haciendo 20. jugando

Ejercicio 3.

1. llegando 2. muriendo 3. moviendo 4. negando 5. sonriendo 6. oliendo
7. despidiendo 8. poniendo 9. reuniendo 10. teniendo 11. trayendo
12. interviniendo 13. viendo 14. volviendo

FORMATION (Participles: Past Participle)

Ejercicio 1.

1. hablado 2. comido 3. vivido 4. caminado 5. actuado 6. aprendido 7. conducido
8. almorzado 9. dado 10. movido 11. olido 12. venido

Ejercicio 2.

1. abierto 2. cubierto 3. dicho 4. escrito 5. hecho 6. muerto 7. puesto 8. resuelto
9. vuelto 10. descubierto 11. devuelto 12. supuesto

Ejercicio 3.

1. Ésta es agua bendita. 2. Habían bendecido la comida. 3. Quiero papas fritas. 4. Él había freído las papas. 5. ¡Maldita suerte! 6. Nunca he maldecido a nadie. 7. Llevaba el pelo suelto. 8. Han soltado a los toros. 9. La palabra impresa es muy importante.
10. ¿Has imprimido tu trabajo?

Chapter 6 Verbs II

USAGE (Preterite vs. Imperfect)

Ejercicio 1.

1. pasábamos 2. tenía 3. había 4. alumbraba 5. íbamos 6. Cocinábamos 7. era
8. nos levantábamos 9. salía 10. preparaba 11. Terminábamos 12. ensillábamos
13. nos íbamos 14. llegábamos 15. estaba 16. había

Ejercicio 2.

1. Estábamos 2. oyeron 3. venían 4. había 5. Nos vestimos 6. fuimos 7. veía
8. formamos 9. empezó 10. duró 11. Agarrábamos 12. Logramos

Ejercicio 3.

1. habíamos 2. caían 3. teníamos 4. respetaban 5. cambió 6. Estábamos
7. empezamos 8. imaginamos (OR: imaginábamos) 9. buscamos 10. encontramos
11. Era 12. parecía 13. Era 14. tenía 15. Estaba 16. podía 17. Parecía 18. había
19. sabía 20. tomó 21. ofrecíamos 22. acostumbró 23. adoptó

Ejercicio 4.

1. conocí 2. nos conocimos 3. conocía 4. podías 5. quería, sabía 6. quise, no pude
7. no quiso 8. no quería 9. supiste

USAGE (Compound Tenses)

Ejercicio.

1. Estoy escribiendo una carta. 2. Han estado trabajando allí desde la semana pasada.
3. Estaba comiendo cuando llegaste. 4. Había estado en el sol por tres horas. 5. Había
estado llamando por dos días. 6. Hemos comido. 7. Habremos comido para entonces.
8. Estuve trabajando en la computadora todo el día ayer. 9. Dijo que habría terminado.
10. Pensé que estaría lloviendo para ahora.

USAGE (Ways of Expressing the Future)

Ejercicio.

1. Mañana comeremos (vamos a comer/comemos) en un restaurante. 2. Esta noche
iremos (vamos a ir/vamos) al cine. 3. Te llamaré (voy a llamar/llamo) esta tarde.
4. ¿Qué harás (vas a hacer/haces) esta noche?

USAGE (Conditional: Courtesy)

Ejercicio.

1. ¿Podrías ayudarme con esto? 2. ¿Tendrías tiempo para ayudarme? 3. No deberías hacer eso. 4. Quisiera que vinieras.

USAGE (Conditional: Future of the Past)

Ejercicio.

1. Pensaba que llegarían a tiempo. 2. Creía que lo terminarían pronto. 3. Dijo que lo haría. 4. Sabía que cumpliría con su promesa.

USAGE (Probability)

Ejercicio.

1. No estudiarás lo suficiente. 2. Sería marciano. Estaría enfermo. Algo lo habría asustado. 3. Estará en el sótano. Habrá ido a la tienda.

USAGE (Subjunctive: Nominal Clauses)

Ejercicio 1.

1. trabaje 2. tienes 3. pagues 4. salgamos 5. sirvamos 6. vaya 7. aprendan 8. vemos
9. comes 10. lleve 11. puedan 12. caigan 13. quiera 14. puede 15. dejen 16. sea
17. lleve 18. sorprendan 19. escuches 20. quede
21. debemos 22. levanten 23. gane 24. lleve 25. sea 26. llueva 27. quieran 28. quiere
29. griten 30. llegue 31. controlen 32. vea 33. va 34. haga 35. lleve 36. se callen
37. salga 38. denuncie 39. sabe 40. pague

Ejercicio 2.

1. quiere 2. quiera 3. se levantaba 4. se levante 5. duermas 6. vayas 7. puedan 8. hagas 9. seas 10. griten 11. está 12. esté 13. sepan 14. llame 15. tomes

Ejercicio 3.

1. (Ella) me deja manejar. 2. Espero poder hacerlo. (OR: Ojalá que pueda hacerlo.)
3. Espero que puedas hacerlo. (OR: Ojalá que puedas hacerlo.) 4. Siento que va a llover.
5. Siento que vaya a llover. (OR: Lamento que vaya a llover.) 6. Siento no poder hacerlo.
(OR: Lamento no poder hacerlo.)

USAGE (Subjunctive: Adjectival Clauses)

Ejercicio.

1. calcula 2. sepa 3. pueda 4. puede 5. pueda 6. puede 7. dije 8. digan 9. digan

USAGE (Subjunctive: Adverbial Clauses)

Ejercicio 1.

1. salimos 2. tengas 3. puedas 4. llueva 5. se vaya 6. se arrepienta 7. se acuesten
8. pudo 9. pueda 10. paguen 11. quieras 12. tenía 13. llueve 14. vean 15. digas

Ejercicio 2.

1. Ella no irá a menos que vayamos nosotros. 2. Lo haré con tal (de) que no se lo digas a nadie. 3. Nos iremos tan pronto como te vistas. 4. Él insistirá hasta que ella acepte.
5. No conozco a nadie que pueda hacer eso sin que tú le expliques cómo.

USAGE (Subjunctive: Sequence of Tenses)

Ejercicio 1.

1. No creo que nuestros amigos lleguen mañana. 2. Parece increíble que Raúl viva en Suiza. 3. Me sorprende que los vecinos ya hayan visto esa película. 4. Dudo que ayer hiciera calor. 5. Me sorprende que se haya levantado (OR: se levantara) a las cinco.
6. Parece dudoso que ya hayan terminado a esa hora. 7. Lamento que mi abuelo ya hubiera muerto cuando llegué. 8. Mi padre dudaba que pronto estuviera lista la cena.
9. Mi tía se quejaba de que siempre hiciera frío en el monte. 10. Era imposible que tú bailaras el tango a los cinco años. 11. Temían que los perros se hubieran escapado.
12. A Roberto le molestaba que Luisa nunca les hubiera dicho el secreto a sus hijos.
13. Me sorprendería mucho que hubieran regresado para la medianoche. 14. Yo tenía miedo que Miguel ya hubiera leído esa novela.

Ejercicio 2.

1. pudieran 2. hiciera 3. gustara 4. fuera 5. tuviera 6. quisieras 7. abrieras 8. fuera

Ejercicio 3.

1. Me parecía increíble que cantaran bien. 2. Dudo que ellos caminaran. (OR: hayan caminado; hubieran caminado) 3. Ellos no creyeron que yo hubiera caminado. 4. Ella se quejó de que yo perdiera las llaves. (OR: hubiera perdido) 5. Me alegro que por fin pudiéramos ver la película. (OR: hayamos podido) 6. A él le sorprendió que los perros no hubieran ladrado en toda la noche.

Ejercicio 4.

1. llamaran 2. fueran 3. explicara 4. pudiera 5. fueran 6. pudieras 7. callaran/despertaran 8. se hubiera cortado

USAGE (Subjunctive: *Si* Clauses and *Como Si*)

Ejercicio.

1. hubiera habido (OR: hubiera) 2. se compraría 3. fuera 4. habríamos tenido
5. ayudaría 6. se hubieran visto 7. fuera

USAGE (Subjunctive: *Ojalá*)

Ejercicio.

1. Ojalá que no hubiéramos ido. 2. Ojalá que me hubieras escuchado. 3. Ojalá que comas hoy. 4. Ojalá que me pudiera ver ahora. 5. Ojalá que no lo hayan hecho. 6. Ojalá que lleguemos allá a tiempo. 7. Ojalá que hayan terminado. 8. Ojalá que le guste. 9. Ojalá que lo hayan comprado. 10. Ojalá que me pudiera oír.

USAGE (Subjunctive: Expressions of Leave-Taking)

Ejercicio 1.

1. Que te mejores. (OR: Que te alivies.) 2. Que tengas un buen fin de semana. 3. Que pasen buen día. 4. Que se divierta.

Ejercicio 2.

1. Que te vaya bien. 2. Que le vaya bien. 3. Que les vaya bien. 4. Que os vaya bien.

Ejercicio 3.

1. Que lo pases bien. 2. Que lo pase bien. 3. Que lo pasen bien. 4. Que lo paséis bien.

USAGE (Infinitive and Present Participle)

Ejercicio 1.

1. Beber agua es muy saludable. 2. No les gusta cantar. 3. Pensaban viajar al Caribe este invierno. 4. Se fueron sin decir nada. 5. Eso es lo que te pasa por hablar tanto. 6. Estoy cansado de correr. 7. Al salir, no se les olvide llevarse el paraguas. 8. El anuncio decía: "No fumar".

Ejercicio 2.

1. Ese idioma es difícil de aprender. 2. Es difícil aprender ese idioma. 3. Esa receta es fácil de preparar. 4. Es fácil decir la verdad. 5. Es posible vivir más de noventa años. 6. Algunas cosas son imposibles de cambiar.

Ejercicio 3.

Ninguna de las frases del #3 usaría el participio presente en español.

Ejercicio 4.

(Puede haber variación.) 1. Ése es uno de los problemas mundiales **que está aumentando.** 2. ¡Qué persona más **interesante**! 3. Es una de las expertas **más importantes** en esa materia. 4. Necesito comprar papel **de escribir.** 5. Ese sicólogo dice que todos los problemas de la adolescencia provienen de los dolores **de crecimiento.** 6. Vi al ladrón **que corría.** 7. Toma una foto del jarro **con** líquido azul. 8. La corte quería una cantidad de objetos **que le pertenecieran a ella** (OR: **de ella**). 9. Ahí estaba, **parado** en medio del cuarto. 10. La película fue **aburrida.** 11. Es un juego **divertido.**

12. Encontré el gato **acostado** en la cama.   13. Estaba **sentada** frente a mí en el cine.
14. Este ejercicio es **entretenido.**   15. ¿Tiene agua **potable**?

Ejercicio 5.

Todas las frases del #5 podrían usar el participio presente, porque se trata de verbos en el progresivo y de adverbios.   1. Mira: están **aumentando** el peso.   2. Estaban **dirigiendo** el tráfico para el lado.   3. Se fueron **corriendo.**   4. El conferenciante nos estaba **aburriendo** a todos.   5. Estaban apenas **sentándose** cuando se acabó la película.   6. Estábamos **entreteniéndonos** en la cocina.

Ejercicio 6.

1. Deben haber comido.   2. Tiene que comer más.   3. Pensaban ir a la playa.   4. No tengo nada que ponerme.   5. Ponte el abrigo antes de salir.   6. Para ver esos efectos, hay que ponerse lentes especiales.   7. Estaba contento de verla.   8. Al entrar, se quitaron los zapatos.   9. Mi hermano hizo venir al veterinario.   10. Esas semillas son difíciles de plantar.   11. Ese libro es fácil de leer.   12. Es fácil leer ese libro.   13. Ver es creer.   14. Me prohíbe manejar.   15. A los niños les encanta jugar en el agua.   16. Se fue sin decir nada.
17. Se arrepintieron después de colgar el teléfono.   18. Se separaron sin realmente haber llegado a conocerse.   19. No me impidas moverme (OR: mudarme).   20. Me duele la espalda de haber trabajado tanto en el jardín.

USAGE (Verbs like *Gustar*)

Ejercicio 1.

(Lo que está entre paréntesis no es obligatorio, pero no es incorrecto.)   1. (Tú) le caes bien (a él).   2. (Ellos) me caen bien (a mí).   3. (Nosotros) le caemos bien (a ella).   4. (Ella) les cae bien (a ellos).   5. (Él) nos cae bien (a nosotros).   6. (Ellos) te caen bien (a ti).

Ejercicio 2.

1. —No le caes bien a nadie. —Le caigo bien **a él.** 2. Sí, pero no le caes bien **a ella.** 3. **Ella** te cae bien **a ti,** pero **tú** no le caes bien **a ella.**

Ejercicio 3.

1. A mí. *(Who is interested in magic? Me. OR: I am.)*   2. A mí. *(Whose turn is it to pay the bill? Mine.)*   3. A mí. *(Who liked dinner? Me. OR: I did.)*   4. Yo. *(Who ate more? Me. OR: I did.)*

Ejercicio 4.

1. Lo quiero.   2. Me encantan mis clases.   3. Me gusta tu casa. (OR: Me encanta tu casa.)
4. Me caen bien mis vecinos.

Ejercicio 5.

1. Les hace falta comida.   2. Les quedan dos días.   3. Nos sobró tiempo.   4. Me haces falta.   5. Le faltan veinte centavos.

USAGE (Reflexive Verbs)

Ejercicio 1.

1. Nos aburrimos en la fiesta. 2. ¿Te acordaste de las llaves? 3. Se acostumbró a él muy pronto. 4. Me alegro de verte. 5. Se avergonzó de su mentira. 6. Me bajé del autobús (camión, guagua, bus, ómnibus…) en la tercera parada. 7. Los otros niños siempre se burlaban de mí. 8. Vas a tener que encararte a ese problema algún día. 9. Se dio cuenta de que tenía que despedirse de mí. 10. Todos debemos esforzarnos por mantener el medio ambiente limpio. 11. ¿Cómo se enteró de eso? 12. No te fíes de nadie. 13. Fíjate en sus ojos cuando bailan. 14. ¿Dónde nos vamos a encontrar con él para almorzar? 15. ¿Por qué se mudaron tus padres? 16. ¿Cómo se llama? 17. Por favor no te vayas ahora. 18. No debes meterte con esos niños. 19. Se quedaron con nosotros durante el verano. 20. Se peleó con su padre. 21. Te pareces a mí. 22. Ahora va a ponerse a ladrar. 23. Me siento triste hoy. 24. Me siento aquí. 25. Me sentí triste ayer. 26. Me senté aquí ayer. 27. Me sentía triste cuando oía esa canción. 28. Me sentaba aquí. 29. Se quedó con mi libro. 30. Sécate bien.

Ejercicio 2.

1. Me enamoré **de** ella hace mucho tiempo. 2. Se casó **con** él en junio. 3. Ella se reía **de** mí. 4. Se quejan **de** todo. 5. No te preocupes **por** mí. 6. Nos parecemos **a** nuestro padre. 7. Se interesa **por** las carreras de caballo. 8. No te fijes **en** los demás. 9. Él se fiaba **de** todos. 10. Nos esforzábamos **por** hablar bajo. 11. Mi madre se empeñaba **en** que limpiara el cuarto todos los días. 12. Por fin se decidieron **a** salir. 13. Se atrevió **a** dirigirse **a** él después de unos minutos. 14. El vino se convirtió **en** vinagre. 15. Él no puede deshacerse **de** nada. 16. ¿Te das cuenta **de** la hora que es? 17. Se curaron Ø los enfermos. 18. Me citaré **con** el dentista mañana. 19. Se arrepintieron **de** haber dicho eso. 20. ¡Aléjate **de** la calle!

USAGE (Indirect Discourse)

Ejercicio.

1. a. Dice que iremos al cine esta noche. b. Ayer dijo que iríamos al cine anoche. c. Esta mañana dijo que iríamos al cine esta noche. 2. a. Ella supone que yo sé hacerlo. b. Ella suponía que yo sabía hacerlo. c. Ella supuso que yo sabía hacerlo. 3. a. Te digo que yo hice tu trabajo. b. Le dije que yo había hecho su trabajo. c. Me dijo que él (ella) había hecho mi trabajo. 4. a. Te pido que te levantes. b. Me pidió que me levantara. c. Le pedí que se levantara. 5. a. Dice que si pudiera ir ahora, lo haría. b. Dijo que si pudiera ir entonces, lo haría. 6. a. Me preguntó esta mañana si quería que fuéramos la semana entrante. b. Me preguntó el mes pasado si quería que fuéramos la próxima semana. c. Sé que me preguntará si quiero que vayamos la semana entrante. 7. a. Me respondió que si quería comer, que comiera. b. Te estoy diciendo que si quieres comer, que comas. 8. a. Te ruego que te vayas. b. Me suplicó que me fuera. c. Insistieron en que me fuera. 9. a. Siempre me pregunta si sé qué hora es, y yo siempre le contesto que no. b. Me preguntó si sabía qué hora era, y yo le contesté que no. 10. a. El domingo por la tarde siempre nos pregunta si nos gustaría salir a cenar, y nosotros siempre le gritamos que sí. b. Nos preguntó si nos gustaría salir a cenar, y nosotros le gritamos que sí.

Chapter 7 Ser, Estar, Haber, Hacer and Tener

A. SER VS. ESTAR (etc.)

Ejercicio 1.

1. Ese hombre **es** profesor. 2. **Es** importante llegar temprano. 3. Martina **está** de vacaciones. 4. **Está** bien que estudien esta noche. 5. Luisa **es** de Guadalajara. 6. ¿Qué hora **es**? 7. **Es** la una de la tarde. 8. **Son** las siete de la mañana. 9. ¿**Está** claro lo que tienen que hacer? 10. Los pisos en esa casa **son** de madera. 11. Mis padres **están** de acuerdo con nosotros. 12. Esa mujer **está** de gerente esta semana, hasta que regrese la gerente oficial. 13. ¿Para cuándo **es** la próxima composición? 14. Este libro **es** de Mario. 15. La ceremonia para la graduación siempre **es** en el gimnasio. 16. Mis libros **están** en mi casillero. 17. Su hermano **está** en Princeton. 18. Nosotros **estamos** en Boston. 19. Tu mochila **está** en el escritorio. 20. La conferencia **es** a las nueve de la mañana. 21. Esta carta **es** para mi papá. 22. El vuelo **está** por salir. 23. Ese puente **fue** construido por un arquitecto famoso. 24. Las ventanas **están** cerradas. ¿Quieres que las abra? 25. Bertita **está** aprendiendo a caminar.

Ejercicio 2.

1. Liza Minelli **es** delgada. 2. Los cuellos de las jirafas **son** largos. 3. El café de Colombia **es** bueno. 4. Madonna **es** atlética. 5. ¡Qué rico **está** el café esta mañana! 6. Oprah **está** más delgada que hace un año. 7. Mi coche **está** averiado. 8. Su cuarto **está** desordenado hoy —¿qué pasaría? 9. La esposa **está** harta de tener que aguantar sus engaños. 10. El presidente **está** contento con los resultados. 11. —Hola, Quique. ¿**Estás** bien? —No, **estoy** enfermo. Pero ya **estoy** mejor que hace una semana. 12. Esa película **es** aburrida. 13. Mi compañero de cuarto, que por lo general **es** muy platicador, ahora **está** callado. 14. Mi hija **es** más lista que sus amiguitos. 15. Ya es hora de irnos. ¿**Están** listos? ¡Vámonos!

Ejercicio 3.

1. **Hay** veinte estudiantes en esta clase. 2. Los estudiantes **están** sentados cerca de la ventana. 3. **Hay** mucho trabajo que hacer. 4. Los libros **están** en la biblioteca. 5. **Hay** libros en la biblioteca. 6. No **hay** suficientes fondos para cubrir su cheque. 7. ¿Dónde **hay** taxis? 8. Los taxis **están** a dos cuadras de aquí. 9. Ya no **hay** tantos árboles como antes. 10. Las leyes que **hay** no bastan para controlar el crimen.

Ejercicio 4.

1. He estado de rodillas demasiado tiempo. 2. ¿Hace frío en el invierno aquí? 3. Los niños tenían sed. 4. No sé por qué estoy triste. 5. No es que la fiesta sea aburrida, es que la gente está aburrida. 6. ¿Fue firmado tu contrato por el abogado? 7. ¿Cuántos cuartos hay en ese edificio? 8. ¿De dónde eres? 9. ¿Es la conferencia en este edificio?

B. PASSIVE VOICE AND RESULTANT CONDITION

1. El pan **está** cortado. ¿Tú comiste?   2. Las cuentas **son** pagadas por el banco.   3. Yo ya **he** visto esa película cuatro veces.   4. Lo **tengo** todo preparado para los invitados.

D. TIME EXPRESSIONS: COUNTING BACK

1. Hace una hora que estoy aquí. Llevo una hora aquí.   2. Hacía veinte minutos que trabajaban cuando ella entró. Llevaban veinte minutos trabajando cuando ella entró.
3. Hace una semana que lo llamamos. *(No se puede usar **llevar** aquí).*   4. Hacía muchos años que no se cortaba las uñas. Llevaba muchos años sin cortarse las uñas.   5. Hace tres años que mi sobrina aprende el ballet. Mi sobrina lleva tres años aprendiendo ballet.
6. Hace dos meses que vino a visitarnos. *(No se puede usar **llevar** aquí).*   7. ¿Cuánto tiempo hace que esperamos? ¿Cuánto tiempo llevamos esperando?

Appendix 1 Lexical Variations

A. TO APPLY

1. Solicitó una beca. 2. El doctor aplicó presión a la herida para parar la sangre.
3. Aplique este ungüento tres veces al día. 4. Solicitaremos un préstamo en el banco.
5. El puesto que solicitaste ya no existe.

B. TO ASK

1. Te quiero pedir un favor. 2. Le hice una pregunta. 3. Me pidió que la llevara al pueblo.
4. Me preguntó, "De veras tienes dieciséis años?" 5. Le preguntamos si había comido.
6. Nos preguntaron por qué habíamos llamado. 7. No me hagas tantas preguntas.

C. TO ATTEND

1. Asistimos a la conferencia por la tarde. 2. No asistió a clase porque estaba enferma.
3. ¿Puedo atenderlo? 4. Atiende a los invitados, por favor.

D. TO BECOME OR TO GET

1. Me alegro (de) que sea viernes. 2. Los niños se callaron. 3. Se calmó después de eso.
4. Se cansaron de caminar. 5. Me enfermé durante las vacaciones. 6. Se enojaron
porque no escribí. 7. Se envejece rápido en este trabajo. 8. El caballo se tranquilizó
después de la inyección. 9. Me fijé que se había puesto pálida. 10. Se hizo doctor.
11. Quería llegar a ser una ciudadana respetada. 12. La flor se había convertido en fruta.

E. TO GO AND TO LEAVE

1. Vamos a la escuela. 2. Se fue hace una hora. 3. El gato salió. 4. Van a salir esta noche.
5. La enfermera salió a almorzar. 6. Estábamos jugando afuera en el parque, y Luisito se
enojó y se fue. 7. ¿A qué hora sale tu vuelo? 8. ¿Podría dejarme en la esquina, por favor?
9. No me dejas hacer nada. 10. Dejaron de gritar.

F. TO KNOW

1. Te conozco. 2. Conoció a su nueva esposa en México. 3. No conoce la región. 4. Sabe
mi número de teléfono. 5. Saben patinar. 6. Sabíamos que hacía frío. 7. No sabían qué
decir. 8. ¿Sabes qué hora es? 9. ¿Conoces ese hotel? 10. No sabía nadar.

G. TO LEARN

1. Aprendió a bailar. 2. Se enteraron de nuestro secreto. 3. Cuando supe (OR: me
enteré) que estabas aquí, vine en seguida.

H. TO MEET

1. La conoció en la oficina.   2. Entonces decidieron encontrarse por la tarde para discutir el trabajo.   3. Adivina con quién me topé en camino a la biblioteca.

I. TO PLAY

1. Jugaron al tenis toda la tarde.   2. ¿A qué juegas?   3. ¿Tocas la guitarra?   4. No juegues con el violín de tu hermana.   5. Esta noche va a tocar el violín.

J. TO PUT

1. Me puso la mano en el hombro.   2. Me puse las botas.   3. Metió la mano en su chaqueta.   4. Ayúdame a poner la mesa, por favor.   5. La cara se le puso verde.   6. No le metas el dedo en el ojo a tu hermano.

K. TO SERVE

1. No me sirvas tanto arroz, por favor.   2. ¿Cómo puedo servirle?   3. La cena se sirve por lo general a las ocho. Esta noche la serviremos a las siete y media.

L. TO SPEND

1. Gastas más dinero en tus hijos que en ti.   2. Pasé tres horas en este trabajo ayer. 3. Pasó un tiempo en la cárcel.   4. Es terrible desperdiciar el tiempo y el dinero.

M. TO TAKE

1. ¿Qué te gustaría tomar?   2. Llevó su cerveza a la mesa.   3. Tomó el lápiz y se fue. 4. —¿Te podemos llevar? —No, gracias, tomaré el autobús.   5. Esto está tomando demasiado tiempo.   6. Toma. Esto es tuyo.   7. Llevamos la cámara a la tienda.   8. Se llevaron nuestras toallas.   9. Déjame apuntar esto.   10. ¿Quieres que te baje los libros? 11. Subieron la comida al cuarto.   12. Tenemos que sacar la basura.   13. No te quites los calcetines.   14. El examen tendrá lugar aquí.   15. ¿Puedo llevar a un amigo a tu fiesta? 16. TTPB. (Trae tu propia bebida.)

N. TO REALIZE

1. Me doy cuenta de que no puedo realizar tus sueños en un instante.   2. Si realizas todos tus deberes con responsabilidad, te puedes quedar.   3. Se dio cuenta que era infeliz. 4. Se dio cuenta que sus sueños eran imposibles.

O. TO THINK

1. No puedo dejar de pensar en ti. 2. ¿En qué pensabas? 3. ¿Qué piensas de mí? 4. No quiso decirme lo que pensó del taller. 5. Pensamos visitar a nuestros amigos la semana que viene.

P. PEOPLE VS. MACHINES

1. Los niños corrían. 2. Ese motor dejó de andar. 3. Trabajan de nueve a cinco. 4. No funciona así. 5. ¿Cuándo empezó la película? 6. Voy a arrancar el coche para que se caliente. 7. Las luces se apagaron después de las diez. 8. Hace ejercicios todos los días. 9. Podemos resolverlo. 10. Salí corriendo. 11. Se tropezó con su primo en el museo. 12. Las baterías se descargaron. 13. A mi reloj se le acabó la cuerda. 14. Bajó las escaleras corriendo. 15. Se encontraron con sus amigos en el bar. 16. Chocó con la pared. 17. Apaga las luces. 18. Todo salió bien.

Q. *ACABAR* PHRASES

1. Acabé mi trabajo. 2. Acabaron de reparar el puente en octubre. 3. Habrá acabado con la construcción para las tres de la tarde. 4. Acabo de levantarme. 5. Cuando llegué, acababan de comer. 6. El examen se acabó a las diez. 7. Nos acabamos el pan. 8. Se nos acabó el pan.

R. *DESPEDIR* PHRASES

1. Me despidieron ayer. 2. Me despedí de mis amigos. 3. Lo despedí. 4. Me despedí de ella. 5. Nos despedimos en la puerta.

S. TO COME AND TO GO

1. ¿Cuándo vienen a vernos tus padres? 2. Fue al cine. 3. Voy al cine. 4. ¿Puedo ir contigo? 5. — ¡Ven acá, Juanita! —¡Voy! 6. Siempre llegan tarde. 7. No llegues tarde. 8. Lo siento por llegar tarde. 9. ¿Cuándo llegaste?

T. AT

1. Los niños se quedaron **en** casa. 2. Ellos están **en** Nueva York. 3. La clase es **a** las diez, **en** el edificio de Morrill. 4. Me siento mejor **en** este momento. 5. No sé qué decir **a** veces. 6. Me parece que oí pasos. Creo que hay alguien **a** la puerta. 7. Hay alguien **en** la puerta preguntando por ti. 8. Le gusta tener a su amiga **a** su lado.

U. BECAUSE

1. Fui a casa a causa de (por) mi hermano. 2. Tuvieron que cancelar el proceso por las noticias. 3. Tuvieron que dejarlo ir por eso. 4. Perdió la voz por gritar tanto. 5. No salieron porque estaba nevando.

V.   BUT

1. Estudié el idioma, **pero** no me atrevo a hablar.   2. Ese hombre no es mi tío, **sino** mi cuñado.   3. No fueron a Puerto Rico, **sino** a México.   4. Esta clase es interesante, **pero** difícil.   5. No lo compró, **sino que** se lo regaló su hermana.   6. No hablo el idioma, **pero** voy a viajar al país.

W. EXIT VS. SUCCESS

1. Si trabajamos mucho, tendremos éxito.   2. Nuestro éxito depende de nuestro esfuerzo.
3. La salida está a la derecha.   4. A mi abuela le gustaba repasar los sucesos del día después de la cena.

X.   GUIDE

1. Nuestro guía en el museo era un anciano.   2. El guía/La guía era de Venezuela.
3. Encontrará las reglas en la guía.

Y.   ORDER

1. Todo se tenía que colocar en un orden específico.   2. Lo hice porque recibí la orden de arriba.   3. —Hola, me llamo Julia Ruiz. —Hola, Victoria Vargas, a tus órdenes (OR: a sus órdenes).

Z.   TIME

1. ¿Tienes tiempo para hablar conmigo?   2. ¿Qué tiempo hacía?   3. ¿Cuántas veces te lo tengo que decir?   4. Esa vez fue diferente.   5. No me quiso decir qué hora era.   6. Sabía que era hora de levantarme.   7. Estará aquí dentro de un ratito.   8. Nos divertimos.
9. Tuvimos buen tiempo.

AA. WHAT

1. ¿Qué es un "cucurucho"?   2. ¿Cuál es el tuyo?   3. ¿Qué países visitaste?   4. ¿Cómo?
5. Lo que no sabes no te hará daño.

Verb Conjugation Tables

Lista de verbos conjugados

1. actuar	15. concluir	29. estar	43. pedir	57. sentir
2. adquirir	16. conducir	30. forzar	44. perder	58. ser
3. andar	17. contar	31. haber	45. poder	59. soler
4. aprender	18. creer	32. hacer	46. podrir	60. tener
5. avergonzar	19. cruzar	33. ir	47. poner	61. teñir
6. averiguar	20. dar	34. jugar	48. prohibir	62. traer
7. buscar	21. decir	35. llegar	49. querer	63. valer
8. caber	22. dirigir	36. lucir	50. regir	64. vencer
9. caer	23. discernir	37. morir	51. reír	65. venir
10. caminar	24. distinguir	38. mover	52. reunir	66. ver
11. cerrar	25. dormir	39. negar	53. rogar	67. vivir
12. cocer	26. enviar	40. oír	54. saber	68. volcar
13. coger	27. errar	41. oler	55. salir	69. volver
14. comenzar	28. esparcir	42. parecer	56. seguir	

Mini-índice de verbos

(El número de la derecha de cada verbo es el que corresponde al verbo modelo de conjugación. Vea la "Lista de verbos conjugados" para la referencia.)

atribuir	15	boxear	10	castrar	10	clarear	10	completar	10
atrofiar	10	bramar	10	catalogar	35	clarecer	42	complicar	7
atronar	17	bregar	35	catapultar	10	clarificar	7	complotar	10
atropellar	10	brillar	10	catar	10	clasificar	7	componer	47
aturdir	67	brincar	7	causar	10	claudicar	7	comportarse	10
augurar	10	brindar	10	cauterizar	19	clausurar	10	comprar	10
aumentar	10	bromear	10	cautivar	10	clavar	10	comprender	4
auscultar	10	broncear	10	cavar	10	clavetear	10	comprimir	67
ausentar	10	brotar	10	cazar	19	climatizar	19	comprobar	17
auspiciar	10	brutalizar	19	cazcalear	10	coadquirir	2	comprometer	4
autenticar	7	bucear	10	cebar	10	coagular	10	computadorizar	19
autentificar	7	burocratizar	19	cecear	10	coarrendar	11	computar	10
autografiar	26	buscar	7	ceder	4	cobijar	10	computarizar	19
automatizar	19	cabalgar	35	cegar	39	cobrar	10	comulgar	35
autorizar	19	cabecear	10	cejar	10	cocer	12	comunicar	7
avanzar	19	caber	8	celar	10	cocinar	10	concatenar	10
aventajar	10	cablegrafiar	26	celebrar	10	codear	10	concebir	43
aventar	11	cabrear	10	cementar	10	codiciar	10	conceder	4
aventurar	10	cacarear	10	cenar	10	codificar	7	concentrar	10
avergonzar	5	cachetear	10	ceñir	61	coercer	64	conceptuar	1
averiguar	6	caducar	7	censurar	10	coexistir	67	concernir	23
avisar	10	caer	9	centralizar	19	coger	13	concertar	11
avivar	10	cagar	35	centrar	10	cohabitar	10	concienciar	10
ayudar	10	calar	10	cepillar	10	cohibir	48	concientizar	19
ayunar	10	calcar	7	cercar	7	coincidir	67	conciliar	10
azorar	10	calcificar	7	cerciorar	10	cojear	10	concluir	15
azotar	10	calcinar	10	cernir	23	colaborar	10	concomitar	10
azucarar	10	calcografiar	26	cerrar	11	colar	10	concordar	17
azuzar	19	calcular	10	certificar	7	coleccionar	10	concretar	10
babear	10	calentar	11	cesar	10	colegir	50	concurrir	67
babosear	10	calibrar	10	chantajear	10	colgar	53	concursar	10
bailar	10	calificar	7	chapotear	10	colindar	10	condecorar	10
bajar	10	caligrafiar	26	charlar	10	colmar	10	condenar	10
balancear	10	callar	10	chequear	10	colocar	7	condensar	10
balbucear	10	calmar	10	chicanear	10	colonizar	19	condescender	44
barnizar	19	calumniar	10	chiflar	10	colorear	10	condicionar	10
barrenar	10	calzar	19	chillar	10	columpiar	10	condimentar	10
barrer	4	cambiar	10	chinear	10	comadrear	10	condolecerse	42
basar	10	caminar	10	chingar	35	combatir	67	condonar	10
bastar	10	camuflar	10	chirriar	26	combinar	10	conducir	16
batallar	10	canalizar	19	chismear	10	comedirse	43	conectar	10
batir	67	cancelar	10	chismorrear	10	comentar	10	conferir	57
bautizar	19	canjear	10	chismotear	10	comenzar	14	confesar	11
beatificar	7	canonizar	19	chispear	10	comer	4	confiar	26
beber	4	cansar	10	chistar	10	comercializar	19	configurar	10
beneficiar	10	cantar	10	chocar	7	cometer	4	confinar	10
berrear	10	capacitar	10	chocarrear	10	comisionar	10	confirmar	10
besar	10	capar	10	chorrear	10	compactar	10	confiscar	7
bienquerer	49	capitalizar	19	chotear	10	compadecer	42	conformar	10
bifurcarse	7	capitular	10	chupar	10	compadrear	10	confortar	10
blanquear	10	captar	10	chutear	10	compaginar	10	confrontar	10
blanquecer	42	capturar	10	cicatrizar	19	comparar	10	confundir	67
blindar	10	caracolear	10	cimentar	11	comparecer	42	congelar	10
bloquear	10	caracterizar	19	circular	10	compartir	67	congestionar	10
bofetear	10	caramelizar	19	circundar	10	compasar	10	conglomerar	10
boicotear	10	carbonizar	19	circunferir	57	compeler	4	congregar	35
bombardear	10	carcomer	4	circunscribir	67	compendiar	10	conjeturar	10
bordear	10	cardar	10	circunvenir	65	compendizar	19	conjugar	35
borrar	10	carecer	42	circunvolar	17	compenetrarse	10	conllevar	10
borronear	10	cargar	35	citar	10	compensar	10	conmemorar	10
bosquejar	10	caricaturizar	19	civilizar	19	competir	43	conmocionar	10
bostezar	19	casar	10	clamar	10	compilar	10	conmover	38
botar	10	castigar	35	clamorear	10	complementar	10	conmutar	10

A
P
P
E
N
D
I
X

4

◆◆◆

1. ACTUAR
(to act)

Verbo en -AR con cambio de *u → ú*

(Como **acentuar, continuar, evaluar, graduar, insinuar**)

Participio presente: actuando

Participio pasado: actuado

Imperativo: actúa (no actúes), actúe Ud., actuemos, actuad (no actuéis), actúen Uds.

Indicativo				Condicional	Subjuntivo	
Presente	**Imperfecto**	**Pretérito**	**Futuro**	**Presente**	**Presente**	**Imperfecto**
actúo	actuaba	actué	actuaré	actuaría	actúe	actuara
actúas	actuabas	actuaste	actuarás	actuarías	actúes	actuaras
actúa	actuaba	actuó	actuará	actuaría	actúe	actuara
actuamos	actuábamos	actuamos	actuaremos	actuaríamos	actuemos	actuáramos
actuáis	actuabais	actuasteis	actuaréis	actuaríais	actuéis	actuarais
actúan	actuaban	actuaron	actuarán	actuarían	actúen	actuaran
Pres. perfecto	**Pluscuamperf.**		**Futuro perfecto**	**Perfecto**	**Pres. perfecto**	**Pluscuamperf.**
he actuado	había actuado		habré actuado	habría actuado	haya actuado	hubiera actuado

2. ADQUIRIR
(to acquire)

Verbo en -IR con cambio de *i → ie*

(Como **coadquirir, inquirir, perquirir**)

Participio presente: adquiriendo

Participio pasado: adquirido

Imperativo: adquiere (no adquieras), adquiera Ud., adquiramos, adquirid (no adquiráis), adquieran Uds.

Indicativo				Condicional	Subjuntivo	
Presente	**Imperfecto**	**Pretérito**	**Futuro**	**Presente**	**Presente**	**Imperfecto**
adquiero	adquiría	adquirí	adquiriré	adquiriría	adquiera	adquiriera
adquieres	adquirías	adquiriste	adquirirás	adquirirías	adquieras	adquirieras
adquiere	adquiría	adquirió	adquirirá	adquiriría	adquiera	adquiriera
adquirimos	adquiríamos	adquirimos	adquiriremos	adquiriríamos	adquiramos	adquiriéramos
adquirís	adquiríais	adquiristeis	adquiriréis	adquiriríais	adquiráis	adquirierais
adquieren	adquirían	adquirieron	adquirirán	adquirirían	adquieran	adquirieran
Pres. perfecto	**Pluscuamperf.**		**Futuro perfecto**	**Perfecto**	**Pres. perfecto**	**Pluscuamperf.**
he adquirido	había adquirido		habré adquirido	habría adquirido	haya adquirido	hubiera adquirido

3. ANDAR
(to go)

Verbo irregular

Participio presente: andando

Participio pasado: andado

Imperativo: anda (no andes), ande Ud., andemos, andad (no andéis), anden Uds.

Indicativo				Condicional	Subjuntivo	
Presente	**Imperfecto**	**Pretérito**	**Futuro**	**Presente**	**Presente**	**Imperfecto**
ando	andaba	anduve	andaré	andaría	ande	anduviera
andas	andabas	anduviste	andarás	andarías	andes	anduvieras
anda	andaba	anduvo	andará	andaría	ande	anduviera
andamos	andábamos	anduvimos	andaremos	andaríamos	andemos	anduviéramos
andáis	andabais	anduvisteis	andaréis	andaríais	andéis	anduvierais
andan	andaban	anduvieron	andarán	andarían	anden	anduvieran
Pres. perfecto	**Pluscuamperf.**		**Futuro perfecto**	**Perfecto**	**Pres. perfecto**	**Pluscuamperf.**
he andado	había andado		habré andado	habría andado	haya andado	hubiera andado

4. APRENDER

(to learn)

Verbo regular 2ª conjugación

(Como **depender, emprender, meter, prender, responder**)

Participio presente: aprendiendo

Participio pasado: aprendido

Imperativo: aprende (no aprendas), aprenda Ud., aprendamos, aprended (no aprendáis), aprendan Uds.

Indicativo				Condicional	Subjuntivo	
Presente	**Imperfecto**	**Pretérito**	**Futuro**	**Presente**	**Presente**	**Imperfecto**
aprendo	aprendía	aprendí	aprenderé	aprendería	aprenda	aprendiera
aprendes	aprendías	aprendiste	aprenderás	aprenderías	aprendas	aprendieras
aprende	aprendía	aprendió	aprenderá	aprendería	aprenda	aprendiera
aprendemos	aprendíamos	aprendimos	aprenderemos	aprenderíamos	aprendamos	aprendiéramos
aprendéis	aprendíais	aprendisteis	aprenderéis	aprenderíais	aprendáis	aprendierais
aprenden	aprendían	aprendieron	aprenderán	aprenderían	aprendan	aprendieran
Pres. perfecto	**Pluscuamperf.**		**Futuro perfecto**	**Perfecto**	**Pres. perfecto**	**Pluscuamperf.**
he aprendido	había aprendido		habré aprendido	habría aprendido	haya aprendido	hubiera aprendido

5. AVERGONZAR

(to shame)

Verbo en -AR con cambio de *u* → *ü* frente a E; *z* → *c* frente a E

(Como **desvergonzarse**)

Participio presente: avergonzando

Participio pasado: avergonzado

Imperativo: avergüenza (no avergüences), avergüence Ud., avergoncemos, avergonzad (no avergoncéis), avergüencen Uds.

Indicativo				Condicional	Subjuntivo	
Presente	**Imperfecto**	**Pretérito**	**Futuro**	**Presente**	**Presente**	**Imperfecto**
avergüenzo	avergonzaba	avergoncé	avergonzaré	avergonzaría	avergüence	avergonzara
avergüenzas	avergonzabas	avergonzaste	avergonzarás	avergonzarías	avergüences	avergonzaras
avergüenza	avergonzaba	avergonzó	avergonzará	avergonzaría	avergüence	avergonzara
avergonzamos	avergonzábamos	avergonzamos	avergonzaremos	avergonzaríamos	avergoncemos	avergonzáramos
avergonzáis	avergonzabais	avergonzasteis	avergonzaréis	avergonzaríais	avergoncéis	avergonzarais
avergüenzan	avergonzaban	avergonzaron	avergonzarán	avergonzarían	avergüencen	avergonzaran
Pres. perfecto	**Pluscuamperf.**		**Futuro perfecto**	**Perfecto**	**Pres. perfecto**	**Pluscuamperf.**
he avergonzado	había avergonzado		habré avergonzado	habría avergonzado	haya avergonzado	hubiera avergonzado

6. AVERIGUAR

(to ascertain)

Verbo en -AR con cambio de *u* → *ü* frente a E

(Como **aguar, amortiguar, apaciguar, atestiguar, santiguar**)

Participio presente: averiguando

Participio pasado: averiguado

Imperativo: averigua (no averigües), averigüe Ud., averigüemos, averiguad (no averigüéis), averigüen Uds.

Indicativo				Condicional	Subjuntivo	
Presente	**Imperfecto**	**Pretérito**	**Futuro**	**Presente**	**Presente**	**Imperfecto**
averiguo	averiguaba	averigüé	averiguaré	averiguaría	averigüe	averiguara
averiguas	averiguabas	averiguaste	averiguarás	averiguarías	averigües	averiguaras
averigua	averiguaba	averiguó	averiguará	averiguaría	averigüe	averiguara
averiguamos	averiguábamos	averiguamos	averiguaremos	averiguaríamos	averigüemos	averiguáramos
averiguáis	averiguabais	averiguasteis	averiguaréis	averiguaríais	averigüéis	averiguarais
averiguan	averiguaban	averiguaron	averiguarán	averiguarían	averigüen	averiguaran
Pres. perfecto	**Pluscuamperf.**		**Futuro perfecto**	**Perfecto**	**Pres. perfecto**	**Pluscuamperf.**
he averiguado	había averiguado		habré averiguado	habría averiguado	haya averiguado	hubiera averiguado

7. BUSCAR
(to look for)

Verbo en -AR con cambio de *c* → *qu* frente a E

(Como **acercar, explicar, justificar, sacar, significar**)

Participio presente: buscando

Participio pasado: buscado

Imperativo: busca (no busques), busque Ud., busquemos, buscad (no busquéis), busquen Uds.

Indicativo				Condicional	Subjuntivo	
Presente	**Imperfecto**	**Pretérito**	**Futuro**	**Presente**	**Presente**	**Imperfecto**
busco	buscaba	busqué	buscaré	buscaría	busque	buscara
buscas	buscabas	buscaste	buscarás	buscarías	busques	buscaras
busca	buscaba	buscó	buscará	buscaría	busque	buscara
buscamos	buscábamos	buscamos	buscaremos	buscaríamos	busquemos	buscáramos
buscáis	buscabais	buscasteis	buscaréis	buscaríais	busquéis	buscarais
buscan	buscaban	buscaron	buscarán	buscarían	busquen	buscaran
Pres. perfecto	**Pluscuamperf.**		**Futuro perfecto**	**Perfecto**	**Pres. perfecto**	**Pluscuamperf.**
he buscado	había buscado		habré buscado	habría buscado	haya buscado	hubiera buscado

8. CABER
(to fit)

Verbo irregular

Participio presente: cabiendo

Participio pasado: cabido

Imperativo: cabe (no quepas), quepa Ud., quepamos, cabed (no quepáis), quepan Uds.

Indicativo				Condicional	Subjuntivo	
Presente	**Imperfecto**	**Pretérito**	**Futuro**	**Presente**	**Presente**	**Imperfecto**
quepo	cabía	cupe	cabré	cabría	quepa	cupiera
cabes	cabías	cupiste	cabrás	cabrías	quepas	cupieras
cabe	cabía	cupo	cabrá	cabría	quepa	cupiera
cabemos	cabíamos	cupimos	cabremos	cabríamos	quepamos	cupiéramos
cabéis	cabíais	cupisteis	cabréis	cabríais	quepáis	cupierais
caben	cabían	cupieron	cabrán	cabrían	quepan	cupieran
Pres. perfecto	**Pluscuamperf.**		**Futuro perfecto**	**Perfecto**	**Pres. perfecto**	**Pluscuamperf.**
he cabido	había cabido		habré cabido	habría cabido	haya cabido	hubiera cabido

9. CAER
(to fall)

Verbo irregular

(Como **decaer, recaer**)

Participio presente: cayendo

Participio pasado: caído

Imperativo: cae (no caigas), caiga Ud., caigamos, caed (no caigáis), caigan Uds.

Indicativo				Condicional	Subjuntivo	
Presente	**Imperfecto**	**Pretérito**	**Futuro**	**Presente**	**Presente**	**Imperfecto**
caigo	caía	caí	caeré	caería	caiga	cayera
caes	caías	caíste	caerás	caerías	caigas	cayeras
cae	caía	cayó	caerá	caería	caiga	cayera
caemos	caíamos	caímos	caeremos	caeríamos	caigamos	cayéramos
caéis	caíais	caísteis	caeréis	caeríais	caigáis	cayerais
caen	caían	cayeron	caerán	caerían	caigan	cayeran
Pres. perfecto	**Pluscuamperf.**		**Futuro perfecto**	**Perfecto**	**Pres. perfecto**	**Pluscuamperf.**
he caído	había caído		habré caído	habría caído	haya caído	hubiera caído

10. CAMINAR
(to walk)

Verbo regular 1ª conjugación

(Como **acabar, comentar, enamorar, interesar, tardar**)

Participio presente: caminando | **Participio pasado:** caminado

Imperativo: camina (no camines), camine Ud., caminemos, caminad (no caminéis), caminen Uds.

Indicativo				Condicional	Subjuntivo	
Presente	**Imperfecto**	**Pretérito**	**Futuro**	**Presente**	**Presente**	**Imperfecto**
camino	caminaba	caminé	caminaré	caminaría	camine	caminara
caminas	caminabas	caminaste	caminarás	caminarías	camines	caminaras
camina	caminaba	caminó	caminará	caminaría	camine	caminara
caminamos	caminábamos	caminamos	caminaremos	caminaríamos	caminemos	camináramos
camináis	caminabais	caminasteis	caminaréis	caminaríais	caminéis	caminarais
caminan	caminaban	caminaron	caminarán	caminarían	caminen	caminaran
Pres. perfecto	**Pluscuamperf.**		**Futuro perfecto**	**Perfecto**	**Pres. perfecto**	**Pluscuamperf.**
he caminado	había caminado		habré caminado	habría caminado	haya caminado	hubiera caminado

11. CERRAR
(to close)

Verbo en -AR con cambio de e → ie

(Como **acertar, calentar, despertar, quebrar, sentar**)

Participio presente: cerrando | **Participio pasado:** cerrado

Imperativo: cierra (no cierres), cierre Ud., cerremos, cerrad (no cerréis), cierren Uds.

Indicativo				Condicional	Subjuntivo	
Presente	**Imperfecto**	**Pretérito**	**Futuro**	**Presente**	**Presente**	**Imperfecto**
cierro	cerraba	cerré	cerraré	cerraría	cierre	cerrara
cierras	cerrabas	cerraste	cerrarás	cerrarías	cierres	cerraras
cierra	cerraba	cerró	cerrará	cerraría	cierre	cerrara
cerramos	cerrábamos	cerramos	cerraremos	cerraríamos	cerremos	cerráramos
cerráis	cerrabais	cerrasteis	cerraréis	cerraríais	cerréis	cerrarais
cierran	cerraban	cerraron	cerrarán	cerrarían	cierren	cerraran
Pres. perfecto	**Pluscuamperf.**		**Futuro perfecto**	**Perfecto**	**Pres. perfecto**	**Pluscuamperf.**
he cerrado	había cerrado		habré cerrado	habría cerrado	haya cerrado	hubiera cerrado

12. COCER
(to cook)

Verbo en -ER con cambio de o → ue; c → z frente a A y O

(Como **descocer, destorcer, retorcer, torcer**)

Participio presente: cociendo | **Participio pasado:** cocido

Imperativo: cuece (no cuezas), cueza Ud., cozamos, coced (no cozáis), cuezan Uds.

Indicativo				Condicional	Subjuntivo	
Presente	**Imperfecto**	**Pretérito**	**Futuro**	**Presente**	**Presente**	**Imperfecto**
cuezo	cocía	cocí	coceré	cocería	cueza	cociera
cueces	cocías	cociste	cocerás	cocerías	cuezas	cocieras
cuece	cocía	coció	cocerá	cocería	cueza	cociera
cocemos	cocíamos	cocimos	coceremos	coceríamos	cozamos	cociéramos
cocéis	cocíais	cocisteis	coceréis	coceríais	cozáis	cocierais
cuecen	cocían	cocieron	cocerán	cocerían	cuezan	cocieran
Pres. perfecto	**Pluscuamperf.**		**Futuro perfecto**	**Perfecto**	**Pres. perfecto**	**Pluscuamperf.**
he cocido	había cocido		habré cocido	habría cocido	haya cocido	hubiera cocido

13. COGER
(to take hold of)

Verbo en -ER con cambio de *g* → *j* frente a A y O

(Como **acoger, encoger, escoger, proteger, recoger**)

Participio presente: cogiendo | **Participio pasado:** cogido

Imperativo: coge (no cojas), coja Ud., cojamos, coged (no cojáis), cojan Uds.

Indicativo				Condicional	Subjuntivo	
Presente	**Imperfecto**	**Pretérito**	**Futuro**	**Presente**	**Presente**	**Imperfecto**
cojo	cogía	cogí	cogeré	cogería	coja	cogiera
coges	cogías	cogiste	cogerás	cogerías	cojas	cogieras
coge	cogía	cogió	cogerá	cogería	coja	cogiera
cogemos	cogíamos	cogimos	cogeremos	cogeríamos	cojamos	cogiéramos
cogéis	cogíais	cogisteis	cogeréis	cogeríais	cojáis	cogierais
cogen	cogían	cogieron	cogerán	cogerían	cojan	cogieran
Pres. perfecto	**Pluscuamperf.**		**Futuro perfecto**	**Perfecto**	**Pres. perfecto**	**Pluscuamperf.**
he cogido	había cogido		habré cogido	habría cogido	haya cogido	hubiera cogido

14. COMENZAR
(to begin)

Verbo en -AR con cambio de *e* → *ie*; *z* → *c* frente a E

(Como **empezar, recomenzar, tropezar**)

Participio presente: comenzando | **Participio pasado:** comenzado

Imperativo: comienza (no comiences), comience Ud., comencemos, comenzad (no comencéis), comiencen Uds.

Indicativo				Condicional	Subjuntivo	
Presente	**Imperfecto**	**Pretérito**	**Futuro**	**Presente**	**Presente**	**Imperfecto**
comienzo	comenzaba	comencé	comenzaré	comenzaría	comience	comenzara
comienzas	comenzabas	comenzaste	comenzarás	comenzarías	comiences	comenzaras
comienza	comenzaba	comenzó	comenzará	comenzaría	comience	comenzara
comenzamos	comenzábamos	comenzamos	comenzaremos	comenzaríamos	comencemos	comenzáramos
comenzáis	comenzabais	comenzasteis	comenzaréis	comenzaríais	comencéis	comenzarais
comienzan	comenzaban	comenzaron	comenzarán	comenzarían	comiencen	comenzaran
Pres. perfecto	**Pluscuamperf.**		**Futuro perfecto**	**Perfecto**	**Pres. perfecto**	**Pluscuamperf.**
he comenzado	había comenzado		habré comenzado	habría comenzado	haya comenzado	hubiera comenzado

15. CONCLUIR
(to conclude)

Verbo en -IR con cambio de *i* → *y*

(Como **atribuir, construir, distribuir, excluir, huir**)

Participio presente: concluyendo | **Participio pasado:** concluido

Imperativo: concluye (no concluyas), concluya Ud., concluyamos, concluid (no concluyáis), concluyan Uds.

Indicativo				Condicional	Subjuntivo	
Presente	**Imperfecto**	**Pretérito**	**Futuro**	**Presente**	**Presente**	**Imperfecto**
concluyo	concluía	concluí	concluiré	concluiría	concluya	concluyera
concluyes	concluías	concluiste	concluirás	concluirías	concluyas	concluyeras
concluye	concluía	concluyó	concluirá	concluiría	concluya	concluyera
concluimos	concluíamos	concluimos	concluiremos	concluiríamos	concluyamos	concluyéramos
concluís	concluíais	concluisteis	concluiréis	concluiríais	concluyáis	concluyerais
concluyen	concluían	concluyeron	concluirán	concluirían	concluyan	concluyeran
Pres. perfecto	**Pluscuamperf.**		**Futuro perfecto**	**Perfecto**	**Pres. perfecto**	**Pluscuamperf.**
he concluido	había concluido		habré concluido	habría concluido	haya concluido	hubiera concluido

16. CONDUCIR
(to conduct)

Verbo en -IR con cambio de $c \rightarrow zc$ frente a A y O; $c \rightarrow j$

(Como **deducir, introducir, producir, reducir, traducir**)

Participio presente: conduciendo | **Participio pasado:** conducido

Imperativo: conduce (no conduzcas), conduzca Ud., conduzcamos, conducid (no conduzcáis), conduzcan Uds.

Indicativo				Condicional	Subjuntivo	
Presente	**Imperfecto**	**Pretérito**	**Futuro**	**Presente**	**Presente**	**Imperfecto**
conduzco	conducía	conduje	conduciré	conduciría	conduzca	condujera
conduces	conducías	condujiste	conducirás	conducirías	conduzcas	condujeras
conduce	conducía	condujo	conducirá	conduciría	conduzca	condujera
conducimos	conducíamos	condujimos	conduciremos	conduciríamos	conduzcamos	condujéramos
conducís	conducíais	condujisteis	conduciréis	conduciríais	conduzcáis	condujerais
conducen	conducían	condujeron	conducirán	conducirían	conduzcan	condujeran
Pres. perfecto	**Pluscuamperf.**		**Futuro perfecto**	**Perfecto**	**Pres. perfecto**	**Pluscuamperf.**
he conducido	había conducido		habré conducido	habría conducido	haya conducido	hubiera conducido

17. CONTAR
(to tell, to count)

Verbo en -AR con cambio de $o \rightarrow ue$

(Como **acostar, costar, encontrar, mostrar, probar**)

Participio presente: contando | **Participio pasado:** contado

Imperativo: cuenta (no cuentes), cuente Ud., contemos, contad (no contéis), cuenten Uds.

Indicativo				Condicional	Subjuntivo	
Presente	**Imperfecto**	**Pretérito**	**Futuro**	**Presente**	**Presente**	**Imperfecto**
cuento	contaba	conté	contaré	contaría	cuente	contara
cuentas	contabas	contaste	contarás	contarías	cuentes	contaras
cuenta	contaba	contó	contará	contaría	cuente	contara
contamos	contábamos	contamos	contaremos	contaríamos	contemos	contáramos
contáis	contabais	contasteis	contaréis	contaríais	contéis	contarais
cuentan	contaban	contaron	contarán	contarían	cuenten	contaran
Pres. perfecto	**Pluscuamperf.**		**Futuro perfecto**	**Perfecto**	**Pres. perfecto**	**Pluscuamperf.**
he contado	había contado		habré contado	habría contado	haya contado	hubiera contado

18. CREER
(to believe)

Verbo irregular

(Como **descreer, leer, poseer, proveer, releer**)

Participio presente: creyendo | **Participio pasado:** creído

Imperativo: cree (no creas), crea Ud., creamos, creed (no creáis), crean Uds.

Indicativo				Condicional	Subjuntivo	
Presente	**Imperfecto**	**Pretérito**	**Futuro**	**Presente**	**Presente**	**Imperfecto**
creo	creía	creí	creeré	creería	crea	creyera
crees	creías	creíste	creerás	creerías	creas	creyeras
cree	creía	creyó	creerá	creería	crea	creyera
creemos	creíamos	creímos	creeremos	creeríamos	creamos	creyéramos
creéis	creíais	creísteis	creeréis	creeríais	creáis	creyerais
creen	creían	creyeron	creerán	creerían	crean	creyeran
Pres. perfecto	**Pluscuamperf.**		**Futuro perfecto**	**Perfecto**	**Pres. perfecto**	**Pluscuamperf.**
he creído	había creído		habré creído	habría creído	haya creído	hubiera creído

19. CRUZAR
(to cross)

Verbo en -AR con cambio de z → c frente a A y O

(Como **abrazar, bostezar, especializar, lanzar, reemplazar**)

Participio presente: cruzando | **Participio pasado:** cruzado

Imperativo: cruza (no cruces), cruce Ud., crucemos, cruzad (no crucéis), crucen Uds.

Indicativo				Condicional	Subjuntivo	
Presente	**Imperfecto**	**Pretérito**	**Futuro**	**Presente**	**Presente**	**Imperfecto**
cruzo	cruzaba	crucé	cruzaré	cruzaría	cruce	cruzara
cruzas	cruzabas	cruzaste	cruzarás	cruzarías	cruces	cruzaras
cruza	cruzaba	cruzó	cruzará	cruzaría	cruce	cruzara
cruzamos	cruzábamos	cruzamos	cruzaremos	cruzaríamos	crucemos	cruzáramos
cruzáis	cruzabais	cruzasteis	cruzaréis	cruzaríais	crucéis	cruzarais
cruzan	cruzaban	cruzaron	cruzarán	cruzarían	crucen	cruzaran
Pres. perfecto	**Pluscuamperf.**		**Futuro perfecto**	**Perfecto**	**Pres. perfecto**	**Pluscuamperf.**
he cruzado	había cruzado		habré cruzado	habría cruzado	haya cruzado	hubiera cruzado

20. DAR
(to give)

Verbo irregular

Participio presente: dando | **Participio pasado:** dado

Imperativo: da (no des), dé Ud., demos, dad (no deis), den Uds.

Indicativo				Condicional	Subjuntivo	
Presente	**Imperfecto**	**Pretérito**	**Futuro**	**Presente**	**Presente**	**Imperfecto**
doy	daba	di	daré	daría	dé	diera
das	dabas	diste	darás	darías	des	dieras
da	daba	dio	dará	daría	dé	diera
damos	dábamos	dimos	daremos	daríamos	demos	diéramos
dais	dabais	disteis	daréis	daríais	deis	dierais
dan	daban	dieron	darán	darían	den	dieran
Pres. perfecto	**Pluscuamperf.**		**Futuro perfecto**	**Perfecto**	**Pres. perfecto**	**Pluscuamperf.**
he dado	había dado		habré dado	habría dado	haya dado	hubiera dado

21. DECIR
(to say)

Verbo irregular

Participio presente: diciendo | **Participio pasado:** dicho

Imperativo: di (no digas), diga Ud., digamos, decid (no digáis), digan Uds.

Indicativo				Condicional	Subjuntivo	
Presente	**Imperfecto**	**Pretérito**	**Futuro**	**Presente**	**Presente**	**Imperfecto**
digo	decía	dije	diré	diría	diga	dijera
dices	decías	dijiste	dirás	dirías	digas	dijeras
dice	decía	dijo	dirá	diría	diga	dijera
decimos	decíamos	dijimos	diremos	diríamos	digamos	dijéramos
decís	decíais	dijisteis	diréis	diríais	digáis	dijerais
dicen	decían	dijeron	dirán	dirían	digan	dijeran
Pres. perfecto	**Pluscuamperf.**		**Futuro perfecto**	**Perfecto**	**Pres. perfecto**	**Pluscuamperf.**
he dicho	había dicho		habré dicho	habría dicho	haya dicho	hubiera dicho

22. DIRIGIR

(to direct)

Verbo en -IR con cambio de *g* → *j* frente a A y O

(Como **afligir, exigir, fingir, surgir, urgir**)

Participio presente: dirigiendo | **Participio pasado:** dirigido

Imperativo: dirige (no dirijas), dirija Ud., dirijamos, dirigid (no dirijáis), dirijan Uds.

Indicativo				Condicional	Subjuntivo	
Presente	**Imperfecto**	**Pretérito**	**Futuro**	**Presente**	**Presente**	**Imperfecto**
dirijo	dirigía	dirigí	dirigiré	dirigiría	dirija	dirigiera
diriges	dirigías	dirigiste	dirigirás	dirigirías	dirijas	dirigieras
dirige	dirigía	dirigió	dirigirá	dirigiría	dirija	dirigiera
dirigimos	dirigíamos	dirigimos	dirigiremos	dirigiríamos	dirijamos	dirigiéramos
dirigís	dirigíais	dirigisteis	dirigiréis	dirigiríais	dirijáis	dirigierais
dirigen	dirigían	dirigieron	dirigirán	dirigirían	dirijan	dirigieran
Pres. perfecto	**Pluscuamperf.**		**Futuro perfecto**	**Perfecto**	**Pres. perfecto**	**Pluscuamperf.**
he dirigido	había dirigido		habré dirigido	habría dirigido	haya dirigido	hubiera dirigido

23. DISCERNIR

(to discern)

Verbo en -IR con cambio de *e* → *ie*

(Como **cernir, concernir**)

Participio presente: discerniendo | **Participio pasado:** discernido

Imperativo: discierne (no disciernas), discierna Ud., discernamos, discernid (no discernáis), disciernan Uds.

Indicativo				Condicional	Subjuntivo	
Presente	**Imperfecto**	**Pretérito**	**Futuro**	**Presente**	**Presente**	**Imperfecto**
discierno	discernía	discerní	discerniré	discerniría	discierna	discerniera
disciernes	discernías	discerniste	discernirás	discernirías	disciernas	discernieras
discierne	discernía	discernió	discernirá	discerniría	discierna	discerniera
discernimos	discerníamos	discernimos	discerniremos	discerniríamos	discernamos	discerniéramos
discernís	discerníais	discernisteis	discerniréis	discerniríais	discernáis	discernierais
disciernen	discernían	discernieron	discernirán	discernirían	disciernan	discernieran
Pres. perfecto	**Pluscuamperf.**		**Futuro perfecto**	**Perfecto**	**Pres. perfecto**	**Pluscuamperf.**
he discernido	había discernido		habré discernido	habría discernido	haya discernido	hubiera discernido

24. DISTINGUIR

(to distinguish)

Verbo en -IR con cambio de *gu* → *g* frente a A y O

(Como **extinguir**)

Participio presente: distinguiendo | **Participio pasado:** distinguido

Imperativo: distingue (no distingas), distinga Ud., distingamos, distinguid (no distingáis), distingan Uds.

Indicativo				Condicional	Subjuntivo	
Presente	**Imperfecto**	**Pretérito**	**Futuro**	**Presente**	**Presente**	**Imperfecto**
distingo	distinguía	distinguí	distinguiré	distinguiría	distinga	distinguiera
distingues	distinguías	distinguiste	distinguirás	distinguirías	distingas	distinguieras
distingue	distinguía	distinguió	distinguirá	distinguiría	distinga	distinguiera
distinguimos	distinguíamos	distinguimos	distinguiremos	distinguiríamos	distingamos	distinguiéramos
distinguís	distinguíais	distinguisteis	distinguiréis	distinguiríais	distingáis	distinguierais
distinguen	distinguían	distinguieron	distinguirán	distinguirían	distingan	distinguieran
Pres. perfecto	**Pluscuamperf.**		**Futuro perfecto**	**Perfecto**	**Pres. perfecto**	**Pluscuamperf.**
he distinguido	había distinguido		habré distinguido	habría distinguido	haya distinguido	hubiera distinguido

25. DORMIR
(to sleep)

Verbo en -IR con cambio de *o → ue* y *o → u*

Participio presente: durmiendo | **Participio pasado:** dormido

Imperativo: duerme (no duermas), duerma Ud., durmamos, dormid (no durmáis), duerman Uds.

Indicativo				Condicional	Subjuntivo	
Presente	**Imperfecto**	**Pretérito**	**Futuro**	**Presente**	**Presente**	**Imperfecto**
duermo	dormía	dormí	dormiré	dormiría	duerma	durmiera
duermes	dormías	dormiste	dormirás	dormirías	duermas	durmieras
duerme	dormía	durmió	dormirá	dormiría	duerma	durmiera
dormimos	dormíamos	dormimos	dormiremos	dormiríamos	durmamos	durmiéramos
dormís	dormíais	dormisteis	dormiréis	dormiríais	durmáis	durmierais
duermen	dormían	durmieron	dormirán	dormirían	duerman	durmieran
Pres. perfecto	**Pluscuamperf.**		**Futuro perfecto**	**Perfecto**	**Pres. perfecto**	**Pluscuamperf.**
he dormido	había dormido		habré dormido	habría dormido	haya dormido	hubiera dormido

26. ENVIAR
(to send)

Verbo en -AR con cambio de *i → í*

(Como **ampliar, confiar, enfriar, rociar, vaciar, variar**)

Participio presente: enviando | **Participio pasado:** enviado

Imperativo: envía (no envíes), envíe Ud., enviemos, enviad (no enviéis), envíen Uds.

Indicativo				Condicional	Subjuntivo	
Presente	**Imperfecto**	**Pretérito**	**Futuro**	**Presente**	**Presente**	**Imperfecto**
envío	enviaba	envié	enviaré	enviaría	envíe	enviara
envías	enviabas	enviaste	enviarás	enviarías	envíes	enviaras
envía	enviaba	envió	enviará	enviaría	envíe	enviara
enviamos	enviábamos	enviamos	enviaremos	enviaríamos	enviemos	enviáramos
enviáis	enviabais	enviasteis	enviaréis	enviaríais	enviéis	enviarais
envían	enviaban	enviaron	enviarán	enviarían	envíen	enviaran
Pres. perfecto	**Pluscuamperf.**		**Futuro perfecto**	**Perfecto**	**Pres. perfecto**	**Pluscuamperf.**
he enviado	había enviado		habré enviado	habría enviado	haya enviado	hubiera enviado

27. ERRAR
(to wander)

Verbo en -AR con cambio de *e → ye*

(Como **aberrar**)

Participio presente: errando | **Participio pasado:** errado

Imperativo: yerra (no yerres), yerre Ud., erremos, errad (no erréis), yerren Uds.

Indicativo				Condicional	Subjuntivo	
Presente	**Imperfecto**	**Pretérito**	**Futuro**	**Presente**	**Presente**	**Imperfecto**
yerro	erraba	erré	erraré	erraría	yerre	errara
yerras	errabas	erraste	errarás	errarías	yerres	erraras
yerra	erraba	erró	errará	erraría	yerre	errara
erramos	errábamos	erramos	erraremos	erraríamos	erremos	erráramos
erráis	errabais	errasteis	erraréis	erraríais	erréis	errarais
yerran	erraban	erraron	errarán	errarían	yerren	erraran
Pres. perfecto	**Pluscuamperf.**		**Futuro perfecto**	**Perfecto**	**Pres. perfecto**	**Pluscuamperf.**
he errado	había errado		habré errado	habría errado	haya errado	hubiera errado

28. ESPARCIR
(to scatter)

Verbo en -IR con cambio de *c → z* frente a A y O
(Como **fruncir, uncir, zurcir**)

Participio presente: esparciendo | **Participio pasado:** esparcido

Imperativo: esparce (no esparzas), esparza Ud., esparzamos, esparcid (no esparzáis), esparzan Uds.

Indicativo				Condicional	Subjuntivo	
Presente	**Imperfecto**	**Pretérito**	**Futuro**	**Presente**	**Presente**	**Imperfecto**
esparzo	esparcía	esparcí	esparciré	esparciría	esparza	esparciera
esparces	esparcías	esparciste	esparcirás	esparcirías	esparzas	esparcieras
esparce	esparcía	esparció	esparcirá	esparciría	esparza	esparciera
esparcimos	esparcíamos	esparcimos	esparciremos	esparciríamos	esparzamos	esparciéramos
esparcís	esparcíais	esparcisteis	esparciréis	esparciríais	esparzáis	esparcierais
esparcen	esparcian	esparcieron	esparcirán	esparcirían	esparzan	esparcieran
Pres. perfecto	**Pluscuamperf.**		**Futuro perfecto**	**Perfecto**	**Pres. perfecto**	**Pluscuamperf.**
he esparcido	había esparcido		habré esparcido	habría esparcido	haya esparcido	hubiera esparcido

29. ESTAR
(to be)

Verbo irregular

Participio presente: estando | **Participio pasado:** estado

Imperativo: está (no estés), esté Ud., estemos, estad (no estéis), estén Uds.

Indicativo				Condicional	Subjuntivo	
Presente	**Imperfecto**	**Pretérito**	**Futuro**	**Presente**	**Presente**	**Imperfecto**
estoy	estaba	estuve	estaré	estaría	esté	estuviera
estás	estabas	estuviste	estarás	estarías	estés	estuvieras
está	estaba	estuvo	estará	estaría	esté	estuviera
estamos	estábamos	estuvimos	estaremos	estaríamos	estemos	estuviéramos
estáis	estabais	estuvisteis	estaréis	estaríais	estéis	estuvierais
están	estaban	estuvieron	estarán	estarían	estén	estuvieran
Pres. perfecto	**Pluscuamperf.**		**Futuro perfecto**	**Perfecto**	**Pres. perfecto**	**Pluscuamperf.**
he estado	había estado		habré estado	habría estado	haya estado	hubiera estado

30. FORZAR
(to force)

Verbo en -AR con cambio de *o → ue*; *z → c* frente a E
(Como **almorzar, esforzar, reforzar**)

Participio presente: forzando | **Participio pasado:** forzado

Imperativo: fuerza (no fuerces), fuerce Ud., forcemos, forzad (no forcéis), fuercen Uds.

Indicativo				Condicional	Subjuntivo	
Presente	**Imperfecto**	**Pretérito**	**Futuro**	**Presente**	**Presente**	**Imperfecto**
fuerzo	forzaba	forcé	forzaré	forzaría	fuerce	forzara
fuerzas	forzabas	forzaste	forzarás	forzarías	fuerces	forzaras
fuerza	forzaba	forzó	forzará	forzaría	fuerce	forzara
forzamos	forzábamos	forzamos	forzaremos	forzaríamos	forcemos	forzáramos
forzáis	forzabais	forzasteis	forzaréis	forzaríais	forcéis	forzarais
fuerzan	forzaban	forzaron	forzarán	forzarían	fuercen	forzaran
Pres. perfecto	**Pluscuamperf.**		**Futuro perfecto**	**Perfecto**	**Pres. perfecto**	**Pluscuamperf.**
he forzado	había forzado		habré forzado	habría forzado	haya forzado	hubiera forzado

31. HABER
(to have)

Verbo irregular (*Para la conjugación de "hay", vea la 3ª persona de cada tiempo excepto el presente del indicativo.)

Participio presente: habiendo

Participio pasado: habido

Imperativo: ha (no hayas), haya Ud., hayamos, habed (no hayáis), hayan Uds.

Indicativo				Condicional	Subjuntivo	
Presente	**Imperfecto**	**Pretérito**	**Futuro**	**Presente**	**Presente**	**Imperfecto**
he	había	hube	habré	habría	haya	hubiera
has	habías	hubiste	habrás	habrías	hayas	hubieras
ha (hay*)	había*	hubo*	habrá*	habría*	haya*	hubiera*
hemos	habíamos	hubimos	habremos	habríamos	hayamos	hubiéramos
habéis	habíais	hubisteis	habréis	habríais	hayáis	hubierais
han	habían	hubieron	habrán	habrían	hayan	hubieran
Pres. perfecto	**Pluscuamperf.**		**Futuro perfecto**	**Perfecto**	**Pres. perfecto**	**Pluscuamperf.**
he habido	había habido		habré habido	habría habido	haya habido	hubiera habido

32. HACER
(to do)

Verbo irregular

(Como **deshacer, rehacer, satisfacer**)

Participio presente: haciendo

Participio pasado: hecho

Imperativo: haz (no hagas), haga Ud., hagamos, haced (no hagáis), hagan Uds.

Indicativo				Condicional	Subjuntivo	
Presente	**Imperfecto**	**Pretérito**	**Futuro**	**Presente**	**Presente**	**Imperfecto**
hago	hacía	hice	haré	haría	haga	hiciera
haces	hacías	hiciste	harás	harías	hagas	hicieras
hace	hacía	hizo	hará	haría	haga	hiciera
hacemos	hacíamos	hicimos	haremos	haríamos	hagamos	hiciéramos
hacéis	hacíais	hicisteis	haréis	haríais	hagáis	hicierais
hacen	hacían	hicieron	harán	harían	hagan	hicieran
Pres. perfecto	**Pluscuamperf.**		**Futuro perfecto**	**Perfecto**	**Pres. perfecto**	**Pluscuamperf.**
he hecho	había hecho		habré hecho	habría hecho	haya hecho	hubiera hecho

33. IR
(to go)

Verbo irregular

Participio presente: yendo

Participio pasado: ido

Imperativo: ve (no vayas), vaya Ud., vamos (no vayamos), id (no vayáis), vayan Uds.

Indicativo				Condicional	Subjuntivo	
Presente	**Imperfecto**	**Pretérito**	**Futuro**	**Presente**	**Presente**	**Imperfecto**
voy	iba	fui	iré	iría	vaya	fuera
vas	ibas	fuiste	irás	irías	vayas	fueras
va	iba	fue	irá	iría	vaya	fuera
vamos	íbamos	fuimos	iremos	iríamos	vayamos	fuéramos
vais	ibais	fuisteis	iréis	iríais	vayáis	fuerais
van	iban	fueron	irán	irían	vayan	fueran
Pres. perfecto	**Pluscuamperf.**		**Futuro perfecto**	**Perfecto**	**Pres. perfecto**	**Pluscuamperf.**
he ido	había ido		habré ido	habría ido	haya ido	hubiera ido

34. JUGAR
(to play)

Verbo en -AR con cambio de *u* → *ue*; *g* → *gu* frente a E

Participio presente: jugando   **Participio pasado:** jugado

Imperativo: juega (no juegues), juegue Ud., juguemos, jugad (no juguéis), jueguen Uds.

Indicativo				Condicional	Subjuntivo	
Presente	**Imperfecto**	**Pretérito**	**Futuro**	**Presente**	**Presente**	**Imperfecto**
juego	jugaba	jugué	jugaré	jugaría	juegue	jugara
juegas	jugabas	jugaste	jugarás	jugarías	juegues	jugaras
juega	jugaba	jugó	jugará	jugaría	juegue	jugara
jugamos	jugábamos	jugamos	jugaremos	jugaríamos	juguemos	jugáramos
jugáis	jugabais	jugasteis	jugaréis	jugaríais	juguéis	jugarais
juegan	jugaban	jugaron	jugarán	jugarían	jueguen	jugaran
Pres. perfecto	**Pluscuamperf.**		**Futuro perfecto**	**Perfecto**	**Pres. perfecto**	**Pluscuamperf.**
he jugado	había jugado		habré jugado	habría jugado	haya jugado	hubiera jugado

35. LLEGAR
(to arrive)

Verbo en -AR con cambio de *g* → *gu* frente a E

(Como **abrigar, cargar, entregar, obligar, pagar**)

Participio presente: llegando   **Participio pasado:** llegado

Imperativo: llega (no llegues), llegue Ud., lleguemos, llegad (no lleguéis), lleguen Uds.

Indicativo				Condicional	Subjuntivo	
Presente	**Imperfecto**	**Pretérito**	**Futuro**	**Presente**	**Presente**	**Imperfecto**
llego	llegaba	llegué	llegaré	llegaría	llegue	llegara
llegas	llegabas	llegaste	llegarás	llegarías	llegues	llegaras
llega	llegaba	llegó	llegará	llegaría	llegue	llegara
llegamos	llegábamos	llegamos	llegaremos	llegaríamos	lleguemos	llegáramos
llegáis	llegabais	llegasteis	llegaréis	llegaríais	lleguéis	llegarais
llegan	llegaban	llegaron	llegarán	llegarían	lleguen	llegaran
Pres. perfecto	**Pluscuamperf.**		**Futuro perfecto**	**Perfecto**	**Pres. perfecto**	**Pluscuamperf.**
he llegado	había llegado		habré llegado	habría llegado	haya llegado	hubiera llegado

36. LUCIR
(to shine)

Verbo en -IR con cambio de *c* → *zc* frente a A y O

(Como **relucir, translucirse, traslucir**)

Participio presente: luciendo   **Participio pasado:** lucido

Imperativo: luce (no luzcas), luzca Ud., luzcamos, lucid (no luzcáis), luzcan Uds.

Indicativo				Condicional	Subjuntivo	
Presente	**Imperfecto**	**Pretérito**	**Futuro**	**Presente**	**Presente**	**Imperfecto**
luzco	lucía	lucí	luciré	luciría	luzca	luciera
luces	lucías	luciste	lucirás	lucirías	luzcas	lucieras
luce	lucía	lució	lucirá	luciría	luzca	luciera
lucimos	lucíamos	lucimos	luciremos	luciríamos	luzcamos	luciéramos
lucís	lucíais	lucisteis	luciréis	luciríais	luzcáis	lucierais
lucen	lucían	lucieron	lucirán	lucirían	luzcan	lucieran
Pres. perfecto	**Pluscuamperf.**		**Futuro perfecto**	**Perfecto**	**Pres. perfecto**	**Pluscuamperf.**
he lucido	había lucido		habré lucido	habría lucido	haya lucido	hubiera lucido

37. MORIR

(to die)

Verbo en -IR con cambio de *o → ue*; participio pasado irregular

Participio presente: muriendo

Participio pasado: muerto

Imperativo: muere (no mueras), muera Ud., muramos, morid (no muráis), mueran Uds.

Indicativo				Condicional	Subjuntivo	
Presente	**Imperfecto**	**Pretérito**	**Futuro**	**Presente**	**Presente**	**Imperfecto**
muero	moría	morí	moriré	moriría	muera	muriera
mueres	morías	moriste	morirás	morirías	mueras	murieras
muere	moría	murió	morirá	moriría	muera	muriera
morimos	moríamos	morimos	moriremos	moriríamos	muramos	muriéramos
morís	moríais	moristeis	moriréis	moriríais	muráis	murierais
mueren	morían	murieron	morirán	morirían	mueran	murieran
Pres. perfecto	**Pluscuamperf.**		**Futuro perfecto**	**Perfecto**	**Pres. perfecto**	**Pluscuamperf.**
he muerto	había muerto		habré muerto	habría muerto	haya muerto	hubiera muerto

38. MOVER

(to move)

Verbo en -ER con cambio de *o → ue*

(Como **doler, llover, morder, promover, remorder**)

Participio presente: moviendo

Participio pasado: movido

Imperativo: mueve (no muevas), mueva Ud., movamos, moved (no mováis), muevan Uds.

Indicativo				Condicional	Subjuntivo	
Presente	**Imperfecto**	**Pretérito**	**Futuro**	**Presente**	**Presente**	**Imperfecto**
muevo	movía	moví	moveré	movería	mueva	moviera
mueves	movías	moviste	moverás	moverías	muevas	movieras
mueve	movía	movió	moverá	movería	mueva	moviera
movemos	movíamos	movimos	moveremos	moveríamos	movamos	moviéramos
movéis	movíais	movisteis	moveréis	moveríais	mováis	movierais
mueven	movían	movieron	moverán	moverían	muevan	movieran
Pres. perfecto	**Pluscuamperf.**		**Futuro perfecto**	**Perfecto**	**Pres. perfecto**	**Pluscuamperf.**
he movido	había movido		habré movido	habría movido	haya movido	hubiera movido

39. NEGAR

(to deny)

Verbo en -AR con cambio de *e → ie*; *g → gu* frente a A y O

(Como **cegar, fregar, regar, renegar, restregar**)

Participio presente: negando

Participio pasado: negado

Imperativo: niega (no niegues), niegue Ud., neguemos, negad (no neguéis), nieguen Uds.

Indicativo				Condicional	Subjuntivo	
Presente	**Imperfecto**	**Pretérito**	**Futuro**	**Presente**	**Presente**	**Imperfecto**
niego	negaba	negué	negaré	negaría	niegue	negara
niegas	negabas	negaste	negarás	negarías	niegues	negaras
niega	negaba	negó	negará	negaría	niegue	negara
negamos	negábamos	negamos	negaremos	negaríamos	neguemos	negáramos
negáis	negabais	negasteis	negaréis	negaríais	neguéis	negarais
niegan	negaban	negaron	negarán	negarían	nieguen	negaran
Pres. perfecto	**Pluscuamperf.**		**Futuro perfecto**	**Perfecto**	**Pres. perfecto**	**Pluscuamperf.**
he negado	había negado		habré negado	habría negado	haya negado	hubiera negado

40. OÍR
(to hear)

Verbo irregular

Participio presente: oyendo | **Participio pasado:** oído

Imperativo: oye (no oigas), oiga Ud., oigamos, oíd (no oigáis), oigan Uds.

Indicativo				Condicional	Subjuntivo	
Presente	**Imperfecto**	**Pretérito**	**Futuro**	**Presente**	**Presente**	**Imperfecto**
oigo	oía	oí	oiré	oiría	oiga	oyera
oyes	oías	oíste	oirás	oirías	oigas	oyeras
oye	oía	oyó	oirá	oiría	oiga	oyera
oímos	oíamos	oímos	oiremos	oiríamos	oigamos	oyéramos
oís	oíais	oísteis	oiréis	oiríais	oigáis	oyerais
oyen	oían	oyeron	oirán	oirían	oigan	oyeran
Pres. perfecto	**Pluscuamperf.**		**Futuro perfecto**	**Perfecto**	**Pres. perfecto**	**Pluscuamperf.**
he oído	había oído		habré oído	habría oído	haya oído	hubiera oído

41. OLER
(to smell)

Verbo en -ER con cambio de o → hue

Participio presente: oliendo | **Participio pasado:** olido

Imperativo: huele (no huelas), huela Ud., olamos, oled (no oláis), huelan Uds.

Indicativo				Condicional	Subjuntivo	
Presente	**Imperfecto**	**Pretérito**	**Futuro**	**Presente**	**Presente**	**Imperfecto**
huelo	olía	olí	oleré	olería	huela	oliera
hueles	olías	oliste	olerás	olerías	huelas	olieras
huele	olía	olió	olerá	olería	huela	oliera
olemos	olíamos	olimos	oleremos	oleríamos	olamos	oliéramos
oléis	olíais	olisteis	oleréis	oleríais	oláis	olierais
huelen	olían	olieron	olerán	olerían	huelan	olieran
Pres. perfecto	**Pluscuamperf.**		**Futuro perfecto**	**Perfecto**	**Pres. perfecto**	**Pluscuamperf.**
he olido	había olido		habré olido	habría olido	haya olido	hubiera olido

42. PARECER
(to seem)

Verbo en -ER con cambio de c → zc frente a A y O

(Como **agradecer, conocer, crecer, merecer, nacer**)

Participio presente: pareciendo | **Participio pasado:** parecido

Imperativo: parece (no parezcas), parezca Ud., parezcamos, pareced (no parezcáis), parezcan Uds.

Indicativo				Condicional	Subjuntivo	
Presente	**Imperfecto**	**Pretérito**	**Futuro**	**Presente**	**Presente**	**Imperfecto**
parezco	parecía	parecí	pareceré	parecería	parezca	pareciera
pareces	parecías	pareciste	parecerás	parecerías	parezcas	parecieras
parece	parecía	pareció	parecerá	parecería	parezca	pareciera
parecemos	parecíamos	parecimos	pareceremos	pareceríamos	parezcamos	pareciéramos
parecéis	parecíais	parecisteis	pareceréis	pareceríais	parezcáis	parecierais
parecen	parecían	parecieron	parecerán	parecerían	parezcan	parecieran
Pres. perfecto	**Pluscuamperf.**		**Futuro perfecto**	**Perfecto**	**Pres. perfecto**	**Pluscuamperf.**
he parecido	había parecido		habré parecido	habría parecido	haya parecido	hubiera parecido

43. PEDIR
(to ask for)

Verbo en -IR con cambio de e → i

(Como **competir, despedir, medir, repetir, servir**)

Participio presente: pidiendo		**Participio pasado:** pedido

Imperativo: pide (no pidas), pida Ud., pidamos, pedid (no pidáis), pidan Uds.

Indicativo				Condicional	Subjuntivo	
Presente	**Imperfecto**	**Pretérito**	**Futuro**	**Presente**	**Presente**	**Imperfecto**
pido	pedía	pedí	pediré	pediría	pida	pidiera
pides	pedías	pediste	pedirás	pedirías	pidas	pidieras
pide	pedía	pidió	pedirá	pediría	pida	pidiera
pedimos	pedíamos	pedimos	pediremos	pediríamos	pidamos	pidiéramos
pedís	pedíais	pedisteis	pediréis	pediríais	pidáis	pidierais
piden	pedían	pidieron	pedirán	pedirían	pidan	pidieran
Pres. perfecto	**Pluscuamperf.**		**Futuro perfecto**	**Perfecto**	**Pres. perfecto**	**Pluscuamperf.**
he pedido	había pedido		habré pedido	habría pedido	haya pedido	hubiera pedido

44. PERDER
(to lose)

Verbo en -ER con cambio de e → ie

(Como **atender, defender, encender, entender, tender**)

Participio presente: perdiendo		**Participio pasado:** perdido

Imperativo: pierde (no pierdas), pierda Ud., perdamos, perded (no perdáis), pierdan Uds.

Indicativo				Condicional	Subjuntivo	
Presente	**Imperfecto**	**Pretérito**	**Futuro**	**Presente**	**Presente**	**Imperfecto**
pierdo	perdía	perdí	perderé	perdería	pierda	perdiera
pierdes	perdías	perdiste	perderás	perderías	pierdas	perdieras
pierde	perdía	perdió	perderá	perdería	pierda	perdiera
perdemos	perdíamos	perdimos	perderemos	perderíamos	perdamos	perdiéramos
perdéis	perdíais	perdisteis	perderéis	perderíais	perdáis	perdierais
pierden	perdían	perdieron	perderán	perderían	pierdan	perdieran
Pres. perfecto	**Pluscuamperf.**		**Futuro perfecto**	**Perfecto**	**Pres. perfecto**	**Pluscuamperf.**
he perdido	había perdido		habré perdido	habría perdido	haya perdido	hubiera perdido

45. PODER
(to be able)

Verbo irregular

Participio presente: pudiendo		**Participio pasado:** podido

Imperativo: puede (no puedas), pueda Ud., podamos, poded (no podáis), puedan Uds.

Indicativo				Condicional	Subjuntivo	
Presente	**Imperfecto**	**Pretérito**	**Futuro**	**Presente**	**Presente**	**Imperfecto**
puedo	podía	pude	podré	podría	pueda	pudiera
puedes	podías	pudiste	podrás	podrías	puedas	pudieras
puede	podía	pudo	podrá	podría	pueda	pudiera
podemos	podíamos	pudimos	podremos	podríamos	podamos	pudiéramos
podéis	podíais	pudisteis	podréis	podríais	podáis	pudierais
pueden	podían	pudieron	podrán	podrían	puedan	pudieran
Pres. perfecto	**Pluscuamperf.**		**Futuro perfecto**	**Perfecto**	**Pres. perfecto**	**Pluscuamperf.**
he podido	había podido		habré podido	habría podido	haya podido	hubiera podido

A
P
P
E
N
D
I
X

4

46. PODRIR o PUDRIR Verbo irregular
(to rot)

Participio presente: pudriendo | **Participio pasado:** podrido

Imperativo: pudre (no pudras), pudra Ud., pudramos, pudrid (no pudráis), pudran Uds.

Indicativo				Condicional	Subjuntivo	
Presente	**Imperfecto**	**Pretérito**	**Futuro**	**Presente**	**Presente**	**Imperfecto**
pudro	pudría	pudrí; podrí	pudriré; podriré	pudriría	pudra	pudriera
pudres	pudrías	pudriste	pudrirás	pudrirías	pudras	pudrieras
pudre	pudría	pudrió	pudrirá	pudriría	pudra	pudriera
pudrimos	pudríamos	pudrimos	pudriremos	pudriríamos	pudramos	pudriéramos
pudrís	pudríais	pudristeis	pudriréis	pudriríais	pudráis	pudrierais
pudren	pudrían	pudrieron	pudrirán	pudrirían	pudran	pudrieran
Pres. perfecto	**Pluscuamperf.**		**Futuro perfecto**	**Perfecto**	**Pres. perfecto**	**Pluscuamperf.**
he podrido	había podrido		habré podrido	habría podrido	haya podrido	hubiera podrido

47. PONER Verbo irregular
(to put) (Como **componer, disponer, oponer, proponer, suponer**)

Participio presente: poniendo | **Participio pasado:** puesto

Imperativo: pon (no pongas), ponga Ud., pongamos, poned (no pongáis), pongan Uds.

Indicativo				Condicional	Subjuntivo	
Presente	**Imperfecto**	**Pretérito**	**Futuro**	**Presente**	**Presente**	**Imperfecto**
pongo	ponía	puse	pondré	pondría	ponga	pusiera
pones	ponías	pusiste	pondrás	pondrías	pongas	pusieras
pone	ponía	puso	pondrá	pondría	ponga	pusiera
ponemos	poníamos	pusimos	pondremos	pondríamos	pongamos	pusiéramos
ponéis	poníais	pusisteis	pondréis	pondríais	pongáis	pusierais
ponen	ponían	pusieron	pondrán	pondrían	pongan	pusieran
Pres. perfecto	**Pluscuamperf.**		**Futuro perfecto**	**Perfecto**	**Pres. perfecto**	**Pluscuamperf.**
he puesto	había puesto		habré puesto	habría puesto	haya puesto	hubiera puesto

48. PROHIBIR Verbo en -IR con cambio de *i → í*
(to prohibit) (Como **cohibir**)

Participio presente: prohibiendo | **Participio pasado:** prohibido

Imperativo: prohíbe (no prohíbas), prohíba Ud., prohibamos, prohibid (no prohibáis), prohíban Uds.

Indicativo				Condicional	Subjuntivo	
Presente	**Imperfecto**	**Pretérito**	**Futuro**	**Presente**	**Presente**	**Imperfecto**
prohíbo	prohibía	prohibí	prohibiré	prohibiría	prohíba	prohibiera
prohíbes	prohibías	prohibiste	prohibirás	prohibirías	prohíbas	prohibieras
prohíbe	prohibía	prohibió	prohibirá	prohibiría	prohíba	prohibiera
prohibimos	prohibíamos	prohibimos	prohibiremos	prohibiríamos	prohibamos	prohibiéramos
prohibís	prohibíais	prohibisteis	prohibiréis	prohibiríais	prohibáis	prohibierais
prohíben	prohibían	prohibieron	prohibirán	prohibirían	prohíban	prohibieran
Pres. perfecto	**Pluscuamperf.**		**Futuro perfecto**	**Perfecto**	**Pres. perfecto**	**Pluscuamperf.**
he prohibido	había prohibido		habré prohibido	habría prohibido	haya prohibido	hubiera prohibido

49. QUERER
(to want)

Verbo irregular

(Como **bienquerer**)

Participio presente: queriendo | **Participio pasado:** querido

Imperativo: quiere (no quieras), quiera Ud., queramos, quered (no queráis), quieran Uds.

Indicativo				Condicional	Subjuntivo	
Presente	**Imperfecto**	**Pretérito**	**Futuro**	**Presente**	**Presente**	**Imperfecto**
quiero	quería	quise	querré	querría	quiera	quisiera
quieres	querías	quisiste	querrás	querrías	quieras	quisieras
quiere	quería	quiso	querrá	querría	quiera	quisiera
queremos	queríamos	quisimos	querremos	querríamos	queramos	quisiéramos
queréis	queríais	quisisteis	querréis	querríais	queráis	quisierais
quieren	querían	quisieron	querrán	querrían	quieran	quisieran
Pres. perfecto	**Pluscuamperf.**		**Futuro perfecto**	**Perfecto**	**Pres. perfecto**	**Pluscuamperf.**
he querido	había querido		habré querido	habría querido	haya querido	hubiera querido

50. REGIR
(to rule)

Verbo en -IR con cambio de e → i; g → j frente a A y O

(Como **colegir, corregir, elegir, reelegir**)

Participio presente: rigiendo | **Participio pasado:** regido

Imperativo: rige (no rijas), rija Ud., rijamos, regid (no rijáis), rijan Uds.

Indicativo				Condicional	Subjuntivo	
Presente	**Imperfecto**	**Pretérito**	**Futuro**	**Presente**	**Presente**	**Imperfecto**
rijo	regía	regí	regiré	regiría	rija	rigiera
riges	regías	registe	regirás	regirías	rijas	rigieras
rige	regía	rigió	regirá	regiría	rija	rigiera
regimos	regíamos	regimos	regiremos	regiríamos	rijamos	rigiéramos
regís	regíais	registeis	regiréis	regiríais	rijáis	rigierais
rigen	regían	rigieron	regirán	regirían	rijan	rigieran
Pres. perfecto	**Pluscuamperf.**		**Futuro perfecto**	**Perfecto**	**Pres. perfecto**	**Pluscuamperf.**
he regido	había regido		habré regido	habría regido	haya regido	hubiera regido

51. REÍR
(to laugh)

Verbo irregular

(Como **freír, refreír, sofreír, sonreír**)

Participio presente: riendo | **Participio pasado:** reído

Imperativo: ríe (no rías), ría Ud., riamos, reíd (no riáis), rían Uds.

Indicativo				Condicional	Subjuntivo	
Presente	**Imperfecto**	**Pretérito**	**Futuro**	**Presente**	**Presente**	**Imperfecto**
río	reía	reí	reiré	reiría	ría	riera
ríes	reías	reíste	reirás	reirías	rías	rieras
ríe	reía	rió	reirá	reiría	ría	riera
reímos	reíamos	reímos	reiremos	reiríamos	riamos	riéramos
reís	reíais	reísteis	reiréis	reiríais	riáis	rierais
ríen	reían	rieron	reirán	reirían	rían	rieran
Pres. perfecto	**Pluscuamperf.**		**Futuro perfecto**	**Perfecto**	**Pres. perfecto**	**Pluscuamperf.**
he reído	había reído		habré reído	habría reído	haya reído	hubiera reído

52. REUNIR

Verbo en -IR con cambio de *u → ú*

(to assemble)

Participio presente: reuniendo | **Participio pasado:** reunido

Imperativo: reúne (no reúnas), reúna Ud., reunamos, reunid (no reunáis), reúnan Uds.

Indicativo				Condicional	Subjuntivo	
Presente	**Imperfecto**	**Pretérito**	**Futuro**	**Presente**	**Presente**	**Imperfecto**
reúno	reunía	reuní	reuniré	reuniría	reúna	reuniera
reúnes	reunías	reuniste	reunirás	reunirías	reúnas	reunieras
reúne	reunía	reunió	reunirá	reuniría	reúna	reuniera
reunimos	reuníamos	reunimos	reuniremos	reuniríamos	reunamos	reuniéramos
reunís	reuníais	reunisteis	reuniréis	reuniríais	reunáis	reunierais
reúnen	reunían	reunieron	reunirán	reunirían	reúnan	reunieran
Pres. perfecto	**Pluscuamperf.**		**Futuro perfecto**	**Perfecto**	**Pres. perfecto**	**Pluscuamperf.**
he reunido	había reunido		habré reunido	habría reunido	haya reunido	hubiera reunido

53. ROGAR

Verbo en -AR con cambio de *o → ue; g → gu* frente a E

(to beg)

(Como **colgar, descolgar**)

Participio presente: rogando | **Participio pasado:** rogado

Imperativo: ruega (no ruegues), ruegue Ud., roguemos, rogad (no roguéis), rueguen Uds.

Indicativo				Condicional	Subjuntivo	
Presente	**Imperfecto**	**Pretérito**	**Futuro**	**Presente**	**Presente**	**Imperfecto**
ruego	rogaba	rogué	rogaré	rogaría	ruegue	rogara
ruegas	rogabas	rogaste	rogarás	rogarías	ruegues	rogaras
ruega	rogaba	rogó	rogará	rogaría	ruegue	rogara
rogamos	rogábamos	rogamos	rogaremos	rogaríamos	roguemos	rogáramos
rogáis	rogabais	rogasteis	rogaréis	rogaríais	roguéis	rogarais
ruegan	rogaban	rogaron	rogarán	rogarían	rueguen	rogaran
Pres. perfecto	**Pluscuamperf.**		**Futuro perfecto**	**Perfecto**	**Pres. perfecto**	**Pluscuamperf.**
he rogado	había rogado		habré rogado	habría rogado	haya rogado	hubiera rogado

54. SABER

Verbo irregular

(to know)

Participio presente: sabiendo | **Participio pasado:** sabido

Imperativo: sabe (no sepas), sepa Ud., sepamos, sabed (no sepáis), sepan Uds.

Indicativo				Condicional	Subjuntivo	
Presente	**Imperfecto**	**Pretérito**	**Futuro**	**Presente**	**Presente**	**Imperfecto**
sé	sabía	supe	sabré	sabría	sepa	supiera
sabes	sabías	supiste	sabrás	sabrías	sepas	supieras
sabe	sabía	supo	sabrá	sabría	sepa	supiera
sabemos	sabíamos	supimos	sabremos	sabríamos	sepamos	supiéramos
sabéis	sabíais	supisteis	sabréis	sabríais	sepáis	supierais
saben	sabían	supieron	sabrán	sabrían	sepan	supieran
Pres. perfecto	**Pluscuamperf.**		**Futuro perfecto**	**Perfecto**	**Pres. perfecto**	**Pluscuamperf.**
he sabido	había sabido		habré sabido	habría sabido	haya sabido	hubiera sabido

55. SALIR
(to go out)

Verbo irregular

(Como **sobresalir**)

Participio presente: saliendo

Participio pasado: salido

Imperativo: sal (no salgas), salga Ud., salgamos, salid (no salgáis), salgan Uds.

Indicativo				Condicional	Subjuntivo	
Presente	**Imperfecto**	**Pretérito**	**Futuro**	**Presente**	**Presente**	**Imperfecto**
salgo	salía	salí	saldré	saldría	salga	saliera
sales	salías	saliste	saldrás	saldrías	salgas	salieras
sale	salía	salió	saldrá	saldría	salga	saliera
salimos	salíamos	salimos	saldremos	saldríamos	salgamos	saliéramos
salís	salíais	salisteis	saldréis	saldríais	salgáis	salierais
salen	salían	salieron	saldrán	saldrían	salgan	salieran
Pres. perfecto	**Pluscuamperf.**		**Futuro perfecto**	**Perfecto**	**Pres. perfecto**	**Pluscuamperf.**
he salido	había salido		habré salido	habría salido	haya salido	hubiera salido

56. SEGUIR
(to follow)

Verbo en -IR con cambio de *gu* → *g* frente a A y O; *e* → *i*

(Como **conseguir, perseguir, proseguir**)

Participio presente: siguiendo

Participio pasado: seguido

Imperativo: sigue (no sigas), siga Ud., sigamos, seguid (no sigáis), sigan Uds.

Indicativo				Condicional	Subjuntivo	
Presente	**Imperfecto**	**Pretérito**	**Futuro**	**Presente**	**Presente**	**Imperfecto**
sigo	seguía	seguí	seguiré	seguiría	siga	siguiera
sigues	seguías	seguiste	seguirás	seguirías	sigas	siguieras
sigue	seguía	siguió	seguirá	seguiría	siga	siguiera
seguimos	seguíamos	seguimos	seguiremos	seguiríamos	sigamos	siguiéramos
seguís	seguíais	seguisteis	seguiréis	seguiríais	sigáis	siguierais
siguen	seguían	siguieron	seguirán	seguirían	sigan	siguieran
Pres. perfecto	**Pluscuamperf.**		**Futuro perfecto**	**Perfecto**	**Pres. perfecto**	**Pluscuamperf.**
he seguido	había seguido		habré seguido	habría seguido	haya seguido	hubiera seguido

57. SENTIR
(to feel)

Verbo en -IR con cambio de *e* → *ie*; *e* → *i*

(Como **arrepentirse, divertir, mentir, preferir, sugerir**)

Participio presente: sintiendo

Participio pasado: sentido

Imperativo: siente (no sientas), sienta Ud., sintamos, sentid (no sintáis), sientan Uds.

Indicativo				Condicional	Subjuntivo	
Presente	**Imperfecto**	**Pretérito**	**Futuro**	**Presente**	**Presente**	**Imperfecto**
siento	sentía	sentí	sentiré	sentiría	sienta	sintiera
sientes	sentías	sentiste	sentirás	sentirías	sientas	sintieras
siente	sentía	sintió	sentirá	sentiría	sienta	sintiera
sentimos	sentíamos	sentimos	sentiremos	sentiríamos	sintamos	sintiéramos
sentís	sentíais	sentisteis	sentiréis	sentiríais	sintáis	sintierais
sienten	sentían	sintieron	sentirán	sentirían	sientan	sintieran
Pres. perfecto	**Pluscuamperf.**		**Futuro perfecto**	**Perfecto**	**Pres. perfecto**	**Pluscuamperf.**
he sentido	había sentido		habré sentido	habría sentido	haya sentido	hubiera sentido

58. SER — Verbo irregular
(to be)

Participio presente: siendo | **Participio pasado:** sido

Imperativo: sé (no seas), sea Ud., seamos, sed (no seáis), sean Uds.

Indicativo				Condicional	Subjuntivo	
Presente	**Imperfecto**	**Pretérito**	**Futuro**	**Presente**	**Presente**	**Imperfecto**
soy	era	fui	seré	sería	sea	fuera
eres	eras	fuiste	serás	serías	seas	fueras
es	era	fue	será	sería	sea	fuera
somos	éramos	fuimos	seremos	seríamos	seamos	fuéramos
sois	erais	fuisteis	seréis	seríais	seáis	fuerais
son	eran	fueron	serán	serían	sean	fueran
Pres. perfecto	**Pluscuamperf.**		**Futuro perfecto**	**Perfecto**	**Pres. perfecto**	**Pluscuamperf.**
he sido	había sido		habré sido	habría sido	haya sido	hubiera sido

59. SOLER — Verbo irregular (defectivo)
(to accustom)

Participio presente: | **Participio pasado:**

Imperativo:

Indicativo				Condicional	Subjuntivo	
Presente	**Imperfecto**	**Pretérito**	**Futuro**	**Presente**	**Presente**	**Imperfecto**
suelo	solía	solí			suela	soliera
sueles	solías	soliste			suelas	solieras
suele	solía	solió			suela	soliera
solemos	solíamos	solimos			solamos	soliéramos
soléis	solíais	solisteis			soláis	solierais
suelen	solían	solieron			suelan	solieran
Pres. perfecto	**Pluscuamperf.**		**Futuro perfecto**	**Perfecto**	**Pres. perfecto**	**Pluscuamperf.**

60. TENER — Verbo irregular
(to have) — (Como **atenerse, contener, mantener, obtener, sostener**)

Participio presente: teniendo | **Participio pasado:** tenido

Imperativo: ten (no tengas), tenga Ud., tengamos, tened (no tengáis), tengan Uds.

Indicativo				Condicional	Subjuntivo	
Presente	**Imperfecto**	**Pretérito**	**Futuro**	**Presente**	**Presente**	**Imperfecto**
tengo	tenía	tuve	tendré	tendría	tenga	tuviera
tienes	tenías	tuviste	tendrás	tendrías	tengas	tuvieras
tiene	tenía	tuvo	tendrá	tendría	tenga	tuviera
tenemos	teníamos	tuvimos	tendremos	tendríamos	tengamos	tuviéramos
tenéis	teníais	tuvisteis	tendréis	tendríais	tengáis	tuvierais
tienen	tenían	tuvieron	tendrán	tendrían	tengan	tuvieran
Pres. perfecto	**Pluscuamperf.**		**Futuro perfecto**	**Perfecto**	**Pres. perfecto**	**Pluscuamperf.**
he tenido	había tenido		habré tenido	habría tenido	haya tenido	hubiera tenido

61. TEÑIR
(to dye)

Verbo en -IR con cambio de e → i; pierde la *i* átona de la terminación

(Como **ceñir, desteñir, estreñir, reñir**)

Participio presente: tiñendo

Participio pasado: teñido

Imperativo: tiñe (no tiñas), tiña Ud., tiñamos, teñid (no tiñáis), tiñan Uds.

Indicativo				Condicional	Subjuntivo	
Presente	**Imperfecto**	**Pretérito**	**Futuro**	**Presente**	**Presente**	**Imperfecto**
tiño	teñía	teñí	teñiré	teñiría	tiña	tiñera
tiñes	teñías	teñiste	teñirás	teñirías	tiñas	tiñeras
tiñe	teñía	tiñó	teñirá	teñiría	tiña	tiñera
teñimos	teñíamos	teñimos	teñiremos	teñiríamos	tiñamos	tiñéramos
teñís	teñíais	teñisteis	teñiréis	teñiríais	tiñáis	tiñerais
tiñen	teñían	tiñeron	teñirán	teñirían	tiñan	tiñeran
Pres. perfecto	**Pluscuamperf.**		**Futuro perfecto**	**Perfecto**	**Pres. perfecto**	**Pluscuamperf.**
he teñido	había teñido		habré teñido	habría teñido	haya teñido	hubiera teñido

62. TRAER
(to bring)

Verbo irregular

(Como **atraer, contraer, detraer, distraer, extraer**)

Participio presente: trayendo

Participio pasado: traído

Imperativo: trae (no traigas), traiga Ud., traigamos, traed (no traigáis), traigan Uds.

Indicativo				Condicional	Subjuntivo	
Presente	**Imperfecto**	**Pretérito**	**Futuro**	**Presente**	**Presente**	**Imperfecto**
traigo	traía	traje	traeré	traería	traiga	trajera
traes	traías	trajiste	traerás	traerías	traigas	trajeras
trae	traía	trajo	traerá	traería	traiga	trajera
traemos	traíamos	trajimos	traeremos	traeríamos	traigamos	trajéramos
traéis	traíais	trajisteis	traeréis	traeríais	traigáis	trajerais
traen	traían	trajeron	traerán	traerían	traigan	trajeran
Pres. perfecto	**Pluscuamperf.**		**Futuro perfecto**	**Perfecto**	**Pres. perfecto**	**Pluscuamperf.**
he traído	había traído		habré traído	habría traído	haya traído	hubiera traído

63. VALER
(to be worth)

Verbo irregular

(Como **equivaler, prevaler**)

Participio presente: valiendo

Participio pasado: valido

Imperativo: vale (no valgas), valga Ud., valgamos, valed (no valgáis), valgan Uds.

Indicativo				Condicional	Subjuntivo	
Presente	**Imperfecto**	**Pretérito**	**Futuro**	**Presente**	**Presente**	**Imperfecto**
valgo	valía	valí	valdré	valdría	valga	valiera
vales	valías	valiste	valdrás	valdrías	valgas	valieras
vale	valía	valió	valdrá	valdría	valga	valiera
valemos	valíamos	valimos	valdremos	valdríamos	valgamos	valiéramos
valéis	valíais	valisteis	valdréis	valdríais	valgáis	valierais
valen	valían	valieron	valdrán	valdrían	valgan	valieran
Pres. perfecto	**Pluscuamperf.**		**Futuro perfecto**	**Perfecto**	**Pres. perfecto**	**Pluscuamperf.**
he valido	había valido		habré valido	habría valido	haya valido	hubiera valido

64. VENCER
(to conquer)

Verbo en -ER con cambio de *c* → *z* frente a A y O
(Como **coercer, convencer, ejercer, mecer**)

Participio presente: venciendo

Participio pasado: vencido

Imperativo: vence (no venzas), venza Ud., venzamos, venced (no venzáis), venzan Uds.

Indicativo				Condicional	Subjuntivo	
Presente	**Imperfecto**	**Pretérito**	**Futuro**	**Presente**	**Presente**	**Imperfecto**
venzo	vencía	vencí	venceré	vencería	venza	venciera
vences	vencías	venciste	vencerás	vencerías	venzas	vencieras
vence	vencía	venció	vencerá	vencería	venza	venciera
vencemos	vencíamos	vencimos	venceremos	venceríamos	venzamos	venciéramos
vencéis	vencíais	vencisteis	venceréis	venceríais	venzáis	vencierais
vencen	vencían	vencieron	vencerán	vencerían	venzan	vencieran
Pres. perfecto	**Pluscuamperf.**		**Futuro perfecto**	**Perfecto**	**Pres. perfecto**	**Pluscuamperf.**
he vencido	había vencido		habré vencido	habría vencido	haya vencido	hubiera vencido

65. VENIR
(to come)

Verbo irregular
(Como **convenir, intervenir, prevenir, provenir, reconvenir**)

Participio presente: viniendo

Participio pasado: venido

Imperativo: ven (no vengas), venga Ud., vengamos, venid (no vengáis), vengan Uds.

Indicativo				Condicional	Subjuntivo	
Presente	**Imperfecto**	**Pretérito**	**Futuro**	**Presente**	**Presente**	**Imperfecto**
vengo	venía	vine	vendré	vendría	venga	viniera
vienes	venías	viniste	vendrás	vendrías	vengas	vinieras
viene	venía	vino	vendrá	vendría	venga	viniera
venimos	veníamos	vinimos	vendremos	vendríamos	vengamos	viniéramos
venís	veníais	vinisteis	vendréis	vendríais	vengáis	vinierais
vienen	venían	vinieron	vendrán	vendrían	vengan	vinieran
Pres. perfecto	**Pluscuamperf.**		**Futuro perfecto**	**Perfecto**	**Pres. perfecto**	**Pluscuamperf.**
he venido	había venido		habré venido	habría venido	haya venido	hubiera venido

66. VER
(to see)

Verbo irregular (Como **entrever, prever**; Note: 3ª pers. sing. pres. y el imperativo de **entrever** y **prever** tienen acento: **entrevé, prevé,** etc.)

Participio presente: viendo

Participio pasado: visto

Imperativo: ve (no veas), vea Ud., veamos, ved (no veáis), vean Uds.

Indicativo				Condicional	Subjuntivo	
Presente	**Imperfecto**	**Pretérito**	**Futuro**	**Presente**	**Presente**	**Imperfecto**
veo	veía	vi	veré	vería	vea	viera
ves	veías	viste	verás	verías	veas	vieras
ve	veía	vio	verá	vería	vea	viera
vemos	veíamos	vimos	veremos	veríamos	veamos	viéramos
veis	veíais	visteis	veréis	veríais	veáis	vierais
ven	veían	vieron	verán	verían	vean	vieran
Pres. perfecto	**Pluscuamperf.**		**Futuro perfecto**	**Perfecto**	**Pres. perfecto**	**Pluscuamperf.**
he visto	había visto		habré visto	habría visto	haya visto	hubiera visto

67. VIVIR

(to live)

Verbo regular 3ª conjugación

(Como **compartir, decidir, emitir, permitir, resumir**)

Participio presente: viviendo | **Participio pasado:** vivido

Imperativo: vive (no vivas), viva Ud., vivamos, vivid (no viváis), vivan Uds.

Indicativo				Condicional	Subjuntivo	
Presente	**Imperfecto**	**Pretérito**	**Futuro**	**Presente**	**Presente**	**Imperfecto**
vivo	vivía	viví	viviré	viviría	viva	viviera
vives	vivías	viviste	vivirás	vivirías	vivas	vivieras
vive	vivía	vivió	vivirá	viviría	viva	viviera
vivimos	vivíamos	vivimos	viviremos	viviríamos	vivamos	viviéramos
vivís	vivíais	vivisteis	viviréis	viviríais	viváis	vivierais
viven	vivían	vivieron	vivirán	vivirían	vivan	vivieran
Pres. perfecto	**Pluscuamperf.**		**Futuro perfecto**	**Perfecto**	**Pres. perfecto**	**Pluscuamperf.**
he vivido	había vivido		habré vivido	habría vivido	haya vivido	hubiera vivido

68. VOLCAR

(to tip over)

Verbo en -AR con cambio de *o* → *ue*; *c* → *qu* frente a E

(Como **revolcar, trocar**)

Participio presente: volcando | **Participio pasado:** volcado

Imperativo: vuelca (no vuelques), vuelque Ud., volquemos, volcad (no volquéis), vuelquen Uds.

Indicativo				Condicional	Subjuntivo	
Presente	**Imperfecto**	**Pretérito**	**Futuro**	**Presente**	**Presente**	**Imperfecto**
vuelco	volcaba	volqué	volcaré	volcaría	vuelque	volcara
vuelcas	volcabas	volcaste	volcarás	volcarías	vuelques	volcaras
vuelca	volcaba	volcó	volcará	volcaría	vuelque	volcara
volcamos	volcábamos	volcamos	volcaremos	volcaríamos	volquemos	volcáramos
volcáis	volcabais	volcasteis	volcaréis	volcaríais	volquéis	volcarais
vuelcan	volcaban	volcaron	volcarán	volcarían	vuelquen	volcaran
Pres. perfecto	**Pluscuamperf.**		**Futuro perfecto**	**Perfecto**	**Pres. perfecto**	**Pluscuamperf.**
he volcado	había volcado		habré volcado	habría volcado	haya volcado	hubiera volcado

69. VOLVER

(to return)

Verbo en -ER con cambio de *o* → *ue*; participio pasado irregular

(Como **devolver, disolver, envolver, resolver, revolver**)

Participio presente: volviendo | **Participio pasado:** vuelto

Imperativo: vuelve (no vuelvas), vuelva Ud., volvamos, volved (no volváis), vuelvan Uds.

Indicativo				Condicional	Subjuntivo	
Presente	**Imperfecto**	**Pretérito**	**Futuro**	**Presente**	**Presente**	**Imperfecto**
vuelvo	volvía	volví	volveré	volvería	vuelva	volviera
vuelves	volvías	volviste	volverás	volverías	vuelvas	volvieras
vuelve	volvía	volvió	volverá	volvería	vuelva	volviera
volvemos	volvíamos	volvimos	volveremos	volveríamos	volvamos	volviéramos
volvéis	volvíais	volvisteis	volveréis	volveríais	volváis	volvierais
vuelven	volvían	volvieron	volverán	volverían	vuelvan	volvieran
Pres. perfecto	**Pluscuamperf.**		**Futuro perfecto**	**Perfecto**	**Pres. perfecto**	**Pluscuamperf.**
he vuelto	había vuelto		habré vuelto	habría vuelto	haya vuelto	hubiera vuelto

APPENDIX 4

INDEX

a, 221
  personal, 28, 46, 63
  preposition, 46
    in expressions, 84
    with reflexives, 191
a causa de, 222
acabar, 220
acabar de, 220
  present, 132
  preterite/imperfect, 137
acabarse, 220
accents
  aquel/aquél, 17, 33, 65
  aun/aún, 17
  change with plural, 27, 36
  discourse
    direct, 18
    indirect, 18
  ese/ése, 17, 33, 65
  eso/esto/aquello, 17, 66
  este/éste, 17, 33, 65
  exclamatives, 18
  homonyms, 16
  interrogatives, 18
  monosyllables, 16
  solo/sólo, 17
  weak and strong vowels, 13
  with the imperative, 123–126
actuar (conjugation), 325
adjectival clause, 7, 158
adjective
  demonstrative, 33
  descriptive
    comparative, 40
    formation, 35
    nationalities, 36
    position, 36
    superlative, 42
  function, 3
  possessive
    long, 35
    short, 35
adquirir (conjugation), 325

adverb
  accent on adverbs ending in *-mente*, 15
  function, 3
adverbial clause, 7, 159
ago, 206
al
  with infinitive, 84, 177
andar (conjugation), 325
aplicar vs. *solicitar*, 208
apply, 208
aprender (conjugation), 326
aquel/aquél, 17, 65
article
  definite, 29–30
    omission, 30
    possessives, 30, 60
    with *gustar, caer bien, encantar*, 182
    with infinitive, 175
    with reflexives, 31
  function, 3
  indefinite, 32
    omission, 32
ask, 208
at, 221
aun/aún, 17
avergonzar (conjugation), 326
averiguar (conjugation), 326
be early, 221
be late, 221
because, 222
become, 210
buscar (conjugation), 327
caber (conjugation), 327
caer (conjugation), 327
caminar (conjugation), 328
cerrar (conjugation), 328
clause
  dependent, 7
  independent, 7
  main, 7
  subordinate, 7
    adjectival, 7, 158
    adverbial, 7, 159
    nominal, 7, 150–156
    relative, 7, 158